ADVANCED ENGLISH GRAMMAR

HELEN HOYT SCHMIDT

Iowa State University

Prentice Hall Regents

Library of Congress Cataloging–in–Publication Data

Schmidt, Helen Hoyt.
    Advanced English grammar / Helen Hoyt Schmidt.
      p.   cm.
    Includes bibliographical references and index.
    ISBN 0–13–096942–7 :
      1. English language—Grammar—Problems, exercises, etc.
    2. English language—Textbooks for foreign speakers. I. Title.
PE1112.S34   1995
428.2'4—dc20   94–39080
                                               CIP

Publisher: Tina B. Carver
Director of Production and Manufacturing: David Riccardi
Editorial Production/Design Manager: Dominick Mosco
Editorial/Production Supervisor: Janet Johnston
Production Coordinator: Ray Keating
Cover Coordinator: Merle Krumper
Cover Designer: Jerry Votta
Electronic Art Production: Todd Ware and Rolando Corujo

© 1995 Prentice-Hall Regents

Printed in the United States of America

10 9 8 7 6 5

ISBN 0-13-096942-7

Illustration Credits
All illustrations by the author except as follows:
    Steffen W. Schmidt: pages 3, 46, 55, 102, 207, 235, 255, and 268
    Elizabeth F. Cleveland: pages 236, 307, and 313
    Jennifer Stiles: pages 52 and 185

CONTENTS

Unit I. The Verb System

UNIT II. RELATIVE CONCEPTS

UNIT III. ADVERBIAL CONCEPTS

UNIT IV. NOUN CONCEPTS—NOUN CLAUSES, GERUNDS, INFINITIVES, ABSTRACT NOUN PHRASES

CHARTS and FIGURES

FOREWORD

Advanced English Grammar is a significant contribution to the materials available for the teaching of English structure and usage. It challenges students to reach a high level of understanding and usage ability of the grammar of English in order to prepare them for the reading and writing skills that are demanded of them in university work.

Advanced English Grammar knows its audience: advanced language students engaged in or preparing to begin high-level academic work. The author has been working with these students for twenty years; she is an experienced teacher responding to the needs of her students. This book seeks to push their skills to a level that enables them to compete successfully in academics and in their professions.

The author, Helen H. Schmidt, uses authentic materials that are relevant to the students' academic interest and educational backgrounds—and are as challenging as anything the students will encounter in their actual coursework in their major fields. A great advantage to the use of authentic materials is that students who have accomplished the many tasks in *Advanced English Grammar* will be prepared for the level of difficulty of the materials they have to deal with in their content courses.

Professor Schmidt successfully combines the use of authentic materials with a variety of pedagogical approaches, both inductive and deductive, based on current theories and understandings of the language acquisition process. Concentrating on reading and writing skills, the text effectively teaches students what they need to know about English structure and usage for highly proficient creative language use. It is a commendable text.

Betty Schrampfer Azar
Langley, Washington

PREFACE AND ACKNOWLEDGMENTS

Advanced English Grammar presents advanced grammatical structures in their original academic contexts and prepares students for the complicated academic prose that university students are expected to read and write. In this text, students learn to search for, discuss, analyze, and paraphrase the patterns of English structure that are typical of the textbooks, professional journals, newsmagazines, and newspapers that they will encounter during their studies and careers. The passages used in this book were chosen from real academic sources representing 40 disciplines. Many were selected by international students taking regular academic courses.

Advanced English Grammar is designed to teach grammar in two ways, *inductively* and *deductively*. In *inductive* learning, students draw their own conclusions about how the grammar of English operates by examining many examples of a grammatical structure in the context of its real-world use. In *deductive* learning, students are given grammar rules and then asked to use those rules to read and write grammatical structures. First, the structures taught in each chapter are introduced *inductively* by having students read authentic passages. Students try to identify these structures and discuss what they already know about the grammar. Second, the structures are reinforced *deductively* with explanations and charts. Third, large- and small-group practice and analysis activities lead students to an understanding of how grammar is used by professional writers to express ideas. The goal of the course is for students to develop their own abilities in the use of appropriate grammatical structures in academic writing.

Advanced English Grammar is the result of my twenty years of experience teaching in the Intensive English and Orientation Program at Iowa State University, where students from Latin America, Asia, Africa, and Europe study for undergraduate and graduate degrees in engineering, business, sociology, agriculture, political science, veterinary medicine, architecture, fine arts, and many other disciplines. Over the years, it has become apparent that advanced international students are entering our intensive English program at higher and higher levels of proficiency. At the same time, many university departments are now requiring TOEFL scores of 550 and above. *Advanced English Grammar* is the result of years of preparing courses for such students. The text has been tried and tested successfully with students whose TOEFL scores range from 480 to 585.

I would like to thank my colleagues at Iowa State for their encouragement, and especially Barbara Matthies, our director, without whose reassurance and help, over the years, this project would never have been completed. A special thank you also to Betty Azar for her interest, support, and invaluable advice. Thanks too to the anonymous reviewers whose insights kept me on the track toward the goal of an inductive grammar. And thank you to my husband and children for their patience, reinforcement, and understanding throughout the writing process.

TO THE INSTRUCTOR

Researchers believe that students must notice grammatical structures before they are able to recognize and use them. Teachers assume that by the time students reach an advanced level of English proficiency, they have learned all the important grammatical structures. It has been my experience, however, that students may have learned those structures in a simplified context, and may not recognize them in the context of academic reading materials.

For many years, as grammar teacher of the advanced grammar class in our intensive English program, I brought to class articles and excerpts of academic prose. To my amazement, what I thought to be an obvious example of whatever we were studying at the moment looked like Greek to my students. I soon realized that the unfamiliar aspects of the prose—new vocabulary or embedded clauses—interfered with the students' recognition of all but the most obvious target structures. Students could still see that "which" was the first word in a relative clause, but many could not recognize a participial phrase.

Such experiences led me to the conclusion that advanced students need a text to bridge the gap between the uncomplicated sentence-level recognition of structures and the difficult, embedded academic prose they are expected to understand at the college and graduate school levels. I also believe that once students "notice" the grammatical structures in the complex prose, they will be better prepared to extract meaning from the prose. *Advanced English Grammar* is based on the assumption that students can rediscover, within the academic prose they will be using in the future, the grammar they learned in earlier contexts. At the same time, exposure to typical academic vocabulary will soften the inevitable shock caused by encountering hundreds of pages of reading in an academic class.

Learners fall into two groups: those who are most comfortable with the deductive method of learning and those who are most comfortable with the inductive method. Most grammar books today favor the deductive method, in which the rules of a structure are presented and students then apply those rules to various exercises. *Advanced English Grammar* has been organized to meet the needs of both types of learners. Each chapter begins with **Discovering the Grammar**, one or more inductive exercises in which the student is lead toward a discovery or rediscovery of the grammatical structures that follow. After **Discovering the Grammar** is **Analyzing the Grammar**, inductive exercises designed to get students thinking about grammatical relationships. Following the analysis exercises are charts and explanations of the structures. **Practicing the Grammar** and **Using the Grammar in Writing** exercises follow the explanations. As many exercises as possible have been contextualized. Most of the grammar points to be practiced are introduced within passages taken from academic texts, journal articles, newsmagazines, or newspapers.

You may choose to use the **Discovering the Grammar** exercises early in the lesson as inductive exercises, or after more extensive teacher-centered introductions of the grammar point in question. I have tried to make the text as flexible as possible in this regard. As a teacher, I realize that some classes need a more teacher-centered deductive approach, while other groups thrive on the inductive method.

Learning theorists believe that we learn by building schema. Schema have been defined as models that the brain builds and then uses to identify new experiences in order to build new schema. I like to think of the grammar schema as templates or patterns against which new structures are judged and either recognized and sent on for further processing, or not. If schema theory is valid, we as teachers should be able to help students build up a library of templates so that they can quickly recognize and process complicated grammatical structures. This means that we need to integrate activities to exercise all parts of the brain. Some experts say that activities like brainstorming, open-ended tasks, guessing, drawing, mental imaging, and tactile manipulation stimulate the right brain, and activities like analyzing, verbalizing, recall, and ordering stimulate the left brain.

Advanced English Grammar uses as many of the two kinds of activities as possible. Students are asked to analyze extremely complicated structures: take them apart, manipulate them, categorize them, paraphrase them, order them, discuss them, and brainstorm about what the authors might be trying to communicate.

We teachers need to shake up the very advanced students. We can show them that the English language is not necessarily divided neatly into the kinds of sentences and paragraphs they've seen in their previous ESL texts. We can help them see that a word is not always one part of speech, that independent and subordinate clauses are not always in one piece, that sentences throughout a passage are related in many ways. All these native speakers take for granted. Our templates instantly recognize myriad combinations of clauses and phrases. Indeed, after twenty years of teaching, I find I recognize and answer a TOEFL question in about three seconds. Native speakers of English probably do the same with thousands of complex structures.

An informal test of a near-native speaker showed that he could fill in the following template in five minutes with a very close approximation of the original sentence (below). Try it yourself.

This _____ es that, from the _____ _____ings
when an _____ _____ed all the _____
_____ and _____ _____ , manufacturing has
grown to _____ a system with _____ _____s
that _____ in a _____ _____ .

Near-native speaker's sentence:
This *indicates* that, from the *new find* ings
when an *industry fail* ed all the *competition tests*
and *quality controls*, manufacturing has grown to
become a system with *low profit* s
that *shrink* in a *major recession*.

Original sentence:
This recognizes that, from the simple beginnings
when an artisan provided all the necessary mental
and physical output, manufacturing has grown to
become a system with many components
that interact in a dynamic manner.

The near-native speaker's answers are not particularly meaningful, but he said that with more time he could have improved his answers. The point here is that his schema or template "knew" what kinds of words to use to fill in the blanks. It would then be up to the analytical part of his brain to analyze for meaning and make it logical. This quality of prediction is basic to the template concept. *Advanced English Grammar* is intended to help students develop the ability to predict what to expect and to use the resulting templates to recognize the thousands of new sentences they will encounter.

The template idea is of course a variation of a cloze test, the difference being that a template contains key words, phrases, endings, and punctuation that trigger our recognition processes. We know instantly that an "es" at the end of a blank means plural noun, that an "ed" means simple past tense verb or participle, that "when" signals a time clause, and that "from" signals a prepositional phrase. If we can build these recognition processes in our advanced ESL students, they will be more fully prepared to deal with the language.

The goal of *Advanced English Grammar* is to help advanced ESL students bridge the gap between the relatively simple structures they recognize when they start the course and the most complicated structures they will need to recognize in their academic, business, and professional careers. Through the exercises provided, students will build up their store of templates and thus be better prepared for a life of reading and writing in English.

The American philosophy of education requires all undergraduates to spend their first two years acquiring a broad-based education, meaning that every student must study a little of everything. We have to take certain courses and pass them whether we like the courses or not. For this reason, I have included passages from as many academic areas as possible. Many of the passages and sentences were taken from articles chosen by students in the Iowa State University Intensive English Program. The articles represent a cross section of academic fields and interests.

Advanced English Grammar is designed for use in large or small groups of students. Many students like to work individually and recite their answers to the large group in the time-honored manner. This class teaching plan covers a lot of material in a short period of time and provides an opportunity for the quiet, less aggressive students "to show their stuff." In our intensive program, my method has been to alternate between a deductive and an inductive approach, large-group teacher-centered days and small-group discussion days. On small-group days, I divide the class into small groups of four or five students, ask them to compare answers they have prepared for homework, or to work together to answer questions for about 30 minutes. Then we discuss the different groups' and individuals' answers as a large group for the next 20 minutes. This method works well in a class of fifteen to twenty-five students.

Some instructors may worry that using an inductive approach will take a lot of preparation time. One of my colleagues who class-tested the text in the ISU intensive English program told me that she had avoided extensive preparation by assigning the exercises to small groups to work on in class. She was able to use the time when the students were working to figure out the answers she felt would be appropriate. She says that she didn't feel she had to be prepared to defend particular grammar rules, and she was able to say "I am not sure about that point, but I'll find out" because she and the students were in the same boat. That is, they were looking at a professional writer's choices, not at hard and fast rules. As a native speaker and ESL instructor, she played the role of adviser, helping everyone to keep an open mind to various possible answers. The students apparently appreciated the freedom they were given. One student returned to visit a year later and told her he had really enjoyed those small-group grammar discussions.

My students enjoy small-group work, too. I also find that it works well if students have not done the exercises as homework. Since solutions to problems posed by the exercises are often not definite, students benefit enormously from discussing the different possibilities. While more time-consuming, small-group work offers students an ideal situation in which to discuss grammar in a meaningful way. Therefore, the text is communicative in the sense that students are encouraged to analyze, compare, and discuss every aspect of what they are doing. The teacher may circulate and listen to the discussion, but he/she avoids answering direct questions until students have exhausted every possible means. Brainstorming can take time. Arguments are to be encouraged, although you may have to step in with an "answer" to head off a dogmatic student on the wrong track. Students need to realize that there can be several possible "correct" answers.

Toward the end of the class hour, you can stop the small-group work to lead a wrap-up discussion that includes the whole class. Depending on the size and composition of the class, students might enjoy taking turns leading a discussion. I have found three effective wrap-up methods.

1. I write the exercises on the board while the students are analyzing them and then take answers from the floor as to how to label, or paraphrase, or combine the sentences.
2. Individual students write each of the sentences on the board, or one student from each group writes the group's solutions on the board for class discussion.
3. I provide overhead transparencies of an exercise on which the small groups can put their answers. Then the transparencies are presented by the students to be compared by the class as a whole.

The aim is to make the activities as varied as possible. Creative teachers will probably devise all kinds of ways for the students to show off their small-group work.

Another important part of the course is analysis of written material from the students' own fields of interest. Early in the course each student should be helped to locate a journal article of at least three pages to analyze along with the exercises in the text. (Special "research" questions are provided at the end of every unit for this purpose.) Students will find that different fields have different writing conventions. Some fields use more passive voice than others. Some fields use more adverbial clauses; others use more noun clauses. Some, like philosophy, use such deeply embedded sentences that even native speakers have trouble reading them. This is all exciting information for students and gives them an incentive to keep struggling with the difficulties in order to be ready to read materials from their major fields.

Advanced ESL students are expected to be able to read on a far higher level than they are expected to write. The complex readings that they face require a more highly developed understanding of grammar than they usually have. The most important element in this course is that the students are led to think about grammar in an unusual way. They are not asked simply to get the right answers; they are asked to research the language to try to figure out how it works. As good researchers, they will come up with hypotheses and predictions. The teacher's role will probably be as fellow analyst and native speaker resource of last resort.

Advanced English Grammar consists of ten chapters. Each chapter is organized in the following way:

1. **Discovering the Grammar**—Introductory inductive exercises designed to help students notice and identify particular grammatical structures.
2. **Analysis of the Grammar**—Inductive exercises designed to help students understand how and why the structures are used in academic prose. Students then use this understanding to determine the grammatical rules operating in the structures under consideration.
3. **Charts and Explanations**—Deductive charts, explanations and discussion of the grammatical structures.
4. **Practicing the Grammar**—Exercises to practice the structures in context.

5. **Using the Grammar in Writing**—Paraphrasing, summarizing, synthesizing, and free writing exercises designed to encourage students to use grammatical structures to write meaningful prose.

Each Unit (every second or third chapter) contains:

6. **Preparing for Standardized Tests**—Practice exercises based on TOEFL-like questions that students might encounter. The questions are derived from academic textbooks and articles and cover the grammatical structures from the previous few chapters.
7. **Building Templates**—Analysis exercises in developing prediction skills. Students are given typical passages from academic sources and asked to fill in what structures (or specific words, if they prefer) they might expect to find in the blanks.
8. **Research Projects**—Questions designed to be used to analyze a piece of academic prose of the student's own choosing. This section allows for individualization within a classroom of students at all levels, from undergraduate freshmen to graduate-level Ph.D. candidates. The same article or passage may be used throughout the semester, or students may elect to use several articles.

The text is divided into the following types of activities.

Inductive
1. Discovering the Grammar exercises: Finding and identifying structures in context.

2. Analysis exercises: Distinguishing structures from one another in context—"that" vs. "that," "-ing" vs. "-ing." Discussing academic writing with other students. Speculating about why authors use particular structures. Coming to conclusions about grammar rules.

3. Using the Grammar in Writing exercises

Deductive
1. Charts

2. Explanations of structures

3. Discussions of rules and usage

The inductive exercises are listed below according to increasing degree of difficulty.

- Fill in the blank in context
- Sentence combining and decombining in context
- Multiple-choice practice tests
- Ordering of sentences in a passage

The more difficult exercises use grammatical structures in real-world situations.

- Answering questions using particular grammatical structures
- Predicting—Learning what to expect in academic reading and test taking
- Paraphrasing—rewriting passages in one's own word
- Summarizing—using paraphrased sentences to write a summary of a passage
- Synthesizing—paraphrasing material from two or more sources to write a summary
- Free writing
- Grammatically analyzing an academic article in a particular academic field

This text also includes extensive review chapters and appendices. Because advanced students come from all kinds of backgrounds, before beginning Chapter 1 some students may need a review of the basic components of the language provided in Review Chapters 1 and 2. Examples and exercises are provided with these chapters and Appendices 1 and 2.

Review Chapter 1—A review of the parts of speech and phrases.

Review Chapter 2—A review of clauses and sentences.

Appendix 1—A reference on the use of prepositions.

Appendix 2—A reference on the use of articles.

Appendix 3—A list of the verbs followed by infinitives or gerunds.

If you have any experiences to share, or questions or comments on this book, I would enjoy hearing from you. Suggestions are welcome, and I will consider them for inclusion in future editions.

Helen Hoyt Schmidt
Intensive English and Orientation program
346 Ross Hall
Iowa State University
Ames, Iowa 50011
Telephone (515) 294-3568
FAX (515) 294-0907

TO THE STUDENT

Advanced students who use this text have probably spent years studying English grammar. Nevertheless, many students cannot use that grammar correctly in their writing, and in some cases students cannot recognize grammar structures in their difficult academic reading. The purpose of *Advanced English Grammar* is to help you bridge the gap between your previous studies and the English you will be expected to understand and use during your academic career.

Most of you have studied grammar by learning rules and then practicing them at the sentence level. When you began, the sentences were very easy. As you progressed, the sentences became more and more complex. Even so, your grammar texts so far have probably not involved really long pieces of writing. When you enter a college or university, you will be expected to apply your grammar knowledge to extensive textbook readings (50–100 pages per week per course) and paper-length writing (two or more papers of 5 to 10 typewritten pages per course). For this reason, *Advanced English Grammar* is designed to help you learn to apply your past grammatical training to the real academic world. This text will also introduce you to long, complex reading passages filled with vocabulary that you will need during your academic career.

People seem to be divided into two types of learners. One group learns best by observation, watching or listening to how something is done and then coming to an understanding of the rules for how to do it. The other type of learner prefers to learn the rules first and then apply them to a task. Some people learn best visually; that is, they prefer to see ideas expressed in charts or pictures. Other people learn well verbally and prefer ideas expressed in a written or spoken form. *Advanced English Grammar* has been developed to contain elements that will be helpful to all types of learners.

The exercises in *Advanced English Grammar* are divided into inductive and deductive exercises. Inductive exercises are those in which you will find and identify grammatical structures in the context of textbook and professional journal writing. Deductive exercises are those in which the grammar text tells you the rules which you then apply to academic types of writing. *Advanced English Grammar* is organized so that the grammatical structures are first introduced inductively and then explained deductively. After the explanation, you will work through a number of exercises, beginning with the easiest (using the structures in fill-in-the-blank exercises) and ending with the most difficult (using the structures in free writing).

This textbook is the result of more than twenty years of preparing students to attend university classes. Many of the passages were chosen by my advanced undergraduate or graduate students who were also taking regular university classes. Their choices were sometimes part of a reading assignment and sometimes came from the resources they had chosen with which to write a research paper.

All students studying at a U.S. university are expected to be well rounded, to be able to read and understand material in different fields. An undergraduate is expected to take a broad range of courses his first two years and then to specialize in a major field. Scientists are required to take a few courses in art, history, or literature; literature majors are required to take a few courses in math and science. The American philosophy of education is that all undergraduate and graduate students should have a broad basis of information; we should all know something about everything. As a result, you will be expected to be able to read textbooks, write papers, and pass exams in fields you may not like. I hope that *Advanced English Grammar* will help you meet that challenge so that you will have the opportunity to concentrate your attention on your favorite courses and particular major. Good luck!

UNIT 1

THE VERB SYSTEM

1

THE VERB TENSES

Do you know how many verb tenses there are in English? How many verb tenses do you think an author uses in an article like the following "Mesa Verde refuge rich with history"? Do you think all writers use some tenses more than others or about the same number of all tenses?

Mesa Verde National Park in Colorado contains more than 4,000 ruins of the cliff dwellings of the Anasazi Indian culture that flourished from about A.D. 500 to A.D. 1300.

Discovering the Grammar of the Verb System

Discovery Exercise 1: Identifying Tenses

Read the newspaper article below. Then find and underline all the verb phrases that express time. You may include verb phrases containing modal auxiliaries, but do not include verbals (infinitives, gerunds, or participles used as adjectives).* When you have found all the verbs, look at the chart following the article to see how many times the different tenses appear in the article.

Mesa Verde refuge rich with history

I remember it as if it were yesterday, not 1967. . . . We were young and poor at the time, as opposed to old and poor, but rich in friendships. At any rate, it seemed for several days in that June of 1967, that poor wasn't half enough—there was a real possibility of bankruptcy.

We had sold our family home and a neighboring rental house, which we were buying on contract, to an apartment house developer and had put money down on the house we now live in.

A hitch in the title to the property we were selling rose out of the catacombs where titles live, and it looked for a time as if we might wind up owing for three homes while barely able to make payments on one.

So what did we do? The same thing any sensible young couple would do in similar circumstances. We piled our four young children, our two mothers and ourselves into our 1963 Volkswagen bus and took off on a two-week camping vacation.

The trip, like our circumstances, began disastrously with two days of deluges and a beef stew blown off the camp stove and into the dirt, but finally, like our circumstances, the weather and the trip turned sunny in the end and a good time was had by all.

All of which is a long and roundabout way of telling you that we returned this spring, for the first time since 1967, to Mesa Verde in southwestern Colorado, one of the places our rolling family reunion visited then.

The return was like a visit with an old and valued friend. It was especially pleasant coming right after a float trip featuring heavy exposure to Indian ruins.

The dwellings and granaries and ceremonial structures nestled in the cliffs and dotting the mesa tops of Mesa Verde represent the pinnacle of that Indian culture, called Anasazi, a Navajo word meaning, roughly, ancient ones.

Mesa Verde literature points out that the word Anasazi is not specific, much like the word European.

The development and increasing sophistication of the Anasazi societies—in art, architecture, pottery, tool-making, agriculture, trade, astronomy—have been traced in and around the San Juan River basin from about the time of Christ to about 1300, when all the settlements were abandoned.

---

* For a review of the parts of speech and their functions in sentences, see Review Chapters 1 and 2.

No one is certain what happened to disperse the people, or where they went. It is thought that the Hopi and Zuni peoples of today are the descendants of the ancient ones. There is evidence also of prolonged drought and speculation about invasion.

On our way from Bluff, Utah, where our float trip began and ended, to Mesa Verde we stopped at Hovenweep in Utah near the Colorado border, another Anasazi ruin famous for its tower structures and one I've wanted to see for at least 20 years.

We took several of the self-guiding hikes at both Hovenweep and Mesa Verde.

It is sobering, at the very least, to walk in the vanished footsteps of what was obviously a vibrant, vital, successful society that disappeared virtually without a trace.

(from John Karras, "Mesa Verde refuge rich with history," *The Des Moines Sunday Register*, June 10, 1990, p. 2E. Reprinted with permission of the Des Moines Register and Tribune Company.)

This chart will help you visualize how often a particular tense is used throughout the article "Mesa Verde refuge rich with history." Read the chart and answer the questions that follow it.

MESA VERDE—FREQUENCY OF VERB TENSES

	ACTIVE		PASSIVE	
	SIMPLE	**PROGRESSIVE**	**SIMPLE**	**PROGRESSIVE**
FUTURE				
FUTURE PERFECT				
PRESENT remember live in live is represent points out is are is			is thought	
PRESENT PERFECT have wanted			have been traced	
PAST were seemed visited wasn't was was was		were buying were selling	was had were abandoned	

(continued)

		ACTIVE		PASSIVE	
	SIMPLE		**PROGRESSIVE**	**SIMPLE**	**PROGRESSIVE**
PAST looked might wind up would do piled took off began turned returned	happened went began ended stopped took was disappeared				
PAST PERFECT had sold had put down					

1. Look at the chart above. How many verb tenses are used in "Mesa Verde refuge rich with history"?
2. Which tenses are the most common in the article?
3. Why does the author use past perfect and past progressive?
4. How often does the author choose simple past versus past progressive and past perfect tenses? The usage that you see in this article reflects usage throughout the English language.
5. How often does the author choose active voice versus passive voice?
6. At what points in the article does the author use present tense? Why?
7. What do you think about the lack of present progressive tense in this article?
8. Why does the author use present perfect tense?
9. Write a brief summary analyzing the use of the verb tenses in the article. Use your answers to numbers 1–8 (above) in your answer.

Analyzing Verbs and Verbals

Analysis Exercise 2a: Discriminating between Verbs and Verbals —
-ing versus *-ing*

In the article "Mesa Verde refuge" are several words that end in "-ing" (they are written below). Locate the words in the article, and from their contexts try to figure out if they are used as nouns, verbs, adjectives (participles), or gerunds (nouns). Also try to figure out an explanation for their usage. The first is done for you.

	PART OF SPEECH	CONTEXTUAL EXPLANATION
1. neighboring	adjective(participle)	used in a noun phrase that describes "house"
2. buying		
3. selling		
4. owing		
5. camping		
6. telling		
7. rolling		
8. coming		
9. featuring		
10. dwellings		
11. dotting		
12. meaning		
13. increasing		
14. tool-making		
15. self-guiding		
16. sobering		

Analysis Exercise 2b: Writing Rules

Write some rules about the four kinds of words that end in "-ing." The first one is done for you.

1. Some words ending in "-ing" are verbs. They can be identified as verbs because they appear with auxiliary verb forms in a sentence.

2.

3.

4.

Explanation 1—Verbs and Verbals

Most verbs in the English verb system are made up of phrases. Only simple present and simple past exist as single words. Remember that most verb phrases will contain one or more auxiliary verbs. If you use a verb that ends in "-ing" without an auxiliary, it isn't a verb. It's something else.

Incorrect: John starting on time.

Correct: John is starting on time.

The word "starting" cannot be the verb alone. We must add "is," "was," "has been," "had been," "will be," or another auxiliary verb to make a sentence. It has a main verb and therefore meaning to an English speaker.

Many students have problems with the words ending in "-ing." A word ending in "-ing"

- may be a part of a verb.
- may be a participle (used as an adjective).
- may be a gerund (used as a noun).
- may be a noun (ends in -s).

In order to be a verb, a word ending in "-ing" must have one or more auxiliaries.

Practicing with Verbs and Verbals

Practice Exercise 3

Find the verb phrases in the passages below. Do not include infinitives. How many "true" verbs ending in "-ing" are there in the passages? What function do the other "-ing" words serve in the passages?

The Adult ego state may be shown by attentive eye contact, active listening, a show of confidence, or leaning forward to better understand the other person. The Child ego state may be indicated by slouching, self consciousness, excitement, laughter, helplessness, moist eyes, wringing hands or raising of the hand to ask for permission to speak in a meeting.

Nonverbal communication is expected to support the verbal. But this is not always so. For example, an autocratic manager who pounds his fist on the table, while announcing that from now on participative management will be practiced, certainly creates a credibility gap. Clearly, nonverbal communication may support or contradict verbal communication, giving rise to the saying that actions speak louder than words. (**27:** 699)

MacNeish continued his search for the source of domesticated corn over the next ten years, excavating first in northern Mexico then further south in Honduras and Guatemala. Some sites yielded early corn but not the wild ancestor.

Since similar types were being uncovered in northern and southern Mesoamerica, MacNeish concluded that corn was probably domesticated somewhere in the middle, in central Mexico.

MacNeish had uncovered the beginnings of modern corn but the search for a complete understanding of the process of domestication is still going on today. (**14:** 11–13)

Discussion of Verb Tenses

The English verb system is made up of fourteen active verb tense forms and ten passive verb tense forms (see Chart 1-1). We will see that some of the forms far outnumber others in actual usage.

Verb tenses are used together in a logical way to tell a story or to describe something. We cannot simply begin with any tense we want. We have to have a reason for choosing a particular tense. Suppose our purpose is to describe something that happened once in 1950. We would choose simple past tense. Suppose we want to describe scientific facts. Then we would choose simple present. Each tense provides the means to express our ideas if only we use them correctly.

Different fields of study favor the use of certain tenses. Sciences, for example, favor the simple present tense. The field of history favors the past tenses. Students should be aware of which tenses are most common in their majors so they can use the tenses correctly and interpret the special meanings that may be attached to them in particular contexts.

Tense in the English verb system does not necessarily mean *time* (tense ≠ time). For this reason you need to study the verb tenses in the context of their usage. (Charts 1-1 and 1-2 may be useful as a reference.)

Notice how different tenses are used with different time phrases. For example, with future tense we use "next week," and with present perfect tense we can use "since 1988" or "for 10 years." The chart is blank for the perfect tenses' continuous passive forms because we never use such forms.

Analyzing Verb Tenses

Analysis Exercise 4: Simple Present, Present Progressive, and Present Perfect

Study the following passages. Find the verbs and try to figure out why the author chose the simple present, the present progressive, or the present perfect tenses. Make notes explaining your reasons in the margins. Then, discuss your ideas in class.

> Today, the computer holds enormous potential for people determined to find solutions to mankind's most pressing problems, such as education, the urban crisis, environmental pollution, exploding world population, hunger, natural disaster, and crime.
>
> Presently, city planners are just beginning to use computers to meet the urban crisis. Large parking lots are computer controlled; the computer not only calculates parking fees but also directs individual cars to open parking spaces. Police departments are using a centralized computer to store information on unpaid traffic tickets and stolen cars. (**45: 2**)

CHART 1-1   VERB FORMS

ACTIVE | | PASSIVE

	ACTIVE	ACTIVE (progressive)	PASSIVE	PASSIVE (progressive)
FUTURE	**"will" + base verb** You *will study* English next year.	**"will be" + verb + "ing"** You *will be studying* English all year.	**"will be" + past participle** English *will be studied* in the future.	**"will be being" + past part.** English *will be being studied* forever.
	present "be going to" + base verb You *are going to study* English next week.	**present "be going to be" + verb + "ing"** He *is going to be studying* English all year.	**present "be going to be" + past participle.** English *is going to be studied* in the future.	
FUTURE PERFECT	**"will have" + past participle** You *will have studied* everything you need by 1999.	**"will have been" + verb + "ing"** You *will have been studying* English for many years by 1999.	**"will have been" + past participle** English *will have been studied* by everyone in the world by 3099.	
PRESENT	**base verb/verb + "s"** I *study* English everyday. He *studies* English, too.	**present "be" + verb + "ing"** We *are studying* English this year.	**present "be" + past participle** English *is studied* in many countries.	**present "be being" + past participle** English *is being studied* everywhere nowadays.
PRESENT PERFECT	**"have/has" + past participle** They *have studied* English before. She *has studied* English since 1988.	**"have/has been" + verb + "ing"** They *have been studying* English for 10 years.	**"have/has been" + past participle** English *has been studied* since the middle ages.	
PAST	**verb + "ed"** I *studied* English in high school.	**past "be" + verb + "ing"** She *was studying* English when the phone rang.	**past "be" + past participle** English *was studied* by many groups in the 18th century.	**past "be being" + past participle** Many languages *were being studied* at that time in history.
PAST PERFECT	**"had" + past participle** I *had studied* English for 4 years before I entered the university.	**"had been" + verb + "ing"** She *had been studying* for 24 hours when she fell asleep.	**"had been" + past participle** English *had been studied* for centuries before America was discovered in 1492	

CHART 1-2 VERB TENSE USES

EXAMPLES OF VERB TENSES	COMMON USES	COMMON EXPRESSIONS
FUTURE We *will plant* 1,000 trees tomorrow. We *are going to need* some help.	**FUTURE** Activities that begin in the future. Future events.	**FUTURE** tomorrow, next week, in 1999, in the year 2000, in three months, soon
FUTURE PERFECT The tree near your window *will have grown* to a height of 100 feet by the time (that) you *finish* your studies.	**FUTURE PERFECT** Conjecture, speculation, and plans about something that will happen before another event in the future. (Use present tenses in the time clause.)	**FUTURE PERFECT** by the time (that) . . . by 1999 by next week within a year, week, month . . .
PRESENT Maple trees usually *have* beautiful wood. Our tree *is growing* rapidly this year. Tomorrow we *plant* 100 more.	**PRESENT** 1. *Simple Present*—habits, truths, definitions, future plans and schedules, and generalizations. 2. *Present Progressive*—temporary activities, activities happening at the moment of speaking, and future plans and schedules.	**PRESENT** 1. Often, sometimes, usually, always, generally, never 2. now, this morning, this year, at the moment, while
PRESENT PERFECT Our maple tree *has been growing* ever since 1900. It *has been beautiful* from the moment that it *was planted*.	**PRESENT PERFECT** 1. Connection of past unfinished events to present and perhaps future time (in the mind of the speaker). 2. Generalizations at the beginnings of paragraphs. 3. Transitions between paragraphs to connect past tense events to present and future tense events.	**PRESENT PERFECT** Often, never, scarcely, hardly (ever), rarely, always, frequently, since, ever since, for, lately, from the time (that), from the moment (that) . . .
PAST The maple tree *was planted* in 1900. We planted dozens of trees while I *was growing up*.	**PAST** 1. *Simple Past*—Historical facts, narrative (story telling), finished events. 2. *Past Progressive*—Description of an ongoing event, scene or situation occurring at the same time as a simple past action.	**PAST** 1. ago, in 1860, during, yesterday, last week, when 2. while, as
PAST PERFECT The tree *had grown* two feet by the time (that) it *was* two years old. As soon as it *had been planted*, it *sprouted*.	**PAST PERFECT** Interruptions of a past narrative to include an action or event that occurred earlier than the simple or progressive past events of the story.	**PAST PERFECT** after, by 1776, by the time (that) . . ., no sooner . . . than, hardly . . . when

The human population explosion exemplifies the exponential growth capability possessed by all species. . . . While populations in Japan and the United States are growing at an annual rate of 0.1 percent, until recently Mexico's has been increasing at a rate of nearly 3 percent per year, as have the populations of Iran and Iraq. . . .

Despite the declining fertility of the remaining arable topsoil, world food output is expected to keep up with population growth into the next century. . . . Although overall food production has kept pace with overall population growth, little food usually reaches those who need it most. . . . Although global relief programs may often compensate somewhat for these situations on an emergency basis, populations continue to grow, and poor people are increasingly cultivating the marginal lands. Both trends forbode unprecedented ecological disasters for the future. (1: 1063–1065)

Analysis Exercise 5: Simple Past, Past Perfect, Past Progressive, and Present

Study the following passage. Find the verb phrases. Try to figure out why the author used the simple past, past perfect, past progressive tenses. Make notes in the margins with your explanations. Then, compare your ideas with other students.

Halibut Fisheries

In the North Pacific, fishermen from Canada and the United States first started to exploit the halibut fishery in the 1880s. The halibut catch gradually rose from 1 million pounds in 1888 to about 28 million pounds in 1904, when it began to decline, dropping off by 5 million pounds in 1906. Larger boats were then introduced, venturing farther offshore, and the halibut catch then went up to about 50 million pounds in 1908, when it again tapered off. Then the fishing fleets moved farther into the Gulf of Alaska, and the catch rose to a peak of 69 million pounds by 1915. Between 1915 and 1918, despite these increased efforts, the catch dropped to 38 million pounds. . . . What was happening was that the fishermen from the two countries were overfishing the ability of the halibut fishery to reproduce to maintain itself. . . .

Once the problem was recognized as a biological problem and not a question of the violation of international boundaries, the two states were able to agree in 1930 on the creation of a permanent commission to conserve and therefore help build up the halibut fishery. In a steady rate of growth this was accomplished, and by the 1960s the catch was being sustained at around the rate of 60 to 70 million pounds per year. The fishery had declined previously because the states denied the fact that the fishery—a renewable resource—was being overfished in its ability to renew itself. (12: 105–106)

VERB TENSE USED	ANALYSIS OF TENSE USED

Paragraph 1

Simple past	Used to tell the basic story-line.
Past progressive	Gives information about other past actions going on at the same time, and an interpretation of the events in the story.

Paragraph 2

Simple past	Continues the basic story-line.
Past progressive	Describes an ongoing situation or condition during the time of the story.
Past perfect	Interrupts the basic story-line with information about a previous event.
Past progressive	Interprets and analyzes events that were going on during the story.

Analysis Exercise 6

Compare your answers in Exercise 5 with the table above that describes the passage "Halibut Fisheries" according to verb tense used (*left*) and analysis of verb tense used (*right*). Then analyze "The Maori Emigration" and "Galileo's Observations" in the same way.

The Maori Emigration

A historical illustration of eternal optimism behavior can be seen in the Maori emigration to New Zealand in the fourteenth century. Prior to that time the Maoris were living primarily in the islands of Central Polynesia. New Zealand had been discovered by a Maori explorer named Kupe about A.D. 925. His navigating instructions were passed from generation to generation by word of mouth on how to reach these large, apparently unoccupied islands. As overpopulation in the central Polynesian Islands became inevitable and as the overpopulation resulted in increasing social discontent, plans were made to have a portion of the population move to Ao Tea Roa (The Land of the Long White Cloud), as Kupe had named New Zealand. . . . The Maoris recognized the fact that their original environment was exceeding its capacity to accommodate their population. They were aware of the uninhabited area of Ao Tea Roa in their folklore, and so rather than dealing with the problems in Polynesia, their solution was to move to the vacant area. (**12**: 117)

VERB TENSE USED	YOUR ANALYSIS OF TENSE USED
1. Present	
2. Past progressive	

3. Past perfect

4. Simple past

5. Simple past

6. Simple past

7. Simple past

8. Past perfect

9. Simple past

10. Past progressive

11. Simple past

12. Simple past

Galileo's Observations

[NOTE: Galileo observed the planet Neptune—which he thought was a "fixed" star—234 years before it was discovered to be a planet.]

From January 25 through January 27 Galileo charted the position of SAO 119234 (a fixed star) each night. On the 28th he placed it 29 Jovian radii (Jovian radii = a distance equal to the radius of the planet Jupiter) from Jupiter's center.

At 11:00 that night Galileo charted the position of Neptune for the last time. He took note of it because it was lying beyond SAO 119234 on a straight line drawn through the star and the center of Jupiter. He had also noticed Neptune the night before but had not recorded its position.

On the 28th he commented that the night before Neptune and SAO 119234 had seemed farther apart. Since no overnight change is possible in the relative positions of fixed stars, he must have been puzzled by his recollection.

(from Drake T. Stillman and Charles T. Kowa, "Galileo's Sighting of Neptune," *Scientific American* 243 #6 [December 1980], p. 79. Copyright© 1980 by Scientific American. All rights reserved. Reprinted by permission.)

VERB TENSE USED   YOUR ANALYSIS OF TENSE USED

Paragraph 1

 1.

 2.

Paragraph 2

 1.

 2.

3.

4.

5.

Paragraph 3

1.

2.

3.

4.

Analysis Exercise 7: Present Perfect and Simple Present

Find and underline the verbs in the passage below. Explain the author's choice of the present perfect and simple present tenses. Then discuss your ideas.

> *The Cranberry Harvest*
>
> The development of modern harvesting machinery has contributed substantially to the growth of the cranberry industry. There are two harvesting methods—wet and dry—and the one a grower chooses depends on the intended use of the crop. When cranberries are dry harvested, a mechanical picker is guided around the bog, gently combing berries from their vines with moving metal teeth. During wet harvesting, the bog is flooded and a mechanical water wheel churns up the water to dislodge the berries, which float to the surface to be collected.
>
> (from Howard Spergel, "The Cranberry Harvest," *The Country Journal* [September 1980], p. 42. Reprinted by permission.)

Analysis Exercise 8: Simple Present and Future Perfect

Explain the author's use of the simple present and future perfect tenses. Discuss your ideas in class.

> It is all that mighty human heart that is the object of our study as humanists and as folklorists. If in the pursuit of particular theoretical approaches and specialized research interests we ever forget that, then we will have bartered our birthright for a mess of pottage and will have lost the vision that should have brought us into folklore in the first place.
> (**46**: 156)

Compare the following two sentences. What is the difference in meaning? Which action happens first, "forget" or "barter and lose"?

> If we ever <u>forget</u> that, then we <u>will barter</u> our birthright and <u>lose</u> the vision that <u>should bring</u> us into folklore in the first place.

> If we ever <u>forget</u> that, then we <u>will have bartered</u> our birthright and <u>will have lost</u> the vision that <u>should have brought</u> us into folklore in the first place.

Practicing the Verb Tenses

Practice Exercise 9a

In the following articles, fill in the blanks with your choice of the correct verb tense. Then compare your choices with the authors' choices on page 17.

> *Rain forests denuded faster than estimated*
> *WASHINGTON, D.C.*—Tropical rain forests (*vanish*) _____ 50 percent faster than previously estimated, increasing concerns about global warming, a private environmental research group said Thursday.
> "Every year the world (*lose*) _____ an area of tropical forests almost as big as the state of Washington," said James Gustave Speth, president of World Resources Institute.
> The Institute, which based its report on 1987 data, said that 40 million to 50 million acres of tropical forests (*strip*) _____ each year. In contrast, the United Nations and many governments (*estimate*) _____ that about 28 million acres (*strip*) _____ each year.
> (from "Rain forests denuded faster than estimated," *The Des Moines Register,* June 8, 1990, p. 5A. Copyright © 1990 by the Des Moines Register and Tribune Company. Reprinted with permission.)

> *White World*
> The first team to reach the South Pole by dog sled since 1911 (*announce*) _____ its arrival by satellite last week. "Here we are," the message said. "Hooray." The six-man international team led by American Will Steger (*cover*) _____ 1,992 miles on skis and dog sleds since setting out on July 27. The men (*endure*) _____ winds of more than 100 mph and temperatures as low as minus 45 degrees Fahrenheit. "It was beyond anything I ever thought existed," said Steger.

But this is just the halfway point. The team (*aim*) _____ to be the first to cross the entire Antarctic continent without mechanical help. (*Newsweek,* December 25, 1989, p. 65. Newsweek Inc. All rights reserved. Reprinted by permission.)

Practice Exercise 9b

Compare your answers to the authors' verbs in the original articles. Discuss the differences.

"Rain forests denuded faster than estimated":
  are vanishing, loses, are being stripped, estimate, are stripped
"White World":
  announced, had covered, endured, aims

  1. Are your verb tenses the same as or different from the authors'?
  2. How can you explain the authors' choices?

Practice Exercise 10

Fill in the blanks in the textbook passages below with appropriate verb tenses. Use the verbs given.

[1]   Theory (*be*) _____ a systematic grouping of interrelated principles. Its task (*be*) _____ to tie together significant knowledge, to give it a framework. Scattered data, such as the miscellaneous numbers or diagrams typically found on a blackboard after a group of engineers (*discuss*) _____ a problem, (*be*) _____ not information unless the observer (*have*) _____ a knowledge of the theory which (*explain*) _____ their relationship.

[2]   Although the organization of human beings for the attainment of common objectives (*be*) _____ ages old, a science of management (*be*) _____ just now (*develop*) _____. Since World War II there (*be*) _____ an increasing awareness that the quality of managing (*be*) _____ important to modern life, and this (*result*) _____ in extensive analysis and study of the management process, its environment, and its techniques.

[3]   Science (*explain*) _____ phenomena. It (*base*) _____
on a belief in the rationality of nature—on the idea that relationships can
be found between two or more sets of events. The essential feature of
science (*be*) _____ that knowledge (*discover*) _____
and systematized through the application of scientific method. Thus we
(*speak*) _____ of a science of astronomy or chemistry to indicate
accumulated knowledge formulated with reference to the discovery of
general truths in these areas. Science (*be*) _____ systematized
in the sense that relationships between variables and limits (*ascertain*)
_____ and underlying principles (*discover*) _____.
(**27**: 10, 13)

[4]   Brown's success (*be*) _____ remarkable, considering the
loneliness of the mission and the size of the task. Brown (*change)*
_____ the world. His first study in 1963, when he (*be*) _____
a planner in the Department of Agriculture, (*help*) _____ alert this
nation to the increasing dependence of the rest of the world on North
American food production. From the White House on down to the farmer,
ideas about exports (*change*) _____ by Brown's discoveries. In
1966, when he (*name*) _____ one of the nation's ten outstanding
young men by the Junior Chamber of Commerce, it (*note*) _____
that his article predicting 1965 crop failure in India (*be*) _____
instrumental in launching a huge food rescue mission.
(from Hugh Sidney, "This Man is Changing the World," *The Country Journal*, September 1980, p. 42. Copyright © The Country Journal. Reprinted by permission.)

[5]   **Televised Violence. An indication of the potential impact of TV can be
found in these figures: By the time the average person (*graduate*)**
_____ **from high school, he or she (*view*)** _____ **some
15,000 hours of TV, compared to only 11,000 hours of formal classroom
instruction. In that time he or she (*see*)** _____ **some 18,000 murders and countless acts of violence. (7: 206)**

[6]   Figure 1-1 shows diffusion of sugar molecules from a sugar cube in a container of water. There are eight sugar molecules directly below an imaginary plane and only four above (Fig 1-1 a). An instant later (1-1 b), of the original twelve molecules, there are six above and six below, but the concentration below remains higher because of the arrival of more sugar molecules (x's) from the sugar cube. Until the cube is completely dissolved, this random process of diffusion will continue to increase the

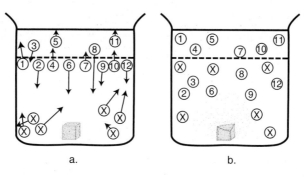

Figure 1-1 Diffusion. Ions and molecules move from regions of high concentration (*left*) across an imaginary line to regions of low concentration until they are evenly distributed. (*right*) (**9:** 116)

number of molecules above the imaginary plane. When the cube is dissolved, diffusion (*result*) _____ in a uniform distribution of molecules throughout the container. (**9:** 116)

[7] Excavations—To build a normal foundation, an excavation is required, and this operation will usually be carried out by some type of power excavation equipment.

The type of foundation to be used for any particular building (*determine*) _____ at the planning stage. The type chosen will depend to a large extent on the soil or subsoil encountered at the site. Soil or subsoil in its natural state is often sufficiently stable to support the foundations of light buildings. Foundations for heavy buildings, on the other hand, (*bring*) _____ to a level with sufficient bearing strength, or to bedrock. . . . In that event, deep foundations (*require*) _____, and these (*discuss*) _____ in a subsequent chapter. (**41:** 33)

Explanation 2—Comparison of Verb Tenses: Important Differences to Remember

Simple present expresses:

1. general truths.
2. scientific facts.
3. customs and habits.
4. planned and scheduled events in the future.
5. the idea of immediacy in
    a. "on-the-spot" news and sports reporting.
    b. observations and summaries of experimental or clinical situations.

6. the meaning "now" with certain verbs:

LINKING VERBS	PERCEPTION VERBS	MENTAL VERBS	EMOTIONAL VERBS	NONACTION VERBS	"SAYING" VERBS
be	*hear*	*agree*	*love*	*belong*	*say*
seem	*feel*	*believe*	*regret*	*contain*	*suggest*
appear	*taste*	*consider*	*care*	*depend*	
	smell	*guess*	*like*	*equal*	
	see	*hesitate*	*admire*	*have*	
		imagine	*hate*	*hold*	
		know	*loathe*	*indicate*	
		prefer		*mean*	
		realize		*need*	
		remember		*owe*	
		suppose		*require*	
		trust		*resemble*	
		want		*tend*	
		wish		*comprise*	

Present progressive

For most tenses the progressive form emphasizes the duration or continuous nature of an event. But in the present tense this is not necessarily true. The progressive form in present tense is reserved for a single action occurring in present time, either "at this moment" or during a period of time that the writer considers to be present time.

> The librarian is sitting at the desk by the door.
> Populations in Japan and the United States are growing at an annual rate of 0.1%.

The "-ing" form may emphasize the temporary quality of that action. The progressive present form may also be used to express a planned future event.

> We are leaving tomorrow.

Sometimes the verbs from the simple present tense group (number 6 above) are used in progressive form. In that case the verb probably changes meaning. For example, "I am seeing a doctor" may mean that I am dating a doctor or that I customarily go to a physician's office for treatment.

Simple past expresses:

1. completed events in the past (one event or repeated events).

> The halibut catch went up to about 50 million pounds in 1908.
> His navigation instructions were passed from generation to generation.

2. duration of a past completed event.

> The halibut catch gradually rose from 1 million pounds in 1888 to 28 million pounds in 1904.

Present perfect is also a past tense but describes the duration of an event from past to present time and possibly includes future, too. The writer who chooses present perfect feels there is a connection to present time and possibly to future although he/she is focusing on the beginning of the event in the past and on the duration or repetition of the event over time from the past to the present.

> the beginning   duration/ repetition of the event
> Since World War II, there has been an increasing awareness of the quality of management.

If there is no time phrase, the decision to use simple past or present perfect depends on how the writer feels about the time involved. If it is a finished event, the writer chooses simple past. Is the action is still in progress? Does it have a connection to now and perhaps the future? Was the action completed only a moment ago? Then the writer chooses present perfect. In this case, the choice of **present perfect progressive** would emphasize the duration and continuous nature of the action and seems to focus on the event or action itself rather than on the beginning of the event or action.

> Bob has been doing the cooking lately.

Sometimes the mental connection to present time is in the mind of the writer and is not obvious from the situation. For example, "I have been to Europe" and "I went to Europe" express the same idea in a general sense, but the first sentence may imply that the writer feels a present mental connection to the idea. Maybe the writer is remembering the trip with pleasure and hopes to visit Europe again. The choice of simple past is more likely when a writer wants to describe a particular time in the past. Simple past would be an appropriate way to begin a past narrative (story), for example. " I went to Europe to study in 1968. In those days it was possible for young people to hitchhike all over the Continent without worrying about safety. Every weekend after classes were over, we hitchhiked to the beach."

Both simple present and present perfect are widely used to express generalizations. Many academic articles begin with a general statement in either simple present or present perfect.

> The computer holds enormous potential.

> The development of modern harvesting machinery has contributed substantially to the growth of the cranberry industry.

Past progressive

Past progressive is used two ways in academic writing. First, it often expresses a past action, situation, or condition simultaneous with another past action.

> By the 1960s, the halibut catch was being sustained at around a rate of 60 to 70 million pounds per year.

It may also express an interpretation and analysis of a series of simple past actions.

> What was happening was that the fishermen from the two countries were overfishing the ability of the halibut fishery to reproduce.

Past perfect

Past perfect expresses events or a situation occurring before other past events. It is often used to interrupt a past narrative to give information about a previous event.

> On January 28 Galileo charted the position of Neptune. . . . He had also noticed Neptune the night before but had not recorded its position.

Future perfect

Future perfect expresses events expected to be finished before a time in the future (specific or not). The future time is usually expressed in the time clause with a simple present tense verb. A phrase indicating future is also possible. Sometimes the expression of that future time is quite vague in academic writing. In Exercise 10, # 5, # 6 and # 7 originally contained verbs in future perfect tense. Why do you suppose the author chose future perfect?

> By the time the average person graduates from high school, he or she will have viewed some 15,000 hours of TV.

> When the cube is dissolved, diffusion will have resulted in a uniform distribution of molecules. . . .

> The type of foundation to be used for any particular building will have been determined at the planning stage.

Analysis of Tenses in a Long Piece of Writing

The purpose of the following exercise is to demonstrate the use of different verb tenses in a longer piece of academic writing. This passage is an introduction to a computer science textbook. As you read the chapter, notice how the verb tenses change as you move from paragraph to paragraph. It is not accidental. The author uses the verb tenses to express specific ideas.

Analysis Exercise 11a

Find and underline the verb phrases in the passage that follows. Do not include gerunds, infinitives, or participles. Then write the names of the tenses you find next to each paragraph, and count the number of times each is used. The first paragraph is done for you.

	TENSE	TIMES USED

Man—The Problem Solver

[1] Since the beginning of time, man has been a problem solver. This ability has made him the dominant species on earth. While solving problems, he has invented tools that have enabled him to change his environment and overcome his physical limitations and human frailties, whereas other species have merely existed as best they can.

present perfect 5

[2] No doubt it was by chance that early man learned to use fire to make his life easier and more comfortable. Perhaps he came across the carcass of an animal that had been killed in a forest fire. Being desperately hungry, he ate some and found it better than raw meat. In time, man learned to start his own fire and was able to enjoy cooked meat whenever he desired. Eventually, he further refined his control of fire and used it as a tool to overcome his physical limitations. He discovered that other animals were afraid of fire and that it could be used as a weapon to compensate for his lack of physical strength. He also learned that fire could provide him with warmth and could make up for his lack of heavy fur. In modern times, man found that fire could be used in a variety of manufacturing processes, such as in the production of iron and steel, and as a means of waste disposal.

[3] One can only guess how the first wheel was invented. Maybe it all began when someone noticed that it was easier to move a block of stone over a rolling log than to push it directly on the ground. Undoubtedly, such an observation led to a series

The Verb Tenses **23**

of logs, where the load was pushed from one log to the next. Somehow, someone found a way to attach the rolling surface directly to the load via axle and wheels. In time man learned to use the wheel as a tool to enhance his abilities and to overcome his physical limitations. He built carts and wagons and trained other animals to pull them so that he could move heavier loads over greater distances. Not satisfied, he invented engines that could power his vehicles so that they could carry more and travel faster. The most notable wheeled vehicle, the gasoline-powered automobile, provides man with a convenient and rapid means of ground travel.

[4]   Man's success in problem solving has also brought him unpredicted side effects and unanticipated problems. His amazing manufacturing processes generate by-products and wastes that contaminate his air, earth and water. His modern automobiles with their internal combustion engines threaten to strangle his larger cities through smog and traffic jams. His modern jet airplanes with their ever-increasing airspeeds and passenger capacities dangerously clog airlanes and jam passenger and baggage handling facilities. Even his miracle medical discoveries produce cruel paradoxes. In some parts of the world, children who are saved by newly discovered medical techniques are in danger of starving to death from lack of food caused by the population explosion.

The Computer—A Problem-Solving Tool

[5]   Today, the computer holds enormous potential for people determined to find solutions to mankind's most pressing problems, such as education, the urban crisis, environmental pollution, exploding world population, hunger, natural disaster, and crime.

[6]   Presently, city planners are just beginning to use computers to meet the urban crisis. Traffic control

projects have been initiated to study the ability of computers to expedite heavy traffic flows and to clear streets ahead of emergency vehicles. Large parking lots are computer controlled, with a computer not only calculating parking fees but also directing individual cars to open parking spaces. Police departments are using a centralized computer to store information on unpaid traffic tickets and stolen cars. With only a radio call, any patrolman in the city can determine within seconds whether an automobile is stolen or whether its driver is wanted for unpaid tickets. Interest is now being shown in using the computer for total city planning. For example, attempts are being made to use a computer to predict how, when, and where a city will expand. With such information, more effective and efficient plans can be developed for city services, such as water distribution and sewage collection, fire and police protection, and street layout and traffic control. In addition, the computer is beginning to be used to solve the problems of the inner city, such as air and water pollution and urban renewal planning.

[7]   The battle against hunger and starvation has just begun to enlist the power of a computer. For example, corn, one of the world's most important food crops, has 20 pairs of chromosomes, each of which has hundreds of genes that influence a plant's growth rate, yield, and disease resistance. In addition, production yields are affected by soil type, plowing, and local growing conditions. Test data from planting experiments from many parts of the world are being fed into a central computer for analysis. Hopefully, the results will reveal how an individual planter can increase his corn production by matching the best available variety of hybrid seed to his own particular growing conditions.

[8]   The effects of the application of computers in medicine are beginning to emerge. Computerized hospital information systems are transmitting

patient data between wards and laboratories, relieving doctors, nurses, and laboratory technicians of time-consuming and error-prone paper work. Computerized intensive care units are being developed, which automatically call attention to potentially serious patient conditions even before the ever-present nurse can sense such changes. Radiologists are using computers to determine radiation dosages likely to be the most effective treatment for cancer patients. Physicians are using computers to analyze electrocardiograms and to diagnose heart ailments.

[9]   Work is just beginning on the control of the natural environment through computers. Meteorologists are improving their weather predictions by using computers to analyze vast amounts of weather data collected by meteorological satellites. Sensors transmit rainfall data from remote unmanned locations to a central computer, which watches for unusual conditions, such as potential flooding. Using a computer, scientists are simulating earthquakes and tidal waves in hope of learning how to predict the occurrence of such devastating natural phenomena.

[10]   Perhaps education is the field in which computers will have their greatest social impact. As population increases, it will be almost impossible to provide enough highly trained teachers. Elementary and high schools must instruct more students and yet insure that each student receives more individual attention enough to guarantee that his performance matches his ability. Junior colleges, universities, and graduate schools must be able to admit and educate all students whose intellect and motivation make them suitable for additional education. The disadvantaged student at all levels must be given additional attention and training so that he can reach his full potential without distracting other students. Workers whose skills are no longer

needed must be retrained so that they can continue to make a contribution to their families and society. These educational problems are challenges not easily solved. Much still needs to be discovered about the learning process itself. Pilot projects indicate that a computer can be a student's personal tutor, guiding him through his lesson, testing him for complete comprehension, and automatically repeating improperly understood material before beginning the next lesson.

[11] The application of the computer to man's most pressing problems will prove its real worth. However, you, the reader, will soon realize that a computer is not an almighty electronic brain. It is a tool—a tool that can help you overcome your human inability to perform rapid mental calculations and to digest masses of information. As with any tool, a computer needs an intelligent human being who knows how to apply it to his problem in the most effective manner. (45: 1–3)

Analysis Exercise 11b: Writing Rules—All Tenses

Based on your analysis of the passage in Exercise 11a, answer each question (rule) below in one sentence. If you can, write your answers in the form of grammatical rules.

RULE 1. What statement can you make about the number of different tenses usually used in a paragraph?

RULE 2. What statement can you make about the tenses that work together within a paragraph?

Analysis Exercise 11c: Discussion Questions

Study the paragraphs in the passage in Exercise 11a again and answer the following questions.

1. What tense begins the passage? Why?
2. Why does the author change to a different tense in paragraph 2?
3. Paragraph 3 includes more than one tense. Why?

4. What function does the first sentence of paragraph 4 have in the passage? (Compare paragraphs 3 and 4 to see which verb tenses are most common.) Why did the author use present perfect tense here?
5. Paragraphs 5, 6, 7, 8, and 9 have some simple present forms mixed with some present progressive forms. Why?
6. Paragraph 10 uses a lot of modal auxiliaries. What is the purpose of this paragraph?
7. What is the function of paragraph 11?
8. When you review the passage as a whole, can you see a pattern in the use of the verb tenses? How did the author develop his ideas? Make an outline of the main ideas and verb tenses for each paragraph.

Explanation 3—Tenses in a Long Piece of Writing

Introductions often begin with verb tenses that express generalizations—present perfect or simple present tense. Writers then tend to discuss the historical background in the past tenses. The next step is usually to move the reader into the present again by using the present perfect. A discussion of contemporary issues may follow in the simple present and present progressive tenses. Suggestions for solutions or future action are often made by using modals, and concluding remarks use simple present and future forms.

FUNCTION OF PARAGRAPH	TENSES USED
Generalization (introduction)	present perfect/simple present
Historical perspectives, background	simple past/past perfect/past progressive
Transitions between past and present time	present perfect
Contemporary issues	simple present/present progressive
Suggestions and solutions	present and future modals
Conclusions	simple present/future

You have seen that writers use the verb tenses for various functions in a piece of writing, and as the purpose of a paragraph changes from the one before, the tenses also change. It is interesting to study how writers use the tenses both within and between paragraphs. There is a pattern to the way tenses work together. Study Chart 1-3.

Explanation 4—Time Frame

CHART 1-3 HOW VERB TENSES WORK TOGETHER

	EXAMPLES	EXPLANATION
To show later events **BASIC TIME FRAME FUTURE** → **Simple Present** To show earlier time relative to Future → Future Perfect	A distorted society looms in the future, a society trapped in the cycle of underdevelopment, stagnation and misery. Projecting current tendencies to **2000**, Latin America will have disintegrated both internally and externally. Of its active population, 44 percent will be in the tertiary sector, but the region will still lack the technological and industrial impetus characteristic of developed nations.	**BASIC TIME FRAME FUTURE—2000** Earlier Time (before 2000) Other Future Events
To show later events **BASIC TIME FRAME PRESENT** → **Simple Present/ Present Progressive** To show earlier time relative to Present → Present Perfect/ Pres. Perfect Progressive	This approach to making the new mass of information more usable **has** much to recommend it, and a number of companies have already adopted it. . . . It **appears** that the future will see multiple intelligence services located throughout an organization so that they can be more responsive to various information needs.	**BASIC TIME FRAME PRESENT** Earlier Time Later Time
To show later events → Past Modals ("would," "might," "could," "was going to") **BASIC TIME FRAME PAST** → **Simple Past/ Past Progressive** To show earlier time relative to Past → Past Perfect	To determine what a fair day's work **was** and to help in finding the best way of doing any given job, the careful study of time and motion **was widely applied** . . . Taylor **emphasized** the . . . . responsibility of managers to design work systems so that workers would be helped to do their best. . . . In concluding his discussion of these principles, Fayol **observed** that he had made no attempt to describe those he had had the most occasion to use, since some kind of codification of principles **appeared** to be indispensable in every undertaking.	**BASIC TIME FRAME PAST** Later Time **BASIC TIME FRAME PAST** Earlier Time

As you study Chart 1-3, you will see that a system of organization is operating in paragraphs that contain more than one tense. First, the writer puts himself/herself into a **basic time frame**—present, past, or future. The writer then can move forward or backward in time relative to the basic time frame. For example, most scientific and business writers put themselves into the basic time frame of the present. The present is a logical choice because the simple present tense expresses facts, habitual actions, truths, and definitions. When the writer wants to express temporary occurrences during an extended period of present time, he/she chooses present progressive. Then, in order to move backward a bit in time but remain connected to the present, the author may choose present perfect; he/she expresses a movement forward in time with future tense and modal auxiliaries like "can" and "may."

A similar system is used by the historical writer. This author chooses the basic time frame of past, the simple past tense. From that specified point in time the writer can move backward relative to that point by using past perfect tense and forward to show later events relative to the basic time frame (a specified past point in time) by using past modals like "would." Ongoing, extended and temporary past events and situations can be expressed with past progressive.

Of course, the writer may want to jump into present time to remind the readers of a fact or definition. If that is the case, the writer will indeed suddenly switch to present tense. On the other hand, if the writer wants to connect the past with the present, he/she will use the present perfect.

Practice Exercise 12

Read the following passage from a Western Civilization textbook, find the verb tenses, and think about the time frames. Then answer the questions that follow the reading.

The Hittites

We saw in Chapter 1 how a northern people, the Hittites, had toppled Hammurabi's dynasty in Babylon. Their capital was Hattusas (modern Boghazköy), the high, arid plateau of north-central Anatolia. They were a ruling Indo-European aristocracy who borrowed from Mesopotamia cuneiform writing, science, conventions in sculpture, the idea of codifying the law, and some Sumerian and Semitic gods. Until 1906 the world knew them only from chance Hebrew and Egyptian references: David's dalliance with Bathsheba, wife of Uriah the Hittite; and the Amarna archives. But in that year German archaeologists discovered the Hittite capital, with massive architecture and 2,500 tablets, in eight languages, of the thirteenth century B.C. Hittite itself, though written in a cuneiform invented

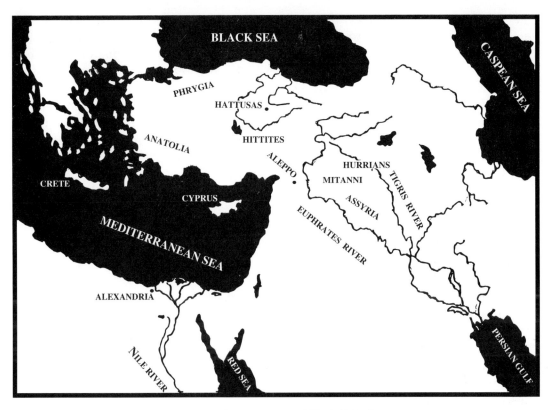

Figure 1-2 The Hittites and Their Neighbors

for Semitic, was an inflected, Indo-European language. The Hittites wrote also in their own hieroglyphs, first deciphered in 1948. These new documents have cast a flood of light on a culture until recently shrouded in darkness.

By the seventeenth century B.C. the Hittites were head of a strong federation. By about 1600 B.C. their king, Mursilis I (c. 1620–1590 B.C.), had established his capital at Hattusas and pushed his conquests as far as Aleppo, in northern Syria. Then for a century, overlapping with Hyksos rule in Egypt, Hittite history is a dark chapter of palace intrigue, murder, invasion, and anarchy. When dawn breaks again under King Telepinus (c. 1525–1500 B.C.), Egypt and the Hittites are apparently partners; at any rate the Hittites did nothing to prevent Thutmose III from invading Mitanni, the land of their aggressive neighbors the Hurrians. But when Amenhotep II made an alliance with Mitanni, Hittite friendship with Egypt was at an end.

The greatest Hittite king, Suppiluliumas (c. 1380–1340 B.C.), occupied the throne while Akhenaton was dallying recklessly in Amarna. As we have seen, he took over the northern part of the Egyptian Empire, and his son

Mursilis II (c. 1339–1306 B.C.), further extended the Hittite federation until it included virtually every Asian state from the Black Sea to Cyprus. At the head of 25,000 men, including the ancestors of the Sea Peoples of a century later, the Hittite King Muwatallis (c. 1306–1282) stopped Ramses II at the Battle of Kadesh. The treaty between them, however, came too late to save either empire. Shortly after 1270 B.C., after the Sea People had destroyed the Hittites, the Mushki (whose King Mitas may have been an ancestor of the Phrygian King Midas of the golden touch) succeeded to the Hittites' dominant position in Anatolia.

(from William L. Langer, ed., *Western Civilization: Paleolithic Man to the Emergence of European Powers* [New York: McGraw-Hill, 1980], pp. 32, 53. Reprinted by permission of McGraw-Hill, Inc.)

1. What is the basic time frame in the passage? What tense is used most? Give an example.
2. How does the author express events that happened earlier than the basic time frame? Give an example.
3. How does the author relate the description of the Hittites to today? Give an example.
4. In the middle of paragraph 2 the author suddenly switches to present tense. Why?
5. In line two of paragraph 3 there is an example of past progressive tense: was dallying. Why does the author use the progressive form?

Explanation 4 (continued)

Most academic writers use the present and past as their basic time frames. A future time frame with future perfect used to express earlier time exists, but is rare. Usually writers avoid the future perfect tense altogether and stick to future and present tenses to express ideas about the future.

To sum up, then, readers need to understand that a writer's choice of tense has the real purpose of communicating meaning. Because the tenses are so closely linked to a specific time frame for meaning, a writer cannot jump from a present perfect tense in one sentence to a past perfect tense in the next unless a basic time frame has been established. Once the basic time frame has been established, all the other verbs in the passage become meaningful because they are relative to that particular point in time.

2

Voice: Active and Passive Sentences

Discovering the Grammar of Passive Voice

Discovery Exercise 1: Review of Passive

Read the following passages and think about the verb phrases. What form are most of the verbs in? Why do you think the author used that form? How many reasons can you think of for choosing that form of the verb? Discuss your reasons in class.

The Athenian Model of Direct Democracy

The government of the ancient Greek city-state of Athens is often considered to be the historic model for a direct democracy. In fact, the system was not a pure system of direct democracy because the average Athenian was not a participant in every political decision. Nonetheless, all major issues, even if decided by the committees of the ruling Council, were put before the assembly of all citizens for a vote. Moreover, about one in six citizens held some political office in any given year. Since positions were

A masterpiece of Greek culture, the Parthenon on the Acropolis in Athens was built between 447 B.C. and 432 B.C.

33

usually held only for one year and were rotated from one citizen to another quite often, most citizens, did, in fact, participate in governing. The most important feature of Athenian democracy was that the legislature was composed of all the citizens. Women, foreigners, and slaves, not being citizens, were excluded. (**39**: 8–9)

Energy in the Body and in Foods

Energy can be transformed from one kind to another, but it can never be created or destroyed. The kinetic energy of water falling down a mountainside can be transformed into the mechanical energy turning the large wheel of a dynamo. This mechanical energy can then be converted to electrical energy and sent through wires into a home, where it can be converted to light energy in a lamp or heat energy in a stove. The chemical energy of food can be converted to the mechanical energy of the beating heart. (**19**: 151)

Functionalism

The functionalist approach in anthropology has been criticized widely for its synchronic view of culture, and its inability to explain change. Additionally, by looking at the way cultural institutions are organized and focusing on social order rather than social change, we tend to develop a conservative bias. If we view a society as existing in harmony, then any change can be likened to disease in an organism, something to be overcome to retain the equilibrium of the social order. . . . It has also been suggested that, contrary to Malinowski's view, not every element in a culture contributes a positive function, and not every element is indispensable. (**14**: 305)

Discovery Exercise 2: Focus on Passive Voice Form

Look at the sentences below. What is the difference between the active and passive verb forms? How do active sentences differ from passive sentences? Write some rules to explain the differences.

ACTIVE VERBS

1. The call number *indicates* the classification of the book.
2. The cards *give* you the information.

3. Most universities *have adopted* the Library of Congress system.

PASSIVE VERBS

1. The classification of the book *is indicated* by the call number.
2. The information *is given* to you by the cards. OR You *are given* the information by the cards.

3. The Library of Congress system *has been adopted* by most universities.

4. The card *will also show* you the edition of the book.

5. You *should take* notes during the event.

6. The catalogers *make* subdivisions by adding a letter and one or more numbers.

4. You *will also be shown* the edition of the book by the card.

5. Notes *should be taken* during the event.

6. Subdivisions *are made* by adding a letter and one or more numbers.

(from Ellen Echeverria, *Speaking on Issues* [Holt, Rinehart and Winston, 1987], pp. 43, 44, 50. Reprinted with permission of Holt, Rinehart and Winston.)

Explanation 1—Passive Voice

- What kinds of verbs can be used in both active and passive sentences?
- What are the functions of the word "by" in passive sentences?

Only transitive verbs can be either active or passive.

| subject | active verb | direct object |
| The call number | indicates | the classification of the book. |

To make an active sentence into a passive sentence, move the previous object to the subject position and the previous subject (now called the agent) to the end of the verb phrase with "by"(or omit the "by" phrase completely). The agent can be a person or a thing that does something to the subject of the passive verb. Use a form of "be" as the auxiliary and the past participle of the main verb.

| subject | passive verb | agent |
| The classification of the book | is indicated | by the call number. |

A second function of a "by" phrase in a passive sentence is adverbial. The "by" phrase explains how something is done.

| subject | passive verb | how articles are listed |
| Journal articles | are listed | by title and author. |

Practicing Active and Passive Forms

Practice Exercise 3: Passive Form

The following passages contain passive verbs. Fill in the blanks with the correct form of the verb given. You may use modal auxiliaries like "can" and "may" if you like. Note how the word "by" is used in these passages.

Basic Chemistry—Matter and energy are fundamental to all living systems. Before the explosion of the first atomic bomb, it (*generally/ believe*) _____ that matter and energy were separate and distinct entities. However, the detonation of the atomic bomb at Alamogordo in the New Mexico desert in 1945 demonstrated Albert Einstein's contention that under certain conditions a small amount of matter (*convert*) _____ into a large amount of energy. In living systems, matter (*not/ convert*) _____ into energy but (*use*) _____ to transfer energy from energy-releasing to energy-using processes.

The Nature of Matter—Chemistry deals with the composition, structure, and properties of matter and the changes it undergoes. All forms of matter (*classify*) _____ as either mixtures or pure substances. A mixture (*compose*) _____ of two or more substances that (*separate*) _____ from one another by physical means, that is, without undergoing chemical change. . . . The components of saltwater (*separate*) _____ by purely physical means; the salt, which (*dissolve*)_____ in the water, (*recover*) _____ simply by evaporating the water. Homogenous liquid mixtures such as saltwater (*call*) _____ solutions.

Pure Substances—A pure substance is a homogeneous form of matter that (*break*) _____ into two or more substances only by a chemical reaction, if at all. Pure substances are of two types. If a substance (*not/separate*) _____ into two or more substances by chemical means, the substance is an element. The substance is a compound if it (*broken*) _____ down into two or more chemical elements. In the past 150 years of research, 106 elements (*discover*) _____ . (**1**: 35–36)

Explanation 2—When to Choose the Active Voice

Research has shown that approximately 70 percent of the verbs in average written English are active. In most cases the active voice causes few problems for the non-native speaker of English. But in some languages, active verbs require animate subjects. In English, we often use active voice with inanimate subjects *when the verb describes an inherent function of a subject.*

subject	verb	object
Something	does something	to something.
A thermometer	measures	temperature.

Inanimate subjects used with active verbs are most common in the physical sciences but can also be found in business and the social sciences. The active verbs in such sentences can be divided into two kinds—causal verbs and explanatory verbs.

Causal verbs appear in a ratio of about 50/50 to explanatory verbs in the social sciences and 70/30 in the physical sciences. They may have inanimate or abstract subjects.*

Cause/effect verbs: *affect, cause, create, kill, prevent, protect*

> (*Business*): If a product does not offer higher quality, a significantly lower price can cause a parity product to be meaningfully different if the market appreciates the improved value.

Change of state or location verbs: *bring, decrease, increase, open, reduce, revolutionize*

Presentation verbs: *give, offer, produce, provide, support, yield*

> (*Physics*): This melt processing technique produces a denser material with long needle-like crystals. This structure overcomes the so-called weak link problem.

Explanatory verbs—*confirm, explain, find, indicate, raise (concerns, etc), reveal, show, suggest*—are more likely to have abstract subjects.

> (*Geology*): Further investigation revealed that most of northern New Mexico was indeed covered by marine sediments.

Practice Exercise 4a: Completing Sentences with Inanimate Subjects and Active Voice

Change the following passive sentences into active sentences with inanimate subjects. After you finish rewriting the sentences, reread them. Which version seems more natural to you, active or passive?

1. "Absolute" ages of rock layers have been provided by recent methods of radioactive dating.

* Adapted from Peter Anthony Master, "Inanimate Subjects with Active Verbs in Scientific Prose," a paper delivered at the International Conference of Teachers of English to Speakers of Other Languages, San Francisco, California, March 8, 1990.

_____"absolute" ages

of _____.

2. The only clue then known to the age of rock formations was provided by fossils.

Fossils _____

_____

3. The imagination is staggered by such an enormous period of time, at an almost unbelievably remote distance in the past.

Such an _____

_____

4. Millions of years are required for these geological processes. (omit "for")

_____

millions of years.

5. On the west side, frequent elevation of the western highlands was caused by periodic vertical motion on a north-south trending fault.

On the west side, _____

on a north-south trending fault _____

_____.

6. Consumers were offered the advantages of both canned and dry dog food by Tender Chunks.

_____ consumers the

advantages of _____.

7. Sometimes a long-lived meaningful difference can be attained by a product even without having the advantage of a sophisticated new form or technological advancement.

Sometimes a product _____

_____ even without having the advantage of _____.

8. Prohibition was addressed by other historical materials.

Other historical materials _____.

9. That our alcohol awareness project was long overdue was suggested by several findings from the questionnaire.

Several findings from the _____

_____.

10. The ceramic oxide is reoxygenated underneath by the process, and its properties are actually enhanced.

The process _____

and _____ its properties.

Discussion: Many students feel that the passive versions are "better," yet the authors who wrote the original sentences chose active voice.

Practice Exercise 4b

Go back through the sentences above, find the verbs, and look them up in the dictionary if you need to. Then separate them into the two categories below according to their type.

CAUSAL VERBS   EXPLANATORY VERBS

Practice Exercise 5: Rewriting Passive Sentences—Inanimate Subjects with Active Voice

Rewrite the following sentences with an inanimate subject and an active verb.

1. The location of an ancient beach is probably indicated by the sandstone.

2. Sediments were carried into the sea that lay in their midst by rivers and streams in Pennsylvania times.

3. That the sediments included much feldspar and other minerals common in granite rock has been shown by examination of sedimentary rock.

4. A revision of ideas about the extent of the Mississipian seas was necessitated by these discoveries. (**32**: 22–29)

Explanation 3—When to Choose the Passive Voice

Most sentences (about 70%) in academic English are in active voice, but writers may choose passive for the following reasons.

- The agent is unimportant or unknown.

   At General Motors' testing track near Milford, Mich., the giant automaker's J-car, which will be released next May or June, is being put through punishing road tests.

- The topic of the paragraph necessitates the use of the topic in the subject position.

> An estimated 40 TW of *solar power* is captured by the green leaves of plants. The overall efficiency of utilization of light energy through photosynthesis on an annual basis is only a fraction of a percent, but under ideal conditions, many plant species convert a quarter of the absorbed light into chemical energy. (**42**: 170)

- To be indirect, that is, to avoid blame.

Active: I have decided to terminate your employment.
Passive: It has been decided to terminate your employment.

- To avoid a "weak" subject in active voice.

weak: *Everyone* knows that ethanol is an excellent fuel.
strong: *Ethanol* is known to be an excellent fuel for spark-ignition engines but is generally unsuitable for Diesel engines.

- To include a detailed description of a process.

Active: Distillation purifies water.
Passive: Water is purified by heating it to the boiling point, condensing it, and collecting the product in a container.

- To avoid problems with masculine/feminine pronouns.

Active: Each student must include *his/her* name and address on *his/her* application.
Passive: Students' names and addresses must be included on each application.

- To provide cohesion and coherence.

> *Between and within sentences*—It (the level of technology) next moves to the level of *applied sciences* such as *medicine or agronomy. These applied sciences* are generally grounded in several of the general disciplines and attempt to apply general theories to pragmatic problems. *Innovations* are the result of their efforts. And, of course *innovation* as perceived by the applied scientist is generally quite far removed from the *innovation* perceived and used by the practitioner. (**48**: 30)

> *Between paragraphs*—All tractor works manufacturing operations converge in the 19-acre (8ha) Tractor Assembly Building. Subassemblies, parts and components come together on three chassis assembly lines, three final assembly lines and two finish paint and trim lines in the right sequence to keep *assembly operations* moving smoothly.

The complex *assembly process* is made more complicated by the need to custom build *each tractor. Each tractor* that rolls off the assembly line is destined for a particular dealer or customer.

Active voice after passive—Special conveyers then transport the hoods, grille screens, air cleaner stacks and toolboxes to the finish trim line where *the tractors* are completed. *The completed tractors* then must pass a final inspection before they are approved for release to a shipping carrier.

(from a John Deere Tractor brochure, John Deere Tractor Company)

Passive voice after active—The transmission of the essential genetic information between generations depends on the precise replication of the nucleotide sequences of DNA. . . . A sequence on one strand of the DNA molecule (for example CATACTAG) lies immediately opposite a complementary sequence (GTA-ATGATC) on the other strand. Double-strand DNA replicates by unwinding and separating. . . . In the presence of suitable enzymes and free nucleotides a new chain is formed. *Each nucleotide lines up next to its opposite number (C next to G, A next to T). The complementary sequence thus established is then linked end to end* by an enzyme that closes the nucleotide couplings. When the replication process has traveled along the entire length of the original double helix, two new helixes identical with the first one have been formed. (**18**: 23)

Explanation 4—Coherence

Academic writing styles are often extremely complex. The writers put many clauses and phrases into each sentence in order to include as much information as possible. The complexity of the sentence structure thus demands an enormous amount of concentration from the reader. *Coherence* means that all parts of a piece of writing are related to each other. We say that a passage is cohesive if it seems logical and clear. Effective writers try to help their readers by using cohesive devices like transitions, clear reference pronouns, and repetition of key words and phrases. In addition, key concepts (noun phrases) put close together help the reader to follow the main ideas. For example, if a sentence ends with a particular concept (often a noun phrase), the author uses that noun phrase or a synonym as the subject of the following clause or sentence whether that choice demands active voice or passive voice. In fact, both active and passive are useful in achieving coherence.

Effective writers choose whichever voice helps them to put the topic of discussion in the best place to enable the reader to follow the writer's ideas.

Analyzing Cohesion

Analysis Exercise 6

Reread the examples of cohesion in Explanation 3 above to explain what the writers are doing to achieve cohesion.

1. What do the italics indicate?
2. What kinds of phrases are italicized?
3. Where are the phrases placed in relation to one another? (Are they close to or far from one another?)
4. How do the writers achieve this placement? (Hint: look at the verb phrases)
5. After examining the examples, how would you define cohesion?

Analysis Exercise 7: The Passive and Cohesion

The vocabulary in the following passage is extremely complex, but don't worry; you are not expected to understand all the specialized vocabulary. First, read the preliminary explanation about the protein engineering passage. Second, read the protein engineering passage, find the repeated noun phrases and their synonyms in the passage, and connect them with arrows. Some of the repeated noun phrases are subjects of verbs. Find the verb phrases. Then answer the questions below.

- Are the verbs active or passive?
- Why did the author choose the voice (active or passive) that he did?

> *Preliminary explanation*
>
> A protein molecule will adopt its native three-dimensional structure under normal physiological conditions. The transition from nonnative to native structure is called "protein folding." The protein engineers in the following article are discussing their hypothesis that there is a hierarchic architecture in proteins in which four types of structural primitives pack together to form protein superstructures. Scientists believe that there may be a stereochemical code that determines the patterns of folding in protein molecules. As they did their research, the biochemists found that protein molecules can be separated into regions called "domains" that appear to be functionally distinct units.

Protein Engineering Passage

These ideas have been reinforced by the suggestion that exons code for domains.

In our analysis, domains appear as an inevitable consequence of the hierarchical assembly of compact units. Therefore, the strategy adopted in our work has been to analyze proteins of known structure, identifying all continuous-chain compact units of any size. Compact units are natural candidates for study because they are the regions within the protein that have most effectively minimized hydrophobic surface area while maximizing internal atomic contacts. The existence of such units follows from the observation of hierarchic architecture in proteins together with the closepacked nature of the molecular interior.

Compact units found in this way can be classified based upon their structural composition. Many units comprised of helix, sheet, and their superstructure were found. Such units were expected because assemblages of helix and sheet are termed repetitive structures because their residues have repeating mainchain torsion angles (O and U), and their backbone N _ H and C + O groups are arranged in a periodic pattern of hydrogen bonding. (**11**: 168)

Analysis Exercise 8: Using Active or Passive to Create Cohesion

Study the two examples below. The first version of each passage is less cohesive, and the second version is more cohesive. Why do you think this is true? Discuss your ideas in class.

[*Less cohesive*] The smallest unit of an element that can combine with another element is the atom. Three primary components are contained in atoms: protons and neutrons, which are located in the nucleus, and electrons, which move rapidly about in the rest of the space occupied by the atom.

[*More cohesive*] The smallest unit of an element that can combine with another element is the atom. Atoms contain three primary components: protons and neutrons, which are located in the nucleus, and electrons, which move rapidly about in the rest of the space occupied by the atom.

[*Less cohesive*] The weak electrostatic forces that sometimes hold nonpolar molecules to each other are van der Waal's forces, which result from the movement of electrons. At any given instant, the charges on a molecule may not be uniformly distributed, inducing the formation of equal and opposite electric charges in different parts of the molecule. Van der Waal's forces often hold together molecules of the same kind.

[*More cohesive*] The weak electrostatic forces that sometimes hold non-polar molecules to each other are van der Waal's forces, which result from the movement of electrons. At any given instant, the charges on a molecule may not be uniformly distributed, inducing the formation of equal and opposite electric charges in different parts of the molecule. Molecules of the same kind are often held together by van der Waal's forces. (**1**: 37, 50)

Discussion—Did you notice that in Example 1 the passage was more cohesive when the writer put the words *atom* and *atoms* close together? This made it necessary to use active voice in the sentence beginning with *Atoms*. In Example 2, the more cohesive passage has *molecule* and *molecules* as close to each other as possible. This choice made it necessary for the writer to use passive voice in the sentence beginning with *Molecules*. Sentences are often connected in this way in scientific writing.

Using the Verb System to Write Cohesive Passages

Writing Exercise 9: Voice

Using what you have learned so far about how writers can use active or passive voice to create cohesion, change the italicized sentences in the passages below to make them more cohesive.

Radioactive Isotopes

Many common biological elements are readily available as radioactively labeled isotopes. *We can incorporate these isotopes into molecules and use them as tracers in biological reactions or in cells and tissues.* The radiation emitted as the elements decay can be measured by a variety of techniques. One of these, called autoradiography, involves placing a specimen containing labeled radioactive material in close contact with photographic film. *When someone develops the film, it shows a pattern formed by radioactivity in the tissues that have incorporated the label.* All atoms of a particular radioactive isotope have the same likelihood of decaying, whatever their age may be. *We cannot specify the time required for a radioactive isotope to decay completely.* (**1**: 42)

Question: When you wrote a cohesive passage in the exercise above, you probably used passive voice in the rewritten italicized sentences. A sentence in the middle of the passage contains a verb in active voice. It and the sentence before it exhibit the same cohesion. Can you find them?

Adoption and Diffusion of Innovations

The first model to be examined is a macroframework for examining a nation or some other large social grouping as a diffusion system. Three important subsystems are within this general system: innovative, practitioner and communicative. . . . As we've created social organization to develop new ideas, we've created social organization to communicate these ideas. *We have enhanced this communication process through the invention of technical means for multiplying and speedily conveying our messages.*

It requires considerable time, of course, to move across the diffusion system and to translate very general ideas into specific innovations. First, let's examine the first antibiotic drug—penicillin. Like other scientific innovations, the development of penicillin was rooted in the basic assumptions of science and depended upon the peculiar conception of the germ theory of disease. *Louis Pasteur and others in the late 1800s formulated and demonstrated this theory, a product of the general flowering of biological sciences.* (**48**: 30)

Fast Atom Bombardment Mass Spectrometry (FABMS)

Mass spectrometric techniques allow the characterization of a protein by providing information about the molecule's weight and structure. Determining a protein's primary structure is a formidable task, yet it is an essential prelude to comprehensive chemical and biophysical studies. FABMS is rapidly becoming the method of choice for confirming DNA-derived amino-acid sequences for large proteins. *After we deduce a sequence from nucleic acid studies,* the actual protein (either purified from its natural source or by recombinant techniques) is digested by chemical or enzymatic means into predictable fragments. *We then determine the molecular weight of these fragments by FABMS and compare them to the molecular weights predicted from the genetic sequence.*

Nuclear Magnetic Resonance (NMR)

NMR has become an increasingly important method for studying the tertiary structures of proteins in solutions. . . . Proteins have several hundred discrete ^{1}H nuclear resonances, each of which provides structural information. In order to get the most from this data, each resonance has to be individually resolved—not an easy task. But two-dimensional (2D) NMR allows the resonances to be systematically separated. Several novel 2D methods have been developed in parallel with increases in magnetic field strength and computing power—allowing workers to determine the tertiary structure of proteins faster and more accurately.

Before workers can determine the tertiary structure of a protein by NMR, however, it is necessary to assign each resonance in the protein's NMP spectrum. Once workers have made these assignments, a two-dimensional Nuclear Overhauser Enhancement (NOE) Spectrum is obtained.

(from Jeffrey Kelly, "New Tools for Probing Protein Structure," *Bio/Technology* 6 [February 1988], 125–129. Reprinted by permission of Bio/Technology, Nature Publishing Company.)

Using the Verb System in Writing

Writing Exercise 10: Ordering Exercise

Your instructor will reproduce, separate, and hand out the introduction and numbered sentences below. The students individually or in groups then put the sentences together in logical order. After approximately 20 minutes, your instructor will hand out *the clues.* You might want to compare your stories with the real sequence of events in the clues. Imagine that you are writing a news story. The following sentences are about the discovery of an ancient man buried in the ice of a glacier, but they are out of order. Use what you know about time expressions, verb tenses, and cohesion to put the sentences into logical order. You may find more than one way to organize the story logically.

The Iceman: Introduction

In September 1991 a dead man was found in a glacier high in the Alps on the border between Austria and Italy. At first no one realized that he was the mummified corpse of a late Stone-Age man (Neolithic period). He died wearing his buckskins and grass cape. His bow and arrows, a copper ax, and other tools were recovered nearby. His skin, internal organs, and even his eyes are still in place. . . . He is the oldest and best-preserved human body ever found. Scientists have found that he is at least 5,300 years old.

The Iceman

1. In late summer or autumn around 3,300 B.C., a 25- to 35-year-old-man wandering above the treeline at about 10,500 feet took shelter in a natural trench nearly 6 feet deep and 20 feet wide.

2. But nobody rushed to the scene. The melting alpine glaciers had already released six corpses that summer. The others were 20th-century climbers whose bodies had been partially pulverized by the glacier's slow, ponderous movement.

3. Then during the unusually hot European summer of 1991, a pair of German hikers spotted a leathery skull and a shoulder poking out of the glacier and contacted the police.

4. He died there. Exposure to several weeks of cold winds mummified the body. Snowfall froze the mummy, and centuries of snowfall became a glacier.

5. [The rescue caused a great deal of damage to the body.] "Thirty men with picks and compressors worked on him," groans Werner Platzer, dean of physiology at the University of Innsbruck and leader of the team studying the body. "The body froze at night and thawed during the hot sun for days while the rescue effort was under way. They had no idea how old he was." Forensic expert Rainer Henn and his men had no idea that the man they were freeing from the ice could be the most important discovery in modern archeology.

6. Sheltered in the trench, the frozen body was spared most of the shearing forces of the glacier.

7. The iceman's body, however, was virtually undamaged. That is, until his rescue.

8. After Henn found a flint-tipped knife in the slush, he told his assistants to stop working on the body.

9. "When I saw this knife, I had the idea that this man was very old," Henn later reported. "From that moment I ordered all the people to be most careful while getting the body out of the ice."

10. In their haste to ferry the find back to Innsbruck, the recovery team left some material behind. And by the time everyone had collected their wits after the first wave of excitement, ten feet of snow covered the site, sealing it for the winter.

11. It will be many years before the frozen body reveals all of its secrets.

12. Now, a single individual from that shadowy time has emerged from a retreating alpine glacier completely outfitted with clothes, tools and weapons.

13. When the corpse and its bundle of artifacts arrived via helicopter at the University of Innsbruck's Institute of Forensic Medicine in October 1991, the university's dean of prehistory, Konrad Spindler, was on hand. "I felt like Howard Carter staring onto the likeness of King Tut," he recalls.

14. In fact, the find will probably prove to be far more important than the discovery of King Tutankamen, because Tut's 3,344-year-old tomb only served to further illustrate the opulent lives of Egypt's well-known pharaohs.

15. The iceman is nearly 2,000 years older, and his discovery illuminates a far more mysterious time period. Scant traces remain of the people who farmed and hunted in the forests of Europe in the late Neolithic Age.

16. The Iceman has spent most of the last months swaddled in an icy cocoon at the University of Innsbruck's forensic laboratory.

17. Because physical examination of the body endangers it, researchers are developing a comprehensive database that allows them to study the body in detail without touching it.

18. Researchers are reluctant to draw further conclusions about how the Iceman lived and died without more study.

The Iceman: The Clues
- 5,300 years ago: A Neolithic-Age man was walking in the mountains where he died and was covered in ice.
- September 1991: The Iceman was found and rescued by several groups, one of which included forensic expert Rainer Henn.
- October 1991: The Iceman was taken to the University of Innsbruck, where he has been kept frozen. Scientists are studying how he lived. (**15**: 46–88)

Writing Exercise 11: Free Writing

Introduction—Everyone is interested in how human beings first appeared on the earth and how we have developed over millions of years. Archeologists divide the history of man into periods of biological and cultural development. The first hominids lived in East Africa about 4 million years ago. These hominids are generally classed in the genus *Australopithecus*. Our own genus, *Homo*, appeared about two million years ago and our own species, *Homo sapiens*, probably emerged about 250,000 years ago.

Look at the chart below. The goal of this exercise is to write a story about the cultural development of man from his earliest form in the past to the future. Think about what life was like when man first appeared on the earth. Think about the many cultural developments that have occurred since then. Consider these questions as you write.

- What kind of life did the earliest humans have?
- What did they do every day? How did they live?
- When did people change from finding food to growing their own food?
- What was happening during the Bronze Age?
- What had happened by the time humans invented the wheel?
- What wonderful inventions have there been since modern *Homo sapiens* first emerged?
- What is going on nowadays?
- What will mankind be like in the future?

You may use the information in the chart below as well as your own knowledge and imagination. Use the appropriate verb tenses and time expressions to express your ideas.

THE AGES OF MAN

ARCHEOLOGICAL PERIOD	NUMBER OF YEARS AGO	NAME OF FOSSIL	CULTURAL HISTORY NEW DEVELOPMENTS
		OLD WORLD	
Stone Age (Lower Paleolithic)	4,000,000	*Australopithecus* (Africa)	Hunting/Scavenging/ stone tools.
	2,000,000		
	1,800,000	*Homo erectus* (Africa & Asia)	Fire used for cooking, warmth, and protection/ Division of labor—men hunted big game/women cared for children and gathered plant food/ Lived in caves or wooden huts in campsites.
	1,500,000		
	250,000	Earliest *Homo sapiens*	
(Middle Paleolithic)	100,000	Neanderthal man (Africa, Asia, Europe)	Religious beliefs (some worshipped bears). Burial / Many shaped stone tools (flaked).
(Upper Paleolithic)	75,000	Modern *Homo sapiens* (Africa)	Art: cave paintings, decorative objects, personal ornaments/ Many bladed tools, bow & arrow, spear thrower, tiny replaceable blades/ Lived in mobile groups in open camps/ Skin-covered huts, caves, and rock shelters/ Mainly hunters, fishers, and gatherers.
	35,000	Cro-Magnon man	

THE AGES OF MAN *(continued)*

ARCHEOLOGICAL PERIOD	NUMBER OF YEARS AGO	NAME OF FOSSIL	CULTURAL HISTORY NEW DEVELOPMENTS
		NEW WORLD	
(Mesolithic)	14,000 (12,000 B.C.)	Humans moved to the Americas across the Bering Strait	Gradual transition from food collecting to food producing/ More sedentary communities.
(Neolithic)	10,000 (8,000 B.C.)	(Africa, Asia, Europe, the Americas)	Permanent villages/ Domestic plants & animals. Introduction of metal tools/ Writing
Bronze Age	5500 (3500 B.C.)		Cities, states/social inequality/ Metals used regularly (copper & bronze)/mining, smelting & casting/Specialization of labor/ Wooden disk-wheeled vehicles & plows/Extensive trade.
Iron Age	2,900 (900 B.C.)		General use of iron/ Developed economic innovations of Bronze Age/ Warfare with horses and horse-drawn vehicles/ Spoked wheels/ Alphabetic writing.
	A.D. 800		Gunpowder
	A.D. 1900		The Industrial Revolution/ Assembly line production/ Dynamite/ oil + gas fuels/ The internal combustion engine/ The automobile/ The airplane.
	The Present		Nuclear energy/Computers/ Space travel/ Environmental pollution.
	The Future	?	? (**8**: 90)

3

AUXILIARY VERBS

PART I   MODAL AUXILIARY VERBS

Auxiliary verbs are verbs that come before the main verb in the verb phrase. Some auxiliary verbs indicate tense and voice. Some examples:

AUXILIARY VERB	MAIN VERB	ACTIVE/PASSIVE VOICE
is	*leaving*	*active*
has been	*found*	*passive*
will have been	*started*	*passive*

Some auxiliary verbs indicate the intentions, attitudes, or feelings of the writer. Two of the common auxiliaries of this type are modals and similar words that we call semi-modals.

MODALS		SEMI-MODALS
will	*could*	*seem to*
shall	*might*	*need to*
can	*would*	*have to*
may	*had better*	*used to*
should	*would rather*	*ought to*
must		*be going to*
		be able to

Sometimes modals and semi-modals are used together.

MODALS	SEMI-MODALS	MAIN VERB
may	*need to*	*leave*
would	*have to*	*study*
will	*seem to*	*agree*
is	*going to*	*apply*

Discovering the Grammar of Modals

Discovery Exercise 1: Identifying Modals

Read the following selection from an anthropology textbook and find the verbs and modals. Make notes in the margins of how the verbs, modals, and semi-modals are used. Note the tenses and meanings of the modals, what kinds of ideas are expressed in the sentences containing modals, and the time frames in the different paragraphs. After you answer the questions, discuss your findings in class.

The Early Migrations of Our Ancestors

[1]   The basic problem is why humans turned increasingly from small to big game and, before that, why they turned to meat eating in the first place. Most primates are vegetarians in the sense that they live chiefly on fruits, grasses, leaves and other plant foods. But probably many primates and many mammals, for that matter, may become meat eaters under certain circumstances. For example, if a baboon happens to come across a nest of fledgling birds, it may on rare occasions scoop up the contents casually, without breaking stride. In other words, meat eating may be incidental.

[2]   It may also be considerably more than that, however. A male baboon has been observed pursuing a hare in a zigzag dodging course for about seventy yards. The chase lasted more than a minute. It ended when the hare jumped over a log and "froze" motionless on the other side. Only to be picked up and devoured by its pursuer. This tactic fools many predators with poor color vision, and baboons may use it themselves, but in general

Many ordinarily vegetarian primates will eat meat if the opportunity arises.

it plays into the hands of primates whose highly developed color vision helps them to detect motionless objects.

[3]   A more complex event took place a few years ago, when John Pfeiffer, one of the authors of this text, spent several weeks in Kenya with Irven De Vore. One July afternoon they were driving through the Royal Nairobi National Park, looking for baboons as usual and heading for a ford across a shallow stream. Suddenly they saw directly ahead a large male baboon with a freshly killed hare in its mouth, a noteworthy event in itself since meat eating is rarely observed. But there was more to come. A whole troop was crossing the stream, and a few seconds later another large male passed with another hare, and not long after that a third male carrying the remains of a small antelope.

[4]   This was an unusual observation, the only recorded example of multiple killings among primates in the wild. But they had missed seeing, probably by only a few minutes, something even more unusual—how the killings had been carried out. Although further knowledge about predatory behavior is required to account for what happened, De Vore suggests a possible explanation: "The whole troop seemed excited, jittery. Since baboons eat small animals in a matter of minutes these animals must all have been killed recently and almost simultaneously. Perhaps one baboon came upon a hare lying in the grass and picked it up casually, and the sight of the act aroused other baboons to go after hares and other small game in the vicinity. In other words, it might have been a spontaneous flurry of activity, a kind of brief blood-lust episode."

[5]   The episode, of course, represented only one incident in the experience of one troop. It might never again occur again in just that way. A casual killing in the future might arouse troop members as before, but the excitement could peter out quickly if other small animals did not happen to be nearby. On the other hand, if a similar experience did recur, the practice of killing could catch on and be passed along from generation to generation within the troop, and also to other troops occupying the same region. The practice might never become established in another region, either because favorable circumstances do not occur frequently enough or because there is ample plant food.

[6]   Similar influences may have been at work in determining the evolutionary adaptations of early hominids. We bear the marks of vegetarian origins in teeth not specialized for ripping and tearing like those of true carnivores and in the sort of long gut generally associated with a diet of plant food. Furthermore, we still seem to digest vegetable fats better than animal fats. Medical research indicates that an important factor in hardening of the arteries may be the formation of deposits of poorly digested fatty products on inner blood-vessel walls. (**36:** 106–108)

1. Scan the first two paragraphs of the selection.
   a. What is the basic time frame established by the author?
   b. What modals do you find here?
   c. What tenses do they express?
2. Look at paragraphs 3 and 4.
   a. What is the basic time frame?
   b. What modals do you find here?
   c. What tenses do they express?
   d. What do they mean?
3. Read paragraph 5.
   a. What time frame does the author seem to be in?
   b. How do you explain the past tenses in lines 4 and 5?
   c. What modals do you find?
   d. What tense do the modals express?
   e. What do the modals mean?
4. Paragraph 6 begins with a modal.
   a. What time does it express?
   b. What does it mean?
   c. What happens to the time frame in paragraph 6?
5. Read the caption on the illustration.
   a. What modal is used?
   b. What is its meaning?

Discovery Exercise 2: Modal Meanings

Read the following anthropology selection about an early hominid, *Australopithecus*. Starting in the second paragraph, find the modals and semi-modals and describe their tenses and meanings in the margin. (The first one is done for you.) Then look at the passage as a whole. What kind of writing uses so many modals? What is the author trying to communicate? Discuss your ideas in class.

Early Hominids and Their Cultures

[1]   Who or what are hominids, and how do they differ from other hominoids? The hominid family comprises modern humans, their ancestors, and other extinct bipedal hominoids. The family includes at least two genera: *Homo* (including modern humans) and *Australopithecus* (a genus of hominids that lived during the Pliocene and Pleistocene epochs). (**8:** 63))

[2]   According to current thinking, *Australopithecus* adapted to life on the savanna and acquired a taste for red meat. In the beginning it <u>may be</u> that its ancestors ventured out of the forests mainly during

present possibility

times of temporary and relatively mild shortages of fruits and other preferred foods.

[3]   Later on during prolonged dry periods when *Australopithecus* and its forerunners came to stay, they had to find an evolutionary zone for themselves and exploit the natural resources of the savanna to the fullest possible extent. They began competing in earnest with other species—with herbivores and their fellow primates for plant foods and perhaps with other primates, including giant baboons, for sleeping trees. And perhaps the conflicts and occasional killings that resulted from competitive encounters had something to do with promoting an increased awareness of other species as potential prey.

Australopithecus

[4]   Certainly meat might have been especially important in providing a well-balanced diet. As far as plant foods are concerned, grassy savanna lands may offer less protein to vegetarian primates than a forest or woodland environment, and in addition the work of foraging over wider areas in a less abundant environment could have contributed to an increased need for protein. Furthermore, there may have been an expanding need for more protein to nourish an expanding brain.

[5]   Running down small game was probably one of the early methods of obtaining meat. Many animals are swift runners, in relatively short spurts. But then they tend to slow down and stop as if they were going on the assumption that the spurts would be enough to shake off or discourage pursuers. Even larger animals like kangaroos and zebras and wildebeests can be run down by species that do not give up after the first dash but follow persistently, species like wolves and wild dogs and humans.

[6]   Hares are among the animals that can be killed and dismembered in a few moments with teeth and bare hands. But this direct method will not work for other small game. The skins of young antelopes, which must have been a significant source of meat, are so tough that they can be penetrated only with sharp cutting tools, and efforts to get at the meat

may well have led to the regular use of such tools. *Australopithecus* probably first turned to naturally sharp rocks or rocks split as a consequence of bashing bones, or rocks that were hurled at escaping prey and missed and broke as they ricocheted off cliff walls.

[7]　The increasingly frequent use of deliberately shaped stone tools in preference to the ready-made variety, the imitation of accidental chipping and flaking, could have come about in a relatively straightforward manner. It could have been "discovered" several times before being accepted as a tradition to be passed along from generation to generation like meat eating itself. Certainly the result was a new and efficient pattern of behavior, as Leakey demonstrated on a number of occasions. One Christmas Eve at his Olduvai camp an audience of attentive Masai tribesmen watched him spend half a minute making a chopper out of a handy rock, and twenty minutes skinning and cutting up the carcass of a freshly killed antelope. (**36**: 108–11)

[8]　Life as an omnivore demands a much broader understanding of environmental conditions than that of a highly specialized herbivore or carnivore. The Kalahari Bushmen, for example, live in intimate contact with the various flora and fauna upon which their survival depends. Bushmen are highly knowledgeable about more than fifty animal species and about all of the available edible plants. Male and female Bushmen seem to know every inch of the several hundred square miles of land upon which they live, and they can successfully locate and utilize every available food source before competing animals can arrive on the scene. Human survival in a hostile environment requires a great deal of information exchange and interpersonal cooperation.

[9]　The need for cooperation must have impressed itself upon the early hominids almost immediately. A single individual armed with a crude stone weapon would have stood little chance against an elephant or a rhinoceros. A group of cooperating individuals, on the other hand, might succeed in killing a crea-

ture. Of course, hunting could not have played a large role in the day-to-day subsistence plan. Nevertheless, the sharing of meat may have served to promote cooperative bonds between hominid groups. The division of labor between the hunting males and the plant-gathering females further laid the groundwork for social cooperation. By pooling both their labor and the fruits of that labor, our ancestors were able to increase their chances of survival; they were capable of exploiting their environment to the fullest. (14: 128)

Chart 3-1 shows the forms and meanings of modal auxiliaries as they are used in academic discourse.

Analyzing Modals

Analysis Exercise 3: Review of Modals' Forms and Meanings

Discuss the possible meanings of the modal auxiliaries in the following sentences.

Shall   What do the writers of these sentences mean when they choose "shall"?

1. We *shall see* in Sec. 4.4-1 that, if friction effects are negligible, this equals the (true) compressive strength.

2. In this chapter, we *shall review* service properties and dimensional attributes.

3. The Congress *shall have* power to lay and collect taxes on incomes.

4. In all criminal prosecutions, the accused *shall enjoy* the right to a speedy and public trial.

Will   Is there a difference in these two uses of "will"?

5. These technologies *will be discussed* in Chapter 10.

6. Faraday's law tells us that any change in flux through a coil *will induce* an emf in the coil.

Can

7. The GNP *can be taken* as a measure of material well-being.

8. A heat pump *can be used* to heat a building.

CHART 3-1   FORMS OF MODALS IN ACADEMIC DISCOURSE

MODAL MEANING		ACTIVE EXAMPLES		PASSIVE EXAMPLES	
		Present/ Future—Modal + Base Verb	**Past—**	**Present/ Future—Modal + "be" + past participle**	**Past—**
CAN	Ability	I *can speak* English.	I *could speak* English when I was 3.	A piano *can be tuned* with a tuning fork.	A piano *could* easily *be tuned* in 1850.
	Possibility	Temperatures *can fluctuate* rapidly in October.	It *could have been* cold yesterday.	The politician *can be bribed.*	He *could have been bribed* before he won the lottery.
MAY	Possibility	There *may be* an opening in Statistics.	There *may have been* a fire.	She *may be elected.*	He *may have been caught* by the police.
MIGHT	Possibility	The condition *might be* unsafe.	There *might have been* a fire.	He *might be forgotten.*	He *might have been caught* by the police.
COULD	Possibility	Three unsafe conditions *could occur.*	There *could have been* a fire.	You *could be arrested.*	He *could have been prosecuted* severely.
MUST	Logical Deduction Necessity	You *must like* to study. You spend all day in the library. Parents *must provide* for their children.	There *must have been* a fire last night. My parents *had to provide* for us, too.	The building *must be ruined* after the fire. We *must be notified.*	The firemen *must have been exhausted.*
HAVE TO	Necessity	I *have to study* for the test.	I *had to study* last night.	The lab *has to be cleaned.*	The police *had to be notified.*
BE TO	Necessity	The list *is to contain* all of the names.	I *was to go* to the meeting.	The box *is to be filled.*	She *was to be hired.*
SHOULD	Advisability Expectation Prediction	You *should work* hard. The class *should begin* soon. It *should* snow tomorrow.	You *should have studied.* The bus *should have arrived* two hours ago.	The metal *should be heated* to 30°.	The alcohol *should have been cooled.*
OUGHT TO	Advisability Expectation Prediction	All citizens *ought to vote.*	The government *ought to have encouraged* the workers.	The mixture *ought to be heated* for an hour.	The vehicle *ought to have been serviced.*
WILL	Intention Certainty	We *will read* Chapter 5. I *would have repaired* the	circuit, but I was busy.	Your orders *will be*	The plans *would have been*
	condition			*followed* to the letter.	*completed.*
WOULD	Intention Expectation Future Past	The firm which *would continue* dares not fail. The colonies *would develop* after 1650.	The factory *would have remained* in operation until the War.	In that tractor, the battery *would be located* near the carburetor.	In the Roman chariot, the brake *would have been located* near the floor.
SHALL	Intention Mandate	We *shall review* Chapter 10. Congress *shall impose* taxes.			

9. An electrical control circuit for controlling an industrial system *can be broken down* into three distinct parts.

10. An ordinary house wire *can safely carry* only about 30A without overheating.

11. We *cannot afford* to ignore this truth.

May

12. Employment in manufacturing *may well decline* in relative terms.

13. Exceptional natural resources *may,* for a short time, *boost* living standards.

14. Elements of expert programs *may be incorporated* in the control system.

Could What is the difference between "can" and "could"?

15. One *could make* the argument that the mark of an industrially developed nation is the proportionately large contribution of manufacturing to national wealth.

16. The circuit of Fig. 3-1 *could easily be extended* to any number of stages. Such a circuit *could be applied* in an industrial control situation whenever there are several loads which must be energized in a given sequence. (**30**: 173)

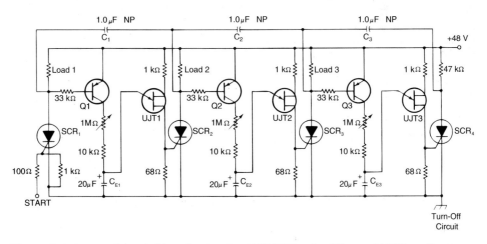

Figure 3-1 Sequential switching circuit using UJT-SCR pairs. When a UJT fires, it causes the next SCR to fire. When that SCR fires, it connects a charged commutating capacitor across the main terminals of the preceding SCR, thereby turning it OFF. (**30**: 172).

17. Surely those who mislabel the classicists *could not have been speaking* of such leading pioneers as Lillian Gilbreth, Seebohm Rountree or Edward Filene.

Have to   What does "have to" mean?

18. These industries and businesses dictate the range of products that manufacturing *has to* provide.

19. The materials and technologies used for making compressor blades *had to change* over the years.

20. Techniques for making very fine, deep holes in very hard materials *had to be developed* too.

21. Consider the average senator who *has to vote* on several thousand different issues during a six-year term.

Must   How do the meanings of "must" relate to the form of the verb?

22. The contribution of manufacturing to the GNP *must be maintained.*

23. The product *must serve* the customer.

24. The status production *must be known.*

25. As climate changed and as human activities changed, there *must have been* many shifts of the margins of the biomes.

26. The ancient engineers of the Middle East *must have been* proud of their irrigation systems that brought water to their fields.

Should   How many meanings of "should" are there?

27. Post-industrial societies *should concentrate* on selected "high technology" industries.

28. A 1-ton refrigeration unit *should be able* to freeze about 10 g. of water per second.

Ought to

29. Harry Truman spoke candidly of the difficulties a president faces in trying to control the executive bureaucracy. . . . Truman went on to say that his job consisted of trying to persuade people to do the things they *ought to have* sense enough to do without his persuading them. (**39**: 420)

Would   How many different meanings of "would" can you find?

30. All European Community members have some form of value-added taxes (VAT). The European Commission wants to equalize these figures. That *would mean* that some members *would have to* raise their VAT and others *would have* to lower theirs. (**33**: 875)

31. One might expect that political science *would have been* the father of a theory of management, since the administration of programs is one of the major tasks of government, and since government itself is the oldest comprehensive form of social organization. (**27**: 31)

32. Mar Greenwal said he *would not discuss* the departure of Mr. Knappman and Mr. Epstein.

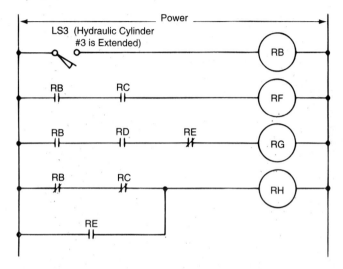

Figure 3-2 A relay logic circuit in which relay coils are controlled by the contacts of other relays. (**30**: 5).

33. In Figure 3-2, the limit switch is mechanically actuated when hydraulic cylinder 3 is fully extended. Hydraulic cylinder 3 *would be located* somewhere in the mechanical apparatus of the industrial system and *would have* some sort of cam attached to it for actuating LS 3. (**30**: 4)

Why is the second "would" separated from the main verb "be"?

34. Another problem often results from the attempt to remedy a situation by applying a principle not designed to cover it. One *would not apply* a theory of metal stress to an engineering problem in which stresses were unimportant, nor *would* one *be* likely to apply a principle of management to a problem of medical diagnosis. (**27**: 9,33)

35. With the tendency of wages to rise faster than labor productivity, the firm which *would continue* to enjoy profits dares not be content to be mediocre, but must aggressively attempt to be more efficient than its competitors.

36. Many people involved in manufacturing have lacked the background that *would have allowed* them to make well-informed decisions.

37. Nathaniel Shaler, head of Harvard's Lawrence Scientific School; M.I.T. economist Francis A. Walker; Columbia's influential Hegelian political scientist, John W. Burgess; and Senator Henry Cabot Lodge used such arguments to propose immigration restrictions. The Rev. Josiah Strong had already provided an immensely popular case for such measures in his l885 work, *Our Country*. Later, the patrician Madison Grant *would draw* on the racial anthropology of De Gobineau and William Ripley to make another influential appeal. (**40**: 225–249)

Explanation 1—Tricky Modals

1. "Can"/"could"/"must" mean possibility, probability, logical deduction, or inference.

   a. In affirmative sentences, "must" expresses a higher probability than "could."

	PRESENT/FUTURE	PAST
100% sure	He *is* on the plane. He *will be* on the plane.	He *was* on the plane.
Logical deduction	He *must be* on the plane.	He *must have been* on the plane.
Expectation	He *should be* on the plane.	He *should have been* on the plane.
Possibility	He *may be* on the plane.	He *may have been* on the plane.
Possibility	He *could/ might be* on the plane.	He *could have been/ might have been* on the plane.
Not sure		

   b. In negative sentences, "can't"/ "couldn't" expresses a higher probability than "must not."

	PRESENT/FUTURE	PAST
100% sure	She *is not* on the plane. She *won't be* on the plane.	She *was not* on the plane.
Improbability	She *can't be/ couldn't be* on the plane.	She *couldn't have been* on the plane.
Logical deduction	She *must not be* on the plane.	She *must not have been* on the plane.
Expectation	She *shouldn't be* on the plane.	She *shouldn't have been* on the plane.
Possibility	She *may not be* on the plane.	She *may not have been* on the plane.
Possibility	She *might not be* on the plane.	She *might not have been* on the plane.
Not sure		

2. "Could"/"be able to" mean ability.
   a. General past ability—"Could" and "be able to" are both appropriate for a general past activity, ability, or talent.

   I *could* swim when I was a child.
   I *was able to* swim when I was a child.

   b. Specific past activity — Only "be able to" is appropriate for a specific past activity or opportunity at a specific time in the past.

   We *were able to* visit Chicago last weekend.
   She *was able to* learn some Chinese in 1980.

3. Archaic modals—"Dare not"/ "need not" are sometimes used in academic writing. (See number 35 in the previous exercise):

   . . . the firm which would continue to enjoy profits dares not be content to be mediocre . . .

Practicing Modals in Context

The following exercises demonstrate the use of modals in the context of a complete piece of discourse.

Practice Exercise 4

The following passage is from an opinion editorial by Kalmay Khalilzad, U.S. Assistant Under Secretary for Defense for Policy Planning from 1990–1992, concerning the United Nations negotiations on Bosnia. The first paragraph contains all of the modal auxiliaries that the writer used. The succeeding paragraphs have blanks to be filled in. The verbs are provided, but you must choose appropriate auxiliary verbs. There are no "right" answers. Several choices may be correct.

The United Nations negotiations on Bosnia . . . have been a failure. Cyrus Vance, the U.N. special envoy, and Lord Owen, the European Community's representative, hope to resolve the crisis through diplomacy alone. . . . President Slobodan Milosevic of Serbia and his Bosnian surrogates have continually duped Mr. Vance and Mr. Owen. . . . Mr. Milosevic has convinced the negotiators that the peace process *would be harmed* if the West took military action or provided arms to the Bosnians. In August, Serbia agreed to put its heavy weapons under U.N. control. . . . Mr. Vance *was to see* that these promises were carried out. . . . Serbia has not lived up to those commitments and has taken control of more towns and areas. . . . Mr. Vance and Lord have given up on Mr. Milosevic's August agreement and last week in Germany they proposed . . . the cantonization of Bosnia along religious lines. The plan contains much of what Serbia has been seeking. . . . Worse, it *would allow* the Serbians to keep their weapons while they negotiate. Meanwhile, Bosnia's Muslims are . . . being pressed to accept conditions that *could lead* to their destruction.

Negotiations between heavily armed Serbians and defenseless Bosnians _____ not produce a fair and lasting settlement. To bring some balance, we _____ demand the fulfillment of the August commitments. If they are not met in two weeks, the U.N. _____ enforce a no-fly zone and begin to arm and train the Bosnians.

Similarly, we _____ insist that Mr. Milosevic begin negotiating with Kosovo's leaders to guarantee autonomy for ethnic Albanians. It _____ be made clear that if he begins "ethnic cleansing," we _____ send arms and perhaps offer air support to the Kosovars and the Bosnians.

Neutralizing Milosevic without going to war _____ require that our threat is real. Stopping him in Kosovo _____ mean stopping him first in Bosnia. To further demonstrate our credibility, President Bush's warning _____ be followed by sending NATO or Western forces to Albania as soon as possible. It's quite likely that this is a decision that President Clinton _____ to make.

Negotiations and sanctions _____ _____ seemed right in April, when the war started, but they have not worked. Serbia _____ know that it _____ _____ to pay a price for its barbarism.

(from Zalmay Khalilzad, "Stop Negotiating with Serbia," *The New York Times*, January 7, 1993, p. A13. Copyright © 1993 by The New York Times Company. Reprinted by permission.)

Practice Exercise 5

In the following passages, fill in the blanks with appropriate modal auxiliaries for the blanks (sometimes one modal works as well as another). You will need to use both active and passive modals, but there are no "right" answers. After you finish, compare your answers.

The value of knowing principles _____ _____ illustrated by several examples. We know from principles that having individuals report to more than one boss involves certain costs and disadvantages, even though the benefits of doing so _____ justify the costs; by knowing principles, we _____ able to minimize these costs. Principles tell us that no manager _____ develop controls without basing them on plans, that managers _____ have organization authority necessary to accomplish the results expected of them, and that no manager _____ develop a meaningful plan without a clear idea of the goal to be accomplished and the future environment premised for its operation. While principles are, as they _____ _____, distilled knowledge, awareness of them _____ help managers avoid mistakes. It is obviously waste-ful for every manager _____ _____ _____ learn these truths from his or her own experience.

Taylor believed that people _____ carefully selected and trained and that they _____ given the work they _____ do best. He had perhaps an idealist's notion that the interests of workers, managers, and owners _____ and _____ _____ harmonized. Moreover, Taylor emphasized the importance of careful advanced planning by managers and the responsibility of managers to design work systems so that workers _____ _____ helped to do their best. But, as he spoke of management, he never overlooked the fact that "the relations between employers and men form without question the most important part of this art." (**27**: 15, 42)

Practice Exercise 6

Fill in the blanks in the following passage with the correct modal auxiliary verbs. Here are the possible number of times each can be used.

would (7)	*could* (3)	*must be* (2)	*might* (2)
would be (2)	*is to be* (1)	*must* (1)	*might be (1)*
should (1)	*may* (2)	*may be* (2)	

Open-Loop Versus Closed-Loop Systems

[1]   Let us start by considering the essential difference between an open-loop system (not self-correcting) and a closed-loop system (self-correcting). Suppose that it is desired to maintain a given constant liquid level in the tank in Figure 3-3 (a). Liquid enters the tank at the top and flows out via the exit pipe at the bottom.

One way to attempt to maintain the proper level is for a human being to adjust the manual valve so that the rate of liquid flow into the tank ex-actly balances the rate of liquid flow out of the tank when the liquid is

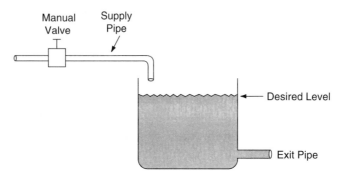

(a)

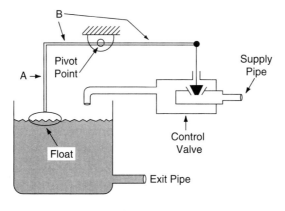

(b)

Figure 3-3 System for maintaining the proper liquid level in a tank. (a) An open-loop system: it has no feedback and is not self-correcting. (b) A closed-loop system: it has feedback and is self-correcting. (**30**: 276).

at the proper level. It _____ require a bit of hunting for the correct valve opening, but eventually the human _____ find the proper position. If he then stands and watches the system for a while and sees that the liquid level stays constant, he _____ conclude that all is well, that the proper valve opening has been set to maintain the correct level. Actually, as long as the operating conditions remain precisely the same, he is right.

The problem is that in real life, operating conditions don't remain the same. There are numerous subtle changes that _____ occur that _____ upset the balance he has worked to achieve. For example, the supply pressure on the upstream side of the manual valve _____ increase for some reason. This _____ increase the input flow rate with no corresponding increase in output flow rate. The liquid level _____ start to rise and the tank _____ soon overflow. (Actually, there _____ be some increase in output flow rate because of the increased pressure at the bottom of the tank where the level rises, but it _____ _____ a chance in a million that this _____ exactly balance the new input flow rate.)

[2]   Assume that the mixing/heating tank _____ be located 30 ft. away from the point where the hot mixture _____ _____ _____ used. There _____ _____ some practical reason for this. For example, it _____ _____ that the mixing/heating tank _____ _____ located indoors and the discharge opening _____ _____ some distance away outdoors. Since there _____ _____ some cooling during the long pipe run, the temperature is measured and controlled at the discharge point rather than inside the tank. This allows the controller to eliminate the effect of cooling in the pipe, which _____ vary widely with outdoor temperature changes.

[3]   It is convenient to imagine the temperatures, because it makes the calculations for proportional band easier to demonstrate. In a real life situation, this _____ mean that the valve _____ never open up to 100%. The error necessary to open the valve that far is beyond the range of the controller. The maximum valve position in this situation _____ _____ 90% open. You _____ check and verify the calculations. (**30**: 275, 320)

Practice Exercise 7: Finding Errors in Verb Phrases

The passage below continues the story about the Iceman, which has been changed to include errors in the verb phrases. Find the errors and correct them. Do not change verbals (participles, infinitives, or gerunds) or any other grammatical structure in the passage.

The Iceman's World

Farming communities spread through the virgin lands of Neolithic Europe some 7,000 years ago. The first farmers slashed and burned hardwood trees, sowed wheat in the clearings, and pasturing their sheep and oxen in the woods. The area was already peopled by a semi-nomadic folk skilled in hunting, tracking, and fishing. The two cultures eventually merged, as the idea and practice of farming spreads throughout Europe. The Iceman reflects this hybridization; he probably subsists on bread, yet will easily be sustaining himself with materials from the surrounding woods.

While the Iceman's body lied preserved in Innsbruck, his belongings are being housed and studying at the Roman-Germanic Central Museum in Mainz, Germany. Under the watchful eye of archaeologist Markus Egg, leather objects have meticulously cleaned, greased, and dehydrated, and must now have been handle. Artifacts of grass have been freeze-dry to dispel moisture. Wooden finds cleaned and bathed in vats of thin, warm, wax, which replace moisture in the wood to prevent rotting.

One of the most remarkable wooden objects found was a long bow, hewn from the strong but flexible heartwood of a Tyrolian yew tree. Yews still grown in the valley below where the Iceman was being found, and in the past this valley was famed for the high-quality bow staves it produced. This, and the fact that the Iceman's bow was unfinished at the time of his death, suggest he has just cut his stave in the valley.
The sheer size of the bow tells us something about the man. Broken in half during the rescue, the bow originally spanning five feet ten inches —seven inches taller than its owner. "You can't making them much bigger than that," says Christopher Bergman, principal archaeologist with 3D/Environmental Services in Cincinnati.

Bergman is an experiential archaeologist who studies prehistoric bows from around the world. He crafts replicas in the same manner as the ancients, and then used them in real world settings to see how they perform. Bergman once has made a five-foot-eight-inch yew bow and says it drew about 90 pounds: To pull the bow string back for firing required the same strength needed to lift 90 pounds with one hand . . .
The bow's underbelly beared marks from the discovery's most striking find, a copper ax. The four-inch blade appears to have been cast from molten metal poured into a mold; when cooled, it had been worked with a hammer. The blade was being hafted in an L-shape crook of yew wood and lashed in place with leather thongs soaked in glue, probably derived from birch tree sap. The ax marks the end of one age and the beginning of another. By 3,300 B.C., stone has been giving away to metal as the material of choice for tools. The technological revolutions arising from the practice of metallurgy would be change the world forever. (**15:** 50, 88)

PART II EMPHATIC AUXILIARY VERBS

Discovery Exercise 8

Read the following passage. What is the purpose of the italicized auxiliary verb?

> Perhaps the most crucial change in early hominid evolution was the development of bipedal locomotion, or walking on two legs. . . . We do not know whether bipedalism developed quickly or gradually, since the fossil record is very skimpy between 8 and 4 million years ago. We *do* know that many of the Miocene anthropoids, judging from the skeletal anatomy, were capable of assuming an upright posture. (**8**: 67)

Explanation 2 —Auxiliaries for Emphasis

A different use for auxiliaries is to express emphasis. Emphatic "do" is used when an author wants to emphasize something that happened or didn't happen. "Do," "does," and "did" are used in combination with another clause or sentence. Other auxiliaries are also stressed to express emphasis in speaking but only "do," "does," and "did" are actually added to a sentence in order to show emphasis in writing.

Practice Exercise 9

Fill in the blanks in the following excerpts with the correct auxiliary to express emphasis.

[1]   Although this study deals more with methods of organizing, initiating, interpreting, and presenting a management audit than with the content of the audit itself, and it is valuable from this point of view, it _____ indicate what a management audit should cover. (**27**: 811)

[2]   While Martindell's American Institute of Management program leaves much to be desired, its pioneering nature deserves praise. It _____ focus attention on controls of overall management and on the results that can be expected from "excellent management." (**27**: 810)

[3]　　It is entirely possible for all the managers of a company to understand psychology and its nuances and yet not be effective in managing. One major division of a very large American company ＿＿＿＿＿＿＿ put its managers from top to bottom through sensitivity training, only to find that the managers had learned much about feelings but little about how to manage. (**27**: 65)

[4]　　Elton Mayo, F. J. Roethlisberger, and others undertook the famous experiments at the Hawthorne plant of the Western Electric Company between 1927 and 1932. . . . They found, in general, that improvement in productivity was due to such social factors as morale, satisfactory interrelationships between members of a work group, and effective management. . . . It should not be inferred from this that prior to the Hawthorne experiments successful managers did not recognize the importance of the human factor, or that management theorists overlooked it.

But what the work of Mayo and his associates ＿＿＿＿＿＿＿ underscore was the need for a greater and deeper understanding of the social and behavioral aspects of management. (**27**: 51)

[5]　　The contact controlled by relay R1 in Figure 3-4(a) does not close immediately. It delays closing until a certain amount of time has elapsed.

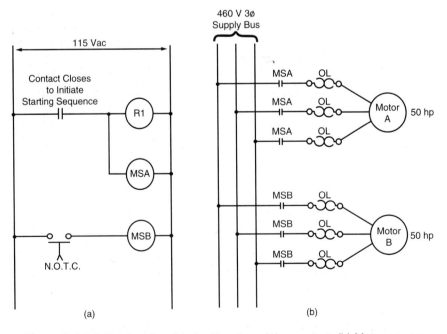

Figure 3-4 (a) Simple relay circuit with a time delay contact. (b) Motor power circuit associated with the relay control circuit in part (a). (**30**: 69).

By the time it _____ close to energize MSB, motor A has reached full speed and has relaxed its current demand. (**30: 68**)

[6]   There is abundant evidence that, until some 200 million years ago, all the continents formed one land mass called Pangaea (a word meaning "all earth"). Gradually, throughout millions of years, this land mass broke apart. The continents drifted apart, collided with each other, and eventually came to occupy their present positions. If you look at a map of the continents, you will see that the continents _____ fit roughly together, like parts of a badly made jigsaw puzzle. The stages of separation are called continental drift. Recent studies of certain types of rocks found on now widely separated coasts of continents seem to confirm that continental drift actually _____ occur. The types and magnetic orientation of the rock particles confirm evidence also presented by fossils of microorganisms. (**9: 136**)

Discovery Exercise 10a: Using Word Order to Express Emphasis

Read the following nine sentences and note the italicized clauses and sentences. Then answer the questions that follow.

1. Managers must not forget that there is some authority they should not delegate. *Nor should they overlook the fact that they must maintain enough authority.*

2. *Seldom do companies or any other kind of organization give procedures planning and control this kind of treatment.*

3. *Only if two identical groups of people with schizophrenia are studied and all treated in exactly the same way,* except that one is given the vitamin, *can sound conclusions be drawn.*

4. High approval ratings for a president, such as Ronald Reagan received in the early months of his administration, can be used to persuade Congress to pass the president's program. *Rarely, however, is public opinion so strongly expressed over a long period of time.*

5. *Not only is the government dependent on popular sovereignty* but the powers of the government are also clearly limited.

6. As you are aware, real life is usually not dramatic, *nor do all events have a neat or an easily understood plot.*

7. *Not until a person has a money income larger than he must spend for immediate needs—that is, a surplus—can he save.*

8. *No longer is it just the customer service rep and the customer looking eye to eye.* Now we have the intrusion of technology.

9. *Only under the assumption that all other things are constant*—no roadblocks, no wrecks, no detours, and so on—*would we predict that taking the freeway is always the quickest way.*

Discovery Exercise 10b: Questions

1. What kinds of words begin the italicized clauses and sentences?
2. Look at the word order in the italicized parts of the sentences. Do the sentences have statement word order or something different?
3. What happens to the auxiliary verbs?
4. In items 1 and 6, look at the part of the passage or sentence that is not italicized. Is it affirmative or negative?
5. Write a statement describing how "nor" is used in items1 and 6. Include information about whether the first part is negative or affirmative.
6. Emphatic sentences beginning with negative words can often be rewritten in normal statement word order with the negative words placed between the auxiliary and the main verb. Which sentences in Exercise 9 can be rewritten in statement word order?

Analyzing Emphatic Auxiliaries

Analysis Exercise 11: Completing a Summary of Emphasis Rules

Complete the summary below.

Emphasis in spoken English is expressed through stress and intonation in the speaker's voice. One way that emphasis can be expressed in written English is through the addition of an _____ _____ such as _____, _____, or _____. In a negative sentence, another way to express emphasis is through the use of _____ words such as _____, _____, or _____ placed at the _____ of the sentence or clause. The word order in the main clause following the negative word, phrase, or clause is _____ word order. The auxiliary verb or "be" is moved in front of the _____ . If there is no auxiliary in the clause, we _____ one. This process is similar to forming a _____ .

CHART 3–2   EXPRESSING EMPHASIS WITH AUXILIARY VERBS AND NEGATIVE WORDS

AUXILIARY VERB EMPHASIS	REGULAR STATEMENT SENTENCE FORM—THE FIRST AND SECOND STATEMENTS ARE OPPOSITES	EMPHATIC SENTENCE FORM — ADD "DO," "DOES," "DID"
Do **Does** **Did**	A thermometer doesn't measure barometric pressure. A thermometer measures temperature. Ancient Eskimos ate enormous amounts of meat. They ate very little fresh produce.	A Thermometer doesn't measure barometric pressure. It *does* measure temperature. Ancient Eskimos ate very little fresh produce, but they *did* eat enormous amounts of meat.
NEGATIVE WORD EMPHASIS	REGULAR STATEMENT FORM—THE NEGATIVE WORD IS BETWEEN THE AUXILIARY AND MAIN VERB	EMPHATIC STATEMENT FORM—THE NEGATIVE WORD MOVES TO FRONT THE CLAUSE—CHANGE CLAUSE TO QUESTION WORD ORDER
Never **Not once** **Only**	One thousand people have *never* attended the lectures. We could predict success *only* under that assumption.	*Never* have one thousand people attended the lectures. *Only* under that assumption could we predict success.
Only if (when)	We will learn their secrets *only if* these people are studied.	*Only if* these people are studied will we learn their secrets.
Rarely **Hardly (ever)** **Scarcely** **Barely**	Public opinion is *rarely* predicted. We had *scarcely* gotten in the door when the phone rang.	*Rarely* is public opinion predicted. *Scarcely* had we gotten in the door when the phone rang.
Seldom	Companies *seldom* give credit without references.	*Seldom* do companies give credit without references.
Not until	The traffic signal was *not* installed *until* the third serious accident occurred.	*Not until* the third serious accident occurred was the traffic signal installed.
No longer	The customer service representative is *no longer* helping the customer.	*No longer* is the customer service representative helping the customer.
Nor "Nor" is used in a clause/ sentence only after a negative clause/sentence.	Managers must *not* forget their employees, and they should *not* overlook their supervisors.	Managers must *not* forget their employers. *Nor* should they overlook their supervisors.

Practice Exercise 12: Writing Emphatic Sentences

Rewrite the following sentences to express emphasis. Use the emphasis words already in the sentences or the words indicated in parentheses.

1. In the past half century the businessman has begun to hold a place of respect.

2. When actions are forbidden by the letter and spirit of the Constitution, they are thereby unconstitutional. (use "only")

3. Restrictions did not accompany the categorical grants until the administration of Franklin Roosevelt.

4. A person cannot save until he has a money income larger than he must spend for immediate needs—that is, a surplus.

5. The amino acids will be used only for their most important function—making proteins if the protein-sparing K calories from carbohydrates and fat are sufficient to power the cells.

6. The political culture not only supports the two-party system, but the parties themselves are adept at making the necessary shifts in their platforms or electoral appeal to gain new members.

7. People are no longer just doing work, following instructions, and waiting for guidance and decisions; they are now individuals with clearly defined purposes.

8. The increased crop yields could not have been accomplished without fuel-driven pumps to irrigate the fields or tractors to draw the implements for planting, cultivating, and harvesting. The food could not have been distributed widely without trucks, trains, ships, and planes, all of which depend on fossil fuels for power. (use "nor")

Preparing for Standardized Tests

Practice Exercise 13

Choose the best answer to complete each sentence below.

1. An airplane designer _____ make a compromise between weight and strength on the one hand and cost on the other.
   a. can to
   b. must
   c. able to
   d. had to

2. Investigation _____ that most of northern New Mexico was once covered by marine sediments.
   a. revealed
   b. was revealed
   c. is being revealed
   d. was reveal

3. The humanists _____ psychologists aware of the importance of psychological needs like the needs for love, self-esteem, belonging, self-expression, and creativity.
   a. have also made
   b. have been made
   c. have also been
   d. had been made

4. The atmosphere extends indefinitely out into space, but only a relatively few feet of it _____ used by living things.
   a. is
   b. are
   c. was
   d. were

5. Making a good replica of a specialized tool and then successfully cutting or scraping with it demonstrate only how it _____ used.
   a. could had been
   b. could being
   c. could have been
   d. could

6. The idea that people seek comfortable or mutually beneficial relationships does not _____ some aspects of interpersonal attraction.
   a. explained completely
   b. explains completely
   c. completely explains
   d. completely explain

7. Neanderthals _____ warfare as well as religion.
   a. may had invented
   b. may have invented
   c. may had been inventing
   d. may have been invented

8. Freud honestly tried to describe what he observed, but what he saw _____ not fully apply to modern men and women.
   a. do
   b. did
   c. had
   d. was

9. Above the timberline much of the vegetation _____ mosses and grasses.
   a. consist of
   b. consists in
   c. consist on
   d. consists of

10. The Isthmus of Panama _____ a barrier to dispersal for organisms in the Atlantic and Pacific oceans.
    a. as
    b. and
    c. in
    d. is

11. Honeybees are native to Europe, Asia Minor, and Africa, and were probably first _____ to the New World in 1622, by English settlers, to Virginia.
    a. in
    b. brought
    c. gave
    d. over

Auxiliary Verbs   **75**

12. At about the time that people _____ more numerous during the period of great glaciations some 8,000 years ago, a curious thing happened.
    a. will have become
    b. had become
    c. were becoming
    d. become

13. The chemical industry _____ very dependent on technical and scientific knowledge for the efficiency of its production capabilities and the profitability of its product line.
    a. that is
    b. even it is
    c. is
    d. it is

14. The word automatic _____ from the Greek and means self-moving or self-thinking.
    a. is derived
    b. was deriving
    c. deriving
    d. that is derived

15. Geologic processes _____ on a geologic time scale.
    a. are operated
    b. operate
    c. operating
    d. being operated

16. By 1931 Tennessee Eastman _____ a process and a market for cellulose acetate yarn.
    a. develop
    b. that developed
    c. had developed
    d. has developed

17. A heat pump _____ to heat a building.
    a. uses
    b. is using
    c. can be used
    d. used

18. Jefferson retired to Monticello in 1809, later _____ the University of Virginia, and developed his interests in education, science, and music.
    a. found
    b. founded
    c. was found
    d. had found

19. The inkblot test, or Rorschach, is one of the oldest and most widely _____ projective tests.
    a. being used
    b. using
    c. used
    d. to be used

20. In any industrial system, the control circuits constantly _____ and process information about conditions in the system.
    a. received
    b. receive
    c. receiving
    d. have received

21. In the Sangre de Cristo Mountains there are some locations where thick sediments _____ a curious repetitive sequence.
    a. are display
    b. displaying
    c. are displayed
    d. display

22. In the course of time organisms have increased in numbers and gradually spread over the earth wherever they _____ a way.
   a. had found
   b. will found
   c. have found
   d. founded

Practice Exercise 14

Find and circle the letter of the *one* error in the following sentences. Then write the correct form above the error.

1. Separation of <u>today's</u> five major continents <u>occurred</u> <u>somewhat</u> more
            a   b   c
   recently than 180 <u>million years</u>.
                    d

2. The herbaceous plants usually <u>blooms</u> more or <u>less</u> simultaneously in
                                  a   b
   the spring, and are <u>well</u> on their way to producing seeds before the
                      c
   trees <u>leaf</u> out.
         d

3. <u>What</u> is necessary, so <u>that</u> a chemical reaction vessel may be designed,
    a   b
   <u>build</u>, and operated <u>successfully</u>, is a satisfactory rate equation.
     c   d

4. As <u>a</u> child, you <u>may had</u> delighted <u>in finding</u> faces and objects <u>in</u> cloud
       a   b   c   d
   formations.

5. <u>Only</u> about 1 percent of <u>the</u> population <u>score</u> above 140 <u>on</u> IQ tests.
     a   b   c   d

6. Roosevelt's first term <u>was illustrated</u> both his preference for
                           a
   <u>conciliating</u> the Republican party leadership and his <u>flair</u> <u>for the</u> grand
       b   c   d
   symbolic gesture.

7. Using gene transfer, scientists <u>can to</u> change <u>a</u> corn variety from one
                                a   b
   <u>that is</u> susceptible <u>to</u> leaf spot disease to one that is resistant.
     c   d

8. Decision making <u>may define</u> as the selection of a course of action
                    a

    intended <u>to bring</u> <u>about</u> a desired state of <u>affairs</u>.
            b   c   d

9. During the period 1899 <u>to</u> 1970, the production index for all
                        a

    manufacturing <u>raised</u> by a factor of 17 <u>while</u> the chemical production
               b   c

    index <u>advanced</u> by a factor of 94^2.
           d

10. History is <u>replete</u> with examples of military leaders who <u>are</u>
              a

    <u>communicating</u> their plans and objectives to their followers, <u>thereby</u>
         b   c

    <u>developing</u> a "unity of doctrine".
        d

11. <u>A</u> concept is a word or idea that <u>represent</u> a class <u>of</u> <u>objects</u>.
     a   b   c d

12. The chemical phenylthiocarbamine (PTC) <u>is tasting bitter</u> to about
                                                a

    70 percent of <u>those</u> <u>tested</u>, and has no taste for <u>the other</u> 30 percent.
               b   c   d

13. Big cats <u>might</u> generally walk away from their <u>kills</u> when human
             a   b

    scavengers <u>or</u> observers <u>appear</u> on the scene.
            c   d

14. Rocks and branches could <u>hardly</u> <u>had</u> served <u>as</u> formidable weapons
                         a   b   c

    <u>against</u> lions and leopards and saber-toothed tigers.
      d

15. Mechanical solutions <u>maybe</u> achieved by trial <u>and</u> error <u>or</u> by <u>rote</u>.
                       a   b   c   d

16. Ben Wattenburg of the American Enterprise Institute <u>in</u> Washington,
                                                   a

    D.C., <u>says</u> the United States is <u>become</u> the <u>world's</u> first "universal
          b   c   d

    nation."

17. Patrick H. Caddell <u>has</u> already worked <u>in</u> five <u>presidential</u> campaigns
                           a   b   c

    by the time he reached <u>age</u> thirty-four.
                              d

18. Between 35,000 and 40,000 years <u>ago</u> <u>the</u> Neanderthal <u>subspecies</u>
                                       a b   c

    disappeared from Europe and <u>replaced</u> by a variety of modern *Homo*
                                         d

    Sapiens, Cromagnon man.

19. Only within the <u>last</u> <u>several</u> decades new <u>laboratory</u> techniques
                        a   b   c

    <u>have unlocked</u> the mystery of the specific design of protein.
              d

20. Robert Fulton, inventor of the steamboat, and Robert Livingston,
    American minister to France, secured a <u>monopoly</u> of steam navigation
                                                a

    <u>on</u> the <u>waters</u> in New York State from the New York legislature <u>since</u>
    b   c   d
    1803.

21. Between 1982 <u>to</u> 1984, the U.S. Department of Agriculture <u>bought</u>
                   a   b

    more than 215 <u>million</u> pounds <u>of</u> honey.
                       c   d

22. The <u>prime</u> importance of the amino acids <u>is reflecting</u> by their <u>uses</u> in
          a   b   c

    <u>the</u> body.
    d

23. The <u>founding</u> fathers <u>could not imagined</u> the ways <u>in</u> which
          a   b   c

    information <u>is</u> disseminated today.
               d

24. Concept formation is part of <u>the</u> process <u>whereby</u> a child classifies and
                                 a   b

    <u>organized</u> experiences <u>into</u> meaningful categories.
         c   d

25. It seems safe to assume that men and women <u>not</u> differ in overall
    a   b

    intelligence, and <u>no</u> significant IQ difference <u>has been found</u>.
                           c   d

26. The statistics for the U.S. chemical industry <u>as a</u> whole, <u>considering</u>

  $\qquad$ a $\qquad\qquad$ b

  both domestic and worldwide activities, <u>presents</u> a picture of massive

  $\qquad$ c

  size and <u>strength.</u>

  $\qquad$ d

27. <u>At</u> the heart of the controversy that <u>was led</u> to the Civil War was the

  a $\qquad\qquad\qquad\qquad$ b

  issue of national government supremacy <u>versus</u> the <u>rights</u> of the

  $\qquad\qquad\qquad\qquad$ c $\qquad$ d

  separate states.

28. By the l980s, the courts <u>have begun</u> to influence cases that <u>involved</u>

  $\qquad$ a $\qquad\qquad\qquad\qquad$ b

  the <u>press's</u> responsibility <u>to</u> law-enforcement agencies.

  $\qquad$ c $\qquad\qquad$ d

29. In the United States there has been a <u>shift</u> away <u>from</u> complex

  $\qquad$ a $\qquad$ b

  carbohydrate <u>foods</u> <u>in</u> 1900.

  $\qquad$ c $\quad$ d

30. Since the 1980s, <u>there</u> <u>was</u> <u>little</u> evidence that men's and women's

  $\qquad$ a $\quad$ b $\quad$ c

  political attitudes are <u>very</u> different.

  $\qquad$ d

Practice Exercise 15

Choose the one best answer for each question about the following passage.

The Importance of Mandatory Imperatives

The state ratifying conventions had couched their proposals, with which Madison had worked, in terms of "ought" and "ought not." Those words sound weak to Americans, who are used to seeing "Congress shall make no law . . . ," "no soldier shall . . . ," and "the accused shall . . . " The oughts and ought nots were typical of the language contained in the English Bill of Rights and in the Virginia Declaration of Rights.

Consider one constitutional amendment proposed by Virginia's state ratifying convention: "That excessive bail ought not to be required, nor excessive fines imposed, nor cruel and unusual punishments inflicted." Madison changed the wording to read, "Excessive bail shall not be required, nor excessive fines imposed, nor cruel and unusual punishments inflicted." This was to become the Eighth Amendment, proposed by Madison on June 8,

1789. The difference between "ought" and "ought not," and "shall" and "shall not," is the difference between effective and ineffective legal language. A *mandatory imperative* was written into the amendments by Madison, and this has probably done more to safeguard the rights of individuals than any other change in the language of the proposed amendments on which he worked. Wishful thinking is not good enough or bold enough. Madison required the language of command. (**39**: 48–49)

1. The main idea of the passage is _____.
   a. strong language is important in legal documents.
   b. it is important to learn the meaning of "ought to" and "shall."
   c. "ought to" and "shall" are synonyms.
   d. Virginia's state ratifying convention used "ought to" instead of shall."

2. According to the passage, Americans are likely to use _____ when they write a legal document.
   a. "have to"   c. "ought to"
   b. "must"   d. "shall"

3. The 8th Amendment to the Constitution used the words _____
   a. "Excessive bail shall be required."
   b. "Excessive bail shall not be required."
   c. "Excessive bail ought to be required."
   d. "Excessive bail ought not to be required."

4. The passage infers that _____
   a. "ought to " means wishful thinking.
   b. "shall" means weakness.
   c. "ought to" means the language of command.
   d. "shall" means the same as the language in the English Bill of Rights.

Analysis Exercise 16: Building Templates for the Verb System

time frames   modals
verb phrases   active/passive

What verb tenses do you expect when you see a passage? Fill in the blanks below with the names of tenses that you would expect to find in the passages. Write the time frames you expect in the left margin.

Example: In l822, Charles Babbage **simple past** the concept of a machine

                that _____ _____ complex computations and

past
[1]   _____ results without human intervention.

                In the past, our manual techniques of collecting, manipulating and disseminating data to achieve certain objectives _____ _____ as data processing. As technology _____ electromechanical machines _____ to do these functions. The term auto-matic data processing (ADP) _____ _____.(**31**: 22)

[2] Today, technology _____ at the point where the electronic computer _____ results formerly accomplished by humans and machines. This _____ as electronic data
____
processing (EDP). (**31**: 8)

[3] Computers _____ _____ a long way since the days of the room-sized ENIAC of the l940s. Technological advances such as large scale integrated (LSI) circuitry _____ _____ both costs and sizes of computer systems. Computer processing speeds _____ _____ at exponential rates. These advances, along with more sophisticated programming languages and techniques,
____
_____ _____ to a tenfold increase in the number of computers installed during the last decade. (**31**: 175)

[4] Jane van Lawick-Goodall _____ her famous research on wild chimpanzees in l960. Three years before she _____ _____ her own way to Africa, driven by an interest in
____
wildlife that _____ back to her childhood.

[5] [*Australopithecus*, a pre-human species, lived 3–5 million years ago.] Adrienne Zihlman of the University of California in Santa Cruz has conducted extensive studies of walking patterns in non-human primates and modern humans as well as relevant fossil material, and concludes: "*Australopithecus* _____ _____ _____ more muscle energy than modern man to perform the same actions. He probably walked with his toes turned out and _____ _____ _____ his weight more on the outside of the foot." (**14**: 61,87)

Research Projects

Every unit in this course will conclude with a research project related to the grammatical structures you have studied. You will choose and analyze a journal article or chapter from a textbook in your major field. The purpose of the exercise is to find and analyze the same grammatical structures that you have studied in your grammar textbook. After you identify the structures, you will determine how they are used in writing in your field. Finally, you will find it interesting to compare and contrast the uses of grammatical structures in your article with those of other students in the class.

Analysis Exercise 17: The Verb System Research Project

This exercise will help you develop a general feeling for the organization, time frames, verb tenses, percentage of active and passive voice, and the number of modal auxiliaries in journal articles in your field. *We will **not** include verbals (infinitives, gerunds, or participial phrases) in this exercise.*

A. ORGANIZATION

Skim through your article.

1. Is it divided into sections?
2. If it isn't organized into sections already, divide it into introduction, body, and conclusion.
3. Write a brief outline of your article. Leave plenty of space to fill in information about the verb phrases in each section.

B. THE VERB SYSTEM

For each section of your article fill in the following information:

Abstract—*Basic Time Frame* (choose one): Past/Present/Future
Other tenses found _____
Number of active verbs _____
Number of linking verbs _____
Number of passive verbs _____
Modal auxiliaries found ("could," "must," etc.) Write them here._____
_____

1. **Introduction**—*Basic Time Frame*: Past/Present/Future

   Other tenses found _____

   Number of active verbs _____

   Number of linking verbs _____

   Number of passive verbs _____

   Modal auxiliaries found _____

   _____

2. **Methods and Materials** or **The Body** (analyze 2 or 3 typical paragraphs)

   Basic time Frame: Past / Present / Future

   Other tenses found _____

   Number of active verbs _____

   Number of linking verbs _____

   Number of passive verbs _____

   Modals found_____

   _____

3. **Results /Discussion**—*Basic Time Frame*: Past / Present /Future

   Other tenses found _____

   Number of active verbs _____

   Number of linking verbs _____

   Number of passive verbs _____

   Modals found_____

   _____

4. **Conclusion**—*Basic Time Frame*: Past / Present/ Future

   Other tenses found _____

   Number of active verbs _____

   Number of linking verbs _____

   Number of passive verbs _____

   Modals found_____

   _____

C. ANALYSIS

Analyze the use of the verb phrases in the different parts of your article (not participial phrases, infinitives, or gerunds). Answer the following questions:

1. What is the general time frame in your article? Is there more than one? Why?
2. Does your article use particular verb tenses for particular sections? Why?
3. How do the verbs function in your article? For example, do parts of your article use more passive than active and linking verbs? Do other parts use more active and linking verbs than passive? Why do you think this is so?

4. When are modals used and why? Are modals more useful in some parts of an article than in others? Why?
5. What is the most interesting use of the verb phrases in your article?
6. Summarize the use of verb tenses, active and passive voice and modal auxiliaries in your article.

D. COMPARISON AND DISCUSSION

Compare your findings with those of the other students in your class.

1. Write the brief outline of your article on the blackboard.
2. Fill in the outline with the information you found in your article.
3. Discuss the reasons why different fields use different tenses, active or passive voice, and modal auxiliaries.

UNIT 2

RELATIVE CONCEPTS

4

RELATIVE CLAUSES, RELATIVE PHRASES, AND CLEFT SENTENCES

PART I   RELATIVE CLAUSES

Discovering the Grammar of Relative Clauses

Discovery Exercise 1: Identifying Relative Clauses

1. Scan the article below to find the underlined clauses. What do we call these clauses? What do we call the word in the underlined clause that connects the clause with the rest of the sentence? One of the clauses has no connector (subordinator). Why?

2. Scan the remaining pages of the article to find more relative clauses. How many different subordinators can you find? What kinds of words (antecedents) come before relative clauses? What do relative clauses do? Finally, write a statement that expresses what relative clauses do.

> *How Farm People Accept New Ideas*
>
> Some farmers will try any new idea that comes along, while others will accept an idea only after it is proven in their neighborhood. A major concern of agricultural leaders is that of narrowing the time gap between the early and late adoptions of recommended practices.
>
> This lag between what is known and what is done by most farmers has been the focus of considerable research in recent years by rural sociologists and others. Despite the many gaps in our present knowledge, there is a need for bringing together and interpreting the results of the various studies for use by agricultural leaders and agencies. The major purpose of this publication is to show the process by which ideas become accepted. This diffusion process will be discussed from three points of view:

The Evaluation Stage

1. The stages through which an individual goes from the time he first learns of an idea until he adopts it, and the media which are most effective at these various stages.
2. Some situational and group influences affecting adoption.
3. Some of the characteristics of farm people as they relate to rate of adoption.

THE DIFFUSION PROCESS

In the Awareness Stage

At this stage the individual knows little about the new idea beyond the fact that it exists.

More people become aware of new ideas from mass communications media than from other sources. Some studies . . . indicate that salesmen are important in creating awareness of new ideas which involve the use of a commercial product. Neighbors and friends are important creators of awareness of new ideas among the lower socio-economic groups . . . It is at the AWARENESS stage that the mass media devices have their greatest impact. The evidence is that for the majority, mass media become less important as sources of information after the individual has become aware of the idea.

In the Interest Stage

At this stage, the individual obtains general information about the idea. ... Mass media still provide information <u>which is timely and readily available</u> from a wide range of sources. Agricultural agencies can provide results of experiment station research ... The channels of communication <u>which rural people will accept as valid</u> are the most influential at this stage.

In the Evaluation Stage

In this stage the potential adopter evaluates the new idea in terms of his own situation ... The data available indicate that as people are evaluating an idea for their own use, they usually consult with neighbors and friends <u>whose opinions they respect.</u>

The earlier adopters tend to depend upon agricultural agencies during this stage. Farm people, in general, go to sources of information <u>which they consider to be dependable for information at this stage.</u> This usually means that the sources are ones <u>with which the farmer has personal contact, i.e. his neighbors and friends</u> ... The potential adopters mistrust some mass media information because they feel that the information is tempered by the business interests of those who are in control of them.

In the Trial Stage

This is the stage where farm people preparing to try out the new idea are primarily concerned with getting information on how to do it and when to do it. Where possible, the new idea or technique is tried on a small scale, i.e., one bushel of hybrid seed corn was planted the first year; commercial fertilizers were used on small plots, etc. At this stage agricultural agencies become more important along with neighbors and friends, who continue to be important sources of information ... Some techniques require "know-how" which the average individual does not have.

Salesmen are important providers of information at this stage when a commercial product is involved.

In the Adoption Stage

This is the stage at which the idea has been completely accepted ... There is some evidence to indicate that adopters seek information to interpret results in relation to their own situation ... An understanding of failures of new practices is as important as interpretation of success. For example, hybrid seed corn use is sometimes discontinued because individuals have used strains unadapted to their climate and soil conditions and have had results that were unsatisfactory.

Diffusion Process Varies with Types of Change

The relative advantage of the new as compared with the old way of doing things is another condition affecting its acceptance. The greater the efficiency ... the greater its rate of acceptance. Another aspect of new practices affecting their rate of acceptance is the relative ease with which they can be demonstrated and communicated.

Some Personal and Social Characteristics Related to Adoption of Practices

The adoption of farm practices is influenced by social and psychological as well as economic factors. Community standards and social relationships provide the general framework wherein the process of change occurs. The extent to which changes are adopted depends upon the values and expectations of the group and upon the extent to which the individual is expected to conform.

The degree to which social contacts are confined to the immediate locality is a factor. The broader one's social orientation, the more likely he is to accept new ideas ... The more education an individual has, the more likely he is to adopt new farm practices. Those with high school training and above tend to adopt new practices earlier than those who have had less formal schooling. Farmers who have children in 4-H clubs or vocational agriculture tend to adopt more approved practices than others.

Individual and family goals and values affect the decisions to adopt or reject new farm practices by providing motivation for individual and family. For example, the high value placed on security, as reflected in owning land debt-free and being reluctant to use borrowed capital, is negatively related to adoption of new practices. People who rate this value highly prefer to use money for paying off debt on their farms. Also new practices involve risks which people who place a high value on security are reluctant to take.

Sequence of Influences in the Adoption of Practices

People may be classified into categories according to the sequence in which they adopt new practices: innovators, community adoption leaders, local adoption leaders, later adopters and nonadopters. Innovators are the first to adopt new ideas.

Community adoption leaders are not the very first to try new ideas, but are among the first to use approved practices in their community areas.

Local Adoption Leaders

These are the people to whom the majority look for information and ideas in their farming operations. They are not necessarily innovators or early adopters, but they do adopt ideas sooner than the majority who look to them for information ... Their leadership is oriented toward their following rather than toward those whom they may consider to be "leaders." ... One of the functions of leaders among farm people is to diffuse new ideas and practices. It is their task to expedite the process of getting ideas from their sources of origin to those who can use them. . . . Later adopters are the majority of the people in the community who adopt new ideas. . . . The later adopters have less education, participate less in community affairs and are older than those who adopt ideas earlier. There are some to whom a practice might apply who never adopt it. They have even less education and social contacts than the later adopters.

In any community, there are always some to whom the practice does not apply and some for whom these generalizations do not hold true. (22: 1–10)

Discovery Exercise 2: *That* versus *that*

In the sentences below, find the relative adjective clauses beginning with "that" and their antecedents (the nouns they modify). Then answer the questions.

- Do all of the *that*s introduce clauses?
- Do all of the *that*s describe or identify nouns?
- What function do you think the *that*s in these sentences serve?

1. Some studies, such as that of hybrid corn in Iowa, indicate that salesmen are important in creating awareness of new ideas.

2. Genetic engineers took a gene from a microorganism that produces a protein that is poisonous to the corn borer, and we placed the gene into the plant-dwelling organism.

3. This is due to the high degree of identification that prevails among intimate associates.

4. The most effective use of the informal leader requires that one work with him on an informal basis.

5. That could save the farmer money.

Discovery Exercise 3a: Punctuation of Relative Clauses

Read the following three passages. Find the relative clauses with commas and compare them to the relative clauses without commas. What are their characteristics? What do you think commas mean in a relative clause? Do you know the names for the clauses with and without commas?

The Root. The functions of the root are to anchor the plant, to absorb and transport nutrients and water, and sometimes to store food and serve in asexual reproduction. Adventitious roots, which do not arise either from the primary seed roots or as branches of later developed roots, often appear at the nodes, or junctions of the stem . . . A protective cap covers the tip. Just behind the region of elongation are the root hairs, which are small projections of the epidermal cells.

(from *The Academic American Encyclopedia*, v. 15 [Danbury, Conn.: Grolier, 1986], p. 335. Reprinted by permission.)

The first coordinator of the NCRPIS was Dr. Max Hoover, who managed the station from 1948 to 1957. The NCRPIS was established as Regional Research Project NC-7, which is entitled "Introduction, Multiplication, Evaluation, Preservation, Cataloguing, and Utilization of Plant Germ-plasm."

(from R.L. Wilson et al., "A Brief History of the North Central Regional Plant Introduction Station and a List of Genera Maintained," Proc. *Iowa Academic Sciences* 92 (2) [1985]: 63–66.)

The high value placed on security is negatively related to adoption of new farming practices. People who rate this value highly prefer to use money for paying off debt on their farms. Also new practices involve risks which people who place a high value on security are reluctant to take. (**22**: 8)

Discovery Exercise 3b: Comparing Punctuation

1. Go back and scan "How Farm People Accept New Ideas." Based on that passage, what might you conclude about the comparative numbers of restrictive clauses (no commas) and nonrestrictive clauses (commas) in the passage and in academic writing?
2. Based on what you've seen in this exercise, in the space below write some rules that explain restrictive and non-restrictive clauses.
3. Compare your rules with the Explanation and charts of relative adjective and relative adverb clauses.

Your Rules for Restrictive and Non-restrictive Clauses

No Commas
　　Types of antecedents:

　　Type of information contained:

Commas
　　Types of antecedents:

　　Type of information contained:

Explanation 1—Relative Clauses

Relative clauses (also called adjective clauses) modify nouns and sometimes whole sentences. They serve as adjectives most often, but sometimes they act like adverbs in that they tell how, where, or when. A relative clause that modifies a complete sentence usually expresses a result.

Chart 4-1 gives examples of relative clauses acting as adjectives and adverbs. These relative clauses follow the nouns they describe and are introduced by subordinating conjunctions (subordinators). The subordinators that serve as direct objects within their relative clauses are frequently dropped. The relative adverb subordinators may also be omitted.

Study Charts 4-1 and 4-2 to review how relative clauses are used in sentences and some of the rules that apply to relative adjective clauses and relative adverb clauses. For an explanation of how relative clauses are formed, see pages 346–349.

Analyzing Relative Clauses

Exercises 4 and 5 review the formation of relative clauses. First you will analyze combined sentences, and then you will decombine (separate) sentences that contain relative clauses into two or more sentences.

Analysis Exercise 4: Review of Formation of Relative Clauses

Study the sentences below. Each number contains three sentences. Compare sentence (c) with (a) and (b) and then describe how the relative clauses in (c) are formed in each case.

1. a. People will change.
   b. People are already well informed.
   c. People who are already well informed will change.

2. a. This is the stage.
   b. The idea has been completely accepted at this stage.
   c. This is the stage at which the idea has been completely accepted.

3. a. People can be classified into categories according to the sequence.
   b. They adopt new practices in the sequence.
   c. People can be classified into categories according to the sequence in which they adopt new practices.

CHART 4-1   EXAMPLES OF RELATIVE CLAUSES

I. RELATIVE ADJECTIVE CLAUSES

NOUN PHRASE		RELATIVE ADJECTIVE CLAUSE				REST OF SENT.
NOUN/PRONOUN	SUBORDINATOR OBJECT IN CLAUSE	SUBORDINATOR SUBJECT IN CLAUSE	SUBJECT OF CLAUSE	VERB PHRASE	COMPLEMENT, ADV., OR OBJ.	
1. Interesting women		who		study	English	live here.
2. Important buyers	(whom)		we	want to meet		arrived last night.
3. The teachers	(to whom)		students	turn (to)	for help	called us.
4. Several students		whose lecture notes		were lost	last week	complained.
5. The library table		whose surface		was scratched		will be repaired.
6. The businessmen	at whose office		we	met	yesterday	were interested.
7. The woman		that		is standing	in line	is my boss.
8. The new book	(that)		I	lent	you	is on sale.
9. A machine		which		handles	money	would be useful.
10. The notes	(which)		she	lost		have been found.
11. The stage	at which		we	discuss	the problem	comes later.
12. The students		each of whom		was called	last night	agreed to help.
13. The professors	(all of whom)		we	selected	for the panel	accepted the offer.
14. The medication	some of which		the doctor	recommended		was unavailable.

II. RELATIVE ADVERB CLAUSES

NOUN PHRASE		RELATIVE ADVERB CLAUSE			REST OF SENT.
NOUN/PRONOUN	SUBORDINATOR	SUBJECT OF CLAUSE	VERB PHRASE	COMPLEMENT, ADV., OR OBJ.	
15. The day	(when)	we	met	in the park	was memorable.
16. The building	(where)	the lecture	was given		had bad acoustics.
17. The reason	(why)	everyone	studies	day and night	must be TOEFL.

CHART 4-2   RULES FOR RELATIVE CONSTRUCTIONS

The Relative Adjective Clause

1. A relative adjective clause must contain at least a subject and a verb.
2. A relative adjective clause usually follows a noun or pronoun and identifies or describes it. The noun is called the antecedent.
3. A relative adjective clause may appear anywhere in the sentence but is usually placed after the noun it modifies.
4. A relative adjective clause typically begins with a subordinator (relative pronoun) like "who," "whom," "whose," "which," or "that."
5. The subordinator may act as the subject or object of the relative adjective clause.
6. A subordinator used as an object may be omitted.
7. A relative adjective clause may be restrictive (no commas) or nonrestrictive (commas, or sometimes dashes).
8. Restrictive adjective clauses use "who," "whom," "whose," "which," or "that" as subordinators. Some authors prefer "that" in restrictive clauses.
9. A restrictive adjective clause identifies the noun or pronoun it modifies. It is essential to the meaning.
10. Nonrestrictive relative adjective clauses use the subordinators "who," "whom," "whose," and "which." "That" should not be used after a comma.
11. A nonrestrictive relative adjective clause adds useful information but is not essential to the meaning of a sentence.
12. Nonrestrictive relative adjective clauses appear after proper nouns (names of people and places) and after nouns previously identified in a passage.

The Relative Adverb Clause

1. A relative adverb clause must contain at least a subject and a verb.
2. A relative adverb clause usually follows a noun or pronoun and identifies or describes it. The noun is the antecedent.
3. A relative adverb clause may appear anywhere in the sentence but is usually placed after the noun it modifies.
4. A relative adverb clause typically begins with the subordinators (relative adverbs) "when," "where," or "why."
5. The subordinator in an adverbial clause cannot act as the subject or object of the relative clause. It acts as an adverb.
6. The relative adverb subordinator may be omitted.
7. A relative adverb clause may be restrictive(no commas) or nonrestrictive (commas, or sometimes dashes).
8. Restrictive relative adverb clauses use "when," "where," and "why" as subordinators.
9. A restrictive relative adverb clause identifies the noun it modifies. It is essential to the meaning of the sentence.
10. Nonrestrictive relative adverb clauses use "when," "where," and "why."
11. A nonrestrictive relative adverb clause adds useful information but is not essential to the meaning of the sentence.
12. Nonrestrictive relative adverb clauses appear after nouns meaning time or place.

EXCEPTION:

13. One kind of nonrestrictive relative clause modifies an entire clause, not a single noun phrase. It has the meaning of a result or "a fact which." Example: John left the party early, *which irritated his wife.*
    See pages 346–349 for a chart on how relative clauses are formed.

Relative Clauses and Phrases; Cleft Sentences   **97**

4. a. A person must understand the values and aspirations of the people.
   b. He must work with the people.
   c. A person must understand the values and aspirations of the people with whom he must work.

5. a. Farmers usually consult with neighbors and friends.
   b. They respect the neighbors' and friends' opinions.
   c. Farmers usually consult with neighbors and friends whose opinions they respect.

6. a. The informal leaders have contacts and influence with people.
   b. No other channels can provide the contacts and influence with people.
   c. The informal leaders have contacts and influence with people which no other channels can provide.

Analysis Exercise 5: Sentence Decombining

Find the relative clauses in the following passage. Then decombine the sentences that contain the relative clauses. Discuss how you made two or more separate sentences.

A Running Tradition

With the possible exception of lacrosse, running, especially long-distance running, has been the sport most closely identified with the American Indian. Reports from the late 19th century routinely refer to Indians who ran 100 miles or more in a single day.

Indians of the Southwest were perhaps the most famous of all runners. The Hopi and the Zuni were recognized by numerous writers as outstanding distance runners. Stevenson (1904) reported that she "has never known the Zunis to lose a footrace with other Indians or with the champion runners of the troops at Fort Wingate, who sometimes enter into races with them." The widespread acclaim received by outstanding runners is suggested by Hayden (1862). He reported that "those who have shown great fleetness and powers of endurance [among the Mandan Indians] received additional reward in the form of praise by the public crier, who harangues their names through the village for many days afterwards" (p. 430).

Authors of the 19th century who traveled among the western Indians frequently referred to their great running accomplishments, particularly in the ball race. In the ball race, which was also called the stick kick race, the runner was required to continually kick a ball or other object in front of him. Blasiz (1933–1934) reported that among the Tarahumare "endurance races of various lengths were promoted, some of which reached a distance of 145 miles." According to Bennet and Zingg (1935), the name Tarahumare may be translated as "footrunners" (p. 3). The most important of all games of this group is the kick-ball race, which often lasted two days and a night. When night races were run, the course was lighted with torches. (34: 68–72)

Practicing Relative Clauses

Practice Exercise 6: Subordinators in Relative Clauses

Fill in the blanks in the passages below with the correct subordinators and prepositions if they are necessary. How are the commas used in the relative clauses?

During the twentieth century, the boldest and most imaginative combatants in the quest of fixing the origins of the Indian entered the arena: a fervent group arguing that the first Indians were survivors of the lost civilization of Atlantis. . . .

The concept of Atlantis goes back to Plato (427–347 B.C.). . . . According to these dialogues, Solon, an esteemed statesman (1) _____ lived about two centuries before Plato, heard about Atlantis from Egyptian priests (2) _____ possessed written records concerning this large island continent. . . . Plato described Atlantis as "the heart of a great and wonderful empire," the home of the "noblest race of men (3) _____ ever lived."

Atlantis's sinking "nine thousand years" before Solon (639–559 B.C.) comes to 11,600 years ago, (4) _____ is precisely the date determined by eminent oceanographic geologist Dr. Cesare Emiliani of the University of Miami for the last worldwide flooding. . . .

Edgar Cayce, the American (5) _____ psychic healing talents have been acknowledged by many, and (6) _____ prophecies have been studied by researchers from many different scientific disciplines, in 1940 predicted that a small part of Atlantis would rise again in 1968 to 1969 near the small island of Bimini in the Bahamas area of the Caribbean. And in 1968, parts of what appeared to be submerged walls or roads and possibly some buildings *were* found in the Atlantic near Bimini. (17: 31–33)

Hubble shows evidence of planets forming

Embryonic solar systems, churning with dust and the promise of new planets, have been spotted around distant stars by the Hubble space telescope, boosting the idea that there may be other worlds like Earth orbiting stars like the sun.

"We have found a place (7) _____ it is very possible that there will be planets within the next few million years," Edward Weiler, program scientist for the space telescope, said Wednesday. "This takes us closer to the final proof that there are other planets (8) _____ there could be life."

Photos taken by the telescope of a small section of the Orion Nebulae detect at least 15 stars surrounded by protoplanetary disks, or bands of dust of the type (9) _____ is thought to form planets. The constellation is about 500 light years from Earth—very close in astronomical terms—and is part of the Milky Way Galaxy, (10) _____ includes the sun.

Stephen Strom, a University of Massachusetts astronomer (11) _____ specializes in the study of star formation, said the Hubble photos confirm the long-held belief by many astronomers that a disk of dust (12) _____ _____ planets can evolve exists around most stars as they form.

Earlier studies, using an infrared detector on a satellite, pinpointed four stars (13) _____ appeared to be surrounded by protoplanetary disks. Strom said the theory is that over time individual grains in the dust disk clump together.

These clumps join others, forming boulders, (14) _____ collide with other boulders, forming larger and larger bodies and taking more and more material from the disk.   Eventually, the disk material forms into planets.

(from "Hubble Shows Evidence of Planets Forming," *The Des Moines Register,* December 17, 1992, p. 1A. Copyright © 1992 by Associated Press. Reprinted with permission.)

Practice Exercise 7: Sentence Combining

Combine the sentences marked as *main clause, 2nd clause, 3rd clause,* and so forth, into new sentences containing relative clauses.

One of the major problems appears to be the tendency for top managers and personnel specialists to apply their own scale of values of challenge and accomplishment to other people's personalities. However, (*main clause*) some people are challenged by jobs. (*2nd clause*) The jobs would appear unconscionably dull to many of us. (*main clause*) In one company, an employee felt he had one of the most important jobs in the company. (*2nd clause*) He had spent his life doing no more than keeping daily records of orders received.

Motivational Techniques—In the first place, money can never be overlooked as a motivator. . . . Another interesting special application of motivation is the "positive reinforcement" approach. This approach holds that individuals can be motivated by properly designing their work environment and praising their performance. (*main clause*) One technique is the increased awareness and use of participation. (*2nd clause*) The technique has been given strong support as the result of motivation theory and research. There can be no doubt that only rarely are people not motivated by being consulted on action affecting them. (**27**: 652, 648)

West Virginia Forest Industries Camp is a one-week environmental education program that is coordinated each summer by West Virginia University's division of forestry. (*main clause*) The program's goal is to help participants develop a philosophical attitude. (*2nd clause*) The attitude views the environment. (*3rd clause*) People live as a total system in the environment. (*4th clause*) The system has as its major component a natural system. (*5th clause*) The social, political, and economic systems are imposed upon the natural system.

(from Burris Bammel, Lei Lane, and Gene Bammel, "Gender Differences During an Environmental Camp," *Journal of Environmental Education* 17, 3 [Spring 1986]: 8–1.)

(*main clause*) The brain and spinal cord are enclosed within the body framework of the skull and the vertebral column. (*2nd clause*) The brain and spinal cord comprise the central nervous system. (*main clause*) The brain consists of two cerebral hemispheres, the brain stem, and the cerebellum, and occupies the cranial cavity within the skull. (*2nd clause*) In the base of the skull are numerous openings for the passage of blood and vessels.

The Spinal Cord—The longitudinal fibers in the spinal cord and brain stem are arranged in more or less definitely circumscribed functional groups. Every ascending pathway of conduction consists of chains of neurons. The neurons are linked together in series in the chains. The first neurons in these chains terminate peripherally in receptors. (*main clause*) The second neurons in the chain are the nuclei of termination. (*2nd clause— use "whose"*) The axons of the nucleii of termination ascend to reach centers in the brain stem or cerebellum. Descending pathways of conduction also form a chain of neurons linked together in series. (*main clause*) The lateral funiculi of the spinal cord contain many fiber-tracts. (*2nd clause*) All of the fiber-tracts cannot be considered in detail here. (**21**: 551, 558)

Practice Exercise 8: Punctuation of Restrictive and Nonrestrictive Relative Clauses

Use the rules you know to punctuate the following passages that include nonrestrictive or restrictive clauses. Think about how important the clauses are to the identification and meaning of the antecedent. Discuss your reasons for putting commas where you did.

[1]   Northwest Airlines Flight 650 lifted off from Fargo, N.D., early one morning last week and made a safe landing, but when the plane, a Boeing 727, landed in St. Paul, three members of the cockpit crew were met by an air-

port police supervisor and an official of the Federal Aviation Administration who immediately placed all three men under what the FAA later termed a "citizen's arrest." The reason: according to FAA officials, all three members of the cockpit crew had allegedly gone out drinking at a local bar during their layover in Fargo which would violate an FAA rule that says aviators may not fly within eight hours of consuming alcohol.
(from "Flying and Alcohol Do Not Mix," *Newsweek*, March 19, 1990, p. 27.)

[2]   **Many types of lasers are available, but they all operate on the principle from which they get their name, *light amplification by stimulated emission of radiation*. The concept of stimulated emission which we soon discuss was first presented clearly by Einstein in 1917. It was not until 1953, however, that the concept was applied to laserlike devices. In that year a microwave laser which is called a *maser* was developed. Lasers which use light rather than microwaves were first conceived and constructed in 1958. (2: 744)**

[3] Scientists say *Gigantopithecus* was a massive ape, towering over everything that walked and crawled the ancient bamboo forests of south Asia. It stood 11 feet tall and weighed 800 pounds. . . . "It's a true 20th-century scientific dilemma," said Russell Ciochon, a University of Iowa anthropologist who will lead the expedition into a series of unexplored caves in Vietnam. "Why was this, the largest ape of them all, the only primate not to have survived the Ice Age?" The theory is the ape was hunted and killed by *Homo erectus* (Stone Age man) and that may have led to its extinction.

The trip has attracted the attention and support of the National Geographic Society which is sending along a film crew. The four-member expedition team which will include Ciochon, U. of I. graduate student Katerina Semendsferi and Professor John Olsen and Mary Kay Gilliland from the University of Arizona is the result of five years of preparation and negotiation with the Vietnamese. . . .

The giant ape has been considered one of nature's mysteries since 1935 when the first evidence—a handful of huge teeth—was found accidentally by a German anthropologist in a Hong Kong pharmacy. . . . Five years later three fossilized giant ape jaws

Gigantopithecus

were located in caves. With the jaws which are about the size of a human skull scientists began to grasp the immensity of the animal.

Ciochon asked the Chinese for permission to visit the area in 1983 but was turned away. A friend who flew American air raid missions over North Vietnam during the war told Ciochon that similar areas existed in that country.

Research team members believe if they find *Gigantopithecus*'s bones they will be able to determine its anatomy and to learn what caused its extinction. (4:1B)

Using Relative Clauses in Writing: Defining Summaries and Paraphrases

A **summary** is used to report what someone else has written in a condensed, concise form that is easy to understand. It gives the essentials in as few words as possible and may use the author's original words.

A **paraphrase** is an exact *re*statement of another person's writing. It should not use the author's original words. To paraphrase means to say or write in your own words what someone else has said or written. Paraphrasing is an extremely important skill to develop for your academic career. Paraphrasing may be used to take notes or to write a summary of another piece of writing.

Writing Exercise 9: Paraphrasing and Producing Relative Clauses

Read the passage below.

> *Dreams and Beyond—A Separate Reality*
>
> *Question: What do people dream about?*
>
> Calvin Hall, a noted authority on dreams, has collected and analyzed over 10,000 dreams. Hall (1966) found that most dreams are extensions of everyday experience. The favorite dream setting is familiar rooms in a house. Action usually takes place between the dreamer and two or three other people with whom the dreamer is emotionally involved—friends, enemies, parents, or employers. Actions are also predominantly familiar: running, jumping, riding, sitting, talking, and watching. About half of the recorded dreams had sexual elements. Dreams of flying, floating, and falling occur less frequently. Hall also found that if you're dreaming more now, you may be enjoying it less. UJnpleasant emotions such as fear, anger, and sadness are more frequent in dreams than pleasant emotions. (7: 156, 157)

Now, using relative clause subordinators, paraphrase the passage. Use each subordinator only once. Leave the blank empty if it is possible to omit the subordinator.

Calvin Hall, _____ is a famous dream psychologist, studied more than 10,000 dreams _____ he found to be based on everyday experience. Rooms _____ are familiar in a house are a common theme. Friends, parents, or enemies _____ relationships to the dreamer are important are usually part of the action in a dream. Some common actions

_____ people dream include sitting, running, and talking. One reason _____ we probably don't enjoy our dreams if we dream a lot is that the most common emotions, _____ are fear, anger, and sadness, are the most common emotions in dreams, too.

Writing Exercise 10: Paraphrasing on Your Own

Read the following paragraphs, which continue "Dreams and Beyond."

[2]   Since so many of the elements of dreams are familiar, it might seem that they are woven exclusively from the vast array of sensory images experienced each day. However, attempts to influence the content of dreams show that this is not the case. In one experiment subjects wore red goggles for a week so that they saw only red during the day. Although the red in their dreams increased, blue, green, and other colors also continued to appear. People paralyzed by accidents and thus confined to wheelchairs continue to have dreams in which they walk or run (as well as dreams in which they are in the chair). (Dement, 1972).

[3]   Charles Tart (1969) has recently called attention to two types of dreaming that differ markedly from the normal dream. The first of these has been called the "high" dream. In the high dream, the individual dreams he or she has taken a psychedelic drug like LSD or mescaline and then experiences the sensory distortion, brilliant colors, and feelings of panic or ecstasy that occur when a drug is actually taken. These are so vivid that the person may lose track of the fact that he or she is dreaming. Some prior experience with a psychedelic may be necessary for recognizing a high dream. It is, therefore, unclear how many people have had such experiences.

[4]   A second unusual form of dreaming, which may relate to the high dream, has been called the lucid dream. This is a dream in which the dreamer "wakes" from an ordinary dream and feels capable of ordinary thought and action but remains in the dream world. The lucid dream, in other words, seems to the dreamer as real as everyday experience.

[5]   *Interpreting Dreams*—Sigmund Freud's book *The Interpretation of Dreams* (1900) opened a whole new world of psychological investigation. Prior to Freud, most psychologists considered dreams a meaningless carryover of waking thoughts or the result of indigestion. Upon analyzing his own dreams, Freud felt that many represented wish fulfillment. Thus, a student who is angry at a teacher may dream of successfully embarrassing the teacher in class; a lonely person may dream of romance; or a hungry child may dream of food. Although Freud's view of dreaming is attrac-

tive, there is evidence against it. For example, volunteers in a study of the effects of prolonged starvation showed no particular increase in dreams about food and eating. (7: 156)

Complete the following paragraphs to paraphrase paragraphs 2, 3, 4, and 5 of "Dreams and Beyond." When you are finished, review your work. Did you use relative clauses? Which parts could you rewrite with relative clauses?

2. According to research, it is not possible to predetermine what we dream. There was one experiment in _____ the subjects _____ all day. However, at night they had dreams _____. Other evidence shows that people _____ still dream about walking and running.

3. and 4. Charles Tart has described two dreams _____ from normal dreams. The "high" dream is a dream _____ _____. The person _____ is not sure whether he/she is awake or dreaming. The person _____ a lucid dream _____ _____.

5. Sigmund Freud, _____ *The Interpretation of Dreams* in 1900, believed _____. For example, _____ _____. However, psychologists _____ before Freud believed _____. More recently, in 1950, volunteers _____ .

PART II   RELATIVE PHRASES—ADJECTIVE PHRASES

Discovering the Grammar of Relative Phrases

Discovery Exercise 11: Identifying Modifying Clauses and Phrases

In the following excerpt there are many examples of adjective clauses and phrases. Some phrases are in the form of present or past participles; others are in the form of prepositional or noun phrases in apposition to (following and modifying) a noun. See how many adjectives, adjective phrases, and relative adjective clauses you can find. Discuss your findings in class.

One Hundred Percent American

There can be no questions about the average American's Americanism or his desire to preserve this precious heritage at all costs. Nevertheless, some insidious foreign ideas have already wormed their way into his civilization without his realizing what was going on. Thus dawn finds the unsuspecting patriot garbed in pajamas, a garment of East Indian origin, and lying in a bed built on a pattern which originated in either Persia or Asia Minor. He is muffled to the ears in un-American materials: cotton, first domesticated in India; linen, domesticated in the Near East; wool from an animal native to Asia Minor; or silk whose uses were first discovered by the Chinese. All these substances have been transformed into cloth by methods invented in Southwestern Asia. . . .

In his bathroom the American washes with soap invented by the ancient Gauls. Next he cleans his teeth, a subversive European practice which did not invade America until the latter part of the eighteenth century. He then shaves, a masochistic rite first developed by the heathen priests of ancient Egypt and Sumer. The process is made less of a penance by the fact that his razor is of steel, an iron-carbon alloy discovered in either India or Turkestan. Lastly he dries himself on a Turkish towel. (**29:** 326–327)

Discovery Exercise 12: Forming Modifying Phrases from Relative Clauses

Study the pairs of sentences below. The A sentences contain relative adjective clauses. The B sentences contain modifying phrases that are derived from the relative clauses. Can you write a rule that explains how the modifying phrases are derived from relative adjective clauses?

A. The unsuspecting patriot is garbed in pajamas, which is a garment of East Indian Origin.

B. The unsuspecting patriot is garbed in pajamas, a garment of East Indian origin.

A. All these substances have been transformed into cloth by methods which were invented in Southwestern Asia.

B. All these substances have been transformed into cloth by methods invented in Southwestern Asia.

A. The unsuspecting patriot who is lying in a bed that was built on a   pattern which originated in Persia is garbed in pajamas, a garment of East Indian origin.

B. The unsuspecting patriot lying in a bed built on a pattern originating in Persia is garbed in pajamas, a garment of East Indian origin.

Explanation 2—Forming Phrases from Relative Clauses

Relative adjective clauses are often reduced into phrases. Sometimes they become single adjectives or prepositional phrases; sometimes they become appositives (noun phrases); and sometimes they become past or present participial phrases. Modifying phrases are derived in a number of ways.

Relative clauses containing "be" can be reduced to several types of phrases by deleting the relative pronoun and "be."

To a prepositional phrase modifier:

The people *who are in the far corners of the earth* will come together.
The people *in the far corners of the earth* will come together.

To an adjective phrase modifier:

There is something *which is weird about this situation.*
There is something *weird about this situation*

To a noun phrase modifier (appositive):

Richard MacNeish, *who is an archaeologist at the Peabody Museum*, is here.
Richard MacNeish, *an archaeologist at the Peabody Museum*, is here.

To a participial phrase expressing the same time as the main verb:

Active. Relative clauses containing verbs with *be* + verb-*ing* (present or past tense) may become participial phrases. The relative pronoun and *be* are deleted.

The students *who are studying* English will pass the TOEFL.
The students *studying English* will pass the TOEFL.

Several countries *that were attending the conference* signed the treaty.
Several countries *attending the conference* signed the treaty.

We will see campuses *which have been improving classes.*
We will see campuses *improving classes.*

Relative clauses containing other verbs (simple past or present tense) may be changed into present participial phrases.

Marie is the student *who lives with me now*.
Marie is the student *living with me now*.

Ann was the student *who lived with me then*.
Ann was the student *living with me then*.

Passive. Relative clauses containing a passive form of a verb may be reduced to participial phrases by deleting the relative pronoun and the first "be" verb.

The texts *that were chosen* have been added to the list.
The texts *chosen* have been added to the list.

The employees *that were being considered* arrived safely.
The employees *being considered* arrived safely.

To a participial phrase expressing earlier time than the main verb:

Relative clauses containing past perfect tense may be reduced to participial phrases by deleting the relative pronoun and changing "had" to "having."

Active (simple form)

The student *who had applied early* was accepted immediately.
The student *having applied early* was accepted immediately.

  (progressive form)

The student *who had been considering* a job for months left school.
The student *having been considering* a job for months left school.

Passive

The student *who had been accepted* left home.
The student *having been accepted* left home.

Discussion of Participial Phrases

Relative adjective clauses are just one way to modify or describe the nouns in a sentence. Professional writers have many ways to modify nouns. Some of the most common modifiers appear in the explanation above. Relative clauses may be reduced to single adjectives, adjective phrases, prepositional phrases, noun phrases, and participial phrases. When the reduced part is only one word long, that word (adjective, noun, or participle) may be placed in front of the noun that it modifies. For example:

Relative clause— John Smith, *who is chairman*, called the meeting to order.
Appositive— John Smith, *chairman*, called the meeting to order.
Noun modifier— *Chairman* John Smith called the meeting to order.

Practicing Modifying Clauses and Phrases

Practice Exercise 13: "One Hundred Percent American" (continued)

See how many more relative clauses, adjective phrases, prepositional phrases, noun modifiers (appositives), and participles you can find in the rest of the article.

Returning to the bedroom, the unconscious victim of un-American practices removes his clothes from a chair, invented in the Near East, and proceeds to dress. He puts on close-fitting tailored garments whose form derives from the skin clothing of the ancient nomads of the Asiatic steppes and fastens them with buttons whose prototypes appeared in Europe at the close of the Stone Age. This costume is appropriate enough for outdoor exercise in a cold climate, but is quite unsuited to American summers and heated houses. Nevertheless, foreign ideas and habits hold the unfortunate man in thrall even when common sense tells him that the authentically American costume of G-string and moccasins would be far more comfortable. He puts on his feet stiff coverings made from hide prepared by a process which can be traced back to ancient Greece, and makes sure that they are properly polished, also a Greek idea. Lastly, he ties about his neck a strip of bright-colored cloth which is a vestigial survival of the shoulder shawls worn by seventeenth-century Greeks. He gives himself a final appraisal in the mirror, an old Mediterranean invention, and goes downstairs to breakfast.

Here a whole new series of foreign things confronts him. His food and drink are placed before him in pottery vessels, the popular name of which—china—is sufficient evidence of their origin. His fork is a medieval Italian invention and his spoon a copy of a Roman original. He will usually begin the meal with coffee, an Abyssinian plant first discovered by the Arabs. . . . Whereas the Arabs took their coffee straight, he will probably sweeten it with sugar, discovered in India; and dilute it with cream, both the domestication of cattle and the technique of milking having originated in Asia Minor.

If our patriot is old-fashioned enough to adhere to the so-called American breakfast, his coffee will be accompanied by an orange, domesticated in the Mediterranean region, a cantaloupe domesticated in Persia, or grapes domesticated in Asia Minor. He will follow this with a bowl of cereal made from grain domesticated in the Near East and prepared by methods also invented there. From this he will go on to waffles, a Scandinavian invention, with plenty of butter, originally a Near-Eastern cosmetic. As a side dish he may have the egg of a bird domesticated in Southeastern Asia or strips of the flesh of an animal domesticated in the same region, which have been salted and smoked by a process invented in Northern Europe. **(29: 326–327)**

We will return to participial phrases and work with them in more detail in Chapter 6 after we have reviewed adverbial clauses because participial phrases are also derived from adverbial clauses of time and cause.

PART III CLEFT SENTENCES—ANOTHER WAY TO EXPRESS EMPHASIS

Discovering the Grammar of Cleft Sentences

Discovery Exercise 14: Identifying Cleft Sentences

Study the sentences below and then make a statement about how the "that" clauses function in the sentences. When there are two clauses, the underlined part shows you where to look. As you examine the sentences, ask yourself:

- What word begins each sentence?
- Are there antecedents to the "that" clauses? What kinds of words precede the "that" clauses (ignore the words between commas)?
- Can these "that" clauses be turned into "which" clauses?
- Can these clauses be defined as relative clauses?
- Why do writers use this type of construction?

1. It is the human need to combine words, sounds, colors, shapes and movements into aesthetically satisfying patterns that separates us most clearly from the rest of the animal kingdom.

2. It is this need, or the satisfaction of it, that answers Ives' s question.

3. It is the section on the naming of sensations that has received the most attention, and there has been seen in it a revolt against, and a complete reversal of, the Cartesian framework.

4. It is by using this definition of democracy that various authoritarian regimes—the Soviet Union, China Cuba, and certain European, Asian and Latin American dictatorships—have been able to claim that they were democratic.

Discovery Exercise 15: Not . . . but Sentences

Read the following sentences and compare them to the sentences in Exercise 14. Pay particular attention to the underlined sections. What do the sentences in Exercises 14 and 15 have in common? What is different about them?

1. The most marvelous thing is one can actually see the activity of the brain cell networks that differ from activity to activity. <u>It was not that this was unanticipated but that it is concrete now, for the first time.</u>
   (from Philip J. Hilts, "Photos Show Mind Recalling a Word," *New York Times,* November 11, 1991, A1.)

2. The argument that the entire recombinant DNA approach to gaining an understanding of the complexities of higher genetic systems is misbegotten. <u>The argument is not that the approach may not work but that its alleged huge risks are unnecessary</u> because less risky, although slower, means are available. (**18**: 28)

Explanation 3—Cleft Sentences

Writers in English need ways to show emphasis. We have already seen that auxiliary verbs and negative words can be used to show emphasis. The cleft sentence is also used for this purpose in academic writing.

Cleft sentences look much like adjective clauses, but are used to emphasize a particular element in a sentence, usually a noun phrase. Look at the examples below.

Affirmative cleft

        strong emphasis
1. It is the *personnel manager* who hires the employees.
      ("not someone else" is unstated but understood)
(normal statement)   The personnel manager hires the employees.

      strong emphasis
2. It is *time* that we need. ("not money" is understood)
(normal statement)   We need time.

      strong emphasis
3. It is *through education* that we will succeed.
      ("not through government handouts" is understood)
(normal statement)   We will succeed through education.

Negative cleft

slight emphasis   **strong emphasis**
4. It is *not* the foreman who hires the employees *but* the *personnel manager.*

(normal statement)   The foreman does not hire the employees; the manager
                                      hires the employees.

slight emphasis   **strong emphasis**
5. It is *not* money that we need *but* time.

(normal statement)   We do not need money. We need time.

slight emphasis   **strong emphasis**
6. It is *not* through government handouts that we will succeed *but* through
    education.

(normal statement)   We will not succeed through government handouts.
                                      We will succeed through education.

The cleft sentences above can be described this way:

It+"be" + **strongly emphasized element** + "that" + clause + (*not* + phrase or clause)
                (usually a noun but may be   "who"
                a prepositional phrase)

It+"be" + *not* + **slightly emphasized element** + "that" + clause + *but* + **emphasized**
                                                                  "who"   **element**

Practicing Cleft Sentences

Practice Exercise 16: Rewriting Sentences into Cleft Sentences

Rewrite the following sentences as cleft sentences to express emphasis. You should
decide which element (noun or prepositional phrase) needs to be emphasized.

Statement: This need or the satisfaction of it answers Ives's question.
Cleft sentence: It is this need or the satisfaction of it that answers Ives's ques-
                         tion.

1. The price of washing machines relative to all other prices is important for
    determining the relationship between price and the quantity demanded.

2. James Madison devised a government scheme—sometimes called the
    Madisonian model—to achieve the separation of powers.

3. Synapse is effected through contact between these terminal bulbs and
    cell bodies or dendrites of other neurons.

4. The member states refuse to act through the diplomatic device of the
    United Nations.

5. (Rewrite the underlined sentence only.) While weaknesses and difficulties may appear at any level of management, effective and perceptive management demands that all those responsible for the work of other regard themselves as managers. <u>The term is used in this sense in this book.</u>

6. (Rewrite all of the sentences in this passage.) Complacency leads a professional pilot to abuse his or her time off by working, not resting. Complacency makes a pilot fail to appreciate the challenge of landing at a VFR airport surrounded by mountains on a dark night. Indeed, complacency lulls us into thinking each and every flight will not require all of our skills and experience.

Practice Exercise 17a: Rewriting *not . . . but* Sentences

Find the emphasized elements in the cleft sentences below. Then rewrite the cleft sentences as normal statements. You can change them any way you like.

1. The first settlers encountered not a vacant continent but scattered Indian tribes of great variety.

2. The emphasis in American folklore study has been not on the national character but on the character of the different groups that make up our society.

3. The problem was that the artistic achievements of numerous Americans still went unrecognized—not because they lacked merit but because they did not fall into the established categories of American folk art.

4. I am convinced that we generate and transmit folklore not because we belong to a particular nation or to a particular group—not because we are Westerners, logger, Catholics, or Finns—but because we are human beings dealing with recurring human problems in traditional human ways.

5. Both true and quasi-18-bit systems can offer improved measured performance, not necessarily because they have higher resolution but because nonlinearity is reduced.

6. The link between randomization and normally distributed observations is not well defined, but seems to be justified on the basis of considerable experience.

7. An anthropologist will spend weeks tracing a lead to the answer. The sociologist cannot afford to become so deeply involved. This is not to condemn either discipline but to point out a basic difference between them.

Analysis Exercise 17b: Other Ways to Express *not . . . but*

Two other ways are used to express the same meaning as "not . . . but." In the sentences below, find the words or punctuation marks that are used instead of "but." Then rewrite the sentences as normal statements.

1. There is an idea that the words for sensations get their meaning by referring to sensations as private objects (something each person has a personal experience with). This is not to deny that there are such sensations; it is to comment on our ways of understanding how we speak of them.

2. English restrictions upon American trade did not so much stifle as divert it into a peculiar triangular pattern.

Preparing for Standardized Tests

Practice Exercise 18: Understanding Relative Clauses

Choose the lettered sentence that is closest in meaning to the original statement.

1. This method yields a coarse, granular polycrystalline material whose current carrying ability is severely limited.
   a. The scientists are limited in their ability to carry current.
   b. The scientists cannot carry the current.
   c. The polycrystalline material does not carry current well.
   d. the polycrystalline material limits its ability to carrying current.

2. Nerve fibers which conduct impulses toward the cyton are termed dendrites; those which conduct impulses away from the cyton to terminate in relation to other cytons are called axons.
   a. An axon conducts impulses toward the cyton.
   b. An axon conducts impulses away from the cyton.
   c. Cytons terminate in relation to other cytons.
   d. Dendrites conduct impulses away from nerve fibers.

3. The weather-induced variability in production, and the wildly fluctuating grain prices which accompany it, are annoying and frustrating to the developed countries, but they can be disastrous to the very poor countries living on the edge of subsistence.
   a. If weather produces changes in production, grain prices go up and down, irritating rich countries, but underdeveloped countries may lose everything.
   b. Weather hardly affects grain prices, and the developing countries are irritated by it.
   c. Grain prices change along with fluctuation in the variable development of poor countries.
   d. Grain price changes are annoying and disastrous to developed countries.

4. The post-revolutionary Articles of Confederation largely embodied republican confederalism, and the extent to which the Constitution departed from it was controversial from the outset of the nation.
   a. The Constitution was extensively different from the outset.
   b. The Articles of Confederation and the Constitution caused controversy.
   c. The Constitution departed from the controversy at the outset of the nation.
   d. The differences between the Constitution and the Articles of Confederation caused controversy.

5. The internal organs of the body generally are supplied by fibers of both sympathetic and parasympathetic divisions, the functional effects of which are mainly antagonistic.
   a. The sympathetic and parasympathetic division fibers work together.
   b. The sympathetic division fibers and parasympathetic division fibers affect the internal organs.
   c. The sympathetic division fibers and parasympathetic division fibers work against each other.
   d. The functions of the internal organs are supplied with parasympathetic and sympathetic fibers.

6. The extent to which changes are adopted depends upon the values and expectations of the group and upon the extent to which the individual is expected to conform.
   a. Conformity and individual expectations determine the range of adoption of changes there will be.
   b. Group expectations of individual conformity and the values and expectations of the group will determine how many changes will be adopted.
   c. Groups adopt values and expectations to a great extent.
   d. Adoptions of individuals and groups depends on conformity and expectations.

Practice Exercise 19: Finding Errors

Choose the one error in each sentence below. Circle the error and then write the correct form above it.

1. The upper layers of the open sea that there is light enough for photosynthesis are deficient in nutrients.

2. The light-producing organs, that may produce light of different colors, probably serve to identify species to one another.

3. The id is like a blind king whose power is awesome but whom must rely on others to carry out his orders.

4. Interest in hypnosis began in the 1700s with Frank Mesmer (who name is the basis for the term *mesmerize*).

5. The first industrial revolution began with little concern for the very people whose made the revolution possible.

6. The most conspicuous of the herbivores is the moose, that is common in open, marshy areas of the taiga.

7. Most of the animals of the tundra are insects in that, like the plants, are dormant most of the year.

8. Toward the middle of the 19th century, some functions of the worker were taken over by machines which mechanical components such as cams and levers were ingeniously arranged to perform relatively simple and repetitive tasks.

9. *Caddis* fly larvae construct cases around their bodies by which protect them from the current and weigh them down, or they spin nets.

10. One of the first group approaches was developed by J. L. Moreno (1953), that called his technique "psychodrama."

11. Estuaries are bodies of water partially cut off from the sea which fresh water from the land mixes with salt water from the sea.

12. A biome is a community in which covers a large geographic area, where the life forms are different from those of other climatic areas.

13. Animals whose live in the desert usually avoid the heat of the day; most are nocturnal (active at night) or crepuscular (active around twilight).

14. Most laboratory research on operant learning takes place in some form of conditioning chamber (also called a "Skinner box," after B.F. Skinner, that invented it for experiments in operant conditioning).

15. The association of sleepwalking and sleeptalking with the deeper stages of sleep seems to explain why sleeptalking makes little sense and why a sleepwalker which is awakened is confused and remembers little.

UNIT 3

ADVERBIAL CONCEPTS

5

ADVERBIALS EXPRESSING RELATIONSHIPS OF TIME, PLACE, SITUATION, CAUSE, EFFECT, AND PURPOSE

PART I   ADVERBIALS OF TIME, PLACE, AND SITUATION

Discovering the Grammar of Adverbials

What are adverbials? Are they single words, phrases, or clauses? How do you identify an adverbial? Can you give some examples? How many adverbial clauses would you expect to see in one sentence? Discuss what you already know about adverbials and then do the following exercise.

Discovery Exercise 1: Identifying Adverbials

Skim the following passages and find examples of adverbial constructions (single words, conjunctions, transitions, phrases, and adverbial clauses expressing adverbial ideas). After the class has identified which structures are adverbials and which are not, discuss the questions in Exercise 2.

> *Early Man in the Americas*
>
> The questions of who the American Indians* are, whether they evolved in the Western Hemisphere, and, if not, where they came from (and

---

* "Native American" and "American Indian" refer to the indigenous people of North America. Some groups prefer "Native American," other groups prefer "American Indian," and still others prefer "Indigenous Peoples." This textbook uses both "American Indian" and "Native American" as they were used in the original passages.

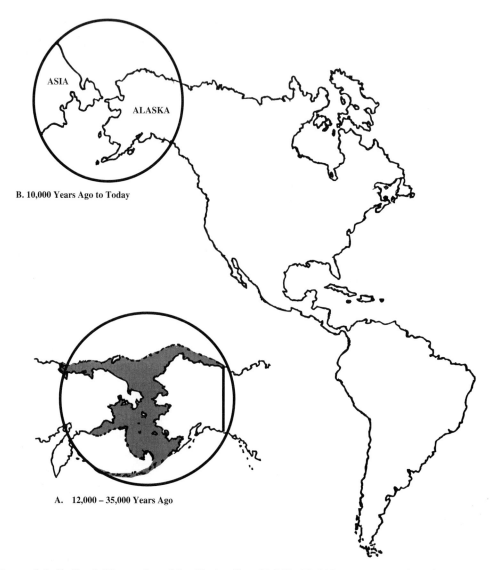

Figure 5-1 (*bottom*). The region of the Bering Sea 12,000–35,000 years ago, when the gray area was a land bridge between North America and Eurasia. (*top*). The region of the Bering Sea from 10,000 years ago to the present. There is no land bridge today. (**9:** 135)

when), have intrigued the white man ever since the time of Columbus. As stated earlier, questions of race and of precise places and times of departure from the Old World persist, but today there is little doubt among scientists where the earliest known inhabitants of the New World came from and how they entered the Americas. Since no remains have ever been found in the Western Hemisphere of a pre-*Homo sapiens* type of man, it is now generally accepted that humans did not evolve in North or

South America as they did in the Old World, but that the first of them crossed into present-day Alaska from northeastern Asia at least 12,000 to 15,000 years ago, and possibly long before that. During the Wisconsin glaciation of the Ice Age, when much of the water of the oceans became congealed in the great icepack glaciers, the sea levels fell and at times were from 250 to 300 feet lower than they are today. As the waters receded, a land bridge connecting northeastern Asia and Alaska came into existence. . . .

From time to time, animals and men could have passed back and forth with ease across this Bering land bridge, which in reality was more than a bridge, since at its maximum expanse of treeless tundra was as wide as approximately one-third the distance across the present-day United States. . . . Some experts have speculated that the earliest migrants could have reached North America during the Sangmon Interglacial period before the Wisconsin glaciation. That would have been 75,000 years ago! But most scientists, while not ruling out the possibility of such an early entry into the Western Hemisphere, are more conservative and provide estimates that range from 12,000 to 35,000 years ago or slightly earlier. . . .

Eventually, the different groups moved down the eastern side, or perhaps both sides of the Continental Divide, hunting game along the mountains into Central and South America and wandering eastward after animals across the plains and through the forests and lowlands of both continents. . . . Meanwhile, behind them, according to the same theory, glacial action sealed the routes they had followed south from Alaska and isolated them for thousands of years from the people who had remained in that northern region. During that time, the Bering land bridge was submerged and then reappeared. When the land was again above water, new peoples bringing more advanced material traits from Asia may have crossed into Alaska. By about 15,000 to 12,000 years ago, passage was again opened between Alaska and more southern areas of the continent, and migrations south may have occurred again in northwestern North America. . . . Whenever the first peoples came, however, all overland travel from Asia to America would have ended by 10,000 years ago when the land bridge disappeared for the last time.

The inhabiting of the New World was a long and gradual process, requiring, according to some authorities, perhaps as much as 25,000 years for man to spread from Alaska to Cape Horn at the southern tip of South America. . . . Although population would have been sparse, and much distance would have separated many of the nomadic bands, some of the newcomers no doubt collided here and there with earlier arrivals, sometimes combining with them and sometimes forcing them into less desirable or accessible parts of the country. (**24**: 37–39)

During the past five years, a startling new rush of archaeological discoveries, new dating techniques and the recognition of hitherto unknown tool manufacturing techniques show that the Indians were in the Americas much, much earlier than suspected—as early as 500,000 years ago. These astounding discoveries have thrown off all our accepted notions of the way North America and perhaps the world evolved. . . . Since, according to previous theories, there were no fully modern men anywhere in the world 70,000 years ago, these new American discoveries, mostly from North America, point to the astonishing thesis that men like ourselves, subspecies *Homo sapiens sapiens*, made their world debut in the Americas, instead of in Europe.

New information has come from far below the earth's surface, from depths of fifteen to sixty feet, much deeper than the few feet usually dug by archaeologists in the Americas. Steam shovels working on housing sites, steep rain-etched gulleys, and exploratory shafts have penetrated a thick earthen veil to offer a glimpse of these ancient times. . . .

Ironically, ten years ago the famed Dr. Louis Leaky stood alone when he suggested that there was an ancient prehistoric bounty to be found in the Americas. . . . Until recently it has been an accepted fact that successive waves of nomadic Asian hunters unwittingly wandered across the now submerged Bering Land Bridge. . . . But now it seems more likely that if the first modern men did cross the Bering Bridge to settle in a new continent, they traveled from the Americas to Europe and Asia. . . . The American Indians may have even been responsible for the sudden appearance of cave-dwelling Cro-Magnon man in Europe, one of the most celebrated events in mankind's history. For decades, archaeologists have known that rather suddenly, 35,000 years ago, the crude Neanderthals were replaced throughout Europe by fully modern Cro-Magnon man. . . . American Indians, who migrated to Europe, may have been the Cro-Magnon. (**17**: 17–19)

Discussion Questions

1. How did you identify the adverbial clauses and phrases?
2. Was your prediction of how many adverbials would be in a single sentence accurate? How many adverbial clauses and phrases can appear in one sentence, do you suppose?
3. Do you feel there are more or fewer adverbials in historical writing than in other types of writing? Why do you think this might be true?
4. Is there anything different about the adverbials in this passage from adverbials you have studied in the past? Which structures seem unusual or confusing?

Explanation 1—Adverbials and Cohesion

Cohesion means that different parts of something stick together. Coherence is a synonym for cohesion, but it relates more to the order and consistency of ideas and statements. It means that all parts of a piece of writing are clearly related to one another in a logical sequence. Transitions are the words and phrases that writers use to compose a coherent piece of writing. We saw in Chapter 3 that judicious use of active and passive voice can help a writer achieve cohesion. Transitions also show relationships between ideas. Most transitions are adverbials. Adverbial clauses and phrases and coordinating conjunctions express a great many relationship concepts: time, place, concession, opposition, comparison, cause, effect (result), purpose, condition, and manner. These adverbial clauses and phrases are introduced by subordinating conjunctions, coordinating conjunctions, conjunctive adverbs, and prepositions. Adverbials of this kind provide one means of connecting ideas to each other. Such connections give coherence to a piece of writing. You will find a list of some subordinators, conjunctions, and transitions in Table 5-1 on page 126.

Most of the adverbial clauses and phrases can appear both at the beginnings of sentences (1st position) and later toward the middle or ends of sentences after the main clause (2nd position). These clauses and phrases may be described as "reversible" when either the main clause or the subordinate clause can appear first in the sentence. For example, the subordinator "after" is reversible: "After we study, we will eat" and "We will eat after we study" are both possible sentences. A few clauses and phrases appear only in 2nd position, and still others like "so . . . that" and "such . . . that" appear in particular, fixed parts of a sentence and cannot be moved around.

Adverbial clauses and phrases are introduced by subordinating conjunctions, and compound sentences are connected by coordinating conjunctions and conjunctive adverbs. Adverbial clauses are used to construct **complex sentences**. A complex sentence is made up of clauses of *unequal* importance. There is a main clause and a subordinate clause. The subordinate clause can be identified by the subordinating conjunction (subordinator). Many of the subordinate clauses and phrases use the same subordinators. For example:

Clause: *When we were ready*, we left for school.
Phrase: *When ready*, we left for school.

Introductory subordinate clauses and phrases are followed by commas. Subordinate clauses and phrases that follow the main clause are **not** usually preceded by commas.

no comma   no comma
We left for school *when we were ready because it was time to go*.

TABLE 5-1

CONCEPT	SUBORDINATORS	CONJUNCTIONS	TRANSITIONS
Time	before, after, while, when	meanwhile	soon, now, later, during, subsequently, at length, eventually, currently, in the future (past), first, second, third, finally, in the meantime
Place			here, there, nearby, next to, in the front (back/middle), in the North (South, East, West)
Summary		hence	in conclusion, finally, in brief, in short, on the whole, in summary
Result		so hence, thus therefore	accordingly as a result of consequently
Cause	because since, as	for	owing to, due to, inasmuch as, in view of, on account of, now that
Purpose	so that in order that		in order to
Contrast	while whereas	but, yet, or however nevertheless nonetheless	conversely, in contrast, on the contrary, contrary to, still, instead, on the one (other) hand
Comparison		likewise	in comparison, similar to, similarly, in the same way, as, like, unlike
Concession	although even though though		naturally, certainly, to be sure, despite, in spite of, regardless of, notwithstanding, no matter + "Wh- word"
Condition	if, as if, as though, unless, when, whenever, where, as long as, so long as, once whether (or not)		assuming (that), given (that), in case (that), in the event (that), just so (that), on condition that, provided (that), providing (that) supposing (that) with, without
Conviction			indeed, admittedly, certainly, clearly, evidently, obviously, patently, plainly
Addition		and	in addition, moreover, and, also, besides, further, furthermore, next, then, finally.
Example			for example, namely, as an illustration, for instance, specifically

CHART 5-1 ADVERBIAL CONCEPTS—TIME/PLACE

SIMPLE SENTENCES	COMPLEX SENTENCES	COMPOUND SENTENCES
TIME RELATIONSHIP		
Adverbial Phrase, Main Clause	Subordinator Subordinate Clause, Main Clause	Clause Conjunction Clause
After studying, we'll go dancing.	After we study, we'll go dancing.	Congress voted; meanwhile, Bush traveled.
Before dancing, we'll study.	Before we go dancing, we'll study.	She hated war; henceforth, they made peace.
When finished, the test seemed easy.	When we studied, we passed.	
Since arriving, we have studied a lot.	Since we arrived, we have studied a lot.	
	As we were studying, the bell rang.	
While studying, John worked hard.	While/whilst we were studying, John came home.	
	As long as we were studying, the radio was on.	
	As soon as we finish, we can go dancing.	
Until 1939, no one suspected a thing.	Until/till you tell me the truth, I won't help you.	
Whenever working, we use the dictionary.	Whenever you lie, I get really mad	
By 1930, women had been given the vote.	By the time you graduate, spring will be here.	
Once finished, he left the office.	Once you learn to swim, you'll never forget how.	
Up to last week, we had never read it.		
Within a year, she will be married.		
Upon seeing her, he screamed.		
During their marriage, they were happy.		
PLACE RELATIONSHIP		
Where necessary, please add punctuation.	Where A is equal to S, the volume is 323.	
Wherever possible, help is offered.	Wherever you go, trouble will follow.	

127

CHART 5-2   ADVERBIAL CONCEPTS—CAUSE/EFFECT

SIMPLE SENTENCES	COMPLEX SENTENCES	COMPOUND SENTENCES
CAUSE/EFFECT **REASON/RESULT** Subordinator Adverbial Phrase, Main Clause	**CAUSE/ EFFECT** **REASON/ RESULT RELATIONSHIPS** Subordinator Subordinate Clause, Main Clause	**CAUSE/EFFECT** Clause Conjunction Clause
Because of their foolishness, the children were lost. Due to her vast fortune, she was able to help the poor. Owing to his wealth, he helped the destitute. As a result of their opinions, they argued about money. In view of their arguments, their friends avoided them.	Because you study constantly, you usually pass. Since you enjoy the winter weather, you should go skiing. As this is the end of the month, we'd better pay the bill. Now that the semester is over, we can relax. Inasmuch as the government requires it, we must comply.	You study constantly; thus, you usually pass. You enjoy the winter; therefore, you should go skiing. It's the end of the month; consequently, we'd better pay. The bill was due; as a result, we'll owe late charges. We were out of town; for this reason, we were late.
Main Clause Adverbial Phrase She had a great fortune, thus assuring his future. The museum was clean, thereby simplifying our task.	As long as you study, you will succeed. In view of the fact that he is new, we will help him. On account of the fact that students need housing, we prepare. As a result of the fact that she was available, the department agreed. On the grounds that he had been cruel, she was granted a divorce. Due to the fact that she was negligent, he demanded the children.	We all enjoy summer weather, so we should plan a trip. The student was homesick, hence he returned home. ; hence, . Hence, **EFFECT/CAUSE** We should plan a trip, for we all enjoy summer weather.

EFFECT/CAUSE

RESULT/REASON

Adverbial phrase   Main Clause

(In order) to agree, we will meet every day.

If necessary, we will meet every day.

Whether intentional or not, his failure was obvious.
Unless studying, he goes to the library.
In case of rain, the game is postponed.

Main Clause   Adverbial Phrase

He walked as if in a dream.
They ran as though possessed.

PURPOSE RELATIONSHIPS

So that we can come to an agreement, we will meet every day.
In order that we can agree, we will include an arbitrator.

RESULT RELATIONSHIPS

She has so much money that she can help the poor.
You have so many friends that you could run for president.
It is such a beautiful day that I can't study.
They are such idiots that they'll never get it right.

CONDITION RELATIONSHIPS (REAL AND UNREAL)

Subordinator Subordinate Clause, Main Clause

If you study, you will pass.
If you studied, you would pass.
Even if you don't study, you will pass.
Provided that you study, you will pass.
As long as you study, you will pass.
Whether or not you study, you will pass.
Unless you study, you won't pass.
In case you study, you'll pass.
If only you study, you'll pass.
(Only if you study, will you pass.)
So long as you don't cheat, you will succeed.

MANNER RELATIONSHIPS (REAL AND UNREAL)

Main Clause Subordinator Subordinate Clause

She looks as if she is sick.
You look as if you had just seen a ghost.
He acted as though he were the King of England.

You should study; otherwise you won't pass.
You should study, or you won't pass.
You could pass, but you don't study.

CHART 5–3 ADVERBIAL CONCEPTS—CONCESSION, COMPARISON/CONTRAST

SIMPLE SENTENCES	COMPLEX SENTENCES	COMPOUND SENTENCES		

SIMPLE SENTENCES

Adverbial Phrase, Main Clause

<u>Although</u> studying everything, we won't pass.

Though only a child, she was a genius.
<u>Despite</u> his illness, he worked hard.
<u>In spite of</u> her family, she left town.
<u>Regardless of</u> the hour, they will leave immediately.
<u>Notwithstanding</u> the delay, they will go.

<u>While</u> helpful, he was unfriendly.

<u>Unlike</u> my children, I am left-handed.
<u>Different from</u> last year, we are taking a vacation.
<u>Instead of</u> studying, I plan to work.
<u>In contrast to</u> last year, next year will be dry.
<u>Contrary to</u> popular thought, the President was effective

COMPLEX SENTENCES

CONTRAST RELATIONSHIP—CONCESSION
Subordinator Subordinate Clause, Main Clause

<u>Although</u> they study everything, they won't pass.
<u>Even though</u> we studied all day, we didn't pass.
<u>Though</u> you tried very hard, you didn't pass.
<u>Despite</u> the fact that they tried, they failed.
<u>In spite of</u> the fact that we studied, we failed.

CONTRAST RELATIONSHIP—OPPOSITION
<u>While</u> you like studying, I like sports.
<u>Whereas</u> we support law, the people believe in revolt.
<u>Where</u> some people enjoy winter, others hate it.

COMPOUND SENTENCES

Clause Conjunction Clause

We won't pass; <u>however</u>, we studied everything.

We didn't pass; <u>nevertheless</u>, we had studied.
We didn't pass; <u>nonetheless</u>, we had studied.
We didn't pass, <u>but</u> we had studied everything.
We won't pass, <u>yet</u> we study every day.

You like studying; <u>however</u>, I like sports.
They support law; <u>nonetheless</u>, the people believe in revolt.
They will be suppressed; <u>nevertheless</u>, they will fight.
Some people enjoy winter; <u>all the same</u>, others hate it.
Some people enjoy winter; <u>even so</u>, others hate it.
Some people enjoy winter, <u>but</u> others hate it.
Some people enjoy winter, <u>yet</u> others hate it.
Some people enjoy winter, <u>still</u> others hate it.

We won't go to the museum; <u>instead</u>, we'll go to the movies.
He is smart; <u>on the other hand</u>, they are stupid.
Last year was wet; <u>in contrast</u>, next year will be dry.
Last year was hot; <u>conversely</u>, this year is cool.

COMPARISON RELATIONSHIPS

Phrase	Main Clause	Main Clause Subordinator Subordinate Clause	Clause Conjunction Clause
Like his father, Gregory works in government.	Gregory works in government.	Gregory works in government (just) as his father did in 1950.	Greg works in government; similarly, his father does too.
Similar to mammals, reptiles breathe oxygen.	Similar to mammals, reptiles breathe oxygen.	Just as mammals breathe oxygen, so do reptiles.	Greg studied politics; likewise, John wants to study politics.

Clause	Comparative	Clause
This book has more pages than the other book has.		
The legal system has fewer options than the military code has.		
Automobiles are lighter than trucks are.		
Motorcycles have less passenger room than cars have.		
This machine runs as well as the other one does.		
The examination in that course is the same as last year's was.		

Phrase	Main Clause
Both in school and out, students enjoy parties.	Both in school and out, students enjoy parties.

Compound sentences are made up of independent clauses of *equal* importance. Two independent clauses are joined with a comma and a coordinating conjunction or a semicolon, a conjunctive adverb and a comma to form a compound sentence.

independent clause   comma   conjunction   independent clause
Winter in the Midwest is cold**,**   *but* summer in the Midwest is hot.

independent clause   semicolon   conjunctive adverb   comma
Winter in the Midwest is cold**;**   *however,* summer in the Midwest is hot.

In this text we will refer to both coordinating conjunctions and conjunctive adverbs as conjunctions.

Some compound sentences can be rewritten as **complex sentences** with little or no change in meaning.

subordinate clause   comma   main clause
Although winter in the Midwest is cold**,** summer in the Midwest is hot.

main clause   no comma   subordinate clause
Summer in the Midwest is hot *although* winter in the Midwest is cold.

An interesting aspect of the study of adverbial subordinating conjunctions and coordinating conjunctions is that different academic fields favor particular subordinators. Another observation has been that some subordinators, like "although" and "as," and coordinating conjunctions, like "but" and "however," appear everywhere, with the result that synonyms like "even though" and "while" are less common. Many of the subordinators and conjunctions that receive equal importance in grammar books are nearly nonexistent in the texts and articles studied here.*

These observations are important to you as you enter a particular academic field. As a new member of a field, you need to learn the common writing conventions in that field. In order to "be" an engineer, you will have to learn to "read and write" like an engineer.

As you work through this chapter, you will see examples of most of the subordinators and conjunctions. You need to remember that they do *not* appear in equal numbers in the real world and that you will need to pay special attention to the readings in your field of interest to see which subordinators and conjunctions are most commonly used.

* For a complete review of parts of speech —including types of conjunctions, phrases, clauses and sentences —see Review Chapters 1 and 2.

Analyzing Concepts Expressed Through Adverbial Clauses, Phrases, and Conjunctions

Analysis Exercise 2a: Time Relationships—Sentence Combining with *before, after,* and *henceforth*

Complete each passage by combining A with B (and C with D) into sentences containing subordinating or coordinating conjunctions to express time relationships. You may use *before/ after/ henceforth*, if they are appropriate. Use the Adverbial Concepts charts for help.

> Psychologists perform experiments with animals and people in order to find out how we learn.

[1] Many experiments have demonstrated that curiosity is a strong drive in animals as well as people. Learning to learn is another interesting cognitive effect. It can be demonstrated by an animal experiment. A monkey is given the problem of which of two objects has a raisin underneath it.
A. 1st Action—a large number of trials
B. 2nd Action—The monkey learns that a treat is always found under the cup, regardless of position.

[2] Motor skills can be thought of as long chains of responses assembled into smooth and practically automatic performance. Motor skills are not lost as rapidly as are many other kinds of learning.
A. 1st Action—ten weeks without practice
B. 2nd Action—People who learned a new motor pattern (keeping a pointer on a rotating target) showed little loss of skill.
C. 1st Action—years without practice
D. 2nd Action—Perhaps you have observed how well you were able to type, roller skate, swim, ride a bicycle, and so forth.

[3] To aid motor-skill learning, begin by learning units that can be practiced with some success.
A. 1st Action—When learning to play piano, simple sequences of notes and hand positions should be mastered.
B. 2nd Action—more difficult passages (7: 198, 200, 201, 202)

Analysis Exercise 2b

In this passage fill in the blank with *before, after,* or *henceforth*.

[4] Industrialists were less than pleased with Roosevelt's determination to mediate between conflicting groups, conciliating all and enforcing a mystical harmony of interests for the general welfare. Business leaders had

further cause for alarm when in 1905, Justice Oliver Wendell Holmes reversed the E.C. Knight decision (1895) by evolving the "stream of commerce" doctrine. Manufacturing was now to fall within the regulatory power of Congress. In spite of the President's assurances of impartiality, corporate leaders now worried that the courts would _____ have to enforce Congress's apparent policy of small-unit, proprietory forms of business enterprise.

(from Christine Bolt, *History of the U.S.A.* [London: Macmillan, 1974], 202.)

Explanation 2—Conjunctions to Express Time Relationships

The words "before," "after," and "henceforth" express the idea of earlier action and later action. Notice the punctuation.

Before

                      main clause   subordinate clause
Clause: There are a number of sessions *before a new game begins.*
                    (earlier action)   (later action)

                                  subordinate phrase
Phrase: There are a number of sessions *before a new game.*

After

                 subordinate clause   comma main clause
Clause: *After there are a number of sessions,* a new game begins.
                 (earlier action)   (later action)
               subordinate phrase comma   main clause
Phrase: *After a number of sessions,* a new game begins.

Henceforth

               clause   semicolon conjunction comma   clause
Coordinate   He never wanted to fight; *henceforth,* he will make peace.
clauses: (meaning "from that time to the future or from then on")

Separate
sentences: He never wanted to fight. He will *henceforth* make peace.

Analyzing Time Relationships

Analysis Exercise 3

In the passages that follow, find the sentences with adverbial clauses or phrases of time. Then answer the questions about each passage.

[1]   *Rural Greece*—Grapevines and wheat are cultivated for domestic use. Wine making begins in September, after the grain harvest, and involves the whole family. Everyone goes to the fields to gather the grapes into large baskets. After the leaves and stems are removed, the fruit is trampled by the men and the newly pressed grape juice, or *must*, is transferred to barrels. (**8**: 240)

What happens first, A or B?

    a. First, the grapes are trampled by the men and the newly pressed grape juice is transferred to barrels, and then the leaves and stems are removed.

    b. First, the leaves and stems are removed, and then the grapes are trampled by the men and the newly pressed grape juice is transferred to barrels.

[2]   *Rural Vietnam*—In the dry season, the farmer decides what sort of rice crop to plant—whether of long or short maturation. The seed beds are prepared as soon as the rains have softened the ground in May. The soil is turned over and broken up as many as six separate times, with two-day intervals for "airing" between each operation. While the soil is being plowed and harrowed in this way, the rice seeds are soaked in water for two days to stimulate sprouting. Before the seedlings are planted, the paddy is plowed once more and harrowed twice in two directions at right angles. (**8**: 241)

Tell whether the following statements are true (T) or false (F).

    a. The seedbeds are prepared first and then the rains soften the ground.

    b. The rice seeds are soaked in water at the same time as the soil is plowed.

    c. The seedlings are planted after the paddy is plowed once more and harrowed twice in two directions at right angles.

[3]   *Marking the Onset of Marriage*—Many societies have ceremonies marking the beginning of marriage. The Kwoma of New Guinea practice a trial marriage followed by a ceremony that makes the couple husband and wife. The girl lives for a while in the boy's home. When the boy's mother is satisfied with the match and knows that her son is too, she waits for a day when he is away from the house. Until this time, the girl has been cooking only for herself, while the boy's food has been prepared by his womenfolk.

Now the mother has the girl prepare his meal. The young man returns and begins to eat his soup. When the first bowl is nearly finished, his mother tells him that his betrothed cooked the meal, and his eating it means that he is now married. At this news, the boy customarily rushes out of the house, spits out the soup, and shouts, "Faugh! It tastes bad! It is cooked terribly!" A ceremony then makes the marriage official. (8: 317)

True or false?
  a. The boy's mother and other women in the family cook for the boy until the boy and his mother are satisfied with the match.
  b. After the boy is away from the house, the mother, who has decided that she and the boy are satisfied with the match, has the girl prepare his meal.
  c. After the boy has eaten most of his soup, the mother tells him that he is married.
  d. Boys in Kwoma like only their mother's cooking.

[4]   *Personality and Cultural Patterning*—One of the most important theoretical approaches to personality and cultural patterning was introduced by the psychiatrist Abram Kardiner. . . . His theory was that as a result of sharing basic childhood experiences, adults in a population share patterns of behavior and personality. This approach has been applied by other anthropologists since it was first developed in the 1930s, with the result that today we understand a great deal about the psychological dimensions of culture, and why personality can vary so greatly from one group to another. (14: 303–304)

Approximately how long has Kardiner's theory been applied?

[5]   *Ijaw Women's Associations*—Women in West Africa often participate in marketing and trade, which allows them to be financially independent of men. Among the Ijaw of southern Nigeria, only women in the northern part of this society are organized into associations. Once a married woman shows herself capable of supporting a household independent of her mother-in-law, which she does by marketing and trading, she has to belong to the women's association linked to her husband's patrilineage. (8: 366)

When does a northern Ijaw woman join the women's association linked to her husband's patrilineage?

Analysis Exercise 4a: More Time Relationships—Sentence Combining with
when, whenever, while, as, as long as, or *meanwhile*

In the following passages, combine the underlined phrases and sentences into sentences containing appropriate subordinators or conjunctions. (Combine A with B, C with

D, and E with F.) You may use *when, whenever, while, as, as long as*, or *meanwhile*. The underlined clauses and phrases are not necessarily in the correct order. Use the Adverbial Concepts Charts 5-1, 5-2, and 5-3 for help. After you have finished, discuss how the relationships between clauses change with the choice of different subordinators or conjunctions.

[NOTE: Dr. Omar Khayyam Moore of Yale university has designed a special lab to study children. In his lab children "play" with a "talking typewriter."]

[1]   In Dr. Moore's lab an encounter with the "talking typewriter" begins the first time a child presses a key. At first typing is fairly random. (A) The child's attention starts to wander. (B) A curtain is removed from the screen above the "typewriter." A single letter appears and the letter is named over the loudspeaker. (C) A child finds the right key. (D) The correct letter is printed, and a voice names it again. (E) The machine pronounces the word. (F) A child has correctly typed all three letters of a word such as "dog." (**7:** 185)

[2]   Many psychologists believe that learning depends upon the concept of "reinforcement." Generally speaking, reinforcement is associated with pleasure, comfort, rewards, or an end to discomfort. Psychologists define a reinforcer as any object or event that increases the probability of a response. (A) A reward or pleasant event follows an action. (B) Positive reinforcement takes place. (C) Dealing with humans. (D) An effective reinforcement may be anything from an M & M (chocolate candy) to a pat on the back. (**7:** 187)

[3]   One of the most useful lessons to be derived from psychological studies is the value of feedback. Feedback (information about what effect a response has had) plays a particularly important role in human learning. Feedback is valuable academically, too. You can add to this feedback on your own. (A) Studying. (B) You can arrange to "take" a test several times. (**7:** 191)

Child and Computer

[4] Observational learning, modeling, is an efficient way of learning. A seemingly simple task such as throwing a small pot could take pages and pages to describe in words, and beginners would still not know how to proceed. Learning by observation fills an important need. For example: (A) <u>A skilled potter centers a ball of clay on the wheel and deftly pulls it up into a vase form.</u> (B) <u>The class of beginners watches intently.</u> Such instructions simply cannot be effectively passed on verbally.(7: 198)

[5] In economics, we can define equilibrium in general as a point from which there tends to be little or no movement. Equilibrium is a stable point. The equilibrium point occurs where the supply and demand curves intersect or cross. (A) <u>There is a shock.</u> (B) <u>Equilibrium can change.</u>

[6] The Problem of Labor Market Shortages—The chairman of the Senate Labor and Human Resources Committee, Senator Edward Kennedy stated, "For the first time since World War II, America is about to enter a period of prolonged labor shortages—a shortage of both workers and skills." Is it possible for a shortage to exist in the labor market? Yes, in the short run. Specialized labor is relatively fixed in supply in the short run. (A) <u>We can predict a shortage.</u> (B) <u>There is an increase in the demand for a specific type of labor such as engineers, nurses, school teachers, or more general categories such as skilled labor.</u> (**33**: 97)

[7] The greatest advances in manufacturing control have been made by the introduction of numerical control (NC). NC is the use of symbolically coded instructions for the automatic control of a process or machinery. The hardware for basic NC includes the machine control unit (MCU). . . . The simplest MCU moves first the x and then the y actuator by the prescribed distances. . . . (A) <u>The program is performed.</u> (B) <u>The program position is reached.</u> (C) <u>A slightly more complex system also moves first in one and then the other direction, but this time with full control of the rate of movement.</u> (D) <u>An operation such as cutting, milling or welding takes place.</u> **37**: 23)

Analysis Exercise 4b

Fill in the blanks in the following passage.

In February 1977, the Select Committee on Nutrition and Human Needs of the U.S. Senate published its *Dietary Goals for the United States.* . . . To achieve these goals, the Committee suggested that we change our food-selection patterns. . . . The publication of these Dietary Goals raised a storm of controversy. . . .

Nutrition Today, the popular publication of the Nutrition Today Society, devoted its November/December 1977 issue to a survey of opinions of the nation's top health professionals. . . . The responses to the Nutrition Today survey make lively reading and are highly recommended. Some responders agreed with the Goals, saying they were long overdue and could only be beneficial. Others found them inexcusably premature and agreed that to adopt them now would be to risk damaging public confidence, reducing support for research and causing actual harm to health, as well as disrupting the food industry and disturbing the nation's economy.

(1.) _____ , the Worldwatch Institute (a private organization) stated that the only known risk of adopting the Goals would be to the food industry, whereas important benefits to the economy would counterbalance this effect. (2.) _____ the debate goes on and research continues, firmer answers to the questions raised above will doubtlessly emerge. (3.) _____, a major benefit that has come out of the Select Committee's report has been—as stated by M. Winick (head of Columbia University's Institute of Human Nutrition)—that they "did an incredibly good job of bringing awareness of nutrition as a major health problem to the people, Congress, and the Executive Branch." (**19: 51**)

Explanation 3—Time Clause and Phrase Conjunctions

The words "when," "whenever," "while," "as," "as long as," and "meanwhile" express the idea of almost simultaneous actions.

When

                subordinate clause comma   main clause
    Clause: *When the child is spanked,* she becomes angry.
  (the actions are almost the same time)

            subordinate phrase comma   main clause
    Phrase: *When spanked,* the child becomes angry.

Whenever

                     comma
    Clause: *Whenever a child is spanked,* he or she becomes angry.
                 (This gives the idea of always.)

                   comma
    Phrase: *Whenever spanked,* the child becomes angry.

While

            main clause   subordinator subordinate clause
    Clause: The response is usually punished *while it is being made.*
             (actions occur at exactly the same time)
            main clause   subordinator subordinate phrase
    Phrase: The reponse is usually punished *while being made.*
               (*while* + progressive verb form)

As

subordinator   subordinate clause   comma   main clause
Clause: *As technology became more complex,* computers improved.
(*As* + simple or progressive verbs) (simultaneous actions)

Clause: *As music is being learned,* a mistake halts the performance.

As long as

main clause   subordinate clause
Clause: A landlord cannot raise rent *as long as the tenants pay.*
(same time action with emphasis on duration of time—implies a time limit)

Meanwhile

independent clause   conjunction   independent clause
Coordinate   Washington crossed the river; *meanwhile,* his troops fought on.
clauses: (simultaneous actions)

NOTE: "Before," "after," "whenever," "while," and "once" + phrase constructions can be reduced to phrases only from sentences with two clauses containing the same subject.

When ***the reward*** *is given,* ***it*** causes a change in behavior.

Whenever ***the reward*** *is given,* ***it*** causes a change in behavior.

After ***the reward*** *is given,* ***it*** causes a change in behavior.

Once ***the reward*** *is given,* ***it*** causes a change in behavior.

Reduced to phrases:

When *given,* the reward causes a change in behavior.

Whenever *given,* the reward causes a change in behavior.

Once *given,* the reward causes a change in behavior.

After *being given,* the reward causes a change in behavior.

"Before" and "after" require "being" + past participle if there was a form of "be" + past participle in the original clause.

Analysis Exercise 5: Sentence Combining with *since, until, once, by (the time that), as soon as, during, up to, within,* or *upon*

Without changing the tense in the following passages, combine the underlined phrases and clauses below into sentences using subordinators, prepositional phrases, or conjunctions of time, *since, until (till), once, by (the time that), as soon as, during, up to, within, upon.* The sentences are not necessarily in order. (Combine A with B, C with D, and E with F.)

[1]   New York, Pennsylvania and Rhode Island proposed the convening of a colonial congress. The First Continental Congress was held . . . on Sep-

tember 5, 1775. It was a gathering of delegates from twelve of the thirteen colonies. . . . The First Continental Congress represented the nation's first formal act of cooperation among the colonies. (A) The Second Continental Congress met in May 1775 (this time all the colonies were represented). (B) Fighting had already broken out between the British and the colonists. (**39:** 30)

[2]   Every schoolchild in America has at one time or another been exposed to the famous words from the Preamble to the United States Constitution. The document itself is remarkable: As constitutions go, it is short. (A) Its ratification on June 21, 1788. (B) Relatively few amendments have been added to the Constitution.

   Congress has considered more than seven thousand amendments to the Constitution. Only twenty-six have been ratified. A reading of Article V of the Constitution reveals that the framers of the Constitution specified no time limit on the ratification process. Congress is to decide what is reasonable. (C) Most proposed amendments have included the requirement that ratification be obtained within seven years. (D) 1919. (**39:** 30, 27, 51)

[3]   By observing a model (someone who serves as an example) a person may learn new responses. For observational learning to occur several things must take place. The learner must pay attention to the model and remember what was done. If a model is successful or rewarded the learner is more likely to imitate the behavior. (A) A new response is tried. (B) Normal reinforcement determines if it will be repeated thereafter. In Dr. Moore's learning lab, the children "play" with a "talking typewriter." After a number of sessions in which typing is fairly random, a single letter appears and the letter is named over the loudspeaker. (C) Children who return to random key pressing suddenly find that the keys no longer work. (D) They press the key corresponding to the letter on the screen.

[4]   Learning is a relatively permanent change in behavior due to past experience with reinforcers. Reinforcers work in two basic ways. Positive reinforcement takes place when a reward or pleasant event follows an action. Negative reinforcement also rewards a response, but it does so by ending discomfort. For example, (A) It pressed the bar and turned the shock off (negative reinforcement). (B) A rat could be shocked mildly through the bottom of the cage. (**7:** 199, 185, 187)

[5]   Marketing Systems—In the early 1950s the marketing era began. Companies became aware of consumer needs and established marketing departments to learn more about them. (A) The 1970 and the 1980s. (B) Many organizations, such as IBM and General Electric, entered the marketing systems era. Organizations may differ in their approach to marketing, but all perform certain important marketing functions.

[6]   Economic Utilities—Economists typically measure the value of a good or service by the utility, or satisfaction, that it creates. Consumers typically select and buy the goods and services that provide them with the greatest utility. The performance of marketing functions generates utilities that increase the value of a good or service to consumers. Place utility creates value by transferring a good closer to the place of consumption. (A) A Maytag clothes washer assembled in Newton, Iowa, has no value to a consumer in Tampa, Florida. (B) It gets to Tampa.

[7]   Relative Prices—Money prices during different time periods don't tell you much. You have to find out relative prices. (Combine A, B, and C.) (A) The distinction between money prices and relative prices is clear. (B) There should be no confusion about the meaning of price increase. (C) A period of generally rising prices.

[8]   Developing a Promotional Strategy—A promotional strategy is like a general's overall battle plan. It tells in broad terms how a firm will use promotion to secure an advantage over competition, to attract buyers, and to capitalize on its resources. (A) The promotional strategy has been established. (B) The firm can develop a set of short- and long-range plans that specify the promotional elements to be used.

[9]   On October 27, 1858, Rowland Macy opened a small dry-goods store on Sixth Avenue in New York. Beginning in 1866, Macy kept adding stores piecemeal until the business eventually occupied the ground space of eleven stores. (A) 1877. (B) The small dry-goods store had been transformed into a full-fledged department store. (**23**: 11, 13, 453, 413)

[10]   Sociological Experiments—What happens when "normal" people are admitted to a mental institution? Are they immediately noticed by the professional staff as being out of place and so discharged? In 1973, D. L. Rosenhan created a field experiment in which he and seven colleagues contrived to get themselves admitted to several mental hospitals. (A) Their entry into the psychiatric ward. (B) They behaved as they normally did. (**35**: 41)

Explanation 4—More Time Clause and Phrase Conjunctions

The words "since," "until (till)," "once," "by the time," "as soon as," "during," "up to," "within," and "upon" express different relationships between clauses and phrases. All of these phrases and clauses may appear before or after the main clause.

Since

Clause:
                subordinate clause   comma   main clause

Clause: *Since independence was declared,* the U. S. has been a pioneer.
      (earlier time established)   (the action takes place after the established earlier
                        time —usually present perfect tense)

         phrase comma   main clause

Phrase: *Since 1776,* we have been a free nation.

Until

             subordinate clause comma   main clause

Clause: *Until there was a drought,* conditions had been favorable.
    (time limit expressed)   (action takes place or a condition exists before
                  the time limit and then stops)

           phrase   comma   main clause

Phrase: *Until this summer's drought,* conditions had been favorable.

Once

           subordinate clause comma   main clause

Clause: *Once avoidance is learned,* it is very persistent.
    (meaning "as soon as")   (action takes place after the subordinate
                    clause or phrase)

        phrase   comma   main clause

Phrase: *Once learned,* avoidance is very persistent.

NOTE: "Until" and "once" + phrase constructions are derived from reduced clauses. Both clauses in the sentence must have the same subject.

    Clause: The meat must be cooked *until it is ready*.

    Phrase: The meat must be cooked *until ready*.

By (the time that)

          subordinate clause   comma   main clause

Clause: *By the time that the war ended,* thousands were homeless.
  (the action in the main clause occurs   (this action started/ existed before
  before the time expressed in   the time expressed in subordinate
    subordinate clause)   clause/ phrase)

            phrase   comma   main clause

Phrase: *By the beginning of 1776,* military encounters were frequent.

As soon as

          subordinate clause   comma   main clause

Clause: *As soon as the battle was over,* the troops went home.
  (establishes the beginning   (action begins immediately after the time
  of the main clause action)   established in the subordinate clause).

During

          phrase   comma   main clause

Phrase: *During the 1640s,* the legislature became bicameral.
   (duration of time)   (what happened then)

Up to

     phrase=until comma   main clause

Phrase: *Up to 1990,* no one would admit there was a recession.
  (establishes a time or date) (situation or action before the time given in
                 the subordinate phrase)

Within

phrase= before then   comma   main clause
Phrase: *Within two months,* Syntex was back in operation.
(end of the time established here)   (this event occurred)

Upon

phrase = as soon as   comma   main clause
Phrase: *Upon their entry into the ward,* they behaved normally.
(this event occurred)

Explanation 5—Sequence of Tense in Adverbial Clauses of Time

Adverbial clauses of time relate the time of the situation or action in the subordinate clause to the time of the situation or action in the main clause. The time in the main clause may be previous to, subsequent to or simultaneous with the time of the subordinate clause.

Compare your knowledge about the sequence of time relationships between clauses with the chart below. This chart shows which tenses and subordinating conjunctions are commonly used together to express particular sequences of actions.

CHART 5-4   TIME CLAUSES AND VERB TENSE

MAIN CLAUSE (LATER ACTION)	SUBORDINATOR	SUBORDINATE CLAUSE (EARLIER ACTION)
Future/Present (simple and progressive)		*Present/ Present Perfect (simple and progressive)* (no future in time clauses)
1. We *will study*	**as soon as**	you *arrive.*
2. We *will be planning* a party	**once**	you *are* here.
3. We always *study*	**after** **when** **whenever**	you *have arrived.*
1. We *will study*	**now that**	we *know* what to do.
2. The students *are pleased*		you *have arrived.*
3. Everyone *is cheering*		the football team *is winning.*
Present perfect		*Present perfect/past*
4. We *have always studied* diligently	**as soon as** **once** **after** **when** **whenever**	you *(have) requested* it.

Past		*Past/Past perfect*
5. We *studied* morning, noon, and night	**as soon as** **once** **after** **when** **whenever**	they *gave (had given)* us the assignment.

MEANING: The action in the subordinate clause happens first.The action in the main clause happens second. The clauses may be reversed.

MAIN CLAUSE (EARLIER ACTION)	SUBORDINATOR	SUBORDINATE CLAUSE (LATER ACTION)
Future/ Present/Present Perfect (simple and progressive)		*Present/ Present perfect (simple and progressive) (no future in time clauses)*
1. George *will take* a shower	**before**	breakfast *is served.*
2. George *takes* a shower	**until/till**	he *runs* out of hot water. he *has run* out of hot water.
3. They *have always studied* diligently	**before** **until/till**	there *is* a test there *is* a test.
Past/ Past Perfect (simple and progressive)		*Past*
4. We *studied* hard	**before** **until/till**	the semester *ended.*
5. John *had promised* to help	**before** **until/till**	he *heard* about the problems.

MEANING: Action in the main clause happens first. Action in the subordinate clause happens second. The clauses may be reversed.

The clause following *until/till* has the meaning of limit or end of the action in the main clause.

SIMULTANEOUS ACTION

MAIN CLAUSE	SUBORDINATOR	SUBORDINATE CLAUSE
Future/ Present (simple and progressive)		*Present (simple and progressive) (no future in time clauses)*
1. The children *will be sleeping*	**when**	you *arrive.*
2. I *will edit* each page	**as** **as long as**	I *am typing.*
3. Students *will study*	**so long as***	the professor *requires* it.
4. We *will be studying*	**while**	the music *is playing.*
5. The men *won't work*		the orchestra *tunes up.*
Present Perfect (simple and progressive)		*Present perfect (simple and progressive)*
6. They *have helped* us	**as long as**	we *have requested* it.
7. They *have been* our friends	**while**	we *have been living* here.

Past (simple and progressive)			*Past (simple and progressive)*

8. She *drove* into the   **as**   the musicians *arrived.*
   parking lot   **while**   the musicians *were tuning up.*

MEANING: The actions of the verbs in both the main and subordinate clauses occur at the same time. The clauses may be reversed.

    * *so long as* is often used when the main clause is negative. The progressive form of the verb is most common after *as* and *while.*

MAIN CLAUSE (LATER ACTION)	SUBORDINATOR	SUBORDINATE CLAUSE (EARLIER ACTION)
Present		*Past*
1. The young woman *feels* happy	**since**	she *got* the job.
Present Perfect (simple and progressive)		*Past*
2. I *have lived* here	**since**	I *was born.*
3. We *have been working*		we *arrived.*

MEANING: Action in the subordinate clause happens first and signals the beginning of action in the main clause. The clauses may be reversed.

Analysis Exercise 6: Using *where* and *wherever* in Sentence Combining

Complete the following passages by combining the two underlined sentences.

[1]   It is now thought that the earth's crust is composed of huge plates, called tectonic plates, on which the continents ride. Studies of the earth's crust suggest that these plates slide by or across one another, or one may slide under another. (place and situation) The two plates slide past one another. (possible result) There may be zones of frequent earthquakes. (9: 136)

[2]   Managers and professionals need to motivate and monitor the work of others. They may face frustration because they lack the power to solve a problem, yet they are often blamed if things go wrong. As managers move higher in an organization, their responsibilities increase along with the job benefits and satisfactions. High-level managers receive high salaries, generous fringe benefits, bonuses, and stock options. (situation/condition) They have some autonomy to carry out projects. (possible result) They may get a sense of accomplishment and satisfaction from their work as well. (35: 381)

(In the following sentence, one of the clauses goes in the blank.)

[3]   Gilbert Ryle thought that ordinary language had to be taken seriously. . . . Ordinary language philosophy was taken further by J.L. Austin (1911–1960). . . . Austin insisted that ordinary language was the begin-all, not the end-all, of philosophy. In some part, this approach owed its

inspiration to Aristotle, who regularly emphasized what is said and how it is said. (fact) <u>An emphasis upon "use" and upon the idea that an account of our understanding of the world can be developed from what is implicit in speaker-hearer identification of things</u> _____ <u>is also to be found in P.F. Strawson (1919).</u>
(definition/ situation) <u>Speaker and hearer are persons.</u> (**20**: 315)

[3]   The kinetic energy of each item of mass entering and leaving a process is a result of the motion of the mass. Accumulation of material within a process entails no significant motion, and thus only the streams entering and leaving contain kinetic energy. If v is the velocity of an item of mass entering or leaving, its kinetic energy is $\frac{1}{2} mv^2$. (definition/condition) <u>m is the mass.</u> (fact) <u>In the food-pound or kilogram-meter unit system, the formula would be written as $\frac{1}{2} (mv\ 2)/g$.</u> (definition/condition) <u>g is the gravitational constant.</u> Work energy appears in several ways in a process. An entering stream must be forced into a continuous process against a constant pressure P. (fact) <u>The work done on the process in this instance is m . P . V.</u> (definition) <u>V is the specific volume of the mass.</u>

    It is likewise true that work is done by the process in forcing an effluent stream out of the process. (fact) <u>Thus, the net work done by the process due to a stream entering and leaving is m $(P_2 V_2 - P_1 V_1)$</u> (definition) <u>The subscript 2 indicates the leaving stream and subscript 1 the entering stream.</u> (**5**: 79–80)

Explanation 6

The words "where" and "wherever" express the idea of place and situation/definition.

Where

                    main clause   subordinator   subordinate clause
Clause: The work done on the process is m.P.V.   *where*   *V is volume.*
        (fact)   (situation/definition of V in this sentence)
          main clause   subordinator   subordinate phrase
Phrase: Please change the spelling of the word *where necessary.*
                            (idea of place)

Wherever

        subordinator subordinate clause comma   main clause
Clause: *Wherever   people   wandered,* they developed organized societies.
    (place=anywhere that)   (what happened there)

subordinator subordinate phrase comma   main clause
Phrase: *Wherever possible,* people developed patterns for behavior.

NOTE: "Where" and "wherever" + phrase contructions are reduced from clauses with an "It" + be + adjective construction.

Wherever it is necessary, we will stop to review the material.
Wherever necessary, we will stop to review the material.

Practicing Adverbial Concepts of Time

Practice Exercise 7: Finding Adverbial Errors

The following passage contains 18 incorrect adverbial subordinators or prepositions of *time*. Find the errors and correct them.

The beginnings of agriculture in the New World are still the object of intensive archeological study. For some time, various authorities have believed that Indians at several different places, independently of each other and at different times, may have learned to domesticate some of the same wild plants. . . .

On 1948 tiny cobs of domesticated corn, between 4,000 and 5,000 years old, were found by archeologists both at Bat Cave in New Mexico and at La Perra Cave in Tamaulipas in northeastern Mexico. While then, archeological work directed by Richard MacNeish in two regions of Mexico has thrown important new light on the entire subject of the start of New World agriculture . . .

Farther south, in caves and rock shelters about Tehuacan in the arid highlands of the central Mexican state of Puebla, a team of experts in many sciences, working with MacNeish, laid bare a sequence of cultural development of the inhabitants of that area, with few interruptions, from approximately 12,000 years ago from A.D. 1500, or historic times. . . . Since about 9,000 years ago, the studies showed, the sparse population in the neighborhood lived predominantly by trapping and hunting small animals, birds, turtles . . . and by gathering wild plant foods. Between about 9,000 and 7,000 years ago, the people shifted considerably more to the collection of wild plants, and when that period began the domestication of certain products, including squashes and avocados. In about 6,000–7,000 years ago a new phase of development was well underway. . . . Once those studies of the MacNeish group, a somewhat similar sequence of development, beginning almost 10,000 years ago, was also revealed by other archeologists working in Mexico's Oaxaca Valley.

In a long time, economies were based primarily on the gathering of wild plants, with supplementary hunting and trapping providing an important second source of food, and the cultivation of wild plants being more of an experimental additive. . . .

While farming ultimately took over and groups settled permanently to till their fields, however, population began to increase and, in time, tended to become concentrated. . . .

Although many persons have tried to estimate how many Indians inhabited the New World as long as 1492, there is no agreement on the figure. . . . After recently, the most knowledgeable students estimated that there were somewhere between 15 and 20 million Indians in the hemisphere upon Columbus arrived, agreeing also that probably only some 850,000 lived within the present boundaries of the contiguous states of the United States, and considerably fewer farther north in Canada and Alaska. The bulk of the population was found below the Rio Grande [in Mexico, Central America, and South America], concentrated most heavily in the regions of the most intensive practice of agriculture. . . . Recent demographic studies in various areas, however, indicate that earlier data are inaccurate and suggest that population estimates be revised upward. . . . Some students believe that the estimates, cited above, may have to be increased possibly as much as ten times. . . once recently, it was thought that somewhat more than 130,000 Indians were in present-day California meanwhile the appearance of white men; now it appears more probable that they were in excess of 350,000.

When the course of the white man's conquest of the New World, Indian numbers changed greatly. . . . The Indian population within the United States (excluding Alaska) declined rapidly whenever by 1860 there remained only some 340,000. As 1910, the figure had declined to 220,000, and the Indian had taken on the popular image of the "vanishing American.". . . Canada, upon, counts 225,000 Indians today, but the figures for Latin America are difficult to agree upon. (24: 49–54)

Using Adverbials of Time and Situation in Writing

One of the most important academic applications of a knowledge of grammatical structures is the ability to paraphrase. In other words, when you know all the different ways to express the adverbial concepts, you will be able to change sentences into your own words and use them in the papers you write.

Writing Exercise 8: Paraphrasing with Adverbials of Time and Situation

Read the following passage and answer the questions. Then write your answers in the form of a summary paragraph.

(NOTE: Since the 1960s, archeologists and anthropologists have discovered that Indians have been living in the New World for as long as 100,000 years, not 10,000 to 12,000 years, as formerly believed.]

The American Indians developed crops that now provide over half of the world's food. The Indians, first-rate farmers, harvested more varieties of plants than were used or even known in any other region of the world. These included corn, beans, squash, pumpkins, amaranth, potatoes, tomatoes, peanuts, pineapples, papayas, manioc, chives, chilies, cashews, sarsaparilla, vanilla beans and cocoa. The Indians also cultivated rubber, chicle (chewing gum), tobacco and cotton.

In addition to this cornucopia, it seems that the Indians were the first to make the miraculous jump from the gathering of wild plants to the development and sowing of domesticated plants. Domesticated wheat and rye first appeared in the Near East 9,000 years ago. Summer squash and pumpkins appeared in the Americas by 8,000 years ago, and corn cobs have been found in Tehuacan, Mexico, dating to 9,000 years ago. But the grinding tools found in the Americas dating to interglacial times (70,000 to 170,000 years ago) indicate a much longer incubation period for the manipulation of plants in the New World than in the Old World. In fact, we have evidence that the Indians had a domesticated plant during interglacial times—corn, or as Indians called it, maize. No wild form of corn has ever been found. In 1954, Dr. Elsa Barghoorn, a botanist at Harvard University, conclusively identified fossil pollen grains from a drill core as being those of corn. These fossil pollen grains came from a depth of two hundred feet below Mexico City and were given an interglacial date of approximately 80,000 years in age. Since this period antedated the accepted appearance of man on the North American continent, the pollen was thought to be that of a wild corn which has since become extinct, even though these pollen grains were indistinguishable from those of modern cultivated corn. With the new interglacial datings for man and grinding tools in the Americas, this fossil corn pollen could easily have come from domesticated corn. [Indian] legend maintains that they had cultivated corn from the start. (**17**: 218–219)

Answer the following questions in your own words. Then put your answers together and write a summary of the passage. Review your summary. Did you use any adverbials of time and situation? If not, which sentences could you change to include adverbial clauses and phrases of time and situation? Discuss your ideas in class.

1. According to the passage, when were Indians first cultivating corn?
2. Why did scientists believe that the pollen grains found by Dr. Elsa Barghoorn came from an extinct wild corn plant?
3. How did the discovery of the grinding tools in the Americas change previous ideas about the domestication of plants?

PART II ADVERBIAL CLAUSES OF CAUSE/EFFECT AND REASON/RESULT

A great many subordinators are used to express cause/effect and reason/result ideas. See the Adverbial Concepts charts on pages 127–131 for a full list.

Analyzing the Grammar of Cause and Effect

Analysis Exercise 9

Fill in the blanks in the following passages to express cause/effect or reason/result according to your analysis of the structure of the sentence, the punctuation, and the relationships involved.

[1] In no society is murder allowed within the smallest type of descent group. On the other hand, killing outside the lineage or the clan may be regrettable, but it is not viewed as a crime. It is interesting to note that the murder of a brother (Cain's murder of Abel) _____ favoritism is the first crime mentioned in the Bible; it was punished by ostracism. Greek law viewed murder of a family member as an unforgivable crime. Perhaps the underlying basis for the strong prohibition against murder within a family exists _____ that is where murder is most likely to occur, as present statistics continue to bear out.

[2] The Hopi Indian clans figure prominently in the Hopi religion. The religion is one in which the unity of the people is evidenced by the interdependence of the clans, _____ each is considered a significant part of the whole. Each clan sponsors at least one of the religious festivals each year and is the guardian of that festival's paraphernalia and ritual. A festival is not exclusive to one clan, _____ all the Hopi clans participate. (**8**: 350)

[3] Manufacturers will eventually find that each additional output of floppy disk production will involve higher and higher costs._____ the only way that floppy disk makers would be induced to produce more and more floppies would be _____ the lure of a higher price market that the floppies could command. (**33**: 77)

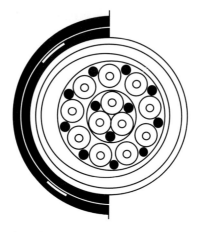

Figure 5-2 Cross section of a 2.8/10.2 copper-aluminum coaxial cable that has a bare copper inner conductor, polyethylene disk insulation spaced at regular intervals on the inner conductor and covered with crimped plastic tape, and a cylindrical outer conductor of aluminum tape, longitudinally welded. (**3:** 359)

[4]   Cables are an integral part of all telecommunications systems. Most systems have been equipped with coaxial cables, but today optical fibers are playing an increasing role. Coaxial cables need to be protected with waterproofing layers. Some large cables use a system of pressurization which sets off an alarm when punctured. A less expensive solution for small diameter coaxial pairs is to fill voids with a powder which swells when moisture enters, _____ forming a moisture barrier.

      Three types of optical fiber cable are in general use. All three types have the advantage that the fibers are free to move transversely in their groove or tube. _____ the fibers are left slightly longer than the cable along its axis, they are not subjected to mechanical strain when the cable is being laid, _____ greatly extending their service life. (**3:** 359–365)

[5]   In the tropical LDC (less developed country), increased investment in agricultural production and distribution will involve many things: higher quality labor through education, new and improved plant varieties through research and development, improved and expanded water management and irrigation, increased production and usage of fertilizer, increased and improved grain storage, government price stabilization programs for farmers and on and on. All these investment activities have one thing in common; they involve the increased employment of scarce resources, _____ they are costly to the society involved. (**6:** 360)

[6]   Emphasis on the equality of every individual before the law is central
to the American system. To ensure that majority rule does not become
oppressive, modern democracies also provide certain guarantees of minority rights. One way to guarantee the continued existence of a representative democracy is to hold free, competitive elections.

_____ the minority always has the opportunity to win
elective office. (**39**: 12)

[7]   The basic problem with punishment is that it is usually aversive

(painful or uncomfortable). _____ people and situations
associated with punishment tend, through classical conditioning, to
also become aversive (feared, resented, or disliked). Generally
speaking, punishment is painful, frustrating, or both. Punishment,

_____, sets up a powerful learning environment for the
promotion of aggression. (**7**: 195)

Explanation 7—Cause Clause and Phrase Subordinators (Conjunctions)

Clause subordinators:

because	*now that*	*whereas**
since	*inasmuch as*	*as long as*
as		

subordinator   subordinate clause   comma   main clause
As there are a multitude of interests, no one group can dominate.
        (expresses the reason or cause)   (expresses the result or effect)

Phrase subordinators (prepositional phrases):

because of	*owing to*
due to	*in view of*
as a result of	

 subordinate phrase   comma   main clause
Due to a multitude of interests, no one group can dominate politics.
(expresses reason or cause)   (expresses effect or result)

Both clauses and phrases of cause are often found after the main clause. The
punctuation rules are not standard in academic publications. When the cause

---

* *Whereas* is most common in legal terminology.

clause or phrase comes *before* the main clause, it is followed by a comma. When the cause clause or phrase comes *after* the main clause, a comma is not needed before the subordinator, but it is used in some publications.

main clause   no comma

Note that negative reinforcement is not punishment because negative reinforcement strengthens a response.

With clause conjunction *for:*

comma conjunction

We'll plan a trip, *for* we all enjoy summer weather.
(expresses result)   (expresses cause)

The conjunction "for" means exactly the same thing as "because." "For" usually appears in the second clause of a sentence preceded by a comma. Some publications also use ". For." In this case, the sentence beginning with "For" follows a sentence of result.

Explanation 8—Result Clause and Phrase Conjunctions

Clause conjunctions:

therefore	*as a result*
thus	*for this reason*
consequently,	*hence*
so	

cause   semicolon   conjunction   comma
or period

A product must fulfill its function ;/. *therefore (thus, consequently),* it must operate.

cause   comma, semicolon conjunction   result
or period

These activities are scarce ,/;/. *hence (so)* they are costly.

Phrase conjunctions:

thereby
thus

reason/cause   comma conjunction   result
(preposition)

The museum was well organized, *thereby (thus)* simplifying our task.

NOTE: The punctuation of "therefore," "thus," "consequently," "as a result," and "for this reason" depends upon where they are in the sentence. They may be preceded by a period if they appear at the beginning of a sentence, or by a semicolon if they appear at the beginning of a clause. They may also appear in the middle of a sentence enclosed by commas.

The punctuation of "hence" varies. "Hence" appears in published books and articles after commas, periods, and semicolons.

Analyzing Some Confusing Words: **Such** *and* **So**

Students are often confused about the many uses of "such" and "so." The next two exercises compare sentences containing most of the uses of "so" and "such." By comparing and contrasting the different uses in context, you will be able to clarify the meanings for yourself.

Analysis Exercise 10a: *Such* versus *such*

The sentences below from a sociology text contain the word "such" used in four different ways. Study the sentences and then answer the questions that follow.

1. Kuhn uses the term *paradigm* to refer to a coherent tradition of scientific laws, theory, application, assumptions, and measurement that forms a distinct approach to problems. . . . The stage becomes set for a scientific revolution when increasing numbers of problems cannot be solved by the existing paradigm and when scientific observations begin to contradict the paradigm. Called anomalies, *such* examples are set aside and ignored for a while. . . . At *such* a time a scientific field may be in crisis, but scientists will not abandon their paradigm until an alternative that explains more than the old one is proposed. (**35**: 480)

2. Today, countries *such* as India, South Korea, and Mexico are struggling to make the transition from an agricultural to an industrial country.

3. Stage theories, proposed by *such* economic thinkers as W.W. Rostow (1960), view nations as going through various stages on the path to development.

4. There is no *such* thing as a free lunch. In ecology, every gain has some cost.

5. Even though the principles stated in this book may not always be established as complete causal propositions, the reader should interpret them as *such*.

6. Today, our intervention in nature to achieve variety and stability has resulted in *such* a complex economic structure that few of us have any direct control over our own food supply.

7. In nature, there is no *such* thing as waste.

8. Mutations are random events. As *such*, very few would be expected to be beneficial.
   a. "Such" + another word sometimes means "for example." Which sentences contain "such" meaning "for example"?
   b. What other word is part of the "such" phrase when it means "for example"?
   c. "Such" sometimes refers back to a previous noun, noun phrase, or sentence. Which sentences contain "such" as a reference? Find and underline the words "such" refers to.
   d. "No such" sometimes means "doesn't exist." Which sentences contain the "no such" idiom, meaning "doesn't exist"?
   e. How are the "no such" phrases different from "such" that refers back to a previous noun phrase or sentence?
   f. "Such" sometimes introduces a result clause and is considered a subordinating conjunction. Which sentence contains a result clause "such"? What other word in the sentence signals the result?

Analysis Exercise 10b: Writing a Summary of *such*

Review the sentences in Exercise 10a and complete the following list of meanings of "such."

"Such" may mean

1.   3.
2.   4.

Analysis Exercise 11a: So versus *so*

The word "so" has many different meanings. The sentences below contain eight different uses of "so." See if you can determine what they mean.

1. Their hope is to try to control the process of development *so* that traditional values are not destroyed by it.

2. Although many sources are eager to lend money to developing nations, they do *so* on terms favorable to themselves.

3. As science improves, *so* should art.

4. Chemically treated fertilizers run off into local streams, rivers and lakes. There the chemicals promote the growth of *so* much algae that fish cannot survive.

5. As much as they might like to change, peripheral areas will find it difficult to do *so*.

6. Jean-Marc Bouvier has found large numbers of artifacts. His main objective is to obtain a clearer picture of the origin and evolution of toolmakers, and *so* far he has dug to a depth of more than twelve feet.

7. There is a long gradual slope, amounting to a very gentle downhill grade and forming the *so*-called continental shelf.

8. If sea levels started dropping today. . . . In a year or *so* sea levels would fall enough to expose some 11,500,000 square miles of land that had once been submerged.

9. The amino acids are attracted or repelled by the charges they carry, *so* the strands tangle into intricate shapes.

10. An organism must maintain its highly organized state. It must repair some types of damage, remove wastes, synthesize certain substances, acquire materials, and *so* on.

Analysis Exercise 11b: Completing a Summary of the Use of *so*

Complete the summary that follows.

a. "So" + _____ means "until now" in sentence number _____.
b. "So" means "therefore" in sentence number _____ .
c. "So" means "approximately" in sentence number _____.
d. "So" means "etcetera" in sentence number _____.
e. "So" + _____ means "something or someone named or known as" in sentence _____.
f. "So" is used to refer to a previous phrase in the sentence in numbers _____ and _____ .
g. "So" + _____ is used to introduce a purpose clause in sentence _____ .
h. "So + _____ + noun + _____ " is used to introduce a result clause in sentence _____ .
i. "So" refers to a previous clause and means "do something also" in sentence number _____ .

Explanation 9—Result Clauses with So . . . That and Such . . . That

so + adjective/adverb + *that* + result clause

                  cause clause
                so   adverb + adjective
These countries are *so* desperately poor *that* they cannot invest.
                            (*that* + result clause)

so much + noncount noun phrase + *that* + result clause

                  cause clause
              so much noun
Iowa produces *so much* corn *that* the world market is affected.
                            (*that* + result clause)

so many + plural count noun phrase + *that* + result clause
so many + plural count noun phrase + *as to* + base verb + phrase

                    cause clause
        so many   noun phrase
So many new students enrolled *that* the bookstore ran out of books.
                      (*that* + result clause)

So many new students enrolled *as to* be a problem for the bookstore.
                (*as to* + base verb + phrase)

such + singular or plural count noun phrase + *that* + result clause

                  cause clause   result clause
Our intervention caused *such* a complex economic structure *that* few could control it.

such + noncount noun phrase + *that* + result clause.

                  cause clause   result clause
The order resulted in *such* confusion *that* no one was able to act.

such + noncount noun phrase + *as to* + base verb

                  cause clause   result phrase
Managers employed a control technique with *such* vigor *as to* negate authority delegations to their subordinates.

NOTE: Result clauses with "so" are more common than those with "such."

A variation of the "so . . . that" + clause, "such . . . that" + clause construction is a "so . . . as to" + base verb, "such . . . as to" + base verb construction.

Practicing So *and* Such

Practice Exercise 12: Sentence Combining with *so* and *such*

Complete the following passages. Combine the lettered sentences with "so . . . that" or "such . . . that" to express result. Combine (A) with (B) and (C) with (D). Look for key phrases (adjectives + nouns, adjectives, or adverbs) to help you decide whether to use "so" or "such." The lettered sentences are not necessarily in the correct order.

[1]   The ability to observe in field research can be enhanced by recording devices, just as the ability to listen in interviews can be aided by a tape recorder. . . . Videotape or film is particularly useful for studying interactions. For example, using film that could be studied frame by frame, Stern (1977) and others were able to observe in caregiver-child interactions whether the caregiver or the child moved first toward the other. (A) To the unaided eye, the movement occurred fast. (B) It was impossible to unravel without the help of a tool to slow down the process. (**35:** 532)

[2]   We are at a critical time in terms of population growth. (A) World population has been growing rapidly, and there is now a large population base. (B) Even a slow rate of growth can rapidly increase the number of people on earth. In the United States although the number of births has been rising in recent years, much of that increase reflects the large number of women of child bearing age. (C) In the 1970s there were many women of child-bearing age. (D) The absolute number of babies rose. (**35:** 532, 341)

[3]   Some sports clearly encourage violence among the players. Football, for example, encourages violence. Indeed, physical contests and violence are part of the game, whether in tackling, blocking, or protecting the quarterback. (A) They were unable to return to the game or to a subsequent game or practice. (B) The National Football League found that each season the 1040 players in the league suffered an average of 1101 severe injuries. (**35:** 615)

[4]   The possibilities of genetic engineering and evolutionary control illustrate the fundamental dilemmas raised by the new capabilities conferred by scientific knowledge. There should be a new, comprehensive assessment of all the issues raised by recombinant-DNA research. . . . Of special importance for early attention is an effective monitoring system for following the actual directions of recombinant-DNA research. (A) The techniques involved in recombinant-DNA research are rich in possibilities, whether for benefit or risk. (B) "Early warning" is essential. (**18:** 33)

[5]   The extensive use of concrete is ample proof of its outstanding characteristics as a building material. (A) It is a familiar material. (B) We take for granted the remarkable process by which cement and water, mixed with a wide range of aggregate materials, are converted into a strong and durable material of almost any desired shape.
(C) Many of the physical and chemical reactions which take place during the setting and aging of concrete are complicated. (D) They are not yet fully understood. This is due in part to the wide range of chemical substances that can exist, partly by design and partly by chance, in any given concrete mix. (**41**: 138)

Explanation 10—So *versus* Very

Sometimes student writers mistakenly use "so" in place of "very" because many people use that form in speaking. The "so" in conversational sentences implies but does not state a result clause.

"I am so tired" means "I am *so* tired *that* I can't do anything."

The result part of the clause is omitted in the first sentence. If you use "so" in this way in speaking, everyone understands that you are implying the rest of the sentence. In formal writing, however, we always use "very" or "extremely" if we omit the "that" result clause.

I am *very* tired. OR I am *extremely* tired. OR I am *so* tired *that* I can't attend the meeting.

Using Adverbial Clauses and Phrases in Writing

Writing Exercise 13: Paraphrasing with Adverbial Clauses and Phrases

First review the adverbial charts on pages 127–131 to find different ways to express adverbial ideas. Second, read the passages below, answer the questions about each passage in your own words, and then use your answers to write a summary of each passage. When you have finished your summary, reread it. How many adverbial clauses and phrases did you use? Discuss your summaries in class.

[1]   The classification "American Indian Languages" is geographical rather than linguistic, since those languages do not belong to a single linguistic

family, or stock, such as the Indo-European or Hamito-Semitic language families. The American Indian languages cannot be differentiated as a linguistic unit from other languages of the world but are grouped into a number of separate linguistic stocks having significantly different phonetics, vocabularies, and grammars.

- How are American Indian languages classified?
- Do American Indian languages have the same linguistic roots?

[2]   There is no part of the world with as many distinctly different languages as the Western Hemisphere. Because the number of Indian languages is so large, it is convenient to discuss them under three geographical divisions: North America, Mexico and Central America, and South America and the West Indies. It is not possible to determine exactly how many languages were spoken in the New World before the arrival of the Europeans, nor how many people spoke these languages.

- Which part of the world has the largest number of different languages?
- How are Indian languages divided?
- How many languages were spoken in the New World before Europeans arrived?

[3]   At the present time, the aboriginal languages of the Western Hemisphere are gradually being replaced by the Indo-European tongues of the European conquerors and settlers of the new world. . . . Apparently there is no role for the American Indian languages as languages of world importance. Moreover, because of the almost total absence of writing and the earlier destruction of most of what writing did exist, the American Indian languages lack great literatures, although they do possess rich oral traditions. The investigation of these languages contributes much to a scientific knowledge of language in general, since these tongues possess a number of linguistic features not otherwise known. Some groups of native Americans in the United States are working to revitalize the languages of their peoples as a result of recently increased ethnic consciousness and feelings of cultural identity.

(from *The New Columbia Encyclopedia* [New York: Columbia University Press, 1975], pp. 85–86).

- What is the present situation regarding American Indian languages?
- Do American Indian languages have great literature? Why or why not?
- What do you think an oral tradition is?
- Are American Indian languages important today?

PART III   ADVERBIAL CLAUSES TO
EXPRESS PURPOSE

Analyzing Clauses of Purpose

Analysis Exercise 14: Sentence Combining with *so that, in order that,* and
in order to

Complete the following passages by combining the sentences to form sentences
expressing purpose. Sentences 1–4 indicate the purpose sentence and the subordinator
to use. In sentences 5 and 6, you should decide which sentence is the purpose sentence and which subordinator to use. As you work, ask yourself the following questions:

- Which auxiliary verbs are common in "so that" clauses?
- What is the difference between "so that," "in order that," and "in order to" in a
  sentence?

1. Use "so that."

   The elite theory perspective on the American political scene sees the
   mass population as uninterested in politics and willing to let leaders
   make the decisions. (A) New members of the elite are recruited through
   the educational system. (B) (purpose clause) The brightest children of
   the masses can allegedly have the opportunity to join the elite strata.
   (**39:** 13)

2. Use "so that."

   Direct democracy in Athens is considered to have been an ideal form of
   democracy because it demanded a high level of participation from every
   citizen. (A) All important decisions were put to a vote of the entire citizenry. (B) (purpose clause) Public debate over potential issues would be a
   constant feature of social life. (**39:** 9)

3. Use "in order to" to combine A and B. Use "so that" to combine C and D.

   (A) Shotgun experiments involve exposing the total DNA of a given organism to restriction enzymes. (B) (purpose) The shotgun experiments
   will obtain many DNA fragments. The fragments are then each recombined with DNA from a suitable vector and the recombinants are randomly reinserted into *E. coli* host cells. (C) The next step is to spread
   the *E. Coli* cells on a nutrient substrate. (D) (purpose) The next step will
   cause each recipient cell, containing a particular inserted foreign
   substance, to grow into a colony. (**18:** 27)

4. Use "so that" to combine A and B. Use "in order to" to combine C and D.

   Professionals are increasingly likely to work in large organizations instead of practicing on their own. Although professional and managerial work is highly varied, it does share some common features. Much of the work involves data, information, problem solving, and dealing with people. (A) Lawyers need to keep abreast of the latest laws and court cases. (B) Lawyers can properly advise clients. (C) Doctors and dentists want to know about new techniques, drugs, and research discoveries (D) Doctors and dentists provide the best available treatment for their patients. (**35:** 381)

5. Combine A and B. Combine C and D.

   Moderate critics of the family reject the assumptions and proposals of both conservatives and radicals, although they accept some of the ideas of both. They assume that traditional family forms and functions did not necessarily suit all individuals. They assume that both men and women have needs for achievement as well as nurture. . . . (A) Their solution is to modify the family. (B) Men and women can both love and work. (C) For example, Juliet Mitchell in her book *Women's Estate* (1971), proposes distinguishing the various functions performed by the family. (D). The functions can be dealt with individually. (**35:** 357)

6. Let's say that it's profitable for this country to produce 20 different models of automobiles. Another country, say, Germany, can also produce these 20 different models. If the U.S. decides, however, to specialize in the production of only 10 models, leaving Germany to specialize in the production of the other 10, the firms in each country will be able to expand their scale of operations and benefit from a greater division of labor. . . . (A) The 10 models that are made abroad can be imported to the United States, and the 10 models made domestically can be exported. (B) Consumers can choose from a total of 20 models. (**33:** 861)

Explanation 11—Purpose Clause and Purpose Phrase Conjunctions

"So that," "in order that," and "in order to" have the same meanings. They introduce the purpose of an action, but they are used with different grammatical structures. "So that" and "in order that" introduce *clauses* that describe the purpose of an action or condition. ("So that" appears more frequently than "in order that.") "In order to" introduces *phrases* of purpose.

Purpose Clause Subordinators

so that
in order that

             main clause
The executive, legislative and judicial powers of government were to be
             (first action)

             subordinator + purpose clause
separated *so that no one branch of government had enough power*
             (expresses the purpose of the first action)

to dominate the others.

NOTE: Sometimes "so" is used alone and "that" is omitted.

Purpose Phrase Subordinators

in order to

subordinator + purpose phrase   main clause
In order to cross any dispersal route, organisms must be able to live in
                            (action necessary for purpose)

the environmental conditions found there.

NOTE: The "so that" and "in order that" clauses and the "in order to" phrase may appear before or after the main clause.

Using Adverbial Concepts for Synthesizing and Summary Writing

---

Writing Exercise 15: Synthesizing Ideas—Using Several Sources to Write a Summary

Read the following three passages about American Indian languages.

[NOTE: Joseph H. Greenberg, a linguist at Stanford University, has been studying languages since the 1950s. In 1987, he published *Language in the Americas* in which he grouped the 150 Native American languages into three groups. His ideas have caused a great deal of controversy in the field of linguistics.]

[1]   Greenberg insists that his method is illuminating the distant past. And a growing number of scientists in other disciplines agree. Two early con-

verts were Stephen L. Zegura and Christy G. Turner II of the University of Arizona. They had studied genetic and dental variation among Native Americans independently of Greenberg. When they heard him lecture on his preliminary findings for Native American languages, they told him that his results closely matched their own. When the biological and linguistic classifications were plotted on a map, they roughly coincided. The main discrepancies came in the Native American populations of the Pacific Northwest, which apparently had a tangled history.

Greenberg and his two collaborators published their findings jointly in 1986 and concluded that the ancestors of Native Americans must have immigrated in at least three discrete waves over the land bridge that once connected Siberia to Alaska. They could not rule out more than three, because additional implanted languages and genes might have left no traces. Exactly which communities of Asia contributed to these waves is hard to say, although Soviet linguists, working independently, have suggested a link between Na-Dene and the languages of northern Caucasia.

Further genetic evidence in support of Greenberg's Amerind hypothesis has since been provided by Douglas C. Wallace of Emory University. "Data we published this year indicate that Greenberg's hypothesis seems correct," Wallace said in an interview in late November. "Our data show, I feel strongly, that the paleo-Indians—Amerinds —are one group."

The combination of genetic and linguistic analysis works particularly well in America, Wallace adds, because it was a blank slate. "The first immigrants who came over the land bridge did not encounter another culture," he says. "I'm not surprised that there are ambiguities in the Old World, because there have been so many mixtures."

(from Philip E. Ross, "Hard Words," *Scientific American*, p. 146. Copyright © 1991 by Scientific American, Inc. All rights reserved. Reprinted with permission.)

[2] "Nearly all American Indians are descendants of a single small band of pioneers who walked across what's now the Bering Strait from Asia 15,000 to 30,000 years ago. . . .

The descendants of this hardy group make up 95 percent of American Indians, including the Mayans, Incas and many others spread throughout North, Central and South America. The exceptions are the Eskimos and Aleuts of the Arctic rim, the Navajos, Apaches and a few others who arrived later, said Douglas Wallace of Emory University in Atlanta.

"It was clearly a small migration," said Wallace of the ancestral group. He based his findings on studies of the genes called mitochondria that are related to the body's energy production. The genes were extracted from blood samples from members of three different Indian groups. . . . The mitochondria, which are separate from the body's other genes, are passed on to children only by mothers, not by fathers.

The research on American Indians showed that the vast majority descended from four women in that original migrating group. "That's a striking finding," said Michael Silverstein, an anthropologist at the University of Chicago who studies American Indian languages. If the finding is confirmed, Silverstein said, it significantly extends the conclusions about Indian origins that can be made using language studies.

In March 1990, anthropologists met in Boulder, Colorado, to debate a suggestion by Joseph Greenberg of Stanford University that most American Indian languages derived from one ancestral language.

(from "Geneticist: Most Indians from 1 Group," *The Des Moines Register,* July 27, 1990. Reprinted with the permission of the Associated Press.)

[3]   Since the publication of *Language in the Americas*, Greenberg has gotten a vote of confidence from within biology. A research team headed by Luigi Luca Cavalli-Sforza, a geneticist at Stanford, completed a global survey of "genetic markers"—variations in proteins and enzymes, for example, that reflect data in a person's DNA. With these markers the researchers sketched a family tree of humankind, depicting the divergence of the world's peoples from a single stock that, they believe, lived in Africa 100,000 years ago. And in the Native American branches of that tree Cavalli-Sforza saw a pattern reminiscent of Greenberg's three-wave scenario for migrations across the Bering Strait.

People who are descended from tribes in Greenberg's Amerind language family, Cavalli-Sforza found, form a fairly homogeneous genetic cluster. . . . The reflection of the three-migration model, and of Greenberg's three-way language classification, Cavalli-Sforza says, is "so sharp in the genetic data that it's really remarkable." (This claim has not gone unchallenged by Greenberg's critics.)

(from Robert Wright, "Quest for the Mother Tongue," *The Atlantic* [April 1991]: 39. Reprinted with permission of the author.)

Synthesizing ideas means using the ideas of more than one author in your own writing. In Exercise 13 you read and summarized a passage on the traditional classification of American Indian languages. Use that information together with the information in writing Exercise 15 to answer the following questions in your own words. Next rewrite your answers as a summary paragraph. When you have finished, review your summary. Have you used any relative and adverbial clauses and phrases? Where could you use such clauses appropriately? Discuss your ideas in class.

1. What has been the traditional way to classify American Indian languages?
2. How has Joseph Greenberg changed the traditional way of classifying American languages?
3. How has another science supported Greenberg's claims? Support your answer with brief examples.

6

PARTICIPIAL PHRASES AND ABSOLUTE CONSTRUCTIONS

PART I   PARTICIPIAL PHRASES

Relative adjective clauses and adverbial clauses of time and cause can be reduced to phrases. When the phrases contain the "-ing " (present participle) or the "-en" (past participle) forms of the verb, they are called participial phrases.

Discovering the Grammar of Participial Phrases

Discovery Exercise 1: Identifying Present Participial Phrases

Study the following sentences. Find the words ending in "-ing" and the phrases that follow. Do not include gerunds. Ask yourself these questions as you work.

- Where are the "-ing" words (present participles) in the sentences?
- The "-ing" words followed by phrases fall into two patterns in the sentences. What are the patterns?
- What words in the sentence do the present participles modify?
- Where are the present participles placed in relation to the words they modify?

1. The federal Smith-Lever Act was passed by Congress, creating the Cooperative Extension Service as we have it today.

2. Beginning with the second round of field experiments, the team starts to introduce new alternatives or to suggest modifications and testing of existing alternatives.

3. This law in effect combined all of the various acts relating to extension into a single bill.

4. In 1913, the Iowa Legislature passed the law authorizing county boards of supervisors to appropriate money to do educational work.

5. The function of the Extension Service is to disseminate useful and practical information on subjects relating to agriculture, home economics and rural and community development to all people in the state.

6. The County Agricultural Extension Districts Law provided for a three-person committee to enter into a memorandum of understanding with the Extension Service setting forth the cooperative relationship between the district and the Extension Service.

7. The chair and secretary must file in January of each year and certify information concerning officers and membership of council with the board of supervisors and county treasurer.

8. Looking over the whole experience, John F.A. Russell, Rainfed Crops Advisor to the Bank, concludes that no one methodology has a monopoly of merits, but "rather that the strengths of different approaches should be recognized, and facilitate cross-fertilization between systems.

Discovery Exercise 2: Making Clauses from Participial Phrases

1. What is the difference between these two sentences?
   a. They must pay sixty thousand dollars for the fiscal year *commencing July 1.*
   b. They must pay sixty thousand dollars for the fiscal year *that commences July 1.*
2. Rewrite numbers 3, 4, and 7 from Exercise 1 in this way.
3. What is the difference between these two sentences?
   a. *Before entering upon the duties of his office,* the councilman will be elected and sworn in.
   b. *Before he enters upon the duties of his office,* the councilman will be elected and sworn in.

   Which sentence(s) in Exercise 1 can be rewritten in this way?
4. Which one of the sentences in Exercise 1 has a participial phrase that modifies the complete sentence and means "result"?

Discovery Exercise 3: Writing Rules for Participial Phrases

Answer the questions below to summarize what you know about participial phrases.

1. Where do participial phrases usually appear in a sentence?
2. How are participial phrases punctuated?

3. What clauses can replace the participial phrases that appear at the beginnings of sentences?

4. What clauses can replace the participial phrases that appear after nouns?

5. According to your answers to the previous questions, what functions can participial phrases perform in a sentence?

Explanation 1—Making Adjective and Adverb Clauses from Participial Phrases

Sometimes sentences with participial phrases (adjective phrases) can be rewritten as sentences with relative adjective clauses.

> They must pay sixty thousand dollars for the fiscal year *commencing July 1.*
> They must pay sixty thousand dollars for the fiscal year *that commences July 1.*

Some participial phrases may be rewritten as adverbial clauses with "as," "while," "when," "before," "after," "because," and "if."

> *Before entering upon the duties of his office,* the councilman will be elected and sworn in.
> *Before he enters the duties of his office,* the councilman will be elected and sworn in.

Analyzing Participial Phrases

Analysis Exercise 4: How Past Participial Phrases Modify

Examine the following passage and

- find the present and past participles used as adjectives.
- find the words that the participles modify. Draw an arrow from each participle to the word it modifies.
- determine which of the past participles below are placed in front of the nouns they modify and which are placed after. Why?
- look for an adjective phrase.

> ### The Elaboration of Material Possessions during the Neolithic Age
> In the more permanent villages that were established after the rise of food production, houses became more elaborate and comfortable, and

construction methods improved. The materials used in construction depended upon whether timber or stone was locally available or whether a strong sun could dry mud bricks. Modern architects might find to their surprise that bubble-shaped houses were known long ago in Neolithic Cyprus. Families in the island's town of Kirokitia made their homes in large, domed, circular dwellings shaped like beehives and featuring stone foundations and mud-brick walls. Often, to create more space, the interior was divided horizontally and the second floor was propped firmly on limestone pillars.

Sizable villages of solidly constructed, gabled wood houses were built in Europe on the banks of the Danube and along the rims of Alpine lakes. Many of the gabled wooden houses in the Danube region were long, rectangular structures that apparently sheltered several family units. In Neolithic times these longhouses had doors, beds, tables, and other furniture that closely resembled those in our society. We know that the people had furniture because miniature clay models have been found at their sites. Several of the chairs and couches seem to be models of padded and upholstered furniture with wooden frames, indicating that Neolithic European artisans were creating fairly sophisticated furnishings. . . .

For the first time, apparel made of woven textile appeared. This development was not simply the result of the domestication of flax (for linen), cotton, and wool-growing sheep. These sources of fiber alone could not produce cloth. Neolithic society developed the spindle and loom for spinning and weaving textiles. True, textiles can be woven by hand without a loom, but to do so is a slow and laborious process, impractical for producing garments. (**8**: 145–147)

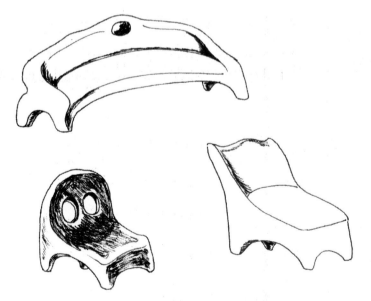

Clay models of furniture found at a Neolithic site in Bulgaria.

Analysis Exercise 5: Other Functions of Participial Phrases

Examine the following sentences and

- find the participial phrases and single participles (both past and present) in the sentences below.
- determine where the participial phrases occur in the sentences below.
- find the words (nouns) that the participles modify. Do all of the participial phrases modify nouns? Which ones *don't* modify nouns?
- determine how the participles that *don't* modify nouns differ.

> *Why Did Food Production Develop?*
>
> We know that an economic transformation occurred in widely separate areas of the world beginning after about 10,000 years ago, as people began to domesticate plants and animals. But why did domestication occur? And why did it occur independently in a number of different places within a period of a few thousand years? (Considering that people depended only on wild plants and animals for millions of years, the differences in exactly when domestication first occurred in different parts of the world seem small.) There are many theories of why food production developed. . . . Gordon Childe's theory, popular in the 1950s, was that a drastic change in climate caused domestication in the Near East. According to Childe, who was relying on the climate reconstruction of others, the postglacial period was marked by a decline in summer rainfall in the Near East and North Africa. As the rains supposedly decreased, people were forced to retreat into shrinking pockets, or *oases*, of food resources, surrounded by desert. The lessened availability of wild resources provided an incentive for people to cultivate grains and domesticate animals, according to Childe. Robert Braidwood criticized Childe's theory. . . . According to Braidwood, there must be more to the explanation of why people began to produce food than simply changes in climate. (**8:** 142)

Explanation 2—Derivation of Participial Phrases

Most participial phrases are derived from two sentences or clauses with the same subject. Participial phrases contain no subject, so the subject in these sentences is understood to be the noun in the main clause nearest the participial phrase.

> These are the technologies *classified as traditional.*
> The law *creating an extension service* was passed in 1898.

Some participial phrases report what an authority has said. These phrases modify the whole sentence, not a particular noun in the main clause:

According to Childe, wild resources provided an incentive to people.

Some participial phrases express a conditional idea similar to "if." These phrases also modify the whole sentence.

Considering that people depended only on wild plants for millions of years, the differences in when exactly domestication first occurred seem small.
Given the circumstances, the economy appears strong.

Some participial phrases modify the complete sentence and express a result:

Policy decisions and relationships interact, *producing conflict*.

Summary: Participial phrases may have the following meanings:

1. Description (derived from an adjective clause).
2. Time (meaning "after" or "while").
3. Cause
4. Result
5. Condition

FORMS OF PARTICIPLES	EXAMPLES	TIME RELATIONSHIP BET. PHRASE AND MAIN VERB
Verb + "ing"	*Running* down the street, the boy fell.	same
Verb + "-en"	*Known* to all, the criminal will flee.	same
"Being" + adjective/noun	*Being a good student,* she reads a lot.	same
"Being" + verb + "-ed"	*Being tired,* the children slept.	same
"Having" + verb + "ed"	*Having passed* the exam, we relaxed.	earlier
"Having been" + verb + "-en"	*Having been chosen* to join, Jo smiled.	earlier
"Having been" + verb + -"ing"*	*Having been waiting* since noon, I left.	earlier

* This form is rarely used. Instead, this would commonly appear as
Having waited since noon, I left.

Position and Meaning

Participial phrases can appear almost anywhere in a sentence.

> *Having applied to Harvard,* Jean was waiting impatiently.
>
> Students *admitted to the university* are lucky.
>
> I saw several students *studying English.*
>
> The students talked all night, *annoying their roommates.*

Participial words and phrases fall into four patterns.

Before nouns	MEANING
The *cleaning* woman is here.	description, kind, or profession
The *developed* countries are rich.	something already finished
The *developing* countries are not.	something happening now

After nouns	
The woman *cleaning* is my mother.	something temporary, happening now
The countries *developed by England* speak English.	something finished; passive, usually longer than one word

At the beginnings of sentences	
Beginning early, the class was over by 10:00.	the idea of cause or time; tells something about the subject; active idea
According to Childe, there was a change in the climate.	the idea that an authority stated; active idea
Considering the situation, the people were lucky.	conditional idea
Given the situation, the people were lucky.	conditional idea
Known by everyone, the author was well received.	the idea of cause, describes the subject; passive idea

At the ends of sentences	
"Equity hierarchies" are extractive systems in their own right, *operating partly out of personal and institutional interests.*	describes the subject "equity hierarchies"; active idea
People cultivated grains, *according to Childe.*	an idea stated by an authority; active idea

The people were lucky, *considering the situation.*	conditional idea
The people were lucky, *given the situation.*	conditional idea
Thus we could conclude that studying equity decision making must involve a detailed examination of the payoffs *expected by the development elite.*	passive idea describing "payoffs"

Punctuation

1. Participial phrases appearing after nouns within a sentence may be restrictive (no commas) or nonrestrictive (commas) in the same way that relative clauses are restrictive or nonrestrictive.

2. A participial phrase (meaning result) at the end of a sentence is separated by a comma.

3. A participial phrase in the initial position is separated by a comma.

4. A participial phrase at the end of a sentence may or may not be separated by a comma. A participial phrase separated by a comma may describe the nearest preceding noun or the subject of the sentence. It may also mean result. Participial phrases in this position are often confusing to the reader.

Analysis Exercise 6: Analyzing Participial Phrases

1. Find all the (past and present) participial phrases in the passages below.
2. Find the noun each participle modifies. Do *all* the participles modify nouns? If not, what is their function?
3. Find the words and phrases that follow the participles.
   • What kinds of words and phrases follow present participles?
   • Look at number 3. You know that participles are derived from verbs and that verbs can have objects. What is the function of the noun phrases that follow the present participial forms in number 3?

Technology, Equity, and Decision-Making

[1]   Inequality both within nations and between systems is the basic premise on which "development experts" and bureaucracies focus their effort. Therefore, we insist that some attention must be paid to the processes by which policy and technology choices, geared to solving inequality, are made. . . .

We will try to develop several arguments pertaining briefly to what Beteille calls distributive issues but concentrating in detail on relation characteristics of inequality.

First, we shall discuss several premises of the most "people"-oriented policy and technology currently in vogue—"appropriate technology." We will also describe a down-flow system of decisions including especially technology decisions and their relation to patron-client relations, widely found in Third World countries. We shall illustrate how public policy decisions and clientelism interact, producing conflict and change but not necessarily equity.

[2] *Relevant Technology and Equity*—It is fashionable these days to invent or rediscover antiquated equipment, especially for agricultural production, and try to sell it to development bureaucrats, farmers and peasants in the less developed countries. British, German and American development experts have given these devices the respectable name of *intermediate* or *relevant* technology.

Let's look at the case of two farmers in Venezuela. The first has four hectares, the second 300, of rich, flat land. What sort of intermediate agricultural devices are they going to find attractive? The first one will clearly not be attracted to anything but elementary tools or devices: those within his reach. A simple "intermediate" tractor would be rather unrealistic. The latter who, judging by the size of his business, may have studied agronomy and visited the U.S. or Europe, is in all likelihood interested in a much more efficient device than the "intermediate" tractor.

[3] *The Patron-Broker-Client Model*—Patron-client relations are vertical social relationships between unequals (or individuals with different resources or goods). These links last over extended periods of time, often covering multiple types of activities or reasons for which the individuals continue the connection. There is also a high degree of reciprocity—of payoffs to both the patron and client, making the arrangement worthwhile for both. The patron nonetheless is clearly the beneficiary—it is a lopsided payoff system. The classic and basic patron-client bond is an informal-dyad, that is to say, a non-legal but mutually understood tie between two people; patron-client "networks" or "pyramids" involving more than one patron and many clients have also been extensively described.

A critical aspect of the patron-client model is first of all the personal nature of the relationship. It thus differs from what we assume are "normal" business transactions or bureaucratic roles which are theoretically rational-legal and highly impersonal. Given the personal quality of clientelism, arguments about efficiency, economic pragmatism, scientifically verifiable logic or superiority may not be as compelling as we think. (**38**: 65–67)

Practicing with Participial Phrases

Practice Exercise 7: Sentence Combining

Find the subordinate clauses that can be changed into participial phrases and rewrite them with participial phrases. You may leave them where they are or move them to another part of the sentence, but first think carefully about where participial phrases are usually placed. The sentences may need a few other minor changes, too. When you are finished, discuss how you chose the clauses that could be changed into participial phrases.

Explanations of Deviance and Crime—For years people have searched for biological reasons that might explain deviant or criminal behavior. The Italian physician Cesare Lombroso (1911) thought that people might be "born" criminals because of certain physical traits. While he was conducting an autopsy of a notorious criminal, it occurred to Lombroso that the deviant's skull looked similar to that of an ape or a primitive human. . . .

Like physical attempts to explain deviance, psychological theories focus on the characteristics of individuals. In general, psychological theories suggest that the tendency to deviate is neither inherited nor inborn, but results from early socialization.

While children are growing up, most children learn from loving parents to curb their antisocial tendencies or to direct them into socially acceptable channels such as sports or music. People who do not have such caring adults in their lives may fail to develop a conscience that guides and controls their impulses.

Durkheim believed that human desires and aspirations, if unchecked, were virtually limitless. In social life, groups usually develop norms that regulate and set limits on human aspirations. But in the state that Durkheim called *anomie*, in which life lacks meaning, people become more aggressive or depressed, which results in higher rates of homicide and suicide.

The theory of differential association attempts to explain how deviant behavior, which includes criminal activity, is transmitted from one generation to another. "Deviant or criminal behavior is learned, just like language, religion, or baseball," said Edwin Sutherland (1937). David Matza (1969) suggests that becoming deviant is usefully understood in terms of the notion of "causal drift," which falls between free will and total determinism. Becoming deviant involves a person who is converted to a particular way of life. . . . Before they decide to convert, people consider themselves in relation to a particular activity.

When we are evaluating the various theoretical approaches to crime and deviance that have been presented here, we cannot conclude that some are correct and others are not. (**35:** 187–91, 199)

PART II   ABSOLUTE CONSTRUCTIONS

Discovering the Grammar of Absolute Constructions

Discovery Exercise 8: Identifying Absolutes

Study the four sentences below. Notice particularly the underlined parts. Then answer the questions.

> Education was mainly provided through private initiative outside New England, <u>with the children of the prosperous benefiting accordingly</u>.

> Until now, video distribution networks have used coaxial cables organized in a true network, <u>with each subscriber being able to receive all the programs transmitted</u>.

> The district known as Aguas Claras consists of four villages, <u>the largest being Ciudad Aguas Claras</u>, and many scattered farms.

> <u>The frontier having been declared closed by the census takers in 1890</u>, appreciation of pioneer exploits and values increased.

1. Are the underlined parts of the sentences above clauses or phrases? Explain how you know.
2. How are the underlined parts of the first two sentences similar?
3. How is the third different?
4. How is the fourth different?
5. Compare the underlined parts of all of the sentences. What do they all have in common? (HINT: Look after the noun phrase.)
6. Look at the four sentences again. This time read the non-underlined parts of the sentences. Are they complete clauses? What kinds do you find?
7. Separate each sentence into two parts. Write the complete clause as one sentence. Then change the remaining phrase into a second sentence.

Sentence #1a.   Education was mainly provided through private initiative outside New England.

   b.   The children of the prosperous *benefited* accordingly.

Sentence #2 a.

   b.

Sentence #3 a.

   b.

Sentence #4 a.

   b.

8. What did you have to do to change the phrases into sentences?

9. Discuss differences between the sentences.

Discovery Exercise 9: Writing a Definition of Absolute Constructions

Use the information that you found in Exercise 8 to write a definition of the absolute constructions that you worked with.

1. How are absolute constructions similar to participial phrases?
2. How are absolute constructions different from participial phrases?

Explanation 3—Derivation of Absolute Constructions

Absolute constructions are derived from two sentences or clauses with different subjects. An absolute construction is a phrase that consists of a subject and participle (verb + "-ing", or verb + "-en") or even no verb form when "being" is deleted. Absolute constructions may also be introduced by "with" or "without." Notice the difference between an absolute phrase and a prepositional phrase.

> absolute phrase   main clause
> With the men banking in town, the tellers were busy.
> prepositional phrase   main clause
> With the banking men in town, the tellers were busy.

In the absolute phrase above, "men banking" means the men are doing something temporary. They will do other things at other times. They may bank other places, too. In the prepositional phrase, "banking men" means a kind of men. Banking is their profession.

Absolute constructions may have the following meanings inferred from context.

1. Further explanation or description (details)

2. Time—"after" or "while"

3. Cause—(sometimes both "after" and cause)

4. Condition

5. Result

CHART 6-1 COMPARISON OF PARTICIPIAL PHRASES AND ABSOLUTE CONSTRUCTIONS

PARTICIPIAL PHRASES		ABSOLUTE CONSTRUCTIONS	
EXPLANATION	EXAMPLE	EXPLANATION	EXAMPLE
Participial phrases are derived from two sentences or clauses with same subjects	The man was tired. The man went to bed.	Absolute constructions are derived from two sentences or clauses with different subjects.	The children were sick. Their parents took them to the hospital.
Participial phrase + main clause	Being tired, the man went to bed.	**Absolute construction** + main clause	The children being sick, their parents took them to the hospital.
	OR		OR
"Being" may be omitted.	Tired, the man went to bed.	"Being" may be omitted.	The children sick, their parents took them to the hospital.
			OR
		"With" may be included.	With the children sick, their parents took them to the hospital.
Participial phrases expressing earlier time are derived from two sentences or clauses with same subjects, one earlier than the other.	Because the Europeans had conquered America, they believed they were superior.	**Absolute constructions** expressing earlier time are derived from two sentences or clauses with different subjects, one earlier than the other.	The Europeans had conquered America. The Indian tribes became discouraged.
Participial phrase + main clause	Having conquered America, the Europeans believed that they were superior.	**Absolute construction** + main clause	The Europeans having conquered America, the Indian tribes became discouraged.

FORMS OF ABSOLUTES	EXAMPLES	AND MAIN VERB
Subject + verb + "-ing"	*(With) the wind blowing,* the tree fell.	same
Subject + verb + "-en"	*The thief caught,* the police pulled back.	same
Subject +"being" + adjective/noun	*Jane (being) late,* the committee waited.	same
(With) + subject +"being" + verb +"-en"	*(With) the baby (being)* tired, we left.	same
Subject +"having" +verb + "-en"	*Mark having passed* the exam, we relaxed.	earlier
Subject +"having been" + verb +"- en"	*Sue having been chosen* to join, Jo smiled.	earlier
Subject +"having been" + verb+"-ing"*	*Jim having been calling all day,* I was worried.	earlier

Position and Punctuation

Absolute constructions are usually at the beginning or end of a sentence, but adjectival types may appear in the middle of a sentence.

> *The frontier having been declared closed by the census takers,* appreciation of pioneer exploits increased.

> The district known as Aguas Claras consists of four villages, *the largest being Ciudad Aguas Claras,* and many scattered farms.

> Education was mainly provided through private initiative outside New England, *with the children of the prosperous benefiting accordingly.*

Absolute constructions are considered nonrestrictive, so they have commas. Some have dashes or parentheses. "With" phrases may have no commas.

Analyzing Absolute Constructions

███

Analysis Exercise 10: Finding Meanings of Absolutes

Find the absolute constructions in the following sentences and then answer these questions:

- What different meanings do the absolutes have?
- Are they more similar to adjectival or to adverbial participial phrases?

1. Suppose that the plants in the greenhouse are arranged on three tables and the treatments are randomly assigned to the three tables, with all plants on a given table receiving one treatment.

* A form that exists but is rarely used.

2. Dreams are usually spaced about 90 minutes apart, with each succeeding dream lasting a little longer.

3. Converters typically come in several grades, the better ones costing considerably more than lesser chips.

4. The above action is repeated in the second stage of the switching circuit, with CE 2 charging through Q2 at a rate determined by the 1-M pot in series with CE2.

5. Bipolar neurons contain two processes, one extending from each pole of the body of the cell.

6. The simple reflexes discussed probably are seldom carried out alone in any adult vertebrate, the nerve impulses probably coming into relationship somewhere along its course with other reflex circuits.

7. The anterior ramus or branch supports the skin, joints, muscles, and bones of the neck, truck, and extremities, the posterior ramus being distributed to the skin and muscles of the back.

8. The frontier having been declared closed by the census takers, appreciation of pioneer exploits increased.

9. Education was mainly provided through private initiative outside New England, with the children of the prosperous benefiting accordingly.

Practicing Relative Clauses, Relative Phrases, and Absolutes

Practice Exercise 11: Finding Errors

The continuation of the Iceman passage below has been changed to include some mistakes in relative clauses, adjective phrases, participial phrases, and absolutes. Find the errors and correct them. Do not change anything else.

The Iceman's World (continued)

The Iceman was an expert at exploiting the natural resources around him; the gear he carried tells us that. Along with his ax, he carried an ash handled knife with a tiny flint blade, just 1½ inches long. "Had we found the blade without the handle attached, "says Konrad Spindler, "we would have assumed it was an arrowhead."

The man also carried a small tool bag that held a bone awl, two flint blades, and what appears to be a flint drill. One of the blades bears pollen traces from some of the 46 species of grass he used to make strings, lashes and other gear. Unique grass artifacts, included a woven sheath for his knife and a voluminous cape, were manufactured as needed. The cape seems to be made from strands of plaited grass on that hung vertically from the collar, as if a poncho were cut into thin ribbons."Runned down to his knees, it looked like a grass skirt in which you would bind around your shoulders," says Egg.

The iceman's equipment includes a U-shaped backpack frame making from hazel wood and the oldest quiver ever found. The quiver contained 12 dogwood arrow shafts and two finished arrows, tipping in expertly chipped flint holding in place with gum deriving from boiled birch tree roots. X-rays of the quiver's interior show a ball of string, a piece of deer antler, and a couple of raw flints. A puzzling tool—a willow dowel with horn or antler runned through the center—may have been used to shape flints. Broad calfskin straps recovering from the glacier may be a belt for the quiver. Somewhere along his trek the Iceman harvested *Piptoporus betulinus*, a birchtree fungus what is used in folk medicine as an antibiotic.

All the equipment was found carefully stashing about 15 feet from the body, just beneath the lip of the trench. . . .

The Iceman was prepared for cold weather. His shoes, oval shapes cutting from what is possible cowhide, cunningly fold up around the foot and leave plenty of space for insulated hay. The hay, from grass that only grows at 10,000 feet in the Alps, was anchoring with grass laces threaded through numerous eyelets. A leather flap on each shoe shielded the laces from moisture.

People at the scene of the find described leather pants that "wound around the legs," but only uncertain fragments survived. The Iceman's jacket, wearing under the grass cape, is also in tatters. Small patches of finely stitched deer hide with the fur is facing out seem to form the torso section, while broader strips probably served as sleeves. The remained fragments show many careful repairs over the jacket's lifetime—and one coarse repair. Egg thinks that the man may have been away from home for quite a while, damaged his coat during his trek, and quickly repaired it before he died. (**15: 88**)

We have all seen how other students can summarize writers' information by paraphrasing what they wrote. The next exercise looks at different versions of the same topic to see how professional writers express themselves using different structures. The exercise contains excerpts from four newspaper articles about the same topic. Paragraphs that discuss the same topics have been juxtaposed so that you can compare and contrast grammatical structures.

Practice Exercise 12: Comparing and Contrasting Versions of a News Story —
A Review of Participles, Relative Clauses, Adjective
Phrases, Appositives, and Absolute Constructions

Find the relative clauses, adjective phrases, participial phrases, appositives, and absolute constructions in the passages below. Then compare the similarities and differences between the passages. First compare only the passages numbered 1 with each other; next, the passages numbered 2 with one another; then, the passages numbered 3; after that, the passages numbered 4; and finally the passages numbered 5. For each group of passages, answer the following questions: What synonyms are used? Which grammatical structures mean the same as other structures? How do the writers express the same ideas using different vocabulary, phrases, and clauses? After comparing the similarly numbered paragraphs, compare *all* the paragraphs to each other to see if you can find even more vocabulary and grammatical structures that have the same meanings.

The World's Oldest Dinosaur

1. Scientists working in Argentina have found the closest thing yet to the grandaddy of all dinosaurs, a dog-sized creature that sprinted after prey on its hind legs.

1. Scientists said they had discovered in the foothills of the Andes mountains what they believed was the worlds's oldest dinosaur—a small, two-legged carnivore which lived 225 million years ago.

2. The dinosaur, named *Eoraptor,* lived at the dawn of the age of dinosaurs— 225 million years ago—but possessed some of the forms and functions that would become more ferocious in *Tyrannosaurus Rex,* the 145-foot-long predator that lived at the close of the age 65 million years ago.

2. Paleontologists said the newly discovered dinosaur, which they named *Eoraptor,* was just a couple of steps from the common ancestor of all dinosaurs.

2. Scientists said they had moved a step closer to identifying the common ancestor of all dinosaurs. . . . It dates back to the beginnings of the dinosaur age 225 million years ago. . . . *Eoraptor* is an early member of the "therapod" group of dinosaurs that included the *Herrasaurus* . . . and the ferocious *Tyrannosaurus* that lived in the final days of the dinosaur age some 65 million years ago. Sereno said the reptile must have lived only 5 to 10 million years after the very first dinosaur, the yet-undiscovered common ancestor with traits generic to all dinosaur species.

3. It has the grasping, three-fingered hands typical of a theropod used to rake flesh from its prey.
(from "Scientists Claim Discovery of World's Oldest Dinosaur," *The Straits Times*, [Singpore], January 7, 1993, p.1.)

3. The *Eoraptor* possessed grasping, three-fingered claws designed to rake flesh from its prey. But it lacked the hinge-like jaw and large pelvic bone common to more developed species.

4. The first clue to the fossil's existence—spotted by Ricardo Martinez, a young paleontologist working with Paul Sereno—was sunlight glinting off two shiny surfaces on a rock, which turned out to be a pair of sharp, serrated, curved teeth.

4. A primitive animal that lived near the dawn of the dinosaur era has been discovered in the Andean foothills, its small snout peeking out of the sand.
(from Tim Friend, "Ancient Eoraptor found on dinosaur family tree," *USA Today*, January 6, 1993, p.1. Reprinted with permission.)

4. The specimen, discovered by an Argentinian student who saw the glint of its tooth in the rubble, was nearly intact.

5. They ruled 165 million years—far longer than mankind's 4-million-year existence—until some catastrophe, possibly the impact of an asteroid, wiped them out.
(from "Bones go back to dinosaur's dawn, *Baltimore Sun Star Tribune*, January 6, 1993, p. 6A. Reprinted by permission.)

5. Dinosaurs roamed the earth for another 165 million years after the appearance of the Eoraptor, disappearing about 65 million years ago.
(from "Scientists Claim Discovery of World's Oldest Dinosaur," Copyright © 1993 Reuters America. Reprinted with permission.)

5. Scientists have theorized that a cataclysm, such as a huge asteroid hitting the earth, caused the climatic changes that killed off the dinosaurs some 65 million years ago. Dinosaurs survived for more than 160 million years, compared to the 4-million-year history of mankind.
(from "Andes dinosaur may be close to original," *Owatonna* [Minnesota] *People's Press,* January 6, 1993, p. 1. Copyright © The Associated Press. Reprinted with permission.)

Apatosaurus

Using a Variety of Grammatical Structures for Paraphrasing

Writing Exercise 13

In Exercise 12, newspaper writers expressed the same ideas with several different grammatical structures and many different synonyms. They also used different word order. In this exercise, use synonyms, word order, and a variety of grammatical structures to put the passage below into your own words. Then discuss your ideas in class.

> New fossil discoveries in Wyoming show that paleontologists . . . could be wrong about the appearance of the hulking sauropods, one of the most familiar groups of dinosaurs, including *Apatosaurus* (commonly called *Brontosaurus*).
>
> The long tails of these huge reptiles, it now seems, were not smooth and unadorned . . . a row of spines ran along the top ridge of the tail, raising speculation that the spines continued along the top of the body and neck as well. . . .
>
> Stephen A. Czerkas, who is co-director of a dinosaur museum being established in Blanding, Utah, reported the discovery at the annual meeting of the Society of Vertebrate Paleontology in Toronto. . . .
>
> The evidence for the tail spikes was uncovered at Howe Quarry, a site near the town of Greybull in northern Wyoming that had produced many dinosaur discoveries earlier this century. . . .
>
> Mr. Czerkas said many conical, spine-line fragments were found in the quarry, some isolated but others connected together, "indicating that their natural positions in life formed a continuous line.". . . More than a dozen examples of spikes were clearly identified, ranging in size from two inches upwards of nine inches.
>
> (from John Noble Wilford, "Familiar Dinosaur May Take New Shape," *New York Times*, November 3, 1992, pp. B5–B8. Copyright © 1992/1993 by The New York Times Company. Reprinted by permission.)

Preparing for Standardized Tests: Relative Clauses, Participial Phrases, Cleft Sentences, Absolutes, and Appositives

Practice Exercise 14

Choose the best answer to complete each sentence below.

1. By the early 1900s, small radical splinter groups were formed, such as the Congressional union _____ Alice Paul.
   a. headed by
   b. heading to
   c. ahead
   d. being heading

2. Members of the American women's suffrage association, _____ , addressed state legislatures, wrote, published and argued their convictions.
   a. finding Stone and others
   b. founded by Stone and others
   c. being found by Stone and others
   d. found by Stone and others

3. The process _____ undesirable characteristics are weeded out and the most desirable characteristics are handed down to succeeding generations is evolution.
   a. is
   b. which
   c. that
   d. by which

4. The concept of comparable worth, _____ , is that women should receive equal pay.
   a. for pay
   b. a payment
   c. or pay equity
   d. paying them

5. Within a few decades, we will no longer be a nation of young people, _____.
   a. with its focus on young people
   b. focus being on young people
   c. being with young people
   d. its focus on young people being

6. _____ , Claude Pepper studied at the University of Alabama and received his law degree from Harvard in 1924.
   a. Borning in Chambers County, Alabama
   b. Born in Chambers County, Alabama
   c. Borned in Chambers County, Alabama
   d. He was born in Chambers County, Alabama

7. Insecticides and fertilizers run off into our streams and lakes, _____
   a. that is how the chemicals become incorporated into the food chain.
   b. by which the chemicals become incorporated into the food chain.
   c. which the chemicals become incorporated into the food chain.
   d. where the chemicals become incorporated into the food chain.

8. Individuals _____ based on ethnic identity may find a common political bond through working for the group's civil liberties and rights.
   a. who join interest groups
   b. groups of interest
   c. join interest groups
   d. which join interest groups

9. We are all influenced by those _____ we are closely associated or whom we hold in great respect.
   a. whose friends
   b. with whom
   c. whom
   d. that

10. _____ , Americans are usually willing to identify themselves on the liberal-conservative spectrum.
    a. Asking them
    b. They asked them
    c. When they asked
    d. When asked

11. One explanation of the diversity of American society is rooted in the concept of the political culture, _____.
   a. which is a set of attitudes about the nation and government
   b. that is a set of attitudes about the nation and government
   c. by which a set of attitudes about the nation and government
   d. it is a set of attitudes about the nation and government

12. _____ , the American Medical Association is now affiliated with more than 2,000 local and state medical societies.
   a. Finding it in 1947
   b. Being found in 1947
   c. Founded in 1947
   d. Having been found in 1947

13. There is no such thing as a neutral political figure _____ everyone agrees with him or her.
   a. who is so fair-minded that
   b. that is fair-minded that
   c. which is so fair-minded that
   d. whose fair mind is that

14. _____ the Declaration of Independence while a member of the Continental Congress, Jefferson was elected to the Virginia House of delegates in 1776.
   a. He drafted
   b. After being drafted
   c. When drafted
   d. After drafting

15. Relevant public opinion for most people is simply public opinion _____ concerning them.
   a. that deals with issues
   b. issues that deal
   c. deals with issues
   d. issues that

16. In 1972 Gary Hart, _____ , asked Patrick H. Caddell, then a senior in government at Harvard University, to join McGovern's presidential campaign.
   a. he was Senator George McGovern's campaign manager
   b. campaign manager and George McGovern
   c. who Senator George McGovern's campaign manager
   d. Senator George McGovern's campaign manager

17. There are very few issues _____ most Americans agree.
   a. on that
   b. that
   c. at which
   d. on which

18. Philip Lieberman, _____ , has carried out some interesting research on the evolution of the speech tract.
   a. who a linguist at Brown University
   b. is a linguist at Brown University
   c. a linguist at Brown University
   d. been a linguist at Brown University

19. _____ , any child born into any society can acquire the language of that community with relative ease.
   a. Exposing given language adequately
   b. Given adequate exposure to language
   c. Exposed adequate given language
   d. Giving adequate exposure to language

20. Roger Brown, a Harvard psychologist, _____ , has shown that the early two-word constructions of children are based on a small number of relationships of meaning.
   a. who pioneered much of the research on language acquisition
   b. whose pioneering much of the research on language acquisition
   c. that pioneered much of the research on language acquisition
   d. pioneered much of the research on language acquisition

21. _____ , starch becomes soluble and can then be easily digested.
   a. Cooking it
   b. With cooking it
   c. While being cooked
   d. While we cooked it

Practice Exercise 15

Find and circle the letter of the one error in the following sentences. Then write the correct form above the error.

1. Assuming Paleolithic people to be too "primitive" for religious
      a   b
   expression, early 19th century archeologists considered the pictures
   in which adorned the ancient cave walls merely decorative.
        c   d

2. One of the largest public interest pressure groups is Common Cause,
                        a   b
   founded in 1968, which goal is to reorder national priorities toward the
        c   d
   public.

3. Several years ago psychologist Joseph Kamiya developed a technique
   by where subjects are signaled by tone or light whenever they produce
        a   b   c
   alpha waves.
      d

4. History is <u>full</u> of examples of scientific ideas <u>being rejecting</u> by the
         a   b

   society <u>in</u> which the scientist <u>operates</u>.
          c   d

5. Sociologists <u>studied</u> science have tried to identify <u>what</u> social features
               a   b

   of scientific groups <u>contribute</u> to their greater or <u>lesser</u> productivity.
                       c   d

6. Where <u>there</u> is maximum competition <u>between</u> research centers,
          a   b

   innovation will be greater, <u>assumed</u> that all rewards are not controlled by
                              c

   <u>a</u> single organization.
   d

7. After <u>a</u> <u>general</u> rise in sea level the clay <u>layer</u>, <u>overlying</u> by the
         a   b   c   d

   sandstone, was then farther from the shore.

8. The <u>exact</u> method by which the cerebrospinal fluid <u>forming</u> is <u>a</u> matter
        a   b   c

   of <u>some</u> dispute.
     d

9. With <u>the</u> number of jobs <u>are</u> increasing <u>much</u> faster in the sunbelt
         a   b   c

   than in the snowbelt, the population <u>shift</u> should continue.
                                  d

10. Fasting is a method <u>of</u> reducing <u>that it</u> requires <u>close</u> medical
                  a   b   c

   supervision <u>in</u> a hospital.
            d

11. A general <u>drop</u> in sea level caused a regression of the sea. The
            a

   limestone in this section <u>no longer</u> covered by seawater, was gradually
                           b

   covered <u>on</u> nonmarine sediments, <u>perhaps</u> clay.
           c   d

12. Carbohydrates are the fuel <u>from that</u> the human body normally <u>derives</u>
                            a   b   c

   most of <u>its</u> energy.
        d

13. Controlled experiments yield specific findings that helps to clarify the
    a.................b............................c
    confusion somewhat.
    ....d

14. Early experiments to teach chimpanzees to verbalize human language
    ....a
    were not notably successful, the absence of vocalizing apparatus certainly
    ....b..c
    has been a factor.
    ....d

15. Only a person knowledgeable in nutrition understands that liquid
    a
    protein products are not a food and that anyone used one of these
    ....b.......................c
    regimens for losing weight is in reality fasting.
    ....d

16. Synthesized in green leaves from carbon dioxide and water using the
    .....a.............................b..............................c
    energy of sunlight, carbohydrate is founded in all parts of plants.
    ....d

17. The inland mountains, near Taos, New Mexico, have an intricate
    ....a....b
    history of ocean basins, shorelines, and river valleys writing in their rocks.
    ....c........d

18. Another useful organism in the fossil record is the ostracod, is a very
    ....a......................................b........c...d
    small crustacean.

19. The atoms of glucose can be rearranged by the plant to form another
    ....a...................................b
    sugar, fructose, that is sweet to the taste.
    ....c.............d

20. Lack of carbohydrate causes ketosis, a condition in which the products
    a.......................................b
    of fat breakdown accumulating in the blood.
    ....c.............d

21. The three sugars are monosaccharides, simple sugars in that stand
    ....a..b...c
    alone, without other sugars.
    ....d

22. The storage form of glucose is starch, <u>it is a substance</u> <u>evolved</u> to feed
                                              a   b
    <u>the</u> next generation of potatoes to guarantee the <u>continuance</u> of the species.
     c   d

Analysis Exercise 16: Building Templates for Relative and Adverbial Concepts

Fill in the blanks below with the names of the words or structures that you would expect to find in the passages. You may choose structures from any of the preceding chapters (relative clause, adverbial clause or phrase, adjective phrase, appositive, cleft sentence, participial phrase,or absolute construction). There are examples in Exercise 17.

[1]   Ruth Fulton Benedict, _____ , studied two North American
       Indian groups, _____ and _____ . The typical Zuni
       was a person _____ and _____ . The Kwakiutl Indians
       were much different. The ideal man among the Kwakiutl was one
       _____ . Child training patterns reinforced this pattern,
       _____ .

           Benedict's study of cultural configurations illustrates how numerous
       aspects of life reinforce the basic pattern of culture, whatever it might be.
       This is not to say that everyone is just like this _____ that it is a
       pattern that describes the typical member of the society.

[2]   Technology, _____ , was the basis of Leslie A. White's theory of
       cultural evolution. To test White's theory of cultural evolution, Marshall
       Shahlins analyzed 14 societies in Polynesia. After _____ ,
       Shahlins was able to divide the Polynesian societies into three different
       categories. Shahlins found what he was looking for, _____ in
       the tools used or the techniques, but in the actual environmental condi-
       tions themselves. Not all cultures went through exactly the same stages,
       but in many cases the stages were similar. It was here _____ he
       felt evolution could be applied most profitably.

[3]   One of the most important figures in leading the way toward a controlled
       method for cultural anthropology was Bronislaw Malinowski.
       _____ , Malinowski was first trained in mathematics but became
       interested in anthropology. He studied in London, then went to the Pacific,
       _____ he was carrying out research when World War I broke out.
       He ended up in Australia, _____ , as a citizen of the German
       nation _____ which Australia was at war, he was subject to

internment for the duration of the conflict. He was, however, able to persuade the officials to allow him to be interned not in Australia,
_____ on a small group of islands to the north, _____
the Trobriands. Malinowski lived in the islands for several years,
_____ the way of life of the natives. _____ from civilization, he was forced to live in native villages, learn their language, and
participate completely in their way of life. (14: 301, 302, 306, 332)

Analysis Exercise 17: Research Project—Relative Concepts

In this exercise you will analyze the academic journal article or textbook chapter you
chose earlier to see if you can find examples of the grammatical structures we have
studied so far in this text. Here are some examples.

Relative clauses	A student *who is caught cheating on a test* is in trouble.
	Law is a system of rules *that are formalized.*
	There was a time *when life was more peaceful.*
Adjective phrases	People *from all over the world* have visited the museum.
	There is something *weird* about this situation.
Participial phrases	The countries *colonized by the British* speak English.
	According to researchers, deviant behavior is learned.
Appositives	Homo erectus, *an ancestor of man,* lived during the Ice Age.
Cleft sentences	It was the president *who hired the manager.*
	It is time *that we need.*
	It is *not* money *that we need, but* time.
Absolute constructions	The children ran to school, *the little ones following the big ones.*

Analyze your academic article. First find and count the relative clauses, adjective
phrases, participial phrases, cleft sentences, appositives, and absolutes in the article. If
your article is very long, choose several typical paragraphs. Fill in this chart with the total
number of each grammatical structure you found in the article. The first line is an example.

FIELD	RELATIVE CLAUSES	ADJECT. PHRASES	PARTICIP. PHRASES	CLEFT SENTEN.	NEG. CLEFT	APPOSI-TIVES	ABSO-LUTES
Biology	20	5	10	0	0	5	1
Your field							

As you analyze your article, try to anwer these questions.

1. Are the grammatical structures that you have found exactly the same as those we discussed in the text? If not, how do they differ?
2. In your article are there many appositives?
3. In your field, which relative constructions seem to be the most common?
4. Which subordinators are the most common in the relative clauses?
5. Are the relative clauses mostly restrictive (no commas) or nonrestrictive (commas)?
6. Did you find any relative clauses that contained another clause or phrase (embedded clauses or phrases) between the subordinating conjunction and the rest of the relative clause?
7. What types of adjective phrases and participial phrases do you find? Do they usually occur at the beginning, end, or in the middle of sentences?
8. Does your article contain any cleft sentences? If so, what element in the sentence is being emphasized?
9. Does your article contain any absolutes? What kinds?

When you write papers in your major, you will probably want to use the conventions that other writers in your field use. Review the results of your research project and briefly summarize the structures that are common in your field.

Last, small groups of students from related fields (Social Sciences, Natural Sciences, Engineering, etc.) fill in the following chart with the results of their research. All students from the same discipline should be grouped together so that the similarities and differences are apparent. Present the final chart to the class (overhead transparency, blackboard, or copied handouts) for discussion.

FIELD	RELATIVE CLAUSES	ADJECT. PHRASES	PARTICIP. PHRASES	CLEFT SENTEN.	NEG. CLEFT	APPOSI- TIVES	ABSO- LUTES
Biology	20	5	10	0	0	5	1

7

ADVERBIAL CONCEPTS OF CONTRAST (CONCESSION/OPPOSITION) AND COMPARISON

PART I   CLAUSES AND PHRASES OF CONCESSION

"Concession" means something a writer admits is true, valid, or certain at the same time that he makes another statement with a different opinion or point of view. The words "although," "even though," "though," "albeit,""despite," "in spite of," "regardless of," "however," "nonetheless," "nevertheless," "but," and "yet" express the concept of concession.

Analyzing the Grammar of Concession

Analysis Exercise 1: Sentence Combining with *although, even though, though, notwithstanding, despite, in spite of, regardless of*

Combine the underlined clauses and phrases with the appropriate subordinators or prepositional phrases into sentences with adverbial clauses and phrases of concession. Use "although," "even though," "though," "notwithstanding," "despite," "in spite of," "regardless of."(See the Adverbial Concepts chart on pages 127–131 for help.) The first one is done as an example. The second gives you clues in parentheses. Decide where to put the subordinators in numbers 3, 4, and 5.

> 1. (valid point) its flaws and weaknesses
>   (author's opinion) Most Americans are proud of their political system and support it with their obedience to their laws, their patriotism, or their votes.

Despite its flaws and weaknesses, most Americans are proud of their political system and support it with their obedience to their laws, their patriotism, or their votes. (**39**: 15)

2. The first constitution of the United States was called The Articles of Confederation.
(true point) The Articles of Confederation had many defects.
(author's opinion) There were also some accomplishments during the eight years of their existence. (**39**: 34)

3. There was a bitter struggle in Massachusetts, but clever politicking by the Federalists brought a close but successful ratification vote on February 6, 1788.
Some historians believe that Anti-Federalists were a majority in the state at that time. (**39**: 47)

4. Life appears to be rare in our solar system.
Life is amazingly common on our planet.

5. their simplicity
viruses vary considerably in form.

Explanation 1—Subordinating Conjunctions and Prepositions of Concession

Although
	subordinator	subordinate clause	comma	main clause
Clause: *Although the organisms may seem the same,* they are different.
(valid assumption)   (writer's opinion)

	subordinator	subordinate phrase comma	main clause
Phrase: *Although apparently the same,* the organisms are very different.

Even though
	main clause	subordinator subordinate clause
Clause: The converter has four connections *even though they don't show.*
(states the fact)   (states how it appears)

Though
	subordinator subordinate clause	comma	main clause
Clause: *Though it was favored by some,* a return to the past was impossible.
(expresses some people's opinion)   (the historical fact)

subordinator
subordinate phrase comma   main clause
Phrase: *Though favored by some,* a return to the past was impossible.

Albeit (formal/old fashioned)

       main clause   comma subordinator   subordinate clause

Clause: There was a close relationship, *albeit experiments did not bring rewards.*

     (fact)   (valid statement)

Other Words That Introduce Phrases

despite   *regardless of*
in spite of *notwithstanding*

     subordinator + subordinate phrase comma + main clause

Phrase *Despite the policemen's efforts,* the victim died.

  (the policemen tried to do something) (this occurred)

These subordinators (prepositions) all mean exactly the same as "although," "even though," "though," and "albeit." All of these phrases can appear before or after the main clause.

USAGE NOTE: "Although" is by far the favorite subordinator in all disciplines and usually appears at the beginnings of sentences with clauses. "Even though" and "though" appear in the middle after the main clause. "Though" is the subordinator usually used with phrases. "Albeit" is very rare and, when it appears, it is preceded by a comma and follows the main clause.

Look again at the examples above and note that the "although" and "though" + phrase construction can be used only with phrases that are reduced from clauses with the same subjects.

Clause: *Although the organisms are apparently the same,* they are different.

Phrase: *Although apparently the same,* the organisms are different.

Clause: A return to the past was impossible *though it was favored by some.*

Phrase: A return to the past was impossible *though favored by some.*

Analysis Exercise 2: Sentence Combining with *however, nonetheless, but, yet, or still*

In the following passages, find the sentences that can be combined with conjunctions to make compound sentences of concession. Use "however," "nonetheless," "but," "yet," "still." Pay careful attention to the punctuation. The sentences are not necessarily in the correct order. As you go over the answers, discuss how you could rewrite the sentences with subordinating conjunctions.

[1] The global communities based on climatic similarities are called biomes. A biome is a community which covers a large geographic area, where life

forms are different from other climatic areas. From the equator to the north and south, you will find tropical rain forest, temperate rain forest, temperate deciduous forest, taiga, tundra and ice. North of the temperate forest is the taiga, a biome characterized by evergreen coniferous trees such as spruce, fir, and pine. Rabbits are also prominent herbivores in the taiga biome. The most conspicuous of the herbivores is the moose, which is common in open, marshy areas of the taiga. (**9:** 127)

[2]   The oceans may be divided into a number of habitats. Many strong-swimming, wide-ranging animals such as tuna and whales live in the open ocean. The open ocean produces only a small fraction of the world's fish catch. (**9:** 113)

[3]   A theoretical outlook is a set of guiding ideas and questions that provides an overall approach to a subject. The existence of seemingly contradictory approaches is not unique to sociology. At the microscopic level it behaves like a particle. Even in the scientific field of Physics, light appears in some ways to be a wave. (**35:** 17)

Fill in the blanks with the appropriate conjunctions.

[4]   According to medical records, there is a man in England who gets by on only 15 minutes to an hour of sleep each night—and feels perfectly fine. _____, this is quite a rarity. The majority sleep on a familiar seven-to eight-hour per night schedule. _____ in the same way that individual needs for food differ, there is considerable variation around the eight-hour average for sleep. (**7:** 149)

[5]   Monetary Policy and Lags—Monetary policy does not suffer from the same lengthy time lags as fiscal policy because the Fed can, within a very short period, put into effect any policy it decides. _____ , researchers have estimated that it takes almost fourteen months for a monetary policy change to become effective measured from the time the economy either slows down or speeds up too much to the time the economy feels the policy change. This means that by the time monetary policy goes into effect, a different policy might be appropriate. (**39:** 531)

Explanation 2—Coordinating Conjunctions of Concession

however
nonetheless
nevertheless

Coordinate Clauses

semicolon or period   conjunction   comma

Light appears to be a wave; *however* (*nonetheless/nevertheless*), it behaves
(this clause expresses how something seems)   (this clause expresses a fact)
like a particle.

Other Conjunctions That Connect Clauses

but
yet
still

comma conjunction

Light appears to be a wave, *but* (*yet*) it behaves like a particle.
(how something seems)   (a fact)

All of these conjunctions mean the same thing and are interchangeable with each other. Also, they often appear first in a sentence, which means that the preceding sentence is closely connected to the meaning of the sentence that the conjunctions begins.

The word "however" also frequently appears later in a clause. In the middle of a sentence it is preceded and followed by commas; at the end of a sentence it is simply preceded by a comma. The two sentences remain closely connected in meaning, as shown in the first two examples below.

> Printed money obviously has little or no value on its own. You can't eat it, drink it, or sleep with it. *However,* it can be exchanged for food, water, lodging and other necessities.

> In some primitive societies, habits may still be acquired and maintained mainly by primary reinforcement. Most of us, *however,* respond to a much broader range of rewards.

> The majority of the 100,000 groups do not strictly fit our description of an interest group because they are not actively seeking to change or influence government policy. *But* we can be sure that the purpose of the roughly 1,200 organizations whose names begin with the word National . . . is to do just this.

NOTE: It is not correct to use both *although* and *but* or *however* and *but* to join the same clauses.

PART II   CLAUSES AND PHRASES OF OPPOSITION

"Opposition" of course means "opposites." Sentences with clauses and phrases of opposition are expressed with "while," "whereas," "where," "in contrast," "on the contrary," "on the other hand," "conversely," "still," "but," "yet," "however," "nonetheless," "nevertheless," "instead of," "unlike," and "different from." It is interesting to note that many of the same conjunctions are used to express opposition as well as concession.

Analysis Exercise 3

Complete the passages below by filling in the blanks with subordinate conjunctions, prepositions, or phrases to complete the passages. Use "while," "whereas," "like," "unlike," or "instead of." Then discuss which sentences could be rewritten as compound sentences with conjunctions like "but," "yet," "however," or "nevertheless."

[1] Both diabetes and hypoglycemia are diagnosed by means of a glucose tolerance test. After fasting overnight the subject is fed a sudden large dose of pure simple carbohydrate, usually a sweet drink. Four or six hours later, the hypoglycemic person is found to have an abnormally low blood glucose level, _____ the diabetic still has hyperglycemia. (**19**: 66)

[2] France is at present building one of the largest interactive video networks. Les Cables de Lyon is installing urban optical cable networks to serve some 420,000 subscribers utilizing $^{85}\!/_{125}$ um multimode optical fibers. Two types of 5-fiber cable are used: one is suitable for laying in plastic tubes, _____ the other can be used for both aerial and underground installation, as well as for runs along exterior building walls. (**3**: 363)

[3] _____ reacting to environmental forces, some companies work to change the environment in which they operate. These marketers attempt to influence government officials, public interest groups, the newsmedia, and other opinion molders in ways that would benefit their companies. The marketing theorist Phillip Kotler has termed this sort of marketing "megamarketing." (**23**: 39)

[4] Many societies do not have lineal (matrilineal, patrilineal, or ambilineal) descent groups—sets of kin who believe they descend from a common ancestor. They are therefore called bilateral societies. The distinctness of the bilateral system of descent is that aside from brothers and sisters, no two persons belong to exactly the same kin group. _____ bilateral kinship, unilineal rules of descent can form clear-cut groups of kin.

[5] Kinship Terminology Systems—The Crow system, named after a North American Indian tribe, has been called the mirror image of the Omaha system (another American Indian tribe). Relatives on the father's side and relatives on the mother's side are grouped differently. _____

the Omaha and the Crow systems, the Iroquois system has different terms for relatives on the father's and mother's sides. (**8**: 342, 343, 354)

Explanation 3—Subordinators of Opposition

While

Clause:
subordinator subordinate clause comma   main clause
While   *principles*   *are*   *useful,*   managers cannot avoid mistakes.
(opposite ideas)

Phrase:
subordinate
phrase   comma   main clause
While helpful, principles are not the answer.
(phrase reduced from two clauses with the same subject)

Whereas
Where (informal)

Clause:
subordinator   subordinate clause   comma   main clause
Whereas   *some*   *vote Democrat,* others vote Republican.
(opposite ideas)

"While" and "whereas" clauses can appear both before or after the main clause. They are preceded by a comma when they are after the main clause.

Some people vacation during the winter, *whereas* (*while*) others prefer summer.

Discovering the Meaning of Tricky Transitions: **On the Contrary, Contrary to,** *and* **On the Other Hand**

One of the most common errors in student writing is the misuse of the phrase "on the contrary." The next exercise will help you clarify its usage and meaning.

Discovery Exercise 4

The following sentences contain three transitions that are often confused: "contrary to," "on the contrary," and "on the other hand." Compare the way each is used. Try to determine how the three transitions differ and what each means. (Hint: When there is a pair of sentences, the first sentence of the pair is the key.) Study the sentence structures and then answer the questions.

- How is "contrary to" different from the other two transitions?
- What is the difference in the sentence structures used with "on the contrary" and "on the other hand"?

Contrary to

> *Contrary to* the expectation of most political analysts, Congress passed a massive tax reform bill in 1986, an election year.

> *Contrary to* popular belief, there are not two types of individuals—those who work in the private and those who work in the public sector.

On the contrary

> The authors have long emphasized that an arbitrary boundary of management knowledge is set for the field of management theory to make our subject "manageable," but this does not imply a closed-system approach to the subject. *On the contrary*, there are many interactions with the system environment. (**27**: 70)

> Indian myths tell us emphatically that the Indians are not just one homogeneous racial group. *On the contrary*, the various Indian groups have had different racial origins, originating in or reaching the Americas in different ways, and at different times. (**17**: 38)

On the other hand

> Historically, economic issues have the strongest influence on voters' choices. When the economy is doing well, it is very difficult for a challenger, particularly at the presidential level, to defeat the incumbent. *On the other hand*, increasing inflation, a rising rate of unemployment, or a high interest rate is likely to work to the disadvantage of the incumbent. If an individual perceives the "new" technology or new organization as interrupting or drastically changing the existing clientelist relationships, the "new" may be viewed with great distrust. *On the other hand*, new technology may under other circumstances be viewed as a "helpful" resource in reinforcing patron-client relations. (**39**: 328)

Explanation 4—Contrary to, On the Contrary, On the Other Hand

Meaning: "Contrary to" introduces a phrase about what most people believe followed by a main clause that expresses what is really true.

Contrary to + phrase   + main clause.
Contrary to expectations, the weather in Florida can be cold.

Meaning: "On the contrary" introduces a sentence that follows a negative clause or sentence. "On the contrary" in this usage really means "in fact," and the sentence repeats and emphasizes affirmatively the meaning of the preceding negative clause. The subjects of both sentences are the same.

negative sentence or clause   *On the contrary* + sentence
The weather in Iowa *isn't* mild. *On the contrary,* it is harsh.

Meaning: "On the other hand" introduces an idea opposite to the sentence before it. The subjects of the two sentences may or may not be the same. If the writer wants to express two opposing ideas, he/she should use "on the other hand."

sentence   + *On the other hand,*   +   sentence
The weather in Florida is mild. *On the other hand,* the weather in Iowa is harsh.

PART III   CLAUSES OF COMPARISON

Analyzing the Grammar of Comparison

Analysis Exercise 5

Fill in the blanks with "as," "like," "just as," "likewise," and "as . . . as" to express ideas of comparison.

[1]   Unemployment—Labor is just _____ any other good or service. If an excess quantity is supplied at a particular wage level, the wage level is too high. By accepting lower wages, unemployed workers will quickly be put back to work. (**33**: 239)

[2]   Future uncertainty and change make planning a necessity. _____ the navigator cannot set a course once and forget about it, so the business manager cannot establish a goal and let the matter rest. (**27**: 170)

[3]   Generally motor skills tend to be retained better than other types of learning, probably because they are less likely to interfere with one another. It is fortunate that motor skills are not lost _____ rapidly _____ are many other kinds of learning. Imagine leaving your car at a garage and returning in two weeks—only to find your driving skills so shot that you are a menace to society on the way home. (**7**: 201)

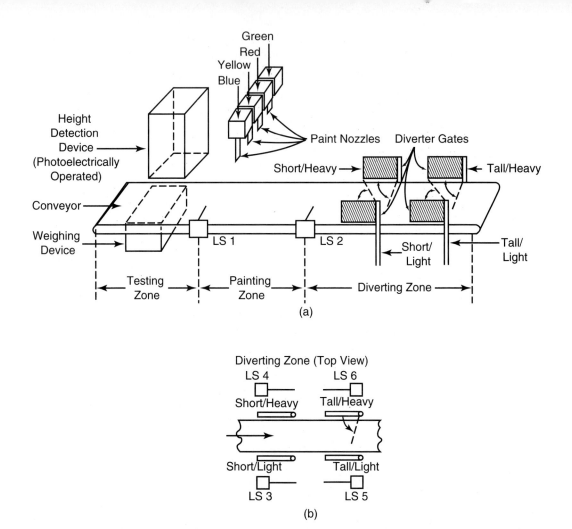

Figure 7-1 (a) Physical layout of a conveyor/classifying system. (b) Top view of the diverting zone, showing the positions of the four diverting gates and the four chute limit-switches. **(30: 6)**

[4]   Relay Logic Circuit for a Conveyor/Classifying System (Figure 7-1)–Manufactured parts of varying height and weight come down the conveyer, moving to the right. A height detector measures the height of each part and classifies it _____ either short or tall, depending on whether the part is below or above a certain prescribed height. _____, a weighing device classifies it _____ either light or heavy depending on whether it is below a certain prescribed weight. **(30: 6–7)**

[5]   Australia—The island continent of Australia has been cut off from connection with all other continents for about 200 million years. The placental mammals such as dogs and cats, in which the female carries the young

Opossum

in her body for a considerable amount of time before birth, reached the continent only very recently. Most of the mammals found in Australia are pouched animals. _____ the opossum of the United States, these animals, called marsupials, give birth to tiny young which then develop in a pouch on the underside of the mother. (**9**: 132)

[6]   History is replete with examples of followers, thereby developing what Mooney calls a "unity of doctrine" in the organization. Even _____ autocratic a commander _____ Napoleon supplemented his power to command with a careful explanation of the purpose of his orders. (**27**: 35)

Explanation 5—Comparative Structures

Comparative structures are extremely common in academic writing. Comparative structures include both adjectives and adverbials. You are familiar with the following forms.

Phrase . . . Clause

> *-er . . . than*   *less . . . than*
> *more . . . than*   *fewer . . . than*

                      comparative adjective phrase + than   + clause
Foreign students seem *more (highly) motivated than other students do.*

> *similar to*   *like*
> *different from* *unlike*

preposition + noun phrase   main clause
Like many people in the world, Americans have a sense of humor.

Like vs. *as*, a cause of major confusion for students

One of the major confusions students have is between "like" and "as." "Like"and "unlike" are comparative prepositions.

Labor is (just) *like* any other good or service.

"As" may be used in the following ways:

1. Comparative in a clause or reduced clause

   As (it was) with many customs in Indian life, the practice of games was dramatically altered in the 19th and 20 centuries.

2. Comparative in phrases with adjectives, adverbs, "much," and "many"

   He is *as* tall *as* the other boy (is).
   We have *as many* exams *as* the other class (does).
   This computer works *as* well *as* that one (works/does).
   A typewriter is *not as* useful *as* a word processor (is).
   A typewriter is *not so* useful *as* a word processor (is).

3. Cause: "as" = "because"

   The farmers are working day and night *as* they hope to get the crops planted before it rains.

4. Effect: "as a result," "as a consequence"

   There have been twenty inches of rain in the last month. *As a result,* the rivers and streams are at flood stage.

5. Condition: "as long as"

   As long *as* you help me, I will be able to finish the work on time.

6. Time: "as" = "while"

   As we were jogging down the street, we met the president.

7. Summary

   As I said before, grammar isn't easy.
   As was discussed in Chapter 5, adverbial clauses can be reduced to phrases.

8. Example: "as" = "such as" or "as an illustration"

   Some flowers, such *as* camellias, require a warm climate.

9. Role, capacity, or function: "As" may be a preposition when it is followed by a phrase indicating role, capacity, or function.

He works *as* a bricklayer.

She is acting *as* a substitute.

As a teacher, I feel that I have some observations to make.

Other Comparatives

(just) as
just as . . . so

Clause: John works in a post office (*just*) *as* his father did.
Just as John's father worked in a post office, *so* does John.
(expresses similarity between clauses)

subordinator + clause

(*Just*) *as* we expected, the manager was fired.

(clause reduced to a past participle)

Phrase: (*Just*) *as expected,* the manager was fired.

Likewise

"Likewise" is a conjunction that is used often in writing. It has the meaning of "also," "similarly," or "in the same way." It can be placed at the beginning of a sentence followed by a comma, between clauses punctuated with a semicolon and comma, or before or after the verb in the second sentence. "Likewise" occurs in the same part of a sentence as "however" does.

There are many kinds of batteries. The ordinary lead-cell battery, the common automobile battery makes use of a chemical reaction to supply energy; *likewise*, this is true of the "dry cell," which is not dry inside in spite of its name. (**2**: 421)

This is *likewise* true of the "dry cell," which is not dry inside in spite of its name.

Likewise, this is true of the "dry cell," which is not dry inside in spite of its name.

Practicing Adverbials of Comparison

Practice Exercise 6: Using Comparatives in a Passage

Fill in the blanks to express ideas of comparison. You may use any of the adverbials in Explanation 5.

Spurred on by the Hawthorne experiments of 1927 and 1932 and the awakened interest in human relations in the 1930s and 1940s, a great many behavioral scientists have taken up the study of management in recent years. _____ will be recalled, the Hawthorne experiments, undertaken by Mayo and Roethlisberger of the Harvard Business School, disclosed that attitudes toward workers may be more important to efficiency and productivity _____ such material factors as rest periods, illumination, and even money. This disclosure _____ well _____ the more basic work done earlier by psychologists and sociologists, resulted in much academic writing by the behavioral scientists. . . .

_____ has already been made clear by the discussion of earlier writers, psychologists have _____ contributed to management understanding through their illumination of the aspects of rational behavior and influence, the sources of motivation, and the nature of leadership. Among the many who have contributed materially to management are McGregor, Likert, Argyris, Leavitt, Blake and Mouton, Sayles, Tannenbaum, Bennis, Fiedler, Stogdill, and Herzberg.

These scholars and others have shown how human beings bring to their tasks aspects of behavior which the effective manager should profitably understand . . . _____, _____ will be pointed out later, the most effective manager is a leader, and understanding how leadership emerges is a key to understanding leadership itself. (**27**: 58–59)

Analysis Exercise 7: Writing Rules About Comparatives

After you correct your answers to Exercises 5 and 6 above, in your own words write some rules that explain the use of "like," "as," "just as," and "likewise."

Explanation 6—Special Comparatives of Proportion

Another structure common in academic writing is the "the ____er, the ____er," or "the more _____ the more _____."

The usual purpose of a battery is to supply energy to charges. In Fig 7-2a we see a battery connected to two plates. The battery places excess charge on the two plates, one positive and one negative. This is a device of considerable practical importance for storage of electric charge. Such a device is called a capacitor (or condenser). We now are interested in how much

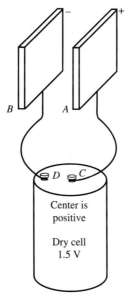

(a)

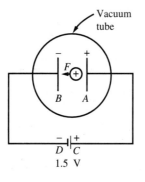

(b)

Figure 7-2 The potential difference from *B* to *A* is 1.5V, the emf of the battery. (**2:** 422)

charge Q resides on one of the plates. The amount of charge on the plate will depend on several factors. *First, the larger the voltage of the battery, the more charge it will put on the capacitor.* Hence, if V is the voltage difference across the capacitor,

$$Q \alpha V$$

Of course, the larger the plate area, the more charge it should hold. In addition, if the plates are brought closer together, the positive plate will attract more negative charge from the battery to the negative plate. (**2:** 427)

The structure of this comparative is more complicated than other structures. Ideally, the writer attempts to make two perfectly parallel phrases or clauses with a comma between. Sometimes there is no verb at all. Look at the examples:

Contrast (Concession/Opposition) and Comparison   **211**

The bigger, the better.

The sooner, the better.

The bigger they are, the harder they fall.

The more you eat, the better you feel.

The less they spend, the more they'll have.

Practice Exercise 8: Finding Comparatives in Context

Examine the following passage from a management text. Find all the comparative struc-tures and mark them. Then answer the questions that follow.

SUMMARY OF MAJOR PRINCIPLES FOR PART 6:

Controlling

Principle of future-directed controls—Because of time lags in the total sys-tem of control, the more a control system is based on feedforward rather than simple feedback of information, the more managers have the oppor-tunity to perceive undesirable deviation from plans before they occur and to take action in time to prevent them.

These two principles emphasize the purpose of control in any system of managerial action as one of ensuring that objectives are achieved through detecting deviations and taking corrective action designed to attain them. Moreover, control, like planning, should ideally be forward-looking. This principle is often disregarded in practice, largely because the present state of the art in managing has not provided for systems of feedforward con-trol. Managers have generally been dependent on historical data, which may be adequate for tax collection and determination of stockholders' earnings, but are not good enough for the most effective control. Lacking means for looking forward, reference to history, on the questionable assumption that "what is past is prologue," is better than not looking at all. But time lags in the system of management control make it impera-tive that greater efforts be undertaken to make future-directed control a reality. . . .

Principle of direct control—The higher the quality of every manager in a managerial system, the less will be the need for indirect controls.

Most controls are based in large part on the fact that human beings make mistakes and often do not react to problems by undertaking their correction adequately and promptly. The more qualified managers are, the more they will perceive deviations from plans and take timely action to prevent them. This means that the most direct form of all control is to take steps to ensure the highest possible quality of managers.

The Structure of Control

Principle of reflection of plans—The more that plans are clear, complete, and integrated, and the more that controls are designed to reflect such plans, the more effectively controls will serve the needs of managers.

It is not possible for a system of controls to be devised without plans since the task of control is to ensure that plans work out as intended. There cannot be doubt that the more clear, complete, and integrated these plans are and the more that control techniques are designed to follow the progress of these plans, the more effective they will be.

Principle of organizational suitability—The more that an organizational structure is clear, complete, and integrated, and the more that controls are designed to reflect the place in the organization structure where responsibility for action lies, the more they will facilitate correction of deviations from plans. (**27**: 822–823)

Analysis of Comparatives of Proportion and Ratio

Analysis Exercise 9: Determining the Meaning

Reread and think about the comparatives like "the more . . . , the more . . ." that you found in the passage in Exercise 8.

- What do they mean?
- In your own words, rewrite the six sentences with "the more . . . , the more" constructions to show that you understand their meanings in the passage.

1.

2.

3

4.

5.

6.

Comparative structures like "the bigger, the better" are not really true comparatives. They are actually expressions of proportion and ratio and cause/effect.

the bigger = the size of something increases
the better = it becomes better
This construction is almost always written as follows:

(NP and VP
may be reversed)

The + comparative adjective or adverb + [(*the, a, Ø*) + noun phrase + verb],

(this part may be omitted)

the + comparative adjective or adverb + [(*the, a, Ø*) + noun phrase + verb].

Ideally, the two phrases or clauses should be parallel. The first clause acts as the "cause" of the second. Sometimes there are three or even four phrases or clauses of ratio. Notice that this is the only sentence in English that does not require a verb.

The higher one's income, the more expensive one's time is.

If conditions occur that drive the measured value out of agreement with the set point, a good system will restore the agreement immediately. The quicker the restoration, the better the system.

The greater the VR1, the faster the capacitor charging rate and the earlier the UJT and triac fire. The smaller the VR1, the slower the charging rate and the later the UJY and triac fire.

Practicing with Comparatives of Proportion and Ratio

Practice Exercise 10

The sentences in this exercise are taken out of context so that you can focus on the grammatical form. Rewrite the sentences below. Make them into sentences of ratio and cause/effect like "the bigger, the better." The first one is done for you.

1. As the rate of interest gets higher, it becomes more expensive to purchase an automobile or a house.
   The higher the rate of interest (gets), the more expensive it becomes to purchase an automobile or a house.
2. As one's income after the cutoff point becomes higher, the effective average social security tax rate on total income becomes lower.
3. The market becomes less organized, so the transaction costs become high.
4. If you study economics more, it is assumed, your expected grade will increase.
5. Historically, as it has become less costly to disseminate information because of technological improvements, transaction costs have fallen more.

6. When the rate of interest rises, it becomes more expensive to invest and the level of desired investment decreases. (this sentence has 3 comparatives)

7. If the thermal resistance becomes larger, the thermal constant becomes large, and more time is necessary to reach a final steady temperature value. (make 3 clauses here)

8. The same holds true for thermal capacity; as the capacity becomes larger, there is more time required to bring the temperature up to a steady value.

Using Adverbial Subordinators of Cause/Effect, Concession, Opposition and Comparison in Writing

Writing Exercise 11: Rewriting Sentences in a Passage

Rewrite the following passage **without** changing the meaning significantly. Replace the underlined words. Find an adverbial conjunction or a transition word of equal meaning and make the appropriate changes in the sentences if necessary. You may decide to omit one or two of the underlined words as you rewrite, but be sure that you do not change the meaning of the passage. Do not choose a conjunction or transition from the same group as the original. For example, if the word is in group A, choose a word from group B, C, D, or E. You may also want to use the Adverbial Concepts Charts in Chapter 5 on pages 127–131.

GROUP A	GROUP B	GROUP C	GROUP D	GROUP E
although	however	despite	in addition	moreover
even though	but	regardless of	conversely	on the other hand
though	nevertheless	in spite of	as a result	besides
while	nonetheless	because of	no matter	further(more)
because	consequently	due to	instead	hence
as	thus	notwithstanding	similar to	accordingly
whereas	and	on the contrary	yet	still

American Indians and Sports

Although sports were often used for recreational purposes and for social relaxation, they also extended deeply into the fabric of the Native American culture. Indian sport was intimately related to ritual and ceremony. In addition to the pure joy involved in participation, sport was used as a means by which the Indians communicated with a higher spirit, seeking blessings on their individual or community welfare. Over the years, activities that began as religious rites often evolved into sport. Nevertheless, sport retained its important cultural significance. This was reflected in the extensive spiritual preparation for sport as well as in the attitude and manner of participating. High standards of sportsmanship and artistic expression prevailed. The placing of wagers was an important aspect of sports contests. Consequently, even extensive sports involvement would not be viewed as overemphasis.

Even though abundant evidence indicates the prominence of sports in the life of Native Americans, the interpretation of this finding is related to one's overall perception of Indian culture. On the one hand, they historically are pictured as stoic, unfriendly, morose, savage and in fact constantly making war on white settlers. However, such reports were most often made by soldiers, missionaries, traders, and others who frequently encountered the Indian in conflict situations. Conversely, they are viewed as friendly, deeply religious, artistic and fond of ceremony and festive occasions. This second characterization seems more consistent than the first with the notion of the importance of sport and games within Indian culture. However, which of the contradictory views is true? Or is there truth in both portrayals.

Regardless of the origin or motivation for the negative portrayals, there is little reason to believe that Indian peoples of the 10th, 15th, or 20th centuries have been predominantly concerned with antisocial activities.

Given the great diversity among Indian cultures throughout America, it is erroneous to imagine a unified picture of Indian sports. Although several games were nearly universal, many others were limited to one tribe . . . Moreover, even where similar games existed, they were often associated with different traditions or cultural significance. Despite these limitations, the most prevalent and popular sports will be presented.

All games and leisure activities among traditional American Indians were categorized by Culin (1907) into either games of dexterity or games of chance. Games of dexterity included active physical contests . . . Betting on athletic contests was a regular practice for both participants and spectators. Gambling in sports was a deeply ingrained tradition and appears to have been universal for tribes on this continent. Betting was used for both relatively minor athletic contests and for major tribal events. The major events, however, led to much heavier wagering. Games of chance, on the other hand, were activities similar to many of our table games of today. They were not dependent upon excellence in strategy but upon "pure chance." Games of chance focused on gambling and including the use of dice, sticks, and other objects was frequently a part of the game.

As with sports and many other customs in Indian life, the practice of games of chance and gambling was dramatically altered during the 19th and 20th centuries. According to the value system of most non-Indians, Indian gambling had an evil connotation. Of course, there had been no such connotation in traditional tribal customs, but the non-Indian value system eventually prevailed because of the influence of colonial religious doctrine and the establishment of regulations by military and political leaders. Consequently, gambling related to games of chance and sports in general, which had been almost universal in the early 1800s, was almost nonexistent by the year 1900. (**34**: xiii, xvii, xix, 141, 142)

Writing Exercise 12: Paraphrasing and Summarizing

Without looking at the "American Indians and Sports" passage again, write down everything you can remember about it as a summary paragraph. Use your own words as much as possible.

Writing Exercise 13: Synthesizing Ideas

Reread the passages on pages 121–124, 150, and 164–166. These passages contain different theories about how early human beings moved between Europe, Asia, and the Americas. Did the earliest people come from Asia to the New World, or did the earliest people move from the Americas to Asia and Europe? Write an essay discussing these theories. Which theory do you believe is true? Use examples from the passages to support your ideas. When you finish your essay, check to see if you used adverbials of contrast and comparison. Are there places in your essay where you could use more? Discuss your ideas in class.

8

ADVERBIAL CLAUSES EXPRESSING CONDITION

Discovering the Grammar of Conditional Sentences

What are conditional sentences? How do you identify them? Discuss what you know about them and then do the first exercise.

Discovery Exercise 1a: Identifying Conditional Sentences

Find the conditional sentences in the passage below. What verb tenses do you see? Are the conditional sentences real or unreal; are they past, present, or future in meaning? What punctuation is there? What does "if any" in number 2 mean?

[1]　　*Scarcity* is a relative concept; scarcity exists for a society because people want more than their resources will allow them to have. As a result, people are forced to choose; if people want literally unlimited goods and services from their limited resources, they must choose which wants to satisfy and which to forgo. In short, society must decide *what* to produce because of scarcity. If wants are severely restricted and resources are relatively superabundant, the question of *what* to produce is trivial—society simply produces everything that everyone wants. Superabundant resources relative to restricted wants also make the question of *how* to produce trivial. If scarcity doesn't exist, superabundant resources can be combined in any manner; waste and inefficiency have no meaning without scarcity. Similarly, *for whom* is meaningless without scarcity; *all* people can consume *all* they want. (**33:** 46)

[2]　　*Substitution Effect*—We assume that people desire a variety of goods and pursue a variety of goals. That means that few, if any, goods are irreplaceable in meeting demand. We are all able to substitute one product

218

for another to satisfy demand. This is commonly called the principle of substitution.

Let's assume now that there are several goods, not exactly the same, or perhaps even very different from one another, but all serving basically the same purpose. If the relative price of one particular good falls, we will most likely substitute in favor of the lower-priced good and against the other similar goods we might have been purchasing. Conversely, if the price of that good rises relative to the price of the other similar goods, we will substitute in favor of them and not buy as much of the now higher-priced good. (**33:** 65)

Discovery Exercise 1b

Compare the conditionals in the following passage with the ones in Exercise 1a. What verb tenses do you see? Are the conditional sentences past or present in meaning? Are the conditionals real or unreal?

One reason for adopting the blade tool-making technique may have been that it made for easy repair of tools. For example, the cutting edge of a tool might consist of a line of razorlike microliths set into a piece of wood. The tool would not be used if just one of the cutting edge's microliths broke off or was chipped. But if the user carried a small prepared core of flint from which an identical-sized microlith could be struck off, the tool could be repaired easily by replacing the lost or broken microlith. (**8:** 100)

Discussion: Real Conditionals—Present, Future vs. Past

Most conditionals that you will see in academic texts are real conditionals in present and future forms. Once in a while, however, you will see real past conditionals like the ones in Exercise 1b. They are useful when an author is describing something that really happened in the past.

Discovery Exercise 2

Find the conditional sentences in the following passage. What tenses do you see? Are they real or unreal? Do you see anything unusual about the verb "be"?

Shotgun experiments involve exposing the total DNA of a given organism to restriction enzymes in order to obtain many DNA fragments. The fragments are then each recombined with DNA from a suitable source and the recombinants are randomly reinserted into a bacterium called *E. Coli.* The result might be unfortunate if the original DNA preparation were to contain genetic material from parasites or from viruses associated with the species under study. For example, shotgun recombinants involving DNA from plant sources could conceivably lead to ecologically dangerous effects if they were to escape into the environment. (**18**: 27)

Explanation 1—Conditionals

Some of the most common adverbial clauses are "if" clauses expressing a condition. Conditional clauses are real (possible, likely) or unreal (impossible, hypothetical). **Real conditional** means that an event is really possible or probable in present or future time or really occurred in the past. **Unreal conditional** means that an event is impossible or highly unlikely to occur in the present or future and did *not* occur in the past.

<blockquote>
subordinate clause comma   main clause

Real   *If* students study, they pass their courses.
(When the first action occurs, the second action, something that is really true, is the result.)
</blockquote>

<blockquote>
Unreal   *If* I were you, I would study hard.
(An impossible situation; the second situation is the hypothetical result of the first.)
</blockquote>

Conditional clauses are different from other adverbial clauses in that verb tenses and modal auxiliaries are used to clarify the reality or unreality of the sentences. For example, we express an unreal present statement using the verb "to be" by using "were" for both singular and plural subjects.

> The result might be unfortunate if the original DNA *were* to contain genetic material from parasites.

Chart 8-1 gives examples of possible combinations of tenses and modal auxiliaries.
    Remember that the adverbial (conditional) clause may appear before or after the main clause.

<blockquote>
main clause   no comma   *if-* clause

You will be able to speak about it with authority if you have knowledge and experience of a particular area.
</blockquote>

"If" is the most common subordinator, but other words and phrases are also used to introduce conditional clauses. These introductory words and phrases are listed in Chart 8-1 on pages 222 and 223.

Reducing If-Clauses

An if-clause may be reduced when it has the same subject as the main clause and the verb *be* (like other adverbial clauses).

> If *you are* ready, *you* may begin.
> *If ready*, you may begin.

Another form of reduction occurs in "if so," "if not," and "if any" phrases. In this type of phrase, "so" or "not" substitute for a previously expressed idea. "Any" is a shortened form of the first part of the if-clause.

> You may need to scrape the wall before you paint it. *If so,* you will need a scraper. *If not*, you may begin to paint immediately.
> That means that few, *if any* goods are irreplaceable in meeting demand.

"If so" means "If you need to scrape the wall before you paint it."
"If not" means "If you do not need to scrape the wall before you paint it."
"If any" means "If there are any goods . . ."

Practicing Conditionals

Practice Exercise 3: Finding Real and Unreal Conditionals

Find the conditional sentences in the following passages. Decide if they are real or unreal and if their meaning is past or present.

[1]   A person learns a culture from the members of his or her group. If you had been born and raised in Japan, you would speak fluent Japanese and feel perfectly comfortable following Japanese customs and traditions. (**14**: 284)

[2]   The American way of life has always been characterized by a number of political subcultures, dividing along the lines of race, wealth, education, religion, sexual preferences, and age. . . . The existence of diverse political subcultures would appear at odds with a political authority concentrated solely in a central government. If the United States had developed into a unitary system, the various political subcultures certainly would have been less able to influence government behavior than they have done and continue to do in our federal system. (**39**: 61, 62)

[3]   The Growth of National-Level Powers—Even if the Great Depression had not occurred, we probably still would have witnessed a growth of national-

CHART 8–1 IF-CLAUSES

Real Conditions

TO EXPRESS:	IF-CLAUSE	MAIN CLAUSE
FUTURE IDEA	**Present tenses** If we leave by ten, If she is eating dinner here, If you plan to be admitted, If you have learned English by next September,	**Future tense** we will arrive by eleven. she should arrive before 6:00. send in your application on time. you can apply to the university.
PRESENT IDEA **PRESENT IDEA—MIXED**	**Present tense** If I am hungry, If she likes English, If you don't understand the examples, If you are having trouble with the exercise,	**Present, present perfect, or past tenses** I usually eat a lot. she has studied it before. you probably didn't read them carefully. you weren't listening to the professor.
	Present perfect tense If Jane has gone, If you have been receiving the checks,	**Present, present perfect, or past tense** John has gone. you mailed us the correct address.
PAST AND PRESENT IDEAS—MIXED **PAST IDEAS**	**Past tense** If you passed the test, If you studied the examples, If I was hungry, If the knife was broken, If they liked the service,	**Present perfect or present** you have been studying hard. you probably understand them now. I ate/ would eat/ used to eat a lot. they could repair it easily. they always left a tip.
	NOTE: Usual meaning = *When, Whenever, If . . . then.* The conditional clause may be in active or passive voice, simple or progressive form. "Can" and "should" are pos- sible. Other words used: *in the event that, on condition that, in case, provided that, suppose, once, unless* = if not.	NOTE: The main clause verb may be imperative, active, or passive voice, simple or progressive form. Present and future modals are possible.

CHART 8-1 IF-CLAUSES
Unreal Conditions

TO EXPRESS:	IF-CLAUSE	MAIN CLAUSE
MOMENT OF SPEAKING OR FUTURE HYPOTHETICAL IDEAS	**Simple past / Past progressive** (active or passive) "Be" = "were" modal "could" If I were you, If I knew the answer, If the book were being used, If he could fly,	**Past modals—Simple / Progressive** (active or passive) "would," "could," "might" I would study every day. I could be writing it on the answer sheet now. it might be ruined by now. he would escape immediately.
UNREAL OR HYPOTHETICAL PAST IDEAS	**Past perfect / Past perfect progressive** (active or passive) "could" perfect form. If I had had a car while I was in California, If they had been driving carefully, If she had been chosen for the position, If he could have gone,	**Past modals—Simple/ Progressive** (active or passive)—"would," "could," "might" I could have visited the Napa Valley. they might not have been injured in the accident. she would have been working in New York. he would have gone.
UNREAL OR HYPOTHETICAL PAST IDEAS MIXED WITH PRESENT OR FUTURE IDEAS	**Past perfect/Past perfect progressive** (active or passive) If we had known about the trip, If you had been studying regularly, If you had been born a king,	**Past modals — Simple/ Progressive** (active or passive) we would be leaving tomorrow. you could attend classes now. you might be ruling your country.
	NOTE: Usual meaning = If . . . then. Other words used: *suppose, supposing that, had, were, could, assume, assuming that*	

level powers as the country became increasingly populated, industrial, and a world power. This meant that problems and situations that were once treated locally would begin to have a profound impact on Americans hundreds or even thousands of miles away. (**39**: 78)

Explanation 2—Occurrence of Real and Unreal Conditional Sentences

Unreal conditional sentences are less common than real conditional sentences in academic writing.

- **Present and future real conditional** sentences occur most often in the hard sciences, economics, and other writing in which the author is speculating about what probably will happen.
- **Past real conditional** is rare but is sometimes used to describe what writers think probably happened in the past.
- **Present and future unreal conditionals** appear in popular scientific articles in which writers speculate about events that haven't happened but might possibly happen, especially something disastrous.
- **Present and past unreal conditionals** are used to give students examples of concepts being explained in a text. Students may be asked to imagine themselves in a particular situation.
- **Past unreal conditional** is used in historical speculative writing in political science, economics, anthropology, or any field that discusses past events.

Practice Exercise 4: Focus on Form—Real Conditionals

Fill in the blanks with the correct forms of the verbs and modal auxiliaries to form *real* conditional sentences. Pay particular attention to the context of the sentences in order to choose the correct tense of the verbs.

[1]   If you (*store*) _____ a cut vegetable or fruit or an opened container of juice, you (*cover*) _____ it tightly with a wrapper that excludes air and (*store*) _____ it in the refrigerator. (**19**: 244)

[2]   It is easy to determine how much the price of an individual commodity has risen: If last year a light bulb (*cost*) _____ 50¢ and this year

it (*cost*) _____ 75¢, there (*be*) _____ a 50 percent rise in the price of that light bulb over a one-year period. (**33**: 168)

[3] In some ancient cultures women were granted a number of rights. In cultures that formed the basis of western civilizations, however, this was not the case. Women were an order apart from male society and had virtually no political or economic rights. For example, if a woman (*become*) _____ widowed, she (*leave*) _____ to find her way back to her father's house or to beg for a living—or, in some cases, to starve. (**39**: 169)

[4] The Ethanol Fermentation Process—The process of making ethanol from corn feedstock is as follows: First, the grain is ground, then mashed and cooked. Enzymes added during the mashing stage convert starch to sugar. The resulting broth is then fermented, using yeast. The process yields a beer (usually of 8%–12% alcohol concentration, by volume) and carbon dioxide. The beer is then distilled to 190 or 191 proof. (Alcohol proof is twice the percent concentration; that is, 200 proof = 100% alcohol.) A dehydration process (*yield*) _____ essentially 200 proof ethanol if anhydrous alcohol (*require*) _____. Denaturing (*not + require*) _____ for ethanol produced on the farm under an experimental permit if the fuel (*use*) _____ within farm boundaries. (**42**: 222)

Practice Exercise 5: Focus on Form—Unreal Conditionals

Fill in the blanks with the correct forms of the verbs and modal auxiliaries to form *unreal* conditional sentences.

[1] Value added is the amount of dollar value contributed to a product by each stage of its production. In Table 8-1 we see the difference between total value of all sales and value added in the production of a donut. We also see that the sum of the values added is equal to the sale price to the final consumer. It is the 15 cents that is used to measure GNP, not the 32 cents. If we (*use*) _____ the 32 cents, we (*be*) _____ double-counting, for we would include the total value of all of the intermediate sales that took place prior to the donut's being sold to its final consumer. Such double-counting (*grossly exaggerate*) _____ GNP if it (*do*) _____ for all goods and services sold. (**33**: 189)

[2] In defining the field of management, it seems imperative to draw some limits for purposes of analysis and research. If we (*be*) _____ to call the entire cultural, biological, and physical universe the field of management, we (*make*) _____ no more progress than (*make*/past form) _____ if chemistry or geology (*undertake*/past form) _____ to cover such a broad field rather than to carve out specific areas for inquiry. As pointed out above, one might say that the field of management should deal with an area of knowledge and inquiry that is manageable. (**27**: 76)

[3] Rockets will never be a cheap and efficient way to lift payloads into space, so alternative and highly speculative technologies are being studied. One is essentially a tether 5,300 miles long, set spinning about its midpoint, which would orbit Earth at a height of 2,600 miles once every three hours. At the lowest part of the swing (just a few miles above the ground) supersonic aircraft could dock with the end. . . . Ivan Bekey of the NASA Office of Space flight sees this system as the forerunner of free-spinning tethers that could lift satellites or spacecraft from low orbit into higher ones or vice versa.

Such a system (*become*) _____ economically attractive if NASA (*be*) _____ to construct a permanent lunar base.
Another structure under discussion called a dynamic "beanstalk" would be built from the ground up but would require a constant expenditure of energy to electromagnetic devices to hold it in place. If its electromagnetic drivers (*be*) _____ to cease operating, the entire tower (*collapse*) _____.

A "beanstalk." The cable would serve as a "space elevator" climbing into the sky. Such a structure could haul 12,000 tons of payload a day into orbit.

(from Gregory Feeley, "Stairways to Heaven," *The Atlantic* 269, no. 3 [March 1992]: 42, 48, 50. Copyright © Gregory Feeley. Reprinted by permission.)

Asteroid: An irregularly shaped object, made of stone or metal, that orbits the sun between Mars and Jupiter. Collisions or chance tugs from Jupiter can knock it across Earth's orbit.
Comet: One of hundreds of chunks of frozen gases and dust that travel in elongated orbits from beyond Pluto to near the Sun.

[4]   A rocky asteroid with a diameter between 30 and 300 feet blows up in a blinding flash when it smacks into the atmosphere, as did the comet or asteroid that exploded over Tunguska, Siberia, one June morning in 1908. Exploding five miles up with the force of 12 megatons, it annihilated reindeer 30 miles away, ignited the clothes of a man 60 miles away and leveled more than 700 square miles of Siberian forest. A sturdier asteroid, one made of nickel and iron rather than stone, would plunge to the ground without exploding. If one the size of the Tunguska rock (*hit*)

_____ the rural United States, calculates John Pike, director of space policy for the Federation of American Scientists, it (*kill*)

_____ almost 70,000 people and cause $4 billion in property damage. It could also flatten buildings 12 miles away, according to the NASA panel. If it (*hit*) _____ an urban area, there (*be*) _____ upwards of 300,000 deaths. If it (*hit*) _____ a seismic zone, it (*trigger*) _____ earthquakes topping 7.5 on the Richter scale.

On March 23, 1989, an asteroid a half mile across missed earth by just 700,000 miles. No one saw it coming; if it (*arrive*) _____ a mere six hours later, it (*wipe out*) _____ civilization. "Earth runs its course about the sun in a swarm of asteroids," says astronomer Donald Yeomans of NASA's Jet Propulsion Laboratory in Pasadena, Calif. "Sooner or later, our planet will be struck by one of them."

(from Sharon Begley, "The Science of Doom," *Newsweek*, November 23, 1992, pp. 56–60. All rights reserved. Reprinted by permission.)

Analysis of Conditionals

Analysis Exercise 6: Comparing and Contrasting Forms—Predicting

Compare the verb tenses and modal auxiliaries you used in the real conditional sentences in Exercise 4 and the unreal conditional sentences in Exercise 5. You probably noticed that the if—clauses in real and unreal conditional sentences have different forms of the verb. Use this knowledge to answer the following questions and predict what verbs will be appropriate in the main clauses.

1. Imagine that you are reading an academic or scientific article and suddenly see a sentence beginning with "If it were possible . . ." Do you expect to see a real or unreal conditional in the main clause?
2. While you are reading the academic or scientific article, you see "if it is possible . . ." What do you expect to see next, a real or an unreal conditional?
3. As you are reading the academic or scientific article, you see a verb with "might" or "could." Is the sentence likely to be real or unreal?
4. While you are reading the academic or scientific article, you see "if + can," or "may," or "should + verb." Is the sentence likely to be real or unreal?

Analysis Exercise 7: Conditionals with *when, suppose,* and *once*

Examine the following sentences. Can you change each into a sentence with "if" and still retain its meaning?

1. When you are searching for a book whose title you know, look it up under the first important word of the title.

2. Suppose you are planning a speech on gun control; you may wish to interview a social science professor.

3. Suppose you had been born in 1500. What would your life have been like?

4. Once you have decided that the book will be useful, check it out.

5. Suppose you were president of your country. What changes would you make?

Discussion

"If," "when," "suppose," and "once" can all introduce real conditional sentences. Such real conditional sentences contain a comma after the "if," "when," and "once" clauses and a semicolon or period after the "suppose" clause.

"Suppose" is also used to introduce unreal conditional sentences.

Practice Exercise 8a: Suppose—Real and Unreal

Fill in the blanks in the following passage, using the correct forms of the verbs in parentheses. "Real" or "unreal" is indicated in brackets in front of each part.

Alfred Kroeber provided an interesting example to illustrate the distinction between the inborn character of most nonhuman behavior and the learned cultural behavior of human beings. [real]Suppose we (*hatch*) _____ some ant eggs on a deserted island. The resulting ant colony (*be*) _____ an exact reproduction of the previous generation of ants, including their social behavior. Ants (*have*) _____ a set of rules they follow in acting together as a group, but these rules (*not/learn*) _____ as a result of interaction with other ants of the previous generation. They (*be*) _____ instinctive and part of the heredity of the ants in each new generation. That is why we can be sure that the newly hatched ants will be and act exactly like their parents' generation, even though they (*never/see*) _____ any members of that generation.

[unreal] Suppose we (*do*) _____ the same with a group of infants from our own society (pretending for the moment that it (*be*) _____ possible). Certainly we (*not/ expect*) _____ the same results— a generation of people just like their parents. Rather the result (*be*) _____ a horde of people essentially without culture. If they (*be*) _____ somehow able to survive (which (*be*) _____ impossible), they (*develop*) _____ their own culture, different from any other way of life on earth. They (*not/speak*) _____ a language that was intelligible to anyone else, nor _____ they (*dress*) _____ or eat or do anything else in a way that reflected their parents' culture. (14: 284–285)

Analysis Exercise 8b

Look back at the passage and answer these questions.

1. How far does the "real" concept extend after the first "suppose"?
2. How far does the "unreal" concept extend after the second "suppose"?

The real and unreal concepts that writers express often extend far into a passage. Conditional ideas are not necessarily limited to the conditional sentences themselves.

Using Conditionals to Write Answers to Academic Questions

Writing Exercise 9

Read the following short passages and then answer the questions, using complete sentences. When you have finished, review your answers. Did you use any conditionals?

[1]   The diet of termites includes cellulose, a substance that they cannot digest. The flagellate protozoans that digest the cellulose of wood particles while living in the gut of termites are good examples of *mutualism*. The termite needs the protozoans to digest the wood that it eats; the protozoans need the termite for shelter and the nutrients it provides. (**1**: 981)

a. What would happen if the termites were experimentally rid of the protozoans?

[2]   In the past half century, there has been a widespread eradication of many predatory animals in various parts of the world. After timber wolves, the natural predator of white-tailed deer were deliberately eliminated from northern Wisconsin by unrestricted hunting, the deer population rose to unprecedented levels. (**1**: 978)

a. What can happen if an animal population rises to extremely high levels?
b. What would happen if the timber wolves were reintroduced into northern Wisconsin?

[3]   A study on species diversity in intertidal zones showed that when all sea stars (starfish) had been removed, the numbers of barnacles and mussels increased greatly. As they competed with each other for the available spaces on rocks, one species of mussel preempted the space,

reducing the number of species of marine invertebrates in these areas from fifteen to eight. (1: 979)

a. How could scientists increase the diversity of marine invertebrates in the intertidal zone?

[4]   In a series of experiments, separate mouse populations with unlimited food and water were established in six 2-by-8-meter boxes. In three of the pens, the food, water, and nesting boxes were scattered throughout the pens; in the other three pens, all the food and water was placed at one end, and all the nesting boxes were crowded together at the other. . . . As the populations grew, so did the fighting among adults. . . . Fighting was often followed by trampling of nests, which led to desertion or cannibalism of litters by the females. Although food was abundant, food intake was reduced and . . . birth rates dropped off. (1: 973)

a. What will happen if the population of mice continues to rise?
b. What might have happened if the populations of mice had not changed in size?
c. If this were a description of human populations and overcrowding, how would it differ? How would it be similar?

Analysis Exercise 10: Identifying Conditional Sentences

Find and underline the conditional sentences in the following case study of a manager in a McDonald's restaurant. Note whether the sentences are real or unreal and present or past in meaning. Then answer the questions that follow.

BACK TO THE CASE

Jim Delligatti could use the management science approach to solve any operational problems that arose. According to the scientific method, Delligatti would first spend some time observing what takes place in one of his restaurants. Next, he would use these observations to outline exactly how the restaurant operated as a whole. Third, he would apply his understanding of restaurant operations by predicting how various changes might help or hinder the restaurant as a whole. Before implementing possible changes, he would test them on a scale to see if they actually affected the restaurant as desired.

If Delligatti were to accept the contingency approach to management, his actions as a manager would depend on the situation. For example, *if* some customers hadn't been served within sixty seconds because the deep-fat fryer had unexpectedly broken down, *then* Delligatti probably would not hold his employees responsible. But *if* he knew that the fryer had broken down because of employee mistreatment or neglect, *then* his reaction to the situation would likely be very different.

Delligatti could also apply the system approach and view each of his restaurants as a system, or a number of interdependent parts that function as a whole to reach desired restaurant objectives. Naturally, each restaurant would be seen as an open system—a system that exists in and is influenced by its environment. Major factors within the environment of a McDonald's restaurant would include customers, suppliers, competitors, and the government. For example, if one of McDonald's fast-food competitors were to significantly lower its price for hamburgers to a point well below what McDonald's was asking for a hamburger, Delligatti might be forced to consider modifying different parts of his restaurant system in order to meet or beat that price.

(from Samuel C. Certo, *Principles of Modern Management*, 4th ed. [Needham Heights, Mass.: Allyn and Bacon, 1989], p. 47.)

1. Did you underline all the sentences in the first paragraph of the case study? They are conditional.Where is the if-clause for the first nine sentences of the passage?
2. What do you notice that is unusual about the conditional sentences in the passage? Do they follow the rules? How are they different? Discuss your ideas with other students in the class.

Explanation 3—Unusual Conditionals

Students at the upper intermediate and advanced level of English usually have a good understanding of conditional rules at the sentence level. Yet, an examination of some typical university-level texts, journals, and newsmagazines reveals that several forms of the conditional do not follow the usual "rules."

- Authentic conditionals may be introduced by words and phrases other than the words we have practiced so far ("if," "when," "once," and "suppose").

  With some help, they might succeed.

  Given one 16- and one 8-bit DAC with equivalent nonlinearity specs, the 18-bit unit will produce less measurable distortion than the 16-bit unit even when only its top 16 bits are used.

  Exceed either parameter and the material ceases to be a superconductor.

  Should a contest be arranged between honey and wheat germ, another favorite item in health food stores, the wheat germ would win hands down.

What remains is not necessarily what the people might have left *had* they *wanted* to give archeologists a clear picture of what was important to them.

Last week Lindow won permission to start his own experiment—*barring* a new court challenge from Rifkin.

- Authentic conditionals make extensive use of the passive voice and continuous forms of the verbs.

    Experts estimate that the vast majority of these fatalities *could have been prevented* and most injuries *reduced* if child restraint systems *had been used.*

    It is clear that if the system *were not moving,* both ropes *would be pulling* up on the pulley and weight.

- Authentic conditionals extend over whole paragraphs or even further. We usually assume that one if-clause is always followed by one result clause, or vice versa. In fact, sometimes this is not true. Authentic conditionals often have an extended result. In this type of paragraph you will see not one result, but several in different sentences.

    Notice that the most important insect herbivore in the monoculture is eaten by a single species of bird. What *would happen if* a disease or bad weather greatly *reduced* the numbers of that bird? The insect *would multiply* unchecked until it depleted its food supply, the crop, but it *would be* too late to save the monoculture. (9: 75)

- Authentic conditionals cause difficulties because authors also sometimes intentionally mix real and unreal conditions within a single sentence. This author shifts from real to unreal.

    There are 10,000 pennies in a jar. One way to estimate the distribution of the dates on the pennies—without examining all 10,000—is to take a representative sample. . . . If the pennies *are very well mixed* within the jar and if you *take* a larger sample, the resulting distribution *would probably approach* the actual distribution of the dates of all 10,000 coins. (39: 206)

- Authentic conditionals can include an if-clause that is only implied.

    The deal would be good for 8 million American farmers and 1 billion Chinese, and it would help solidify diplomatic relations between Washington and Peking, and it was a timely boost for Jimmy Carter. Last week the administration announced that an agriculture negotiating team in China had reached an "agreement in principle" committing the Chinese to buy between 6 million and 9 million metric tons of U.S. grain annually for 3 years, starting in 1981.

    (from "Politics of Grain: Enter the Dragon," *Newsweek*, October 20, 1980, p. 77.)

Practice Exercise 11: Mixed Conditionals

Find the mixed real and unreal conditions below. Why do you think an author writes this way?

> *Real Income Effect*—If the price of some item that you purchase goes down while your money income and all other prices stay the same, your ability to purchase goods in general goes up. That is to say, your effective purchasing power is increased, even though your money income has stayed the same. If you purchase 20 gallons of gas a week at $1 per gallon, your total outlay for gas is $20. If the price goes down by 50 percent, to 50 cents a gallon, you would only have to spend $10 per week to purchase the same number of gallons of gas. If your money income and the prices of other goods remain the same, it would be possible for you to continue purchasing 20 gallons of gas a week and to purchase more of other goods. You will feel richer and will indeed probably purchase a bit more of a number of goods, including perhaps even more gasoline. (**33**: 65)

Practice Exercise 12: Finding Hidden Conditionals in Context

Find the hidden conditionals in the following newspaper article. Does one result clause always follow one conditional clause? Then think about how you could express the hidden conditions another way. Discuss your ideas in class.

> *Without Mass Extinction, Dinosaurs Might Be in Charge*
>
> Ever wonder what the world might be like had dinosaurs escaped extinction 65 million years ago? For starters, an intelligent, lizard-eyed skinhead probably would've released a movie about Jurassic-age mammals who never evolved beyond a rudimentary stage.
>
> Dale Russell, a paleontologist with the Canadian Museum of Nature, Ottawa, believes that had a catastrophic comet or asteroid not exploded into the Yucatan peninsula all those eons ago (the latest extinction theory), the dinosaurs surely would have continued as the ascendant animal on Earth. . . . As long as dinos existed, Russell maintains, mammals would have remained relatively insignificant creatures.
>
> A basic question that underlies Russell's flight of fancy is whether evolution is random. "I don't think it is," he says. "There's a signal in the history of life on Earth, a trend, a pattern, a regularity."
>
> Basically life evolves from the simple to the complex. Evidence of that premise is all around us.

And had an extraterrestrial object not shaken the planet with an explosion Russell describes as 10,000 times more powerful than the force that would be unleashed by the detonation of all the world's nuclear weapons, dinos, he asserts would still be with us.

Working with a sculptor, Russell has conceived a model of what he calls dinosauroid, or dinosaurman, and what would probably be a distant cousin, Troodon. Dino-man and Troodon, Russell believes, would have had a common ancestor.

Dinoman

Troodon, like some other small, meat-eating dinosaurs of the Cretaceous period, had a brain relative to its size far larger than those of contemporary reptiles.

It also had other features we would consider advantageous: It walked on two legs; had a flexible and opposable digit on its three-fingered hands; and its large eyes were set forward, providing stereoscopic vision. Troodon might have been warmblooded, or tepid blooded. . . . In any case, dino-man's metabolic rate most certainly would have increased over the millenia, and at the same time, his size would have diminished to a more human scale.

Russell's dino-man, which eerily resembles drawings of space aliens, is hairless and toothless (with a mouth equipped with biting and chewing surfaces) and has long arms and feet with three toes. . . .

There is no reason to believe, Russell says, that the brain of the dinosaur would not have evolved just as remarkably as that of the human species.

(from Margo Harakas, "Dinoman, "*The Des Moines Register,* June 17, 1993, p. 1T. Copyright © *Sun Sentinel* (Fort Lauderdale). Reprinted by permission.)

Practice Exercise 13: Rewriting Hidden Conditionals

Rewrite the hidden conditionals below. Change them to conditional sentences with if-clauses.

1. Without new facts, induction from them of significant relationships, testing of hypotheses, and development of principles, we would never understand our universe.

2. Had the physical and biological sciences waited, we might still be living in caves.

3. In 1800 B.C. the ruler of Babylonia decreed that anyone caught violating his price-wage freeze would be drowned. Babylonia endured 1,000 years of such price fixing.

4. Scientists testified that genetically engineered organisms, without natural predators or other controls, might spread unchecked, like the chestnut blight or gypsy moth.

5. To the extent that you hold no-interest bearing cash, you will lose because of inflation.

6. Nelson Mandela is 10 months younger than John F. Kennedy would have been, had he lived.

President Nelson Mandela
of South Africa

7. Hume believed that the mind was a kind of theatre where several perceptions successively made their appearance. . . . Given this definition of the mind, it should come as no surprise to learn that Hume debunks the notion of the soul and of the self.

8. Assuming that other things in the economy didn't change, this argument might indeed have been a possible refutation of the law of demand.

9. The way we have drawn the diagram, demand has increased more than supply, so price has gone up from P_e to P'_e. But the converse could have been true, and the price could have fallen.

Analyzing the Meaning of Conditionals

Analysis Exercise 14: Determining the Author's Meaning from Context

Read the following passage and fill in the blanks with the conditional or other verb forms that express the ideas that you think the author intended when he wrote this passage.

On January 1, 1966, federal law mandated health-warning labels for all cigarette packages, and since January 2, 1971, cigarette advertising has been banned on radio and television. . . . Smoking on short-distance (and some longer-duration) airline flights (*ban*) _____ and many insurance companies (*provide*) _____ favorable rates on life and car insurance premiums to nonsmokers.

Thus far, however, the act of smoking itself is perfectly legal, just so long as people do not light up where it is specifically prohibited. What (*happen*) _____ , though, if some states (*be*) _____ to make smoking completely illegal?

One thing that is practically certain, based on past attempts to outlaw alcohol, fireworks, or harmful drugs, is that compliance with such laws (*be/not*) _____ total. Cigarettes and other smoking materials (*smuggle*) _____ into states that had declared their ownership or consumption to be illegal. Entrepreneurs (*ensure*) _____ the survival of a smokers' subculture by fulfilling the demand for tobacco products. . . . Cautionary images of people being fined and possibly imprisoned for the act of lighting up (*appear*) _____ on the nation's television screens. . . . A smokers' civil rights movement (*arise*) _____ quite likely _____ , and the nation's legislatures, courts, and political executives (*embroil*) _____ in efforts by pro- and antismoking forces to enforce or change the laws.

If the ban on smoking really (*be*) _____ successful, we (*expect*) _____ to have a lower rate of smoking-related health problems, such as lung cancer and emphysema. . . . With smoking-related diseases reduced, the nation's medical agenda (*shift*) _____ toward more AIDS- , breast cancer- , or stroke-prevention and the problems of aging. Of course, serious political and economic problems (*be*) _____ almost inevitable in states where large numbers of people in the tobacco-related farm, manufacturing, and service sectors (*thrown out*) _____ of work . . . If some states successfully adopted antismoking statutes, one result (*be*) _____ effective national action to do the same. . . . It should be kept in mind, however, that at least one previous attempt to ban smoking through state legislation (*fail*) _____. Social reformers (*launch*) _____ a campaign to enact anticigarette laws in nine southern and western states before World War I. By 1929, however, increased advertising, women's political emancipation, and illegal liquor consumption (*act*) _____ together with other social forces to blunt that early movement to prohibit cigarette consumption by adults. (**39:** 612)

Using Conditionals in Writing

Writing Exercise 15: Answering Academic Questions with Conditionals

Answer the following questions using the information you learned in Exercise 14. Review your answers to see if you used any conditionals. If you didn't, which answers could also be expressed with conditionals? Discuss the possible answers.

1. What is the purpose of the passage in Exercise 14?
2. According to the author, how would state laws making smoking illegal affect the people in those states?
3. Where else could smoking be made illegal, and when might that happen?
4. Does the author believe that smoking will be banned? How do you know?

Writing Exercise 16: Paraphrasing and Summarizing with Conditionals

Summarize the following passage on sampling techniques by completing the paraphrased sentences that follow it.

> How can interviewing several thousand voters tell us what tens of millions of voters will do? Clearly, it is necessary that the sample of several thousand individuals be representative of all voters in the population. Consider an analogy. Let us say we have a large jar containing pennies of various dates and we want to know how many pennies were minted within certain decades— 1940–1949, 1950–1960, and so on. There are 10,000 pennies in the jar. One way to estimate the distribution of the dates on the pennies without examining all 10,000 is to take a representative sample. This sample would be obtained by mixing the pennies up well and then removing a handful of them— perhaps 100 pennies. . . . If the pennies are very well mixed within the jar and if you take a larger sample, the resulting distribution would probably approach the distribution of the dates of all 10,000 coins.
>
> The most important principle in sampling, or poll taking, is randomness. Every penny or every person should have an equal chance of being sampled. If this happens, then a small sample should be representative of the whole group both in demographic characteristics (age, religion, race, living area, and the like) and in opinions. The ideal way to sample the voting population of the United States would be to put all voter names into a jar—or a computer —and randomly sample, say, 2000 of them. . . . Since this is too costly and inefficient, pollsters have developed other ways to obtain good samples. One of the most interesting techniques is simply to

choose a random selection of telephone numbers and interview the respective households. This technique produces an accurate sample at an inexpensive price. (**39**: 205–206)

(Your paraphrased version):

If we wanted to know how many pennies had been minted within certain decades, _____ a representative sample. If we wanted to get a representative distribution of dates, _____

_____ . It would be possible to nearly get the distribution of all 10,000 coins _____

_____. Sampling people is the same as sampling pennies. The chances of being sampled must be as equal as possible. If we want to give every person an equal chance of being sampled,

_____

random. If poll taking were not truly random, _____ not be truly representative. If _____ , one would put all voter names into a computer in order to _____.

This method may be too expensive. If one wanted a cheap, accurate sample,

_____ .

Writing Exercise 17: Paraphrasing and Summarizing by Answering Questions

Read the following passage about Vitamin C. Then paraphrase it by answering the questions that follow.

Does Vitamin C Prevent Colds?

According to a theory widely publicized by Linus Pauling, vitamin C prevents colds. Pauling's book *Vitamin C and the Common Cold* first came out in 1970. In it, he stated that the RDA (recommended daily allowance) for vitamin C was far too low. RDA amounts will prevent scurvy, but according to Pauling, much larger quantities are necessary to enable the vitamin to perform its other functions, one of which is to protect cells from attack by cold-causing viruses. Pauling says that our ancestors evolved on a vegetarian diet, which provided far more vitamin C than meat eaters consume at present. Because evolution takes place very slowly, our bodies doubtless have not changed since prehistoric times. Therefore, we still need large quantities of vitamin C today. Pauling advocates taking 1g or 2 g (1000 to 2000 mg) of vitamin C per day, about 20 to 40 times the RDA.

Many controlled, double-blind studies on vitamin C and colds have been performed since Pauling's controversial book first came out. A pooling of the data from eight of these showed that there was a difference of a tenth of a cold per year and an average difference in duration of a tenth of a day per cold in those subjects taking vitamin C over those taking the placebo (sugar pill). These are enough data to support the tentative conclusion that the statistical effects of vitamin C, if any, are very small. This does not exclude the possibility that the effects on a few individuals might be considerable. The difficulties of performing research of this kind were shown vividly in one study, in which a questionnaire given at the end revealed that a number of the subjects had guessed the contents of their capsules. A reanalysis of the results showed that those who received the placebo who thought they were receiving vitamin C had fewer colds than the group receiving vitamin C who thought they were receiving placebos! (**19**: 256)

Answer the following questions about the vitamin C passage. Then review your answers to see if you have used any conditional sentences. If not, which questions could you answer with conditional sentences? Rewrite some of your answers and then use all of your answers to write a summary of the passage.

1. What does Linus Pauling's book say about vitamin C?
2. How does Pauling's book compare our needs with our ancestors' needs for vitamin C?
3. What do studies show about the use of vitamin C and the occurrence and severity of colds?
4. How did the questionnaire reveal that this kind of research is difficult?
5. What is likely to happen in a research project on vitamin C and colds if the people take a pill that they think is vitamin C even though it isn't vitamin C?
6. What might happen to people receiving vitamin C pills who think that they are receiving placebos (sugar pills)?

Analyzing Other Ways to Express Hypothetical Ideas

Analysis Exercise 18

Fill in the blanks below with "whether," "as if," or "as though." Notice which sentences are appropriate with "unreal" forms.

John Dun Scotus (1265–1308), a Franciscan philosopher, was tied to Thomas Aquinas (1225–1274) at every stage of development of his own thought. Scotus agreed with Aquinas that ethical conduct is conducted in accord with right reason. . . . Is Scotus' Christian morality simply the arbitrary submission of one's free will to the dictates of God's law?

(1) Scotus does not assign this much weight to the will, _____ the human will or God's will. (2) For Scotus we detect a suspicion of absolute moral judgments, _____ such judgments limit God's ability to change his mind.

Modern philosophy begins with Scottish philosopher David Hume (1711–1776). (3) As far as philosophical reasoning is concerned, Hume is a skeptic. But as far as living in the real world is concerned, he says that it would be absurd to act _____ things and the self _____ not exist. (4) Early modern philosophers could not bring themselves to act _____ contemporary science really did operate simply according to mechanical laws. (5) If we focus on the attempt by early modern philosophy—_____ of the ritualist or empiricist variety—to give a uniform and satisfactory explanation of the objective nature of reality, we would have to admit that it got off to a terrible start from which it never really recovered. (**16**: 81,139,141,140)

(6) Manufacturing is essentially the art of transforming raw materials or, very often, semifinished products into goods and articles (_____ they are means of production or articles of consumption). . . . (7) The product, _____ it be a machine, tool, household machine, building product, computer, automobile, aircraft, chemical processing plant, power station, oil drilling rig, cookware, or soft-drink container, is designed to fulfill its intended function. (**37**: 12)

True epilepsy in dogs occurs, as a rule, in animals aged between one and two years, and has been noted most frequently in cocker spaniels. No one knows if the epileptic dog experiences the aura characteristic of human epilepsy, but (8) some animals have been observed to show signs of uneasiness, or to appear to stare vacantly, _____ they _____ aware of an impending attack. The sequence of events leading up to the suspected epileptic episode should be learned, and an exact description of the seizure should be obtained. (**21**: 565)

Explanation 4—Other Ways to Express Hypothetical Ideas

Whether

	clause	conjunction clause
Real clause:	We will begin at 9:00 *whether* you *are* there or not.
	(implies two or more alternatives)

	subjunctive clause	comma	clause
Unreal clause:	*Whether* it *be* true or false, the idea appeals to everyone.
	(implies doubt)		(all verb tenses possible)

                    subordinator + phrase   comma   clause
    Phrase: *Whether* touch tone or pulse, AT&T provides telephones.

As if
As though
                    linking verb subordinator   subordinate clause
        Real clause: He looks *as though*   he *is* sick.
                                 as if

    Unreal clause: She acts *as if* she *were* the president of the United States.
                                 as though

In academic writing the conjunction "whether" and the subordinators "as if" and
"as though" are similar to the conditional. ("As if" means "as it would be if.") "As
if" and "as though" are very similar to the "if" in conditional sentences and
express real or contrary-to-fact ideas.

"Whether" is used with "real" and "unreal" forms of the verb. In conditional
sentences, the subjunctive form (unreal) is used to express contrary-to-fact and
hypothetical ideas. In the case of "whether," the writer probably uses the subjunctive to express doubt.

Using Adverbials for Synthesizing: Paraphrasing More Than One Source to Write a Summary

You have read about American Indians and sports and games. The following passage and article describe gambling on Indian reservations today.

> *A Brief History of North American Indian Tribes and Gambling in the 1980s*
> American Indians consider gambling to be expressions of tribal sovereignty
> and a means to economic development. Many elders say, "We have always
> gambled, so inclusion of gambling as a past way of life is good."
>
> Indian tribes all over the United States have been running bingo games
> on their reservations for many years. In 1979 the state of Florida sued the
> Miami Seminole Indians for breaking a law prohibiting bingo prizes of more
> than $100. In 1982 a federal appeals court made a historical decision. The
> court ruled that the Seminoles were a sovereign nation; therefore, state civil
> regulation did not apply to them. Within five years, tribes around the nation
> (113 games businesses) were earning $225 million a year. In 1987, the
> Supreme Court ruled that Indians could operate any form of gambling per-
> mitted by a state.
>
> Meanwhile during the '80s, federal funding for Indian reservations was cut
> drastically. Tribes were suffering high rates of unemployment and were heav-
> ily dependent on the government for social services. They desperately needed

other sources of funding. In 1988, Congress approved the "Indian Gaming Act" to use gambling as "a means of promoting tribal economic development, self-sufficiency, and strong tribal governments." Aware that communities with legalized gambling have had problems with an increase in all types of crime, alcoholism, and drug abuse, Congress set up a regulatory commission, the National Indian Gaming Commission (NIGC). It is interesting to note that most tribes were against the Indian Gaming Act prior to its passage because they saw it as an infringement of tribal sovereignty.

(Adapted from D. R. Segal, "Dances with Sharks," *The Washington Monthly* 24: 26–30, March 1992, and an interview with Jerry Stubben, chairman of the American Indian Studies program at Iowa State University and adviser to the Native American Student Association.)

Gambling on the Reservation: Native Americans hope to make casinos pay off

Consecrating the land is an ancient Native American tradition. This week, on the Mashantucket Pequot reservation in Connecticut, a medicine man will stand before a massive boulder. Slow Turtle will bless the grounds and the low-slung building that stands on them—The Foxwoods High Stakes Bingo & Casino. Costing $58 million (a Malaysian company that operates casinos in Asia loaned $55 million), the plush gambling establishment will open on Feb. 15, offering visitors 150 gaming tables, off-track betting, three restaurants, and valet parking. The casino, which will employ 2,300 workers, promises to be a boon to the local economy—and a bonanza for the 200-member tribe. With the opening of Foxwoods, the $41 billion reservation gambling industry enters a new era of sophistication. But the tribes also face stricter regulation, thanks to a crackdown by the recently formed National Indian Gaming Commission (NIGC). Over the past decade, makeshift bingo halls began popping up on reservations; some offered slot machines and other games, which violated state laws. Since Indian reservations are under federal authority, states could do little to stop the trend. On some reservations, corrupt casino managers pocketed profits meant for the tribe, and there was evidence that the mob had tried to horn in. Tony Hope, 50, appointed by President Bush to be NIGC chairman, thinks the mafia scare was overstated, but the need for regulation was clear: in 1988, Congress passed the Indian Gaming Regulatory Act, which created the NIGC. . . . The NIGC's first act angered tribes in the West. . . . The NIGC endorsed existing legislation that banned slot-type machines unless they were approved in a "compact" with the state. That same week, California lawmen had raided gaming halls in the San Diego area and confiscated 230 slot-type video games. Since slots are the most popular form of gambling, tribes believe that Las Vegas was threatened by the competition and pressured for the raid. . . . In California and New Mexico, tribes are petitioning, or suing, the states to allow slot-type machines. . . .

While the gambling wars rage, other gaming halls welcome regulations. "If we had had them back in the 80's," says Albuquerque's "Bingo Bob" Boles, "we wouldn't be facing these problems now." . . . More regulations will be approved in the months ahead. . . .

Despite misgivings, gambling is on the reservation to stay. Seeing casinos as a way to reduce welfare rolls, Minnesota gave 11 tribes the go-ahead to open casinos; last year five of them alone netted $51 million. While many Indians deplore gambling, others believe it should have a chance. "It's like any other freemarket enterprise," says NIGC commissioner Jana McKeag, a Cherokee from Oklahoma. "With good managers and a solid tribal government, it will succeed." Native Americans have a high stake in trying to ensure that payoff: at last count, the average unemployment rate on the nation's reservations stood at 40 percent.

(from J.N. Baker, "Gambling on the Reservation," *Newsweek*, February 17, 1992, p. 29. Newsweek, Inc. Reprinted by permission.)

Writing Exercise 19: Synthesizing to Write an Essay

Read the preceding passage and news article about gambling on Indian reservations. Combine and use all the information you have about American Indians and sports and games to write an essay. Discuss the development of gambling as it relates to Native American cultural traditions. Why, for example, is gambling a logical industry for Native Americans? What is your opinion of these new gambling businesses? What do you think will happen in the future? Review the passage on American Indians and sports (pages 215–217) before you begin. When you have finished, review your work to see how many different types of sentences you used. A variety of structures indicates effective writing.

Preparing for Standardized Tests

Practice Exercise 20

Choose the best answer to complete each sentence below.

1. If the eyes were not limited to "light" sensitivity, "seeing" _____ like getting hundreds of different "channels" at once.
   a. is   c. would be
   b. will be   d. was

2. _____ they are using oxygen, microorganisms are breaking down organic molecules into simpler ones.
   a. Yet   c. As if
   b. While   d. Unless

3. Hearing aids are of no help to a person with nerve deafness _____ can-not reach the brain no matter how loud the sound.
   a. because of auditory messages   c. until auditory messages
   b. because auditory messages   d. due to auditory messages

4. Information processing is very important indeed, _____ it is still only a tool.
   a. but   c. or
   b. and   d. however

5. _____ its edible fruits and its possibility as cattle food, a cactus called prickly pear was transplanted from the Western Hemisphere to Australia.
   a. Because   c. Because of
   b. Although   d. Despite of

6. Competition is based on serving the function at minimum cost; _____ , cost considerations will always enter into the choice of manufacturing processes.
   a. whereas   c. however
   b. hence   d. nevertheless

7. A person who is completely color blind sees the world _____ a black and white movie.
   a. as if it were   c. as if it is
   b. as if it was   d. as if it would be

8. Correlations in psychology are rarely perfect. The closer the correlation coefficient is to + 1.00 or − 1.00, _____ .
   a. the relationship is stronger
   b. the strong relationship is obtained
   c. and there is a strong relationship
   d. the stronger the relationship

9. Determining a protein's primary structure is a formidable task, _____ it is an essential prelude to comprehensive chemical and biophysical studies.
   a. yet   c. once
   b. or   d. if

10. Many strong-swimming, wide-ranging animals such as tuna and whales live in the open ocean; _____ , the open ocean produces only a fraction of the world's fish catch.
    a. thus   c. however
    b. therefore   d. and

11. _____ the human species' destruction of forests of the Mediterranean region, Western people began to clear the deciduous forest of Europe and North America.
    a. Because   c. Therefore
    b. After   d. Until

12. While some people sleep _____ they don't want to, a far greater number have trouble getting enough sleep.
    a. as
    b. after
    c. when
    d. even

13. _____ , modern humans, like their ancient ancestors, will walk long distances, fight, work from sunup to sundown, or even steal or kill to obtain it.
    a. If their deprived of food
    b. If deprived of food.
    c. If they depriving of food
    d. If they are being depriving of food.

14. Evergreen plants shed their leaves individually after the leaves are two or three years old. _____ , in an evergreen forest there is a continual falling of leaves.
    a. Therefore
    b. Even though
    c. But
    d. However

15. The water penny beetle is _____ flat that it appears to be a bump on a stone.
    a. too
    b. as
    c. such
    d. so

16. The animals found in a particular region are called the fauna of that region; _____ , it is correct to say that different biogeographic regions have different faunas.
    a. otherwise
    b. therefore
    c. despite
    d. whereas

17. Lakes and ponds in the temperate zone, _____ , have certain features in common with the oceans.
    a. if they are sufficiently large
    b. if they were sufficiently large
    c. if they had been sufficiently large
    d. if they would be sufficiently large

18. The starling is _____ serious pest in so many ways that it is difficult to calculate the damage it has caused in the cities.
    a. such a
    b. not a
    c. only a
    d. a so

Find and circle the letter of the one error in each of the following sentences. Then write the correct form above the error.

1. Before industrialization <u>many</u> wastes did not exist; only around <u>a few</u>

                                        a   b

    large cities <u>sewage wastes</u> <u>were</u> a problem.
                       c   d

2. <u>Very</u> little money has gone <u>into</u> biological control <u>in spite of</u> it is not
        a   b   c

    profitable for companies to sell a product that reproduces <u>itself</u>.
                                                                 d

3. <u>Unlike</u> clinical psychologists, psychiatrists are also interested <u>in</u>
       a   b

    treating <u>human</u> problems, but they are trained <u>differently</u>.
                   c   d

4. <u>A</u> hypothesis is a description or explanation that remains <u>tentative</u> or
    a   b

    exploratory <u>however</u> it has not <u>yet</u> been adequately tested.
                  c   d

5. The United States now has <u>strict</u> regulations about the introduction of
                                       a

    <u>any</u> animal or plant and severe penalties for violations; <u>unless</u>,
     b   c

    newspapers and magazines often have stories of new organisms which

    have been brought in <u>anyway</u>.
                             d

6. The rods and cones of the eye, <u>like</u> other receptor cells, would respond
                                      a

    less to a constant stimulus <u>were it</u> not for the fact that the eye <u>normal</u>
                                     b   c

    makes <u>thousands</u> of tiny movements every minute.
               d

7. <u>Because</u> striving to satisfy <u>functional</u> requirements, the designer must
         a   b

    be <u>aware of</u> <u>manufacturing</u> implications.
         c   d

8. Despite of intense research, a generalized mechanistic understanding
       a   b
   of proteins remains obscure.
       c   d

9. Whereas a child enters school, the child's friends become an important
       a   b c
   influence on behavior and attitudes.
           d

10. Even if the Great Depression had not occurred, we probably still will
      a   b c
    have witnessed a growth of national-level powers as the country became
    increasingly populated, industrial, and a world power.
      d

11. Even though their ability to channel such nutrients as protein into
      a   b
    different pathways, the cells do have certain basic needs that must be met.
              c   d

12. As not originating with him, block grants were an important part of
      a   b
    President Reagan's new federalism, which he outlined in his first State of
                                      c
    the Union message in 1982.
            d

13. Because of their proven productivity, the elderly have suffered from
      a   b   c
    discrimination in employment for many years.
            d

14. From 1980 to 1988 the snowbelt states of the North increased 35.9
            a
    percent in population overall, or the sunbelt states of the South and West
          b   c   d
    increased 85.8 percent.

15. Only in recent times, perhaps in the last 2,000 years, humans have
                             a   b
    begun to change the environment to produce a food supply that is varied
                                  c   d
    and dependable.

16. A balanced diet is <u>as</u> important <u>for</u> health that it <u>has become</u> a political
                    a   b   c

   <u>issue</u>.
   d

17. Just as an engine would be destroyed if <u>even</u> a cup of liquid gasoline
                                         a

   gave <u>up its</u> energy in a moment, <u>as</u> would the tissues of the body be
        b   c

   damaged if all the energy in a potato <u>were</u> released at once.
                                         d

18. One of <u>mankind's</u> giant steps was acquiring control of fire <u>because</u> this
           a   b

   permitted the cooking of meats and <u>thereby</u> greatly <u>expands</u> the choice of
                                      c   d

   foods.

19. It has been more than <u>half a century</u> since women obtained the right
                          a

   to vote in <u>most</u> countries of the western world, <u>and</u> the number of women
              b   c

   who have held high political positions can be counted on <u>one's</u> fingers.
                                                            d

20. <u>As</u> age was not included <u>within</u> the <u>protections</u> of the 1964 Civil Rights
    a   b   c

   Act, <u>therefore</u> Congress directed the secretary of labor to prepare a report
         d

   on the problems of age discrimination.

21. <u>Before</u> avoidance is <u>learned</u> it is <u>very</u> persistent.
    a   b   c d

22. <u>Alike</u> <u>conventional</u> x-ray techniques, Laue diffraction studies <u>use</u> a
    a   b   c

   multiwave x-ray beam <u>to obtain</u> a complete data set.
                        d

23. Desert temperatures (in air in the shade) may reach 57°C (135°F) at
   <u>midday</u>, <u>so</u> nights may be cool <u>or</u> cold in <u>the</u> desert.
    a   b   c   d

Read the following excerpts from academic journals and textbooks and choose the sentence or sentences that mean the same as the original text or the italicized parts of the text.

Kautilya's Circle Theory of States

1. According to Kautilya, State A is most likely to make alliance treaties with States C. For example, feeling a threat by State B_1, State A would most likely make alliances with States C_1, C_2, and C_{12} against B_1. This means :

   a. State B_1, before feeling a threat, would make alliances with State A against C_1, C_2, and C_{12}.

   b. If State A felt a threat from State B_1, State A would probably make alliances with States C_1, C_2, and C_{12}.

   c. Had State A felt threatened by B_1, State A wouldn't be likely to make alliances with States C_1, C_2, and C_{12}.

   d. State A was feeling a threat by State B_1; otherwise, State A would have made alliances with States C_1, C_2, and C_{12}. (**12**: 30)

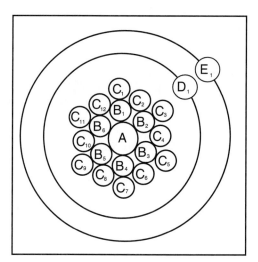

Figure 8-1 Kautilya's Circle Theory of States. (**12**: 30)

2. In attempting to analyze the merits and flaws of the guild system, we should note the protection it gave the consumer against bad workmanship and fraud. This means:

   We should note the protection the guild system gave the consumer against bad workmanship and fraud

a. if we attempt to analyze the merits and flaws of the guild system.

b. after we attempt to analyze the merits and flaws of the guild system.

c. but we need to analyze if the merits and flaws of the guild system are attempted.

d. if we had attempted to analyze the merits and flaws of the guild system.

3. Given his current standing in the grain states, it wouldn't be surprising if candidate Carter were to announce other new agreements sometime before Nov. 4. This means:

a. It won't be surprising if candidate Carter announces other new agreements sometime before Nov. 4 because of his current standing in the grain states.

b. Since he is currently standing in the grain states, it wouldn't be surprising if candidate Carter were to announce other new agreements sometime before Nov. 4.

c. Standing in a current in the given grain states, it wouldn't be surprising if candidate Carter were to announce other new agreements sometime before Nov. 4.

d. No one would be surprised if candidate Carter, because of his current standing in the grain states, were to announce other new agreements sometime before Nov. 4.

4. Once sealed, the new China–U.S. grain deals would ensure about $1 billion worth of export sales yearly for U.S. farmers, tend to encourage steadier production of grains in the long term, and reduce volatility in American markets. This means:

The new China–U.S. grain deals would ensure about $1 billion worth of export sales yearly for U.S. farmers, tend to encourage steadier production of grains in the long term and reduce volatility in American markets

a. since the deal was sealed once.   c. in order to seal the deal.

b. if the deal were sealed   d. as the deal is already sealed.

5. While costs vary with each conversion process, the U.S. Department of Energy estimates that *ethanol could be produced from corn for $0.28/l in a distillery that produced 189 million l annually (99)*. The feedstock corn (at $0.09/kg) represents the largest item ($0.28/l). (42: 170)
The italicized part of the sentence above means:

Ethanol could be produced from corn for $0.24/l

a. unless a distillery produced 189 million l annually.

b. if a distillery produced 189 million l annually.

c. although a distillery produced 189 million l annually.

d. in order to produce 189 million l annually.

6. Without regulation of the technology, says Sharples, "No one can say that, out of 10,000 experiments, one won't turn into a problem." And the problem could be serious. An engineered microbe, for example, that accidentally proved deadly to a beneficial insect would create an ecological upset that could mean millions of dollars of crop loss. This passage means:

   a. The experiments will be a problem because there is no regulation of technology.

   b. Millions of dollars will be lost although there is regulation of technology.

   c. If there is no regulation of technology the experiments won't be a problem.

   d. There may be serious problems if there is no regulation of technology.
   (from Michael Rogers, "Tinkering With Nature," Newsweek, May 26, 1986, p. 54.)

7. Scientists testified that genetically engineered organisms, without natural predators or other controls, might spread unchecked, like the chestnut blight or the gypsy moth. This sentence means :

   a. Genetically engineered organisms could spread unchecked if they don't have natural predators or other controls.

   b. Genetically engineered organisms will spread unchecked even if they have natural predators and other controls.

   c. Genetically engineered organisms will not check their spread if they have natural predators or other controls.

   d. The chestnut blight or gypsy moth could check the spread if they were natural predators or controls for genetically engineered organisms.

8. Once farmers start to purchase seeds and abandon traditional seed, they will become dependent upon purchased seed, thus ensuring their integration into the commodity economy. This sentence means:

   a. Before farmers start to purchase these seeds and abandon traditional seed, they will become dependent upon purchased seeds.

   b. Farmers will become dependent upon purchased seed if they start to purchase them and abandon traditional seed.

   c. If farmers don't start to purchase these seeds and abandon traditional seed, they will become dependent.

   d. Farmers started to purchase these seeds and abandoned traditional seed, so they became dependent upon purchased seed.

9. The need for printed media in Africa, such as have evolved in the West, might have been greater had African social, economic, and political institutions developed along with its technology. This sentence means:
The need for printed media such as have evolved in the West might have been greater

   a. than the social , economic and political institutions that developed along with its technology.

   b. because Africa had developed social, economic, and political institutions along with its technology.

   c. if Africa had developed social, economic and political institutions along with its technology.

   d. as Africa developed social, economic, and political institutions along with its technology.

10. Another example of the folly of equating dollars with defense is the B-1 bomber. *Had the president gone forward with the B-1, as his critics urged, billions would have gone into a weapons system that would have soon been obsolete.* The italicized sentence means:

   a. It was a good idea that the president went forward with the B–1 bomber.

   b. It was too bad that the president went forward with the B –1 bomber.

   c. The president didn't go forward with the B-1 bomber.

   d. The president was urged to go forward with the B-1 bomber in order to save an obsolete weapons system.

   (from Robert J. Bresley, "The Defense Debate: In Search of Illusions, *USA Today*, September 1980, v. 109, no. 2424, p. 9.)

Discussion: Predicting Test Answers

After completing Practice Exercise 22 above, it is useful to go back and discuss how to approach this type of test question. For example, a student can read the first part of a question and, after looking at the conditional verb, make an educated guess about what form should be in the correct choice. If the first verb phrase is a real conditional, then the correct choice should be real as well. This helps eliminate at least two of the possibilities quickly. Going through each question rapidly as a group and asking "What is it, real or unreal?" or "What are we looking for in the answer, real or unreal?" helps to develop the scanning techniques necessary for testing situations.

Analysis Exercise 23: Building Templates for Adverbials

Fill in the blanks in the short passages below with the conjunctions that seem to be logical. There may be many correct answers.

1. On a dark moonless night, allow your eyes to slowly scan the sky
   _____ you find a star off toward the edge of your vision that is
   _____ dim that you can just barely see it. Now, _____
   you look directly at the star (so _____ its image falls on the cones
   of the fovea in your eye), it should appear even dimmer and may actually
   disappear.

2. _____ you sit reading this chapter, receptors for touch and pressure in the seat of your pants are sending nerve impulses to your brain.
   _____ _____ these sensations have been present all
   along, you were probably not aware of them _____ just now. The
   seat-of-your-pants phenomenon is an example of selective attention. We
   are able to "tune in on" any of the many sensory messages bombarding us
   _____ excluding others. (**7**: 85–86, 91)

3. It has been shown that bacteria are able to carry out their functions as decomposers at pressures as high as 1000 times that of the surface;
   _____, organisms adapted to great pressures have difficulties in
   moving to areas with other pressures. They may literally explode
   _____ brought to the surface in dredges of deep-sea biologists.
   _____ the pressure inside has to be the same as the pressure outside at any depth, biologists have built special high-pressure chambers to
   study the organisms brought up from great depths.

4. Altitudinal gradients are environmental gradients that change
   _____ you go higher or lower on earth. For example, the
   higher you go up a mountain, the lower the average temperature becomes,
   and the daily and annual extremes of temperature become greater, too.

5. Recent studies show that coyotes can learn not to attack lambs
   _____ they are given lamb meat treated with a substance that
   makes them sick _____ does not kill them. _____ this
   method of predator control were used, coyotes might go back to
   ontrolling the burrowing animals, _____ the use of poisons
   ich concentrate in food chains might be eliminated. (**9**: 114, 117, 123)

 53   IAL CONCEPTS

Coyote

Analysis Exercise 24: Research Project

Using the academic journal article or textbook passage that you chose for previous research projects, scan your article to find as many conjunctions as you can. Use the Adverbial Concepts charts to help you.

1. Find and mark the subordinating and coordinating conjunctions.
2. Next, look to see what kinds of structures come after the subordinating conjunctions—phrases or clauses. Write some examples of the most common ones:

   Subordinating conjunctions followed by clauses—
   Subordinating conjunctions followed by phrases—
3. Write some typical examples of coordinating conjunctions from your article here.
4. How are the sentences with coordinating conjunctions punctuated? Does your article use semicolons and/or commas to separate independent clauses, or does your article use periods to separate simple sentences that begin with the conjunction?
5. As you scanned your article, did you see any comparatives? Look back through the article to see if you can find examples of structures like "the bigger, the better," "likewise," or "just as." Write the comparatives here.
6. How many examples of conditionals can you find in your article? Are they real or unreal? Would you say that your academic field uses many conditional sentences in writing?

Adverbial Clauses Expressing Condition   **255**

7. Summary—Write a paragraph to summarize the use of adverbial conjunctions in your article. Include the answers to the following questions in your summary.

   a. What can you conclude about the relative numbers of sentences containing adverbials in your field? Are there more or fewer than other types of sentences?

   b. Are there a lot of sentences with one particular subordinator?

   c. Do some sections of your article contain more adverbial conjunctions than the others? If so, why do you think this is true?

UNIT 4

NOUN CONCEPTS—
NOUN CLAUSES, GERUNDS,
INFINITIVES, AND
ABSTRACT NOUN PHRASES

9

NOUN CLAUSES

In this chapter we will begin with noun clauses. What do you know about noun clauses already? For example, what words introduce noun clauses?

Discovering the Grammar of Noun Clauses

Discovery Exercise 1: Identifying Noun Clauses

Read the following passage from an American Government textbook. Find the clauses that begin with the subordinators "what," "that," and "whether," and underline them.

> What makes power rightful varies from time to time and from country to country. In the United States we usually say that a person has political authority if his or her right to act in a certain way is conferred by a law or

The Capitol, the meeting place of the U.S. Congress

a state or national constitution. But what makes a law or constitution a source of right? That is the question of legitimacy. In the United States the Constitution today is widely, if not unanimously, accepted as a source of legitimate authority, but that was not always the case.

Much of American political history has been a struggle over what constitutes legitimate authority. The Constitutional Convention in 1787 was an effort to see whether a new, more powerful federal government could be made legitimate; the succeeding administrations of George Washington, John Adams, and Thomas Jefferson were in large measure preoccupied with disputes over the kinds of decisions that were legitimate for the federal government to make. The Civil War was a bloody struggle over the legitimacy of the federal union; the New Deal of Franklin Roosevelt was hotly debated by those who disagreed over whether it was legitimate for the federal government to intervene deeply in the economy.

In the United States today no government at any level would be considered legitimate if it were not in some sense democratic. That was not always the prevailing view, however; at one time, people disagreed over whether democracy itself was a good idea. In 1787 Alexander Hamilton worried that the new government he helped create might be too democratic, while George Mason, who refused to sign the Constitution, worried that it was not democratic enough. Today, virtually everyone believes that "democratic government" is the only proper kind. Most people probably believe that our existing government is democratic; and a few believe that other institutions of public life—schools, universities, corporations, trade unions, churches—should be run on democratic principles if they are to be legitimate. We shall not discuss the question of whether democracy is the best way of governing all institutions. Rather we shall consider the different meanings that have been attached to the word "democratic" and which, if any, best describes the government of the United States.

(from James Q. Wilson, *American Government* [Lexington, Mass.: D.C. Heath, 1980], p. 6. Reprinted by permission of D.C. Heath and Company.)

Discovery Exercise 2

Answer the following questions.

1. How do you know the groups of words that you chose are clauses?
2. Did you choose any clause that was also a complete sentence? How do the words "what" and "that" function in these sentences?
3. Look at the clauses that are parts of longer sentences. Many of them are in the second parts of the sentences. What words precede the subordinating conjunctions? What parts of speech are they?

4. The word "that" appears after verbs forms and preposition. The "that" clauses function differently in these sentences. What is the difference?

5. The word "whether" appears after two different kinds of words. What are they? How do the "whether" clauses function in these two cases?

6. The first sentence of the passage begins with a "what" clause. How does this clause function in the sentence? (Hint: What kind of word *follows* the clause?)

7. From your observations so far, write some rules for the functions of "what," "that," and "whether" clauses. Can you name them according to their functions?

Discovery Exercise 3: Focus on the Form of Noun Clauses

Compare the sentence pairs below. One kind of construction is italicized in the "a" sentences. Another construction is italicized in the "b" sentences. What are the constructions called and what are their similarities and differences?

1. a. Historians focus on *certain things.*
   b. Historians focus on *why things occurred in the past.*

2. a. Their arguments do not explain *the price increase.*
   b. Their arguments do not explain *how the price increase affected the market.*

3. a. Physical anthropology teaches us *a remarkable fact about people.*
   b. Physical anthropology teaches us *that people are remarkably similar.*

4. a. *The order* is not clear.
   b. *Which came first* is not clear.

5. a. *The reason for the existence of these preferences* is explained by sociologists.
   b. *Why these different preferences exist* is explained by the sociologists.

6. a. *The importance of the election* was *the three major presidential candidates.*
   b. *What was special about the election* was *that there was a third major presidential candidate.*

Explanation 1—Noun Clause Versus Sentence

A sentence with the subject "that" or beginning with a Wh- question word is not the same as a noun clause introduced by the subordinator "what" or "that."

Sentences: subject + verb
What makes power important?
That is the question of legitimacy.

Clauses: subject   verb
What makes power rightful varies from place to place.
subject + verb subordinator noun clause
Most people believe *that our government is democratic.*

In the first two complete sentences, "what" and "that" are the subjects. In the latter two sentences, "what" and "that" introduce clauses. The subordinator "what" may also be the subject of its noun clause, but "that" will almost never be the subject of its clause. The only exception is when the subordinator "that" is omitted and the subject of the clause is the pronoun "that."

subordinator + subject
We believe (that)   that is the problem

Analyzing Noun Clauses

Analysis Exercise 4: *If* versus *if*

Study the sentences below and answer the questions.

[1]   The organic plots on this farm have been non-chemical for fifteen years. The waste from cattle and hogs (manure) is composted and then spread on the field. *If* manure is going to be applied, two weeks at the minimum should elapse before planting to allow for some decomposition. *If* the seed does germinate, the small roots will try to go around the manure concentration. . . . There are problems when spreading manure in the spring. In Iowa it rains every weekend during April. *If* it rains on Easter, it will rain for the next seven Sundays.

[2]   Researchers are now raising the question about nitrogen losses during the composting process and the nitrogen availability in the compost to a corn crop that has a high nitrogen requirement. The soil phosphorus levels are high, and the soil potassium levels are medium. The soil potassium level was 169 pounds per acre in 1967 and has not changed in a closed farm system. The soil phosphorus has increased to a very high level of 80 pounds

per acre during this same time period. Extensive soil, leaf tissue and grain analysis will be recorded over a number of years to see *if* the change in storage technique will change the nitrogen and potassium levels.

[3]   How can farmers raise hogs without huge capital expenditures for buildings, pumps, pits, and tanks that will be rusted out before the depreciation expires? Can't hogs survive without drugs? Our individual isolit farrowing houses, along with the open-front fresh air nursery and finishing units, were built to see *if* hogs could be raised without vaccinations and drugs in the feed. (43: 7–8)

[4]   The new biotechnologies developed in universities are now being commercialized by private companies which are established solely to create profit. For example, private capital directs much of this research toward producing hybrid seeds that are not reproductively stable, thereby forcing farmers to purchase seeds annually. Once farmers start to purchase these seeds and abandon traditional seed, they will become dependent upon purchased seeds, thus ensuring their integration into the commodity economy. This can be very dangerous for a nation *if* seeds are imported. (25: 13)

1. All the sentences above contain if-clauses, but some sentences are different from the others. Change every sentence so that the if-clause comes first. Do all the sentences seem correct?
2. We studied conditional sentences in Chapter 8. Many conditionals contain if-clauses. Which of the sentences are conditional sentences, and which are not conditional sentences?
3. Look again at the sentences that are not conditionals. How did you decide that they are not conditional sentences?
4. When we were studying verbs, we saw that verbs often have objects. Other verb forms (participles, gerunds, and infinitives) also can have objects. What are the objects of the infinitives in the sentences above?
5. Objects of verb forms are usually what part of speech?
6. Are the objects of the infinitives in the sentences single words or clauses?
7. If an object is usually a noun, then what would you call a clause that is an object?
8. What could an if-clause in the middle or toward the end of a sentence be? How do you identify them?
9. What is an if-clause at the beginning of a sentence? Do you know why?

If-clauses may be conditionals or noun clauses. An if-clause following a transitive verb is probably a noun clause. An if-clause at the beginning of a sentence can never be a noun clause. We use "whether" at the beginning of a sentence instead of "if" in a noun clause.

In the preceding exercise we determined that some if-clauses are noun clauses. They act as objects of verbs. Those verbs can be an infinitive or the main verb in the sentence.

Analysis Exercise 5: Identifying Subordinators and Noun Clauses

Study the following passage to find words (subordinators) that can introduce noun claus-es. Also find the verb forms that precede the noun clauses. Then answer these questions.

- Some of the verb forms are followed by clauses. Are these clauses objects? Find the ones that are not objects.
- What do we call clauses that follow the verb "to be"?
- What subordinators introduce the noun clauses?

Recombinant-DNA Research—There has been widespread alarm about the possible risks of recombinant-DNA research. Many critics want to know why *E. coli,* a common bacteria in the human intestine, has been used as a host for recombinant-DNA. One side argues that scientists must be mad to pick a normal human inhabitant (and a sometime human pathogen) to serve as a host for recombinant DNA. The other side argues that no known untoward event has yet resulted from recom-binant-DNA research. The *E. coli* actually used in laboratory research has been so modified genetically that survival outside of laboratory con-ditions is essentially impossible. The use of genetically deficient strains is what is meant by the term "biological containment."

Arguing that time may be needed to "pace" new genetic knowledge to human capacities for putting nature to intelligent use, Robert L. Sincheimer of the California Institute of Technology wonders whether "there are certain matters best left unknown, at least for a time."

It is difficult to know how the problem should be handled. The Na-tional Institutes of Health has set out guidelines on recombinant-DNA research, but no provision has been made for budgeting what may turn out to be the considerable cost for technical surveillance, personnel training, and medical monitoring.

Clifford Grobstein of the *Scientific American* says that the policy challenge we face is whether we can create institutions able to trans-form the fruits of an age into the achievements of an age of intervention. (**18:** 24-31)

Analysis Exercise 6: Writing a Summary of Noun Clauses

Answer the following questions to write a summary of noun clauses.

1. What kinds of verb forms can come before noun clauses?
2. What functions do noun clauses have after various verb forms?
3. What are the subordinating conjunctions that introduce noun clauses?

Practicing Noun Clauses

Practice Exercise 7: Subordinating Conjunctions

Fill in the blanks in the following passages with appropriate subordinating conjunctions.

[1]   *Explanations for Age Differentiation*—Functionalists suggest
_____ in traditional tribal society, much of the tribe's knowledge and wisdom is stored in the memories of tribal elders. They may
remember other tribes were friendly or aggressive in the past,
_____ water was found, or how to deal with a plague of locusts.
In industrial societies, in contrast, the economic activity of most members
is not centered around the land. Individuals can subsist independently of
their elder kin. . . . Often the younger generations know how to do more
things than do the older ones. As a result, it is not functional for such a
society to rely heavily on its older generations. . . .The conflict
perspective stresses _____ the way a society is arranged depends
on the relative power and resources of various groups in it. (**35**: 292)

[2]   An American returning from Upper Volta, in West Africa, remarked
_____ he could leave his bicycle on the ground in a village and it
would still be there a year later. Bicycles are valuable in Upper Volta, but
tribal customs dictate _____ you may and may not do with
something that belongs to someone else. In a pluralistic and highly
complex society like ours, however, there is no one custom dictating
_____ things should be done. (35: 202)

[3]   *Unemployment*—Perhaps the most important link between individuals
and the economy is _____ or not a person has a job at all. The
issue of unemployment has become an important one in recent years. . . .
The unemployment patterns mean _____ certain regions—the
manufacturing Midwest, the construction-related Northwest, and urban
centers with large numbers of minority teenagers — have particularly
high rates of unemployment. (**35**: 385)

[4]   Law as a Means of Social Control—One of the central differences between
modern industrial societies and simple tribal societies is the reliance of
modern societies on law and formal legal systems to manage social
processes that were once handled by tradition, the family, or tribal
customs. This is true about _____ behavior is defined as well as
about other social practices. (35: 201–202)

[5]   Job Performance—Education is the single most important factor in getting a job . . . Theorists differ on _____ this is true, but they agree that for most people, at least some higher education is necessary for a professional or managerial position. Although most social scientists concur that education is needed to help get a job, there is less agreement on _____ it helps a person do that job well. (**35**: 428, 429)

[6]   Perhaps the best definition of culture, as it is used in anthropology, is still the one proposed by Edward B. Tylor more than 100 years ago. . . . First of all, culture is a complex whole. It is a whole, an integrated unit. . . . Second, Tylor's definition tells us _____ culture is "acquired by man" This has several implications, among them _____ culture is not inherited or instinctive, and also _____ culture is unique to the human species. Many anthropologists no longer believe _____ culture is a uniquely human characteristic. . . . A third implication of Tylor's definition is _____ culture is shared and _____ learning takes place within the confines of a group. (**14**: 284–285)

Analyzing Noun Clauses (continued)

Analysis Exercise 8: Functions of Noun Clauses

Since noun clauses play the same roles as single nouns, they will probably occur in other noun positions as well. Examine the sentences below. Then answer the questions.

1. Which came first is not clear.

2. Why these different preferences exist is explained by sociologists such as Ball (1972) and Mitchell (1983).

3. Whether you'll be able to hear a reduction in distortion is yet another question.

4. That the study of human interaction is useful and important cannot be denied.

5. Whoever undertakes a new national review should first carefully examine the current situation, including the actual effectiveness of the regulatory mechanisms provided by the NIH guidelines.

6. What emerges on the new policy agenda, then, is the need for effective policy-oriented research to reduce the current uncertainty as to the risk of particular kinds of experiments.

    a. What do you see in front of the main verb, a clause or a phrase?

    b Find the subject of the main verb and underline it.

    c. What part of speech is the usual subject of a main verb?

    d. Since the subject of the main verb in these sentences is a clause, what part of speech is it?

    e. What function do noun clauses fill in this exercise?

    f. What subordinating conjunctions are used to introduce the noun clauses?

    g. What are the functions of noun clauses that we have seen so far?

Discussion of Noun Clause Functions and Subordinators

We found earlier that noun clauses can act as direct objects, predicate nouns (complements), and subjects in sentences in the same way that single nouns or noun phrases can. The subordinators "if," "that," "whether," "how," "what," "where," "why," "which," and "whoever" are often used to introduce such noun clauses. How do we know which subordinator to use? The following exercises will help you decide which subordinator is appropriate in different situations.

Analysis Exercise 9: Derivation of Noun Clauses—How Statements and Questions Combine

Study how the following statements and questions combine into statements. Try to see what rules are operating. Write a rule that explains how we can combine a statement and a question into one sentence.

1. One of the great debates surrounding American political history is (. . .).

   Was the U.S. Constitution designed to protect all the people against the power of the government?

   One of the great debates surrounding American political history is whether the U.S. Constitution was designed to protect all the people against the power of the government.

2. What gets Henry excited?

   A new product created by his company.

   What gets Henry excited is a new product created by his company.

3. What can you do, once the lamps have come on?

   Adjust the R2 resistance backup to a higher value.

   What you can do, once the lamps have come on, is (to) adjust the R2 resistance backup to a higher value.

African Grazing Mammals

4. Only time will tell (. . .).

   Will the large African grazing mammals turn out to be beneficial in their new environments?

   Only time will tell whether the large African grazing mammals will turn out to be beneficial in their new environments.

5. How does the motor-driven two-position system work?

   Here is (. . .).

   Here is how the motor-driven two-position system works.

6. When was the term "melting pot" first applied to American society?

   No one really knows (. . .).

   No one really knows when the term "melting pot" was first applied to American society.

7. Americans and Europeans value different spectator sports. Why do these different preferences exist?

   (. . .) is explained by sociologists such as Ball (1972) and Mitchell (1983).

   Why these different preferences exist is explained by sociologists such as Ball (1972) and Mitchell (1983).

8. The phlogiston theory could not explain (. . .).

   Why did some materials gain weight after they burned?

   The phlogiston theory could not explain why some materials gained weight after they burned.

Practice Exercise 10: Combining Statement and Question Sentences

Combine the following statements and questions into statements similar to those in Exercise 9.

1. For those most concerned with the security obtained by owning their arms free of debt, one can show (. . .).
   How will the adoption of improved practices contribute toward this end?

2. For those placing a high value upon material conveniences, one can show (. . .).
   How will the adoption of improved methods of farming help obtain these conveniences?

3. The exact nature of the habitat depends upon (. . .).
   Is the shore rocky, sandy, or muddy?

4. The constitution left unsettled the key question of (. . .).
   Who could make such definitions?

5. The ethnocultural American believes that only his conception really captures (. . .).
   Who is he, in the truest, most primordial sense?

6. Integral limit switches inside the motor housing detect (. . .).
   When has the value reached the 180° position, and when has it reached the home position?

7. The Chinese government began a research program attempting to determine (. . .).
   Where did the teeth originate?

8. What is yet to be determined?
   (. . .) is what else happens to the plant when that genetic change takes place.

9. What's special about this one?
   (. . .) is that it could be ready as early as next year.

10. How wealthy are you?
    (. . .) is also associated with your political views.

11. Physical anthropology tells us (. . .).
    What is the basis for behavior? What are the limits upon it? Why should we expect others to behave within those limitations? What variations are possible?

Analysis Exercise 11: How Statements and Statements Combine

Study the following sentences to see how two statements can be combined into one.

1. There is evidence (of . . .).

   Social cliques serve as barriers to the spread of information outside themselves.

   There is evidence that social cliques serve as barriers to the spread of information outside themselves.

2. Reports of evaluation attempts often indicate (. . .).

   Significant gains were made of pre-post testings.

   Reports of evaluations attempts often indicate that significant gains were made of pre-post testings.

Practice Exercise 12: Combining Two Statements

Combine the following pairs of statements into single sentences.

1. The literature confirms (. . .).

   Girls get better grades in elementary and high school.

2. Maccoby and Jackson pointed out (. . .).

   There appear to be no sex differences in learning.

3. Children notice early (. . .).

   Principals as well as math and science teachers are primarily men.

   In school boys are given more opportunities to manipulate science-related apparatus.

4. The problem is (. . .).

   Once a stereotype has been established, it is very difficult to change the image.

5. An interesting feature of relays and contractors is (. . .).

   They naturally tend to provide a differential gap for on-off control.

6. One of man's discoveries was (. . .).

   Fire could be used to frighten or even kill large animals.

Writing a Summary of How to Combine Sentences to Make Sentences with Noun Clauses

Write a statement that describes how to combine statements + questions, and statements + statements, to make sentences with noun clauses. List the appropriate subordinators for each type of noun clause. When should you choose "what," and when should you choose "that" as a subordinator? When should you use "whether"? (See Chart A3—HOW NOUN CLAUSES ARE FORMED—on pages 349–354 for a detailed explanation.)

Explanation 2—What *vs.* That

If you ever have a problem deciding whether to use "that" or "what" as a subordinator, think about the sentence-combining exercises. Remember:

A "that" clause comes from a statement.

A "what" clause comes from a question.

If you can separate the ideas that you want to combine, then you will be able to tell if you have a statement or a question to include.

Analyzing Noun Clauses in Other Roles

We found in earlier exercises that noun clauses can act as objects of verb forms, predicate nouns after "be," and some other linking verbs, and as subjects of sentences. What other roles do nouns play?

Analysis Exercise 14a: **Noun Clauses as Objects of Prepositions**

Study the sentences below. Find the noun clauses and then answer the questions.

- What parts of speech appear directly in front of the noun clauses?
- What do we call a noun that follows a preposition?
- What role does the noun clause play in this exercise?

1. The expressed concerns of the critics have generated a revised agenda for what is now emerging as a broadened second round of policy making.

2. There has been some uncertainty in the Department of Commerce as to how it should be handled.

3. You are the judge of how many times you should rehearse.

4. Two-way information is usually needed to obtain the detailed information on how and when the new technique is to be applied.

Analysis Exercise 14b: Summary of Noun Clauses as Objects of Prepositions

Write a rule that covers the function of the noun clauses that we saw in Exercise 14a.

Analysis Exercise 15: Forms of Noun Clauses

- Circle the words immediately following the italicized subordinators in the noun clauses below. What do you find?
- Which subordinators are followed by the subject of the clause?
- What is different about *"what," "which,"* and *"whoever"*?
- Suppose you wanted to use *who* as the object in a noun clause. What form would you use?

1. . . . *if* the change in storage technique will change the nitrogen and potassium levels.

2. . . . *whether* the farmers would be able to continue to raise these vital crops economically.

3. . . . *that* scientists must be mad to pick a normal human inhabitant...

4. . . . *what* is meant by the term "biological containment."

5. . . . *where* it is shelved in the library.

6. . . . *what* they should look at in the visual.

7. *Whoever* undertakes this new national review . . .

8. . . . *how* it should be handled.

9. . . . *how many times* you should rehearse.

10. . . . *how and when* the new technique is to be applied.

11. . . . *which* came first is not clear.

Discussion: "What," "who(m)ever," and "which" may function as subjects or objects as well as subordinating conjunctions in noun clauses. "If," "whether," "that," "where," "when," and "how" function as subordinators in noun clauses.

Analysis Exercise 16: Anticipatory *it* and *that* Clause Subjects

Study the following sentences from a public-speaking text and answer the questions that follow.

1. It is important that you practice the speech in its entirety, paying special attention to phrase and sentence transitions.

2. It is interesting that people fear public speaking.

3. It is unlikely that they would forget an anecdote because everybody likes to hear stories.

4. It is not recommended that you put too much information in handouts.

5. It is well-known that humans communicate 75 percent of the time.

a. How are the sentences alike?
b. Find the noun clauses. What parts of speech come before the "that" clauses?
c. Rewrite the sentences. Put the "that" clause and everything after it in place of "it." Do the sentences have the same meanings?

Analysis Exercise 17: *Tell* and *that* Clauses

Study the following sentences from a public speaking text and answer the questions.

1. Tell your audience that you are repeating the exact words of your source.

2. Tell the audience that you will elaborate further on, and name the omitted section.

3. The teacher told the student that she said "gonna" instead of "going to."

a. What is the main verb in the sentences?
b. What kinds of words come after the main verb and before the "that" clause? Are they subjects? verbs? direct objects? indirect objects?
c. What role do the "that" clauses play in the sentences? Are they subjects? verbs? objects?
d. What can you say about the relationship between the verb "tell" and the words and clauses that follow it?

Analysis Exercise 18: Writing Rules about *that* Clauses (Noun Clauses)

Answer the following questions to complete some grammatical rules about "that" clauses.

1. Where do "that" clauses usually come in a sentence?
2. If the main verb is "tell," what is between the main verb and the "that" clause?
3. If the subject of the main clause is "it" and the main verb is a form of "be" (or a linking verb), what is in front of the "that" clause?
4. What is the function of "that" clauses that come at the ends of sentences after the subject replacer "it" and a form of "be"?
5. What is the function of "that" clauses that come at the ends of sentences after ordinary subjects and transitive verbs?

Analysis Exercise 19: *That versus that*—Noun Clauses versus Adjective Clauses

Study the following sentences. Notice that each of the sentences has two clauses beginning with "that." One clause is a noun clause and the other is a relative adjective clause. See if you can tell the difference. How do you know which is which?

1. Make sure that you are using synonyms correctly and are employing the correct English equivalent for the vocabulary that you have looked up in the dictionary of your native language.
2. An instructor who reviewed the tape of a speech that a foreign student had delivered told the student that she said "gonna" instead of "going to."
3. When you deliver a speech, you should make sure that you speak at a pace that permits the audience to catch every word.

Analysis Exercise 20: Writing Rules About *that* versus *that* Clauses

Answer the questions to complete rules about noun clauses and relative adjective clauses beginning with "that."

1. What word can you use to replace "that" in adjective clauses?
2. What do adjective clauses usually follow?
3. What do noun clauses with "that" usually follow?
4. If the verb is "tell," what do noun clauses follow?
5. What functions do noun clauses and relative adjective clauses fulfill in sentences? What do they each do?

Practice Exercise 21: Identifying Noun Clauses and Adjective Clauses

Study the following sentences and underline the "that" clauses. Put an **N** above the noun clauses and an **A** above the relative adjective clauses.

1. Some observers suggest that our current scientific flowering is due to the happy bonding of science and technology in our society.

2. Usually no single factor accounts for all the social changes that occur in the world.

3. The institution of science refers to the social communities that share certain theories and methods aimed at understanding the physical and social worlds.

4. Any social activity generates certain social norms that suggest how people should behave, and science is no exception.

5. Although rationality may offer a valuable approach to many problems, it should not be forgotten that rationality may support the interests of certain groups (manufacturing and military interests) more than others (tribal societies, landed aristocracy, or unemployed ghetto residents), and that it may not be the best approach to all situations.

6. Of all the great variety of proteins in living organisms, the antibodies best demonstrate that proteins are specific for one organism.

7. The body, after recognizing that it has been invaded, manufacturers antibodies, and they inactivate the foreign protein.

8. The part of the wheat plant that is made into flour and then into bread and other baked goods is the kernel.

9. We are beginning to understand some of the subterranean forces that elevate enormous sections of the earth's crust to mountainous heights.

Practice Exercise 22: *That* versus *that*

Fill in the blanks in the passage below with any appropriate subordinator. Can you see which clauses are relative clauses and which clauses are noun clauses?

> *'Phantom Algae' Are Linked to Mass Fish Deaths*
>
> Scientists say they have found _____ 'phantom' algae are responsible
> for mysterious mass kills _____ have destroyed millions of fish. . . .
> Because the algae can survive in everything from fresh water to the salinity of

the open sea, the scientists say they suspect _____ these resilient and powerful killers are likely to be quite widespread.

Researchers suggest _____ the phantom algae could be the long-sought culprits in many of the mysterious and increasingly frequent die-offs _____ have cost the world's fishing industry many hundreds of millions of dollars in the last two decades.

The discovery of the phantom-like behavior of these algae has also begun to challenge scientists' understanding of _____ causes the red and brown tides, the best-known examples of population explosions of algae known as algal blooms.

Dr. Ted Smayda, professor of oceanography at the University of Rhode Island, said, "_____ is magnificent about this work is _____ even while there's been tremendous amounts of study about these kinds of events, here suddenly these researchers find an organism _____'s incredibly novel _____ no one's ever found before." According to Dr. Smayda, these phantoms are the first algae _____ have been shown to be capable of photosynthesizing like a plant but _____ can also detect fish and use toxins to prey upon them. . . . Biologists tend to view them as half plant and half animal.

(from "Phantom Algae Are Linked to Mass Fish Deaths," *New York Times*, July 30, 1992. p. A1. Copyright © 1992/1993 by The New York Times Company. Reprinted by permission.)

Analysis Exercise 23a: More Noun Clauses—Appositives

Study the following sentences from different academic texts and journals. They contain underlined "that" clauses that are defined as noun clauses. See if you can figure out what the difference is between these noun clauses and relative adjective clauses. Here are some questions to ask yourself as you examine the sentences below.

- What kind of word precedes the "that" clause?
- Would it be possible to substitute the "that" clause for the word preceding it? Could you say *Noun = "That" clause*?
- Can you substitute "which" for "that" in these clauses?
- Single nouns and noun phrases can follow other nouns and modify them. Do you remember what they are called?
- If single nouns that follow and modify other nouns are called _____, what would you call a noun clause that functions the same way?

1. The fact that humans can adjust to very low intakes [of calcium] makes setting the Recommended Dietary Allowance difficult.

2. The guarantee <u>that blood calcium levels are always maintained</u> might seem to imply that you need make no effort to obtain calcium in your daily diet.

3. Stolypin's semi-official newspaper *Rossia* constantly hammered at the theme <u>that a single national idea, a sense of Russian statehood, should unify state and society.</u>

4. The camp staff places specific emphasis on the eastern hardwood ecosystem and the knowledge <u>that it can be used to produce the goods and services required by people without destroying or degrading its contribution to the environment.</u>

5. The hypothesis, <u>that significant gender differences would occur on the pre-tests but be reduced on the post tests,</u> was accepted for the knowledge tests and rejected for all other tests.

6. Researchers, after reviewing the literature, supported the hypothesis <u>that "there are no differences between boys and girls or men and women that merit differential treatment of one sex over the other."</u>

7. During the delivery of the speech there should exist a "feeling" on the part of both the speaker and the audience <u>that a communication experience is in progress and that the two parties, speaker and audience, are engaged in interaction.</u>

8. If you are able to summarize your ideas without making any major mistakes or hesitating, it is an indication <u>that you are in control.</u>

Analysis Exercise 23b: Explaining Noun Clauses as Appositives

Write a statement explaining the use of "that" clauses (noun clauses) in Exercise 23a. Be sure to include information on punctuation possibilities (compare #5 with the other sentences). How do you explain #7?

Explanation 3—Summary of Noun Clauses in Apposition

NOUN   =   definition of NOUN
The fact   =   definition of fact
The fact / belief / hypothesis   (is)   that . . .

Sometimes there are other modifying phrases between the noun and the appositive "that" clause. See number 7 above.

Noun clauses beginning with "that" may follow certain nouns. When noun clauses beginning with "that" equal their antecedents in meaning exactly, they are called appositives.

When "which" can be substituted for "that" in the clause, it isn't a noun clause; it is a relative adjective clause.

Practice Exercise 24: Noun Clauses in Apposition—*that* versus *that*

Fill in the blanks in the passages below. Can you tell the difference between noun clauses and relative adjective clauses? Can you tell the difference between the noun clauses in apposition and the noun clauses used as direct objects? Can you tell the difference between noun clauses and other *that*s?

[1]   *Speech*—Anatomical evidence tends to support the notion _____ speech was a relatively late development. Studies of the relationship of the pharynx, larynx and esophagus in *Australopithecus* indicate _____ it was incapable of creating certain vowels and consonants.

[2]   Culture—Many anthropologists no longer believe _____ culture is a uniquely human characteristic, and we will discuss this problem in more detail. But the fact _____ culture is acquired is important for understanding why people behave the way they do. . . . The assumption _____ animals could not learn and could not transfer learned behavior to other members of the species has been challenged by studies of Japanese macaques. . . . Anthropologist George Peter Murdock has compiled a list of what he calls cultural universals, basic solutions to the problems of living _____ are found in one form or another in all cultures. (14: 284, 286)

[3]   People are likely to jump to completely erroneous conclusions when interpreting their experiences. For example, a man seated in the center of a car seat sometimes thinks _____ he has been pushed to the side of the car as it rounds a corner. He might even assert _____ the force pushing him sideways was so great _____ it threw him against the side hard enough to injure him. This is nonsense, of course. There was no mysterious ghost pushing him toward the side of the car. Certainly no material object was pushing him in _____ direction. He must therefore be mistaken.

     The same man would not claim _____ a mysterious force suddenly acted on him to throw him violently against the dashboard of the car as it suddenly stopped. He knows _____ his forward momentum could be lost only if some force retarded his motion. Hence, when the car suddenly stopped, he continued going forward until the dashboard of the car began to exert a force on him to stop him from moving forward. This is merely an example of Newton's idea _____ things continue in motion until a force acts on them to stop them. (2: 152)

Study the sentences below. How are they different from all of the previous sentences containing noun clauses?

1. A survey in 1936 revealed that people were suffering from the loss of nutrients from bread. The Enrichment Act of 1942 required that lost nutrients be returned to the flour.

2. Western backers may be concerned that the country be an open market for their own manufactured goods.

3. It is important to realize that a barrier need not be effective against all organisms; nor need it be a solid structure such as a dam.

4. The Senate gave its "advice and consent" to the charter and thus accepted compulsory jurisdiction; but it included the proviso that the United States be free to determine for itself what matters were of an essentially domestic nature and therefore outside the jurisdiction of the Court.

5. The NIH (National Institutes of Health) guidelines are silent on the matter of commercial application other than stipulating that large-scale experiments with recombinants "known to make harmful products" be prohibited unless specially sanctioned.

Explanation 4—Subjunctive Noun Clauses

Noun clauses after certain verbs, adjectives, and nouns that express requests, demands, or urgency contain a base form of the verb (subjunctive). The patterns of such sentences are as follows:

Type 1   subject+ verb + (that) + subject   + base verb
       We   urge   that   the student *consult* an advisor.

Type 2   "it"+ verb(passive) + (that) + subject   + base verb
       It is required   that the student *register* for Chemistry 101.

Type 3   "It" + "be" +   adjective + (that) + subject +   base verb
       It   is   advisable that   the student *pass* the course.

Type 4   "It" + "be" + noun +   (that) + subject +   base verb
       It   is   our suggestion that   the student *study* harder.

Sometimes the modal auxiliary "should" is used in the noun clause as well.

Look at Chart 9-1 to find examples of the noun clauses you have studied.

> Noun clauses as subjects of sentences.
> Noun clauses as objects of verb forms.
> Noun clauses as subjective complements (predicate nouns).
> Noun clauses as objects of prepositions.
> Noun clauses as appositives.

CHART 9–1   NOUN CLAUSES

SUBJECT POSITION

OBJECT POSITION

	DIRECT OBJECT
What the problem is concerns us. How it works will be explained.	We know what the problem is. Please explain how it works.
Who they are is not important. Whoever wants to go will be invited. When he arrives isn't clear. Where she lives is not known. Why it functions is a mystery. That Americans are always in a hurry appears to be true. Whether** we run or not remains the question.	Tell me who they are. I invited whoever* wanted to go. We want to know whom you chose. They will know when you leave. We told them where she lives. I don't understand why it functions. People say (that) he is interesting. We don't know whether (or not) we will run. We don't know if we will run.
NOUN CLAUSES SUBJECT WITH "IT" (used with certain adjectives and verbs) It is important what you study. It seems clear why it functions. It was agreed (that) they would travel. It was not known whether he would run (or not.)	OBJECT OF A PREPOSITION She was afraid of what he would say. We are concerned about how you will live. They complained about where she was living. OBJECT OF A GERUND OR INFINITIVE Our problem is budgeting what we need. We want to know how they finished it. COMPLEMENT POSITION AFTER "BE" The question is how we will go. The query is whether he is honest (or not.) COMPLEMENT IN APPOSITION. The evidence that he was guilty suprised us. The hypothesis that the world is flat is ridiculous.

* Use *whoever* when it is the subject of the noun clause. Use *whomever* when it is the object in the noun clause. See pages 349–354 for a detailed explanation of how to form noun clauses.

** Only *whether* may be used in the subject position. Either "whether" or "if" is possible in the object position.

Analyzing Reduced Noun Clauses

What is the difference between *a* and *b* below? Do they differ in meaning? What can you say about the word "that" as a subordinator?

a. The biggest problem is that manure hauling will slow down planting by 50 percent.
b. The biggest problem is manure hauling will slow down planting by 50 percent.

Can you find where the noun clauses begin in *c* and *d*? Where could you put "that"?

c. Critics say the new technology could spawn ecological disaster and destroy the small farmer.
d. Jeremy Rifkin worries genetic engineers might accidentally release a man-made scourge on agricultural crops dangerous to human health.

Practice Exercise 26a: Reduced Noun Clauses

Study the sentences below. Find the noun clause subordinators. Underline the words after the subordinator. Then answer the questions that follow.

[1]   The National Institutes of Health's Recombinant DNA Advisory Committee (RAC) was considering whether to allow genetic engineering on animal genes. It is not too early, however, to begin the internal consideration of how best to approach the international arena. (**18**: 31)

[2]   A farmer is interested in how to apply the practice; in amounts, time and conditions for application. He obtains more information about the idea and decides whether or not to try it. To be effective in the process, he must know what techniques to use at the different stages and how to mobilize them effectively. (**22**: 3-4)

a. Are the underlined groups of words noun clauses? Why or why not?
b. Rewrite the phrases as noun clauses. What takes the place of a complete verb in the phrases?
c. What happens to the subject of the clause when it becomes a phrase? Why is this possible?

Analysis Exercise 26b: Summary of Reduced Noun Clauses

Answer the following questions to summarize noun clause reduction.

1. How can noun clauses beginning with "that" be reduced?
2. How can noun clauses beginning with "whether," "what," "how," and all of the other wh-words be reduced to phrases?

Using Noun Clauses in Writing—Reported Speech

One of the most common uses of "that" clauses in academic writing is to report what another person has said. Instead of using a direct quotation every time a writer wants to tell what another person has said, the writer will use indirect speech.

Try the following exercise and then discuss when we use present tense to express "truths" and when we don't. Sometimes one tense just "sounds better." Sometimes it depends upon the writer's feelings toward the statement. Sometimes it depends upon the context. Charts 9-2 and 9-3 on pages 286 and 287 contain examples of how we write reported speech using "that" clauses and modals.

Writing Exercise 27: Using Noun Clauses to Report Quotations

Change the following direct quotations into reported speech. Use Charts 9-2 and 9-3 on pages 286 and 287 if you need help.

"All life is an experiment." (Oliver Wendell Holmes)
Oliver Wendell Holmes said that all life was an experiment.

1. Alfonso X declared, "Had I been present at the creation of the world, I would have proposed some improvements."
2. "The goal of all life is death." (Sigmund Freud)
3. "A national debt, if it is not excessive, will be to us a blessing." (Alexander Hamilton.)
4. "If man is not ready to risk his life, where is his dignity?" (Andre Malraux)
5. " All diplomacy is a continuation of war by other means." (Chou En-Lai)

6. "Extreme remedies are very appropriate for extreme diseases." (Hippocrates)

7. "We know accurately only when we know little; with knowledge doubt enters." (Goethe)

8. "When you see a situation you cannot understand, look for the financial interest." (Tom Johnson)

9. "The truth is, we are all caught in a great economic system which is heartless." (Woodrow Wilson)

10. "There were four things from which the Master was entirely free. He had no foregone conclusions, no arbitrary predeterminations, no obstinacy, and no egoism." (Confucius)

11. Thomas Edison: "I am proud of the fact that I never invented weapons to kill."

(from George Seldes, *The Great Quotations* [New York: Pocket Books, 1967]).

Writing Exercise 28: Paraphrasing, Summarizing, and Reporting Speech

Read the following parts of an article about a new use for computers and write a summary of the ideas. Imagine that you have interviewed several experts about the topic. Use reported speech to include what the different people said (in the past) about this amazing new technology. You can rearrange your summary in any way you like.

Step into Another World: "Virtual Reality" Is Virtually Here

It sounds like science fiction. Actually it's a . . . preview of one of the hottest new technologies around: virtual reality (VR), which uses the personal computer to create a world unlike anything humans have ever seen and then puts them into it.

Wearing a helmet that provides a television view and stereo sound, and guiding motion with a joystick or other device, a user can move electronically through a simulation of real life —or something abstract that only a computer can create.

The effect is something like a computerized flight simulator, but far more detailed and realistic. . . . Turn your head and the scene changes accordingly, just as it would in real life. Put your hand into a special electronic glove, and you can "pick up" items you see—but which actually exist only as computer graphics.

Experts are predicting that the VR industry could mushroom into billions of dollars of annual revenue before the end of the decade. "It is going to explode, and the fundamental questions are going to be what are you going to do with it, not how are we going to do it," says Kevin Teixeira, virtual reality project manager at Intel Corp., the Santa Clara, Calif.-based computer chipmaker.

(continued)

Not everyone is so optimistic: Noting that some pioneer companies in the field already are foundering while waiting for the industry to develop, some observers caution that many leading edge technologies like VR evolve into business far more slowly than their proponents envision. And the VR systems already in place are still no substitute for real life—the limited graphics and animation capabilities of today's computers leave most VR systems rather crude. Still, "enough of the technology is here that you can get some crude sort of virtual reality, relatively cheaply, relatively soon," says Steve Ditlea, a New York journalist and consultant who has written extensively about virtual reality.

VR arcade games are already beginning to appear. . . . "This may be the first technology that goes directly from supercomputers to entertainment, with nothing else in between," says Mike Ramsey, senior vice president at Silicon Graphics Inc.

But virtual reality's potential goes way beyond games, proponents of the technology say. . . . The technology could allow doctors to enter computer generated versions of patients to better visualize surgery, creating what some call "Nintendo surgeons." The Pentagon wants virtual reality for simulations and combat planning. Educators are expected to use VR to create "virtual textbooks" in which students could inhabit computerized recreations of the things they are studying.

Fantastic stuff, and it already is raising questions about whether virtual reality can be abused, like a drug. . . . "The problem with virtual reality is that it's a door to another world," says Michael McGreevy, head of NASA's virtual reality research effort. "People might walk through it and decide not to come back."

Even in its more conservative forms, virtual reality can produce a disorienting and nauseating feeling known as "simulator sickness," in which the eyes tell the brain the body is moving, based on the images from the VR system—contrary to the signals from the inner ear, which thinks the body is stationary.

"In virtual reality, what happens is this: We're putting the observer inside the medium," says Tomas A. Furness III, who began working on virtual reality for the air force more than 25 years ago. . . . "Boy, let me tell you, it changes the whole rules." In a way, virtual reality is the ultimate optical illusion. "We can change gravity, we can change the speed of light, we can change the speed of sound," Furness says. "We are all-powerful."

There are already several products that allow architects to convert computerized plans into three-dimensional computer-generated models of buildings and then use virtual reality to "walk" through them. The typical virtual reality set up currently involves four or five major components: a helmet with a miniature television screen, a joystick or ball-like control device, a "Polhemus" sensor that constantly senses the locations of the helmet and control device and transmits the information back to the most important component, a computer. Some systems add a fifth component, a "power glove" that can be used to point at, grasp or move objects in the virtual world.

Researchers are working on lighter, more comfortable devices. "Helmets are Stone Age," declares Ken Pimental, product manager at Sense8. . . . The goal is to come up with a virtual reality interface that is as easy to wear as a pair of glasses. "If the consumer market comes out with some effective, lightweight glasses, it could drive the market, even if it's low quality," says John Latta, president of Fourth Wave, Inc.

The expense of virtual reality systems so far has limited the market for them. Some experts estimate that there are fewer than 1,000 true virtual reality systems in existence, almost all of them in academic, corporate or government laboratories. . . .

Nonetheless, with costs dropping and technology improving, participants in the field are almost uniformly optimistic. . . . Many liken the state of VR to the personal computer business in the late 1970s.

"It's exactly where PCs were about 15 years ago, and I think it's got the potential to be way bigger than PCs," says Ben Delaney, publisher of CyberEdge Journal. . . . "It's crude now, but we're at, I sincerely believe, the birth of an industry."

"It's like the first days of the Wright brothers' airplane. It's crude, but we can get off the ground and have a hell of a thrilling ride," Intel's Teixeira says. "And like the Wright brothers, people can jump in and get involved."

(from Mark Potts, "Step into Another World: 'virtual reality' is virtually here," *Washington Post National Weekly Edition*, Washington, D.C., September 7–13, 1992, p. 21. Reprinted by permission.)

CHART 9–2   DIRECT AND REPORTED SPEECH

	DIRECT SPEECH	REPORTED SPEECH	
	DIRECT QUOTATION	IMMEDIATE REPORTING **Present Tense**	LATER REPORTING **Past Tense**
STATEMENT	"Jeff is creative," says Gartner.	Gartner says (that) Jeff is creative.	Gartner said (that) Jeff was creative.
WH-QUESTIONS	"What work has she done?" asks Price	Price is asking what work she has done.	Price asked what work she had done.
YES/NO QUESTIONS	Does Steve have self confidence?" she asks.	She is asking whether/ if Steven has self-confidence.	She asked whether/ if Steven had self-confidence.
MODAL AUXILIARIES	"We can leave now," she explains. "They will fail, " he claims. We must succeed!" they declare.	She is explaining (that) we can leave now. He claims (that) they will fail. They declare (that) they must succeed.	She explained (that) we could leave then. He claimed (that) they would fail. They declared (that) they had to succeed.
PAST TENSE QUOTATIONS	"The idea was to ease children into adulthood," noted Hamburg.		Hamburg noted (that) the idea had been to ease the children into adulthood.

CHART 9–3   MODALS IN NOUN CLAUSES

EXAMPLES OF SEQUENCE OF TENSES

PRESENT—FUTURE MEANING	PAST MEANING
He <u>says</u> (that) he <u>can</u> write in Chinese.	She <u>said</u> (that) she <u>could</u> swim as a child.
You <u>know</u> (that) she <u>can</u> go with us.	We <u>knew</u> (that) she <u>could</u> go with us.
They <u>claim</u> (that) he <u>might</u> refuse.	We <u>knew</u> (that) he <u>might</u> refuse.
They <u>believe</u> (that)the president <u>may</u> resign.	They <u>believed</u> (that) he <u>might</u> resign.
They <u>say</u> (that) he <u>could</u> do it soon.	They <u>reported</u> that we <u>could</u> go anytime.
We <u>know</u> (that) it <u>must</u> be cold in Alaska.	He <u>said</u> (that) it <u>must have been</u> cold in Alaska last year.
The law <u>states</u> (that) you <u>must</u> get a license.	The law <u>stated</u> (that) you <u>had to</u> get a license last year, too.
People <u>tell</u> me (that) I <u>have to</u> study hard.	Last semester, my adviser <u>told</u> me (that) I <u>had to</u> work hard to pass my courses.
My boss <u>says</u> (that) I <u>am to</u> go to the meeting.	She <u>announced</u> (that) our office <u>was to</u> attend all meetings.
My wife <u>says</u> (that) I <u>should</u> get more sleep than I do.	My mother always <u>said</u> (that) I <u>should</u> get more sleep, too.
My brother <u>says</u> (that) he <u>should be</u> getting a raise soon.	My father always <u>said</u> that he <u>should</u> be getting a raise, too, but he never got a raise. He was a hard worker. I <u>believe</u> (that) he <u>should have gotten</u> a raise.
Everyone <u>knows</u> (that) people <u>ought not to</u> tell lies.	The founders of the United States <u>wrote</u> (that) everyone <u>ought to</u> vote. I <u>think</u> (that) it <u>ought to have been</u> a law.
The professor <u>promises</u> (that) we <u>will</u> finish the textbook.	Last year, all my professors <u>promised</u> (that) we <u>would</u> finish our textbooks, too.
I <u>refuse</u> to believe (that) my best friend <u>would</u> steal money.	One <u>might not expect</u> (that) barbers <u>would have been</u> the original dentists.

10

INFINITIVES, GERUNDS, AND ABSTRACT NOUN PHRASES: EXPRESSING NOUN CONCEPTS AND OTHER IDEAS

PART I   INFINITIVES

Discovering the Grammar of Infinitives

Discovery Exercise 1: Infinitives as Objects

Answer the following questions about the sentences.

- What do we call the italicized words?
- What is their function in the sentences?
- What words are the "subjects" of the infinitives? (Who or what is doing the action of the infinitive?)

1. Critics of modern management prefer *to refer* to the ideal group operation as a "team effort."

2. Would a company president attempt *to make* decisions without taking into account the multitude of influences both inside and outside the company?

3. Consumers often want *to know* what kind of bread is the most nutritious.

4. As more and more foods other than bread are refined and processed, other nutrients may begin *to be lost* from our diet.

5. Olive oil can claim *to be unsaturated,* but not *to be polyunsaturated.*

Discovery Exercise 2: Objects of Verbs as Subjects of Infinitives

Compare the sentences in Exercise 2 with those in Exercise 1. Answer the following questions about the italicized infinitives in the sentences below.

- What do you see between the verbs and their following italicized infinitives ?
- What words are the "subjects" of the italicized infinitives?
- How are the infinitives in numbers 2 and 3 different from number 1?

[1]   Analysis of data results in an estimate but the estimate is in error. We need to estimate the variance of our experimental error (called briefly experimental error variance). Frequently, some writers may refer to the analysis of variance . . . as the design. However, we reserve the word "design" *to describe* the plan for assigning the treatments to the experimental material. (**13**: 272)

[2]   At least since 1914, a judicial policy has existed forbidding the admission of illegally seized evidence at trial. This is the so-called exclusionary rule . . . but the court has allowed illegally obtained evidence *to be used* if it would have been obtained inevitably in the course of the arrest. (**39**: 123)

[3]   The United Nations charter affirmed the principle of self-determination for all peoples although few at the San Francisco conference in 1945 expected that goal *to be totally achieved.*

Analysis Exercise 3: Writing a Summary of Infinitive Patterns

Complete the following patterns of the previous sentences containing infinitives

Exercise 1:   S + V + _____ + rest of the sentence

                                active form

Exercise 2:   S + V + _____ + _____ + rest of the sentence

                                            passive form

                   S + V + _____ + _____ + rest of the sentence

Write the two forms of infinitives you saw in Exercises 1 and 2.

General time: active form _____

General time: passive form_____

Discovery Exercise 4: Infinitives as Subjective Complements

Determine the function of the underlined infinitives in the following passages. (REMINDER: A subjective complement is a predicate noun phrase that follows the verb "be" or a linking verb and that means the same as the subject.)

[1]   The researcher needs to separate sources of variation from explanatory variables. Sorting all sources of variation into four classes seems a useful simplification.

    I. The *explanatory* variables are the objects of the research.

    II. There are extraneous variables which are *controlled*.

    III. There are extraneous uncontrolled variables which are *confounded* with the class I variables.

    IV. There are extraneous uncontrolled variables which are treated as *randomized* variables.

The function of statistical "tests of significance" is to test the effects found among the Class I variables against the effects of the variables of Class IV. . . . The aim of efficient design both in experiments and in surveys is to place as many of the extraneous variables as is feasible into the second class. . . . The aim of randomization in experiments is to place all of the third class into the fourth class. (**26**: 329, 330)

[2]   One way of looking at the difference between the two disciplines (Anthropology and Sociology) is to note that sociology tends to be more quantitative, while anthropology tends to be more qualitative.

Cultural anthropology generally refers to the study of existing peoples . . . its aim is to understand and appreciate the diversity in human behavior and ultimately to develop a science of human behavior. (**14**: 18,16)

Discovery Exercise 5: Subjective Complements—Reversed Word Order

Reverse the word order of the sentences with underlined infinitives in Exercise 4 so that the infinitive and everything after it comes first in the subject position.

The function of statistical tests is *to answer* a question.

To answer a question is the function of statistical tests.

Is there any difference in the meanings of the reversed sentences? This is a good test of whether or not an infinitive is a complement.

Subject = subjective complement

Discovery Exercise 6: Other Infinitive Forms—Passive and Progressive

How are the underlined infinitives in the following sentences different from those in Exercise 4?

[1]   Women appear to hold different attitudes from their male counterparts on a range of issues other than presidential preferences. These differences of opinion appear <u>to be growing</u> and may become an important factor in future elections. (39: 218).

[2]   The exclusionary rule is a judicial policy forbidding the admission of illegally seized evidence at trial. In a recent case in Massachusetts, the court seemed <u>to be loosening</u> the severity of the exclusionary rule. (**39**: 123)

[3]   Suppose that after 50 years of running deficits, the public debt becomes so large that each adult person's tax liability is $50,000. Suppose further that the government chooses (or is forced) to pay off the debt at that time. . . . Nothing says that taxes to pay off the debt must be divided equally; it seems likely that a special tax would be levied, based on ability to pay. But much of this analysis is beside the point. The federal government is not likely <u>to be forced</u> to pay off all its debt at once. (**33**: 314)

Analysis Exercise 7: Infinitive Usage Patterns

Fill in the blanks below to show the infinitive usage patterns in Exercises 4 and 6.

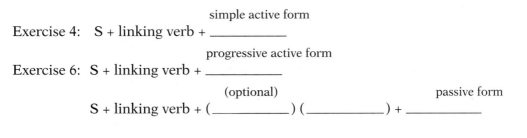

simple active form
Exercise 4:   S + linking verb + _____

progressive active form
Exercise 6:   S + linking verb + _____

                                          (optional)   passive form
          S + linking verb + (_____) (_____) + _____

Discovery Exercise 8a: *It* Subjects

Look at the clauses and sentences with infinitives below. What kinds of words come between the main verb and the underlined infinitives?

[1]   The advantages of the experimental method are so well known that we need not dwell on them here. . . . In many situations experiments are

not feasible, and this is often the case in the social sciences; but it is a mistake to use this situation to separate the social from the physical and biological sciences.

[2]   Actually, much research—in the social, biological, and physical sciences—must be based on nonexperimental methods. In such cases the rejection of the null hypothesis leads to several alternate hypotheses. . . . It is the duty of scientists to search, with painstaking effort and ingenuity, for bases on which to decide among these hypotheses.

[3]   The experimental method has some shortcomings. First it is often difficult to choose the "control" variables so as to exclude all the confounding extraneous variables; that is, it may be difficult or impossible to design an "ideal" experiment.

[4]   In social research, in preference to both surveys and experiments, frequently some design of controlled investigation is chosen. . . . These designs are sometimes called "natural experiments." For the sake of clarity, however, it is important to keep clear the distinctions among the methods and to reserve the word "experiment" for designs in which the uncontrolled variables are randomized. (**26**: 332, 331, 334)

[5]   In the late 1940s and 1950s, it was fashionable for radical socialists to be labeled "one-worlders." The United Nations was thought of as a potential world leadership organization to which all people could turn for political support and stability. (**33**: 470)

Analysis Exercise 8b: *It* Subjects—Reversing Word Order

Reorganize the sentences that contain underlined infinitives in Exercise 8a to place first the infinitive and everything after it. Follow the example below.

> It is a mistake to use this situation to separate the social from the biological sciences.

> To use this situation to separate the social from the biological sciences is a mistake.

Discussion:
What is the function of the infinitive (and everything after it) in the rewritten sentences in Exercise 8b? What kinds of words come after the infinitives in the rewritten sentences above? How did you handle "for radical socialists" in number 5?

Most of the infinitives in the sentences in Exercise 8a are followed by nouns. Number 2 differs slightly because the verb "search" has a preposition "for" as part of the infinitive. The complete infinitive is "to search for." This one is also confusing because it has a parenthetical expression between "search" and "for." However, the word after it is a noun.

Number 4 is also slightly different because the infinitive is followed by an adjective. The adjective in that position is rather formal. "Clear" is placed in that position so that it will not interfere with the prepositional phrase modifying "distinctions."

Infinitives can function as nouns, but because they are also verb forms, they can have objects just like other verbs. The nouns that follow the active infinitives in Exercise 8a are the objects of the infinitives. Sentence 5 has a passive infinitive. Who or what receives the action of the passive infinitive?

Analysis Exercise 9: Infinitives as Subjects

Answer the questions about the following sentences with underlined infinitives. The questions are different for each sentence.

[1]   It is clear that modern decision-makers make more decisions having great consequences in less time than ever before. To discuss decision-making in international politics is to engage in an essentially pre-scientific exercise, one that involves analogy, extrapolation, projection, and reduction from decisional studies of other units and levels of analysis to the international political systems. (**12: 61**)

    a. What is the subject of the sentence with the underlined infinitive?
    b. What is the function of "decision-making"?
    c. What is the function of "in international politics"?

[2]   Hanan C. Selvin advises researchers to refrain from making tests of significance until "after all relevant" uncontrolled variables have been controlled. . . . The control of all relevant variables is a goal seldom even approached in practice. To postpone to that distant goal all statistical tests illustrates that often "the perfect is the enemy of the good." (**26:** 331)

    a. What is the subject of the sentence with the underlined infinitive?
    b. What is the phrase "to that distant goal"?
    c. What is the function of "all statistical tests"?

Infinitives sometimes appear in subject position instead of the more usual "it" subject form. An infinitive subject is singular. Some types of writing may also reverse the object of the infinitive and the prepositional phrase of place or time.

Analyzing Infinitives as Other Parts of Speech

Analysis Exercise 10a: Infinitives as Adverbs

Study the passage below and then do the following:

First, analyze the sentences by finding the subjects, main verbs, infinitives, subjects, and objects of the infinitives.

Second, define the meaning of the infinitive in the sentences.

Third, describe the function of the infinitives in the sentences. Are they functioning as nouns or as something else?

> Types of Experiments—An absolute experiment is conducted to determine the absolute magnitude of a physical constant or the absolute existence or nonexistence of some phenomenon. A comparative experiment, on the other hand, is conducted to compare the relative values of several constants and is concerned with the differences, or perhaps the ratios among them. For example, one successful transmission of the human voice by wireless was enough to establish absolutely that radio programs were possible. On the other hand, many comparative experiments were conducted to arrive at today's design for transmitters and receivers. (13: 269)

Analysis Exercise 10b

Study the underlined infinitive below and determine its meaning and function. Is it different from those in Exercise 10a?

> Secretary of State Henry A. Kissinger posed one of the most difficult questions we face in meeting global problems: "The question is whether or not it is possible in the modern bureaucratic state to develop a sense of long-range purpose and to inquire into the meaning of activity." <u>To understand</u> why it is so difficult to change our individual and national approaches to problem solving, we must look behind present policies into the political, sociological, and psychological factors that motivate men to behave as they do. (12: 69)

Analysis Exercise 10c: Writing a Summary of Infinitive Functions

Write a description of how the infinitives function in Exercises 10a and 10b.

Analysis Exercise 11: Review of Some Infinitive Rules

To complete a review of some of the rules for infinitives that you have found in this chapter, circle the correct words.

1. When a sentence has a(n) active/passive verb, there may be a direct object between the main verb and the infinitive.

2. Direct objects of the main verbs may be noun phrases, pronouns, or infinitives/adjectives.

3. The direct object of the verb may act as the subject/object of the infinitive.

4. Infinitives that follow "be" or a linking verb are called objects/ complements.

5. Infinitive complements have the same meaning as the subject/ object of "be" or the linking verb.

6. Infinitives that follow "It" + "be" + adjective or noun are really the subjects/ objects/ complements in the sentence.

7. Infinitives may have objects, too. The objects of the infinitives may be noun phrases, noun clauses, and pronouns/adjectives.

8. The subject of an infinitive may be the same word as the subject of the main verb, or it may be the direct object of the infinitive/main verb.

9. In addition to acting as subjects, objects, and complements, infinitives also function as main verbs/adverbs.

10. When infinitives function as adverbs, they have the meaning of purpose or in order to/in spite of.

Analysis Exercise 12a: More Uses of Infinitives—Adjectives, Appositives, and Infinitive Complements

Sometimes infinitives function as nouns, sometimes as adverbs, and sometimes even as adjectives, appositives (noun phrases that follow and modifiy nouns), or infinitive complements. (An infinitive complement is an infinitive that follows the direct object of a causative verb: "order," "force," "cause," "get.") Find the infinitives in the passages below and try to figure out their function in each sentence. They may function as subjects, objects, adjectives, appositives, complements, or adverbs.

[1]   We referred briefly to the need for more observations in comparative experiments than in absolute experiments. It is more than a need for several observations. We must have several independent randomizations of treatments to experimental units. Such independent randomizations are called replications. To illustrate the idea of replication, consider designing an experiment to compare the effects of three different plant growth stimulants on green bean plants grown in a greenhouse. In comparative experiments the object is to compare two or more stimuli called treatments. The comparison of treatments ultimately involves comparing two treatments, so let us consider the problem of only two treatments. . . . What factors cause our estimate to be anything other than the true effect? The following list has been useful in trying to answer this question:
1. differences in experimental units
2. errors in applying treatments
3. errors in measuring the response
4. unknown factors
5. factors known but ignored
All of these factors contribute to the experimental error. In judging the significance of our estimate, we need to estimate the variance of our experimental error (called briefly "experimental error variance"). In designing experiments, it is frequently the case that we look ahead to the analysis of variance likely to result from data. (**13**: 271, 272)

[2]   One reason that citizens obey the government is because people believe that it has the authority to make laws. By authority we mean the ultimate right to force compliance with its decisions. In general, Americans believe that laws should be obeyed because they possess the quality of legitimacy, that is, they are appropriate and rightful. Legitimacy implies rightfulness. . . . To say that authority is legitimate is to suggest strongly an obligation to comply with its decision—even a moral obligation. (**39**: 8)

[3]   At each stage of the decision-making process three considerations implicitly or explicitly influence the decisions: what is desired, what can be done, and what must be done. . . . Decision making appears logical and rational when its components are presented theoretically. Yet in real life any number of contingencies may muddy the waters. Most obvious, of course, is the fact that policy makers differ in their assessments of nearly every situation. But differences among policy leaders are only one difficulty to be dealt with in making decisions. (**12**: 62, 63, 64)

[4]   Of the many kinds of current misuses [of statistical tests], this discussion is confined to only a few of the most common. First, there is "hunting with a shotgun" for significant differences. . . . Second, statistical "significance" is often confused with and substituted for substantive

significance. The attempts to use the probability levels of significance tests as measures of the strengths of relationships are very common and very mistaken. (**26**: 336))

[5]   There are two main tasks involved in the work of the cultural anthropologist, to describe the cultures of other peoples and to compare them.

[6]   Most of today's taxonomists, or systematists, as they are also called, use the term natural in a new sense—to refer to systems of classification that reflect the kinships of organisms.

Analysis Exercise 12b

1. Which infinitives in Exercise 12a mean "in order to"?
2. Which infinitive phrases in Exercise 12a function as adjectives?
3. What part of speech is "likely" in passage #1? What word does it modify?
4. Which infinitive functions as part of the main verb?
5. Which infinitives function as appositives?
6. Which infinitive functions as the subject of the sentence?
7. Which infinitive follows the object of a causative verb?
8. Which infinitives are complements?
9. In number 1, what is the function of "to answer"?

Analysis Exercise 13: Subjects of Infinitives

We have seen that infinitives may have "objects" as part of the infinitive phrase. Infinitives may also have "subjects" other than the main subject of the sentence or the object of the verb. One of these can be an "of" phrase in front of the infinitive. Examine the sentences below to see if you can find a fourth kind of "subject" of the infinitives.

1. We are well acquainted with the fact that a certain amount of time is necessary for the voltage across a capacitor to build up to a steady value if a resistor-capacitor circuit is subjected to a sudden change in driving voltage.

2. A certain amount of time is necessary for the thermal capacity to rise to a steady temperature when a thermal resistance-capacity system is subjected to a sudden change in temperature difference.

3. One of the main requirements for an act to be criminal is intent.

4. It is entirely possible for all the managers of a company to understand psychology and its nuances and yet not be effective in managing.

5. It takes longer for people who are relatively unknown to receive credit for their ideas.

6. Although it is still possible for individuals to buy dynamite, machine guns, rifles, and handguns, it is certainly illegal for them to be used in most situations.

Explanation 1—Infinitives and Their Functions in Academic Writing

Infinitives may function as nouns (subjects and objects, as complements, and as appositives). Infinitives may function as adverbs and as adjectives.

CHART 10-1   INFINITIVES AND THEIR FUNCTIONS
FORMS OF INFINITIVES

General time

Active (simple)

    to + base verb
    to see

Active (progressive)

    to + *be* + verb + ing
    to be seeing

Passive (simple)

    to + *be*+ verb past participle
    to be seen

Past time

Active (perfect simple)

    to + *have* + verb past participle
    to have seen

Passive (perfect simple)

    to + *have* + *been* + verb past participle
    to have been seen

THE MOST COMMON PATTERNS OF INFINITIVES IN SENTENCES

1. *subject* + *active verb* + *infinitive* + *(object of infinitive)*
   Consumers   want   to learn   new information.
   Consumers   expect   to be listened to.

2. *subject* + *passive verb* + *infinitive* + *object of infinitive*
   An experiment is conducted   to compare   values.

3. *subject* + *active verb* + *object* + *infinitive* + *(object of infinitive)*
   We   chose   design   to describe   the plan.
   Few   expected   the goal   to be achieved.

4. *subject + causative verb(active)+object + infinitive complement*+ object complement*
   The factors cause   our estimate   to be   a bad idea.

5. *subject*   +   *linking verb* +   *complement*   +   *(infinitive object)*
   The aim   is   to place   variables.
   The court   seemed   to be loosening   the rules.
   The government   is likely   to be forced.

6. *subject*   +   *linking verb + adj./ noun + subject of infinitive + infinitive*   +   *(inf. object)*
   Some time   is   necessary for the voltage   to build up.
   It   is   the duty   of scientists   to find   the key.

7. *subject(obj. of infinitive)*   *linking verb*   *complement*   *(+ subject of infinitive)*
   To search for the key   is   the duty   of scientists.
   To pass the TOEFL   is   necessary.

8. *introductory adverbial phrase +*   *subject + verb +*   *rest of sentence*
   To compensate for revenue losses, a tax was enacted.
   To be deserved,   punishment must be relevant.

NOTE: See appendix for a list of verbs and adjectives that are followed by infinitives.

CHART 10-2 INFINITIVES AND THEIR TIME RELATIONSHIPS TO THE MAIN VERB

General Time Form—Infinitives used as objects of the verb
express the same time or a time future to the main verb

    subject   active verb   infinitive   object of infinitive
1. The president   wanted   *to change*   the rules.
                     (Infinitive is object of main verb)

    subject   active verb   infinitive
2. The rules   needed   *to be changed.*
                (the action of the infinitive affects the subject)

General Time Form —Infinitives used as subjects and complements
express the same time or a time future to the main verb

  active infinitive subject   linking verb   active infinitive
3. *To understand*   is   *to perceive.*
               (same time)

  passive infinitive subject   linking verb   passive infinitive
4. *To be understood*   was   *to be perceived.*
               (same time)

*Exceptions: "make," "have" and "let" are followed by the base form of the verb (*to*-less infinitive). "Have" and "get" are followed by the past participle in passive constructions.

     The professor *made / let / had* the students <u>leave</u>.
     The instructor *will have* the work <u>done</u>.

Infinitives, Gerunds, and Abstract Noun Phrases   **299**

Past Time—Perfect Form—Infinitives used as objects of the verb
express an action earlier than the main verb

subject	linking verb	active perfect infinitive	object of infinitive
5. The president	seems	*to have changed*	the rules.

(action of the infinitive earlier than the main verb)

subject	linking verb	passive perfect infinitive
6. The rules	seem	*to have been changed.*

(action of the infinitive earlier than verb and affects the subject)

subject	passive verb	passive perfect infinitive
7. The landlord	was known	*to have been thrown* out of the apartment.

(actions of the verb and the infinitive affect the subject)
(action of the infinitive earlier than the verb)

SPECIAL NOTE: In some languages a passive verb followed by a passive infinitive (or gerund) means the same as an active verb, in much the same way that a double negative sometimes means an affirmative in English (e.g., *not un*common). This is NOT true of passive verbs followed by passive infinitives (or gerunds) in English. The actions of the verb and the following infinitive are **both** passive.

Using Infinitives in Writing

Writing Exercise 14: Read and React

Briefly summarize the following passage. Then write a critique (your opinion) of the ideas expressed. Last, review your work. Did you use any infinitives? Are there sentences that you could rewrite appropriately with infinitives? Discuss your ideas in class.

Understanding and Controlling Criminal Behavior—In a few years, the genetic keys to understanding and controlling behavior should be known. Through synthesis of the body's own chemicals and time-release implants of powerful therapeutic medications, behavior could be kept in constant check: drugs fighting drugs.

The next step might be the use of nanocomputer implants to keep track of and control the behavior of public offenders. These implants could be placed in the brain and could be equipped with microscopic transmitters to constantly monitor behavior and to send subliminal anti-crime messages to the offender (e.g., "Do what the law requires" or "Help, don't harm"). The nanocomputer could also release control chemicals on a set schedule and even diagnose changes in behavior and take necessary action to calm the individual.

(from Gene Stephens, "Drugs and Crime in the Twenty-first Century," *The Futurist* [May–June, 1992]: 19, 20. Reprinted with permission.)

PART II   GERUNDS

Discovering the Grammar of Gerunds

Read the following passages from an Agricultural Extension Service bulletin, notice the words ending in "-ing," and then answer the questions.

[1]   *The Extension Service*—The Smith-Lever Act, passed by Congress in 1914, provided for the Cooperative Extension Service as a part of the Land-Grant College System. Local people, the state university, and the United States Department of Agriculture cooperated in *planning, financing,* and *carrying* out a system of rural education. It is now the largest system of organized adult education in the world. *Providing* a County Agricultural Extension Council in each district, the law also provides for certain limitations on the powers and activities of the council.
   The law establishes as the sole purpose of the council the dissemination of information. The law establishes the *giving* of instruction and practical demonstrations on subjects *relating* to agriculture. *Training* in home economics subjects has been a part of extension activities since its very *beginning.*

[2]   *Extension and the World Bank*—Rural development personnel in the World Bank are in a strategic position to survey and draw lessons from the whole world mosaic of the various kinds of extension systems. *Looking* over the whole issue, John F.A. Russell, Rainfed Crops advisor to the Bank, concludes that no one methodology has a monopoly of merits. . . . Certain basic principles need to be respected for improved extension performance. First, management must be improved. . . . Second, an integrated approach should be taken to service delivery. . . . Third, extension messages must be made relevant to farmers' needs. *Farming* systems research is *addressing* this issue with multidisciplinary research/extension teams *giving* a needed data base. . . . Fourth, systematic means must be found for *monitoring* and *evaluating* the extension impact. . . . Some cost *savings* can come from more *channeling* of services and *training* to and through groups rather than individuals, and the supplemental use of other media, *including* radio, for example. Finally there is need for stronger farmer participation, both men and women. The farmer adopts or refuses all new technology, *supplementing* research by *fine-tuning* all recommendations to fit perceived needs *supplementing* extension by *advising* interested neighbors. (**10**)

Infinitives, Gerunds, and Abstract Noun Phrases   **301**

a. Nouns can be identified in sentences in several ways. What do you look for in order to identify a noun?

b. Gerunds act as nouns. How can you identify a gerund? Find the gerunds in the passages above.

c. Some of the words ending in "-ing" are participles (adjectives). Find the participles. How did you identify them?

d. Two of the words ending in "-ing" are neither gerunds nor adjectives. What are they?

e. Gerunds and participles are verb forms, so they can have objects. Find the objects of the participles and gerunds. Gerunds and their objects are called gerund phrases. Gerunds and their prepositions are also called gerund phrases.

Discussion: Definition of Gerunds

Gerunds are words ending in "-ing" that are used as nouns. Gerunds may be used as subjects or objects of the main verb or as objects of prepositions. Gerunds may also be used as other parts of speech. Gerunds are always singular.

Discovery Exercise 16: Gerund Phrases as Adverbials

Find the gerunds in the passages below and try to figure out what they do in the sentences. Are they subjects or objects? What do they mean?

[1]   By studying human nature, the variety of peoples in the world today and in the past, and the relationship of the human species to others, we are better able to understand why we behave the way we do. The physical anthropologist gives us valuable information about the uniqueness and limitations of our physical structure. Why are we different from apes, for example?

[2]   No anthropologist can work without an awareness of the past, of what the particular sequence of events was that led to the situation under study. In describing another culture or in comparing aspects of two cultures, the anthropologist dares not ignore the cultural background. Yet there is no doubt that history and anthropology are distinct disciplines.

[3]   The study of language from an anthropological perspective forms a third branch of the discipline—anthropological linguistics. Anthropologists ask questions about language from the point of view of the human species rather than trying to describe the language or its structure. (14: 9, 18, 13)

[4]   People react to information overload by making errors.

[5]   In defining the field of management, care must be taken to distinguish be-
        tween tools and content.

Discovery Exercise 17: Gerunds as Subjective Complements and Appositives

In the sentences below, find the gerunds acting as subjective complements and appositives. Do all of the passages contain gerunds?

[1]   Many different plans have been developed to help the consumer make food
        choices that will ensure an adequate diet. One of the most familiar is the
        Four Food Group Plan. The Four Food Group Plan specifies that a cer-
        tain quantity of food must be consumed from each group. An objective in
        diet planning is to design a balanced diet. Traditionally, balance means
        including foods from the four food groups.

[2]   The food exchange system was first developed in 1950 and revised in 1976.
        It is useful to the consumer who wants to eat well and control calories at
        the same time. The Exchange System sorts the foods of the Four Food
        Group plan into exchanges, groupings that are equal in k calories with
        specific serving sizes. (**19**: 29, 31)

[3]   Co-optation is one of the key social
        processes used to maintain any strat-
        ification system, whether societal or
        organizational . . . "formal co-opta-
        tion requires informal control over
        the cooptated elements lest the unity
        of command and decision be imper-
        iled." These informal controls in-
        clude social favors—inviting people
        for lunch or dinner, playing golf or
        other sports with them, and so forth.
        (**35**: 232)

Golf

[4]   Can you say anything you want about someone else? Not really. Individu-
        als are protected from defamation of character, which is defined as wrong-
        fully hurting a person's good reputation. Defamation of character is called
        slander. Legally, slander is the public uttering of a statement that holds a
        person up for contempt, ridicule or hatred. (**39**: 108)

Question: How did you analyze "groupings" in number 2?

Explanation 2—Gerunds and Their Functions in Academic Writing

Gerunds function as nouns: subjects, objects of verbs, objects of prepositions, subjective complements, and appositives. Gerunds as objects of prepositions function as adverbs.

CHART 10-3 GERUNDS AND THEIR FUNCTIONS

FORMS OF GERUNDS

General time

Active (simple)

   verb + *ing*
   seeing

Passive (simple)

   being + verb past participle
   being seen

Past time

Active (perfect simple)

   having + verb past participle
   having seen

Passive (perfect simple)

   having + *been* + verb past participle
   having been seen

THE MOST COMMON PATTERNS OF GERUNDS IN A SENTENCE

1. *subject* + *active verb* + *gerund* + *(object of gerund)*

   The university   encourages   learning   mathematics.
   The law   establishes   the giving   of instruction.

2. *subject* + *linking verb* + *gerund* + *(object of gerund)*

   Balance   means   including   all foods.

3. *subject* + *(object of gerund)* + *verb* + *rest of sentence*

   Evaluating   the impact   could solve   our problems.

4. *subject* + *verb* + *prep.+ gerund + rest of sentence*

   A systematic means must be found   for monitoring the results.

5. *introductory adverbial phrase*   *subject* + *verb + rest of sentence*

   By advising neighbors,   the farmer helps   his community.

NOTE: Notice that, as in number 1 above, when the gerund is preceded by "the," the object of the gerund is an "of" phrase.

CHART 10-4   GERUNDS AND THEIR TIME RELATIONSHIPS
TO THE MAIN VERB

<u>General Time Form—Gerunds used as objects of the verb</u> express the same time or a time future to the main verb.

　　　　　　subject　　　　verb　　　　　active gerund　　object of the gerund
1. The president　considered　　*changing*　　　the rules.
　　　　　　　　　　　　　　　　　　(Gerund = object of main verb)

　　　　　　subject　　　　verb　　　　passive gerund
2. The president anticipated *being elected.*
　　　　　　　　　　　　　　(Action of gerund affects the subject.)

3. The candidate was last seen *being attacked* by the press.
　　　　　　　　　(Action of the verb and the gerund affect the subject.)

<u>General Time Form—Gerunds used as subjects or complements of the verb</u> express the same time or a time earlier than the main verb.

　　　active gerund subject　　　verb　　active gerund complement
4. *Seeing*　　　　　　　　　is　　　*believing.*
　　　　　　　　　　　　(same time)

　　　subject　　　　gerund object　　　verb　　object
5. *Lowering*　　the interest rates　had　　two effects.
　　　(Action of the gerund is earlier than the main verb.)

　　　passive gerund subject　　　verb　　passive gerund complement
6. *Being seen*　　　　　　meant　　*becoming recognized.*
　　　　　　　　　　　　(same time)

<u>Past Time—Perfect Gerund Form</u> expresses an action earlier than the main verb.

　　　subject　　　　　verb　　active gerund　　　object of gerund
7. The president forgot　*having changed*　the rules.
　　　　　　　　　　(perfect gerund = object of main verb)

　　　subject　　　　　verb　　passive: perfect gerund
8. The candidate understood *not having been elected* as president.
　　　　　　　(Action of gerund affects the subject.)

SPECIAL NOTE # 3: In some languages a passive verb followed by a passive gerund equals an active meaning in much the same way that some double negatives equal an affirmative idea in English. This is not true for a passive verb + passive gerund or infinitive in English. If a passive gerund or infinitive follows a passive verb, the meaning of the sentence remains passive.

#5: Often a gerund subject implies a time earlier than the main verb. We will discuss gerund subjects later.

It is interesting to note that gerunds do not have as many uses as infinitives do in academic writing. This may be because the present participle, not the gerund, fulfills the functions of adjective and verb. In conclusion, then, *infinitives are far more common in academic writing than gerunds are.*

PART III GERUNDS VERSUS INFINITIVES

Explanation 3—Subjects of Gerunds and Infinitives

Gerunds are verb forms and may have subjects in academic writing. You may remember that in spoken English we use a possessive noun or pronoun in front of the gerund as its subject.

> "subject" of gerund
> *Their social* typing may lead to the label being accepted by others.

As we saw earlier, infinitives may have subjects expressed in a "for" phrase.

> "subject" of infinitive
> It would be worthwhile *for you* to study vocabulary for the GRE.

Practicing Gerunds and Infinitives

Practice Exercise 18: Subjects of Gerunds and Infinitives

Find the gerunds and infinitives and their subjects in the following paragraphs.

[1]   Within less than a hundred years, the human body has been invaded by hundreds of new chemicals. It cannot use, detoxify, or expel all of these substances. The changes wrought by the Industrial Revolution have taken only decades but it takes millions of years for evolution to develop systems for handling new substances. An example is the body's handling of alcohol. Your protection against its harmful effects is built into your genes. One of those genes, expressed in your liver, codes for an enzyme that converts alcohol into substances the body can use or excrete. So long as the liver is not overwhelmed with alcohol, the system works efficiently. But alcohol has been around ever since the first fruit ripened and fermented, so there have been millions of years for natural selection to mold a detoxifying system for it. (**19: 8**)

[2] President Harry S. Truman lamented that "I sit here all day trying to persuade people to do things they ought to have sense enough to do without my persuading them."

President Harry S. Truman

Explanation 4—The Difference Between Gerunds and Infinitives as Subjects in a Sentence

Infinitives as Subjects—Infinitives often express purpose and imply a slightly future action. As subjects they may emphasize the act of doing something in an objective, formal way, or they may indicate a purpose.

> (the act)
> *To discuss* decision-making in international politics is to engage in an essentially prescientific exercise.

> (the act)
> *To punish* a man who has tried his hardest to secure a job during a period of acute and extensive unemployment for having insufficient means of support is shocking.

Gerunds as Subjects—Gerunds emphasize the action, the continuous nature of an activity, and often imply something already in progress. A gerund may also express a cause/effect relationship with the verb.

> (action emphasis)
> *Running down* small game was probably one of the earliest methods of obtaining meat.

> (cause)   (effect)
> *The punishing* of a man known to be innocent of any crime shocks our moral consciousness and is seen as a grave injustice.

Infinitives, Gerunds, and Abstract Noun Phrases **307**

Explanation 5—Differences Between Gerunds and Infinitives as Objects in a Sentence

These somewhat general differences in meaning are strongly emphasized when gerunds or infinitives are used as objects and are combined with particular verbs.

A few verbs that take both forms even change meaning.

1st action   2nd action
The manager *tried*   *to fill out* the application.
(He attempted the action and couldn't do it for some reason.)

1st action   2nd action
The manager *forgot*   *to fill out* the application.
(He didn't fill out the application because he forgot he was supposed to.)

The manager *tried filling out* the application.
(He did several things, one of which was filling out the application.)

2nd action   1st action
The manager *forgot*   *filling out* the application.
(He filled out the application in the past and then forgot that he had done it.)

The explanation below helps to explain why.

With certain verbs,

infinitives mean future, unfulfilled actions in relation to the action of the preceding verb.

gerunds mean fulfilled actions (fulfilled before the action of the preceding verb).

2nd action   1st action
The manager *remembered paying* the bill.
(the action was fulfilled before the action of the first, main verb)

1st action   2nd action
The manager *remembered to pay* the bill.
(the action happened after the action of the first, main verb)

The verbs of this type are "try," "remember," "forget," and "regret." "Stop" is used somewhat the same way, but in this case the infinitive means "in order to."

earlier action   later action
He *stopped* (in order) *to fill out* the application.

later action   action already in progress
He *stopped filling* out the application.

A complete list of verbs that take infinitive and gerund objects can be found in Appendix 3.

How and When Gerund and Infinitive Objects Are Used

The following infinitives and gerunds patterns are arranged in order of most common to least common.*

Pattern 1

	subject	verb	infinitive object
	The upper-middle class	aspired	to join upper-class prestige clubs.

Pattern 2

	subject	verb	direct object	infinitive
	People	have used	power and wealth (subject of infinitive)	to maintain their position.

Pattern 3

	subject	verb	gerund object
	The second step	involves	making sure no major changes are made.

Pattern 4

	subject	verb	possessive	gerund object	(object of gerund)
	We	resent	their	social typing	of students.

Note that noun clauses ("that" clauses) are used more than either infinitives or gerunds. They occur *46 percent* of the time.

Knowledge of sentence patterns can help a writer determine the choice of a gerund or infinitive object. Although noun clauses and infinitive objects are used most of the time, you will see gerunds used in your academic reading assignments from time to time.

Practice Exercise 19: Infinitive and Gerund Object Patterns

Study the following sentences and then try to determine what patterns they follow — 1, 2, 3, or 4.

1. A wealthy family seeks to protect the wealth being given to inept family members by establishing trust arrangements and legal and financial advisors.

2. Young people who want to become doctors but are not admitted to medical school may go to other countries.

3. People owning a factory may decide to close it or to move it somewhere else.

*Adapted from M. Celce-Murcia and Diane Larsen-Freeman, *The Grammar Book* (Boston, Mass.: Heinle & Heinle, 1983), p. 433.

4. Social ranking begins to occur when surpluses are generated, and when some individuals own or control appreciably more productive resources than others.

5. Conflict theories try to explain human behavior in terms of how individuals seek to realize their interests.

6. Marx failed to predict the shift from individual capitalists to large corporations.

7. A number of institutions and social processes help to maintain systems of stratification.

8. Peasant workers and new political parties all work to rally supporters to their cause.

9. If new members refuse to go along with the way things have always been done, they may be socially ostracized.

10. Totalitarianism involves the use of state power to control and regulate all phases of life.

11. South African whites have used the power of the state to influence the ideology and the ideas that circulate within the society.

12. Advantaged members of society use their superior power, wealth and influence to maintain their privileged positions.

13. Many people have the mental capacity to become doctors.

14. Ideology does little to restrain their anger.

15. The second step in co-optation involves making sure no major changes are made.

16. The increase in length of the long bones involves a dismantling of the crystals near the ends of the bone to allow for the growth of the collagen and the subsequent reinvasion by mineral crystals.

17. One example is the body's handling of alcohol.

Explanation 5 (continued)—When to Use Infinitives and Gerunds as Objects of Verbs*

We often use **infinitives** after:

1. Nonfactive verbs (express something that hasn't happened yet)
   decide, hesitate, intend, learn, need, prepare, tend, volunteer

*Adapted from Celce-Murcia and Larsen-Freeman, *The Grammar Book*, pp. 434–438.

2. Verbs indicating future
    attempt, deserve, expect, promise
3. Verbs of request/ denial
    ask, beg, claim, decline, demand, refuse, threaten
4. Verbs of emotion
    hope, mean, prefer, struggle, want, wish

5. Verbs of implication (imply the truth or falsity of the statement)
    bother, condescend, fail, happen, hasten, manage, neglect, venture

"She *condescended to give* us permission" implies that she gave us permission.
"She *neglected to give* us permission" implies that she did not give us permission.
    We often use **gerunds** after:

1. Factive verbs (express something that really happened)
    admit, appreciate, finish, legalize, miss, regret, stop

2. Two-word verbs
    insist on, consist of

Discussion: The idea that we can learn which verbs take gerunds and which take infinitives by learning categories of verbs does not help for all verbs. For example, "anticipate" and "avoid" seem to be nonfactive (to indicate something that hasn't happened yet), but they are followed by gerunds.

The manager *anticipated filling out* the application.
The manager *avoided filling out* the application.

To avoid incorrect usage, use every method available to increase your gerunds and infinitives repertoire, but be aware that every rule has exceptions and that some verbs may follow only one of the many explanations.

Practice Exercise 20: Choosing Infinitives or Gerunds

The following passages contain infinitives and gerunds used as subjects, objects, adverbs, or something else. Fill in the blanks with the correct form of the words given. Choose only an infinitive or a gerund. Some sentences contain two consecutive blanks. It would be interesting to discuss how you decided what to put in the second blank.

[1]   *The Main Features of International Organizations*
    All of the international organizations represent diplomatic means for

    (*try*) _____ (*solve*) _____ problems facing
    the international community. The United Nations was created in 1945 as

a diplomatic instrument of states (*facilitate*) _____
the peaceful settlement of disputes and conflicts, (*attack*) _____
economic and social causes of conflict, and (*build*) _____ a
lasting peace. An international commission on control and supervision
was created by the January 1973 Paris Agreement on (*end*)
_____ the war and (*restore*) _____ peace in
Vietnam as one of several devices (*supervise*) _____ the
implementation of the agreement and its protocols.

   If the United Nations does not act, newspaper editorials pro-
claim the ineffectiveness of the organization, or they demand (*know*)
_____ why the United Nations refuses (*act*) _____.
Seldom do these editorials state the fact that the United Nations can do
only what its members want it (*do*) _____. It is the states
through the diplomatic device of the United Nations that refuse (*act*)
_____. (**12**: 290)

[2]   Hume is the first modern philosopher who finds no need (*bring*)
_____ God to the rescue of philosophy; he is the first
modern philosopher who remains true to his principles to their logical
conclusion, without (*attempt*) _____ (*explain*)
_____ away difficulties in his philosophical position
through resort to an "outside factor" such as God.

   Hume recognized the inconsistencies in the positions taken by his
British predecessors, and hoped (*prevent*) _____ these
inconsistencies from (*arise*) _____ in his own philosophy.
He took as his guiding principle the scientific doctrine then current in
which nature could be understood and explained in terms of mechanical
laws, and in his *Treatise of Human Nature* and *An Enquiry Concerning
Human Understanding*, he attempted (*apply*) _____ this
mechanistic doctrine to his investigation into human nature and into
human knowledge. (**16**: 135)

[3]   *Probability* has been defined as the study of the frequency of appearance of a phenomenon in relation to all possible alternatives. The difficulty in (*try*) _____ (*trace*) _____ the origins
of probability is that it began essentially as an empirical science and
developed only much later as a mathematical science. Indeed, probability has twin roots in two fairly different lines of thought: the solution of gambling, or betting, problems and the (*handle*)
_____ of statistical data related to such quantitative

instruments as mortality tables and insurance rates. Let us first exam
ine the wagering problems of (*gamble*) _____ .

Did (*gamble*) _____ develop from game (*play*)
_____ , did it arise from religious activity, or did it arise
from (*wager*) _____? No one knows. . . . Games of chance
are probably as old as the human desire (*get*) _____ something for nothing. (**28**: 623)

Practice Exercise 21: Identifying and Analyzing Perfect Infinitives and Gerunds

Read the passages below and find the perfect forms of the infinitives and gerunds.
When do the actions of the perfect gerunds and infinitives take place in relation to the
main verbs? Discuss their meanings in the context of the sentences.

President John F. Kennedy

[1]   John F. Kennedy, after promising
to take certain measures during a
press conference, is said to have
remarked: "Today I actually made
a little policy."

[2]   Most of those who later contributed to the principles of business management—such as Sheldon, Dennison, Mooney, and Barnard—show no evidence of having been familiar with the work of Fayol.

[3]   Nearly every controversy in this book seems to have closed with a statement saying, in effect, "It's up to you."

[4]   Administrators and bureaucrats who translate words into action have some
opportunity to imprint policy with their own individual interpretations.
This appears to have been the case with the bombing attacks against North

Vietnam ordered by General John Lavalle, commander of U.S. Air Force units in Southeast Asia in the early months of 1972. . . . According to a high-ranking military source close to the incident, Lavalle was known to have received no written orders authorizing the attack. . . . On the other hand, General Lavalle claimed to have believed that his superiors in Saigon were aware of his bombing attacks and tacitly condoned them. (**12**: 67)

[5]   *Labeling Theory*—Labeling theory describes the ability of some groups to impose a label of "deviant" on certain other members of society. The police, for example, have ideas about "typical" juvenile behavior and of who are "good kids" or "punks," partly depending on family background. A person gets labeled "sinner," "queer," "crazy," "junkie." Sometimes called stigmatization, this process involves spoiling someone's identity by labeling him or her in a negative way. . . . Eventually the label may be accepted by others or by the individual. . . . Thus, the process of labeling may produce deviant careers. Other people interpret the present and even the past behavior of stigmatized individuals in terms of their new identities. For example, someone caught cheating on a test is assumed not to have written the excellent paper turned in earlier. . . . Also, having spent time in a juvenile facility or detention center is a serious negative feature of juveniles' records and may hurt their futures. (**35**: 193)

[6]   In 1982 there were 394,380 people imprisoned in federal and state prisons in the United States, and nearly 200,000 more on parole. People get put in jail who have been arrested for a crime, are awaiting trial, and are unable to raise the money required for their bail. Given the delays in the court systems of many cities today, poor people who cannot raise bail may stay in jail for months awaiting trial without ever having been convicted of committing a crime. (**35**: 205)

[7]   The government of the ancient Greek city-state of Athens is often considered to be the historic model for a direct democracy. Direct democracy in Athens is considered to have been an ideal form of democracy because it demanded a high level of participation from every citizen. All important decisions were put to a vote of the entire citizenry so that public debate over political issues was a constant feature of social life. (**39**: 9)

Practice Exercise 22: Using Gerunds and Infinitives in Context

Fill in the blanks in the paragraphs below with the correct forms of gerunds or infinitives .

[1]   Gaming seems (*reach*) _____ such a level of popularity with the Greeks and Romans that it eventually became necessary

(*forbid*) _____ it legally except in certain seasons. Later, during the Middle Ages, the Christian Church launched a campaign against (*play*) _____ with dice and cards, not so much because of the (*gamble*) _____, however, but rather because of the vices of (*drink*) _____ and (*swear*) _____ that seemed (*accompany*) _____ the (*gamble*) _____ .

During the Third Crusade (1190), no person below the rank of knight was allowed (*gamble*) _____ for money, whereas knights and clergy, interestingly enough, could play but were not allowed (*lose*) _____ more than twenty shillings in a twenty-four-hour period. Medieval history is full of such attempts (*prohibit*) _____ or (*limit*) _____ (*gamble*) _____ .

[2]   One might assume that during these several thousand years of (*dice-play*) _____, some elements of a probability theory would have begun (*appear*) _____. Yet no direct link between (*gamble*) _____ and mathematics seems (*observed*/passive form) _____. Apparently no one considered that (*calculate*) _____ the frequency of falls of dice was possible or fruitful or even that each face would turn up with equal frequency.

[3]   The first true mathematical treatment of probability began in the latter part of the fifteenth century and in the early part of the sixteenth century, when some Italian mathematicians began (*consider*) _____ the mathematical chances in certain gambling games. Girolamo Cardano (1501–1576), who was rich in genius and often devoid of principle, was an Italian professor of mathematics and medicine with a most interesting and varied career. Over a period of forty years, Cardan gambled daily. Early in his life he determined that if one did not play for monetary stakes, no compensation would be gained for the time lost in (*gamble*) _____, which could otherwise be spent in such more worthwhile pursuits as (*learn*) _____. Since he did not wish to waste his time in unprofitable activities, he seriously analyzed the probabilities of (*draw*) _____ aces out of a deck of cards and of (*throw*) _____ sevens with two dice. Then he reported the results

of these investigations . . . in a gambler's manual called "The Gambling Scholar," first published in 1539. (*Aid*) _____ his fellow gamblers, he noted, for example, that when (*cut*) _____ a deck the chance of (*obtain*) _____ a certain card is considerably increased by first (*rub*) _____ the card with soap!

[4]   We mentioned earlier that probability had twin roots. . . . Let us consider the (*process*) _____ of statistical data. Statistics has been defined as the science and art of (*gather*) _____ , (*analyze*) _____ , and (*make*) _____ inferences from data. Significant statistical investigations began only when merchants, particularly those representing insurance companies, needed probabilistic estimations of events.

Insurance appears (*create/* passive) _____ as early as Roman times (*protect*) _____ merchant sailing vessels. The first marine insurance companies were established in the fourteenth century in Holland and Italy; by the sixteenth century, it had moved to other countries. . . . (*Put*) _____ these operations on a firm actuarial footing, however, some mathematical determination of probabilities was called for. John Graunt (1620–1674), a London merchant, was the first person (*draw*) _____ statistical inferences from analyses of mass data. The bills of mortality from which Graunt drew his conclusions were originally yearly and weekly reports of the number of burials in various London parishes. They seem (*arise*) _____ as early as 1532 (*keep*) _____ track of the progress of the plague in London. Graunt's work included many conclusions of varying validity and generality. (**28:** 624, 627)

Discussion: Deciding whether to choose a gerund or an infinitive is difficult, but our problems are considerably reduced if we remember a few basic facts:

1. the typical sentence patterns.
2. the relative percentage of usage—infinitives are used most in the object position.
3. the time relationship between the gerund or infinitive and the main verb.
4. sentence cues like articles and prepositions.

Try to develop methods of keeping track of the verb + infinitive/gerund combinations in your own major field. Native speakers of English learn these combinations through repetition, and eventually the combinations become automatic. Speakers of English as a second language can do the same thing if they make an effort to notice and practice the repeated combinations.

Using Gerunds and Infinitives in Writing

Writing Exercise 23: Read and React

Briefly summarize the following passage and then write your reactions to it. How did the idea of a "sober-up" pill make you feel? Do you think it's a good idea? Then reread your summary to see how many gerunds and infinitives you used. Discuss the different possibilities in class. Did you use more infinitives or more gerunds?

A drug now being tested promises to alleviate the massive problems caused by alcohol. RO15-5413, first tested by a Swiss pharmaceutical firm, sobered up heavily intoxicated rats in two minutes. Later tests found that, if the drug was taken before drinking, the rats did not get drunk; if it was taken over a period of time, the rats lost interest in alcohol. Early reports indicate that the same results will be found for human beings, leading to a "sober-up" pill.

Police have expressed concern that a driver might kill someone while under the influence of alcohol and then take a sober-up pill in an attempt to hide the "evidence," but since the drug works by blocking the impact of the alcohol on the brain rather than actually lowering the body's blood-alcohol content, the alcohol in the blood stream should still be detectable with blood tests. Since half of all street crime and traffic fatalities are associated with alcohol, this should be a great boon to curbing the nation's biggest drug problem.

(from Gene Stephens," Drugs and Crime," *The Futurist* [May–June 1992]: 19.)

PART IV   ABSTRACT NOUN PHRASES

A **concrete noun** is a word for an object that you can touch, see, or smell. An **abstract noun** is a word for an idea, emotion, or concept.

Abstract noun phrases are common in academic writing. They are considered to be stronger than either gerund phrases or infinitive phrases. When an abstract noun phrase is possible, many experienced writers will choose it instead of a gerund or infinitive.

Many abstract noun phrases are derived from simple sentences. The predicates of simple sentences (verbs and predicate adjectives) are reduced into noun phrases that may be used the way other noun phrases are used: as subjects, objects, complements, and appositives in other sentences. Some abstract noun phrases are derived from "it"-fronted noun clause sentences.

Simple sentence	The supply curve shifts rapidly.
Abstract noun phrase	the rapid supply curve shift
Simple sentence	The police cracked down heavily on drug sellers.
Abstract noun phrase	The heavy police crackdown on drug sellers
Sentence	It is interesting that people fear public speaking.
Abstract noun phrase	people's interesting fear of public speaking

Analysis Exercise 24a: Forming Abstract Noun Phrases

Study the examples above of how sentences can be changed into abstract noun phrases and then change the following sentences into abstract noun phrases.

1. Consumers discover information easily.
2. Similar circumstances prevailed before 1914.
3. The market failed miserably.
4. The government produced and operated centers for inoculation free.
5. Political changes occur frequently.
6. Television magnifies violence enormously.
7. College attendance has increased dramatically.
8. Functionalist and conflict sociologists differ significantly.
9. Education has expanded dramatically in the U.S.
10. Some occupations and organizations practice discrimination.

Analysis Exercise 24b: Questions About Abstract Noun Phrase Formation

Think about what you did when you changed the sentences above into abstract noun phrases and answer the following questions. Then write a summary of your answers.

1. Which word in the sentence do you change to the abstract noun?
2. What becomes of the subject of the sentence when it is changed to an abstract noun phrase? (More than one way is possible in the sentences above.)
3. What happens to the adverb?

4. What happens to the direct object?

5. When there is a direct object and a subject, what happens to each?

Analysis Exercise 25: Changing Abstract Noun Phrases into Sentences

Examine the following abstract noun phrases and decide which ones can be expressed better in sentence form. They are all possible, but some of the sentences do not have exactly the same meanings as the phrases.

1. the income redistribution programs

2. unemployment insurance benefits

3. government health care services

4. the military's exercise of power and authority

5. the existence of a centralized state

6. the rapid expansion of education

7. the existence of a bureaucratic state

Analysis Exercise 26: Writing a Summary of Abstract Noun Phrase Rules

Fill in the blanks below to complete the rules for abstract noun phrases.

Many abstract noun phrases are derived from verbs and predicate adjectives in simple sentences. The original subject of the simple sentence usually appears in three ways in the abstract noun phrase: in an _____ phrase; a _____ phrase , or a _____ form of a noun.

An object in the original sentence usually becomes an _____ phrase. An "-ly" adverb in the original sentence becomes an _____ in the abstract noun phrase.

Explanation 6—Abstract Noun Phrase Formation

To change a simple sentence into an abstract noun phrase, we usually use the following equivalents (parallels).

1. The original subject of a simple sentence = a prepositional phrase or a possessive noun.

2. An object in the original sentence = a prepositional "of" phrase.

3. Adverbs = adjectives.

4. The original verb = an abstract noun.

Exceptions and additions:

1. An adverb with no "-ly" ending does not change.

    He arrived *late* = His *late* arrival

2. "Very" in the sentence becomes "great" in the abstract noun phrase.

3. Subjects of abstract noun phrases can appear as noun modifiers:

    the *police* crackdown

  or with other prepositions:

    the difference *between* functionalists and conflict sociologists

Discussion: Usage of Noun Clauses, Infinitives, Gerunds, and Abstract Noun Phrases

All of the following sentences are grammatically correct, but some are preferable to others. Do you have a preference?

Noun clauses

  It pleased the stockholders that the company promptly negotiated the contract.

  That the company promptly negotiated the contract pleased the stockholders.

Infinitive

  For the company to promptly negotiate the contract pleased the stockholders.

Gerund

  The company's promptly negotiating the contract pleased the stockholders.

Abstract noun phrases

  The company's prompt negotiation of the contract pleased the stockholders.

  The prompt negotiation of the contract by the company pleased the stockholders.

Experts say that noun phrases are stronger than infinitives or gerunds and that writers should always choose them. But too many abstract noun phrases make a sentence hard to read, as do too many noun clauses.

Whether gerunds or infinitives are used as objects is usually determined by the preceding verb, but what about gerunds and infinitives as subjects? Why would an author choose one over the other? Do writers say to themselves, "Here I'm going to use a noun clause"? The answer is "probably not." Native speakers don't usually analyze structure unless someone tells them that a sentence is confusing.

After many years in a field, writers seem to pick up the writing conventions (the style and usage) used by other writers in that field. Students begin the process in university classes when their professors tell them that they should express an idea one way or another. Let's look at some examples from different fields.

Noun clauses—Philosophy, Political Science, and Economics
Philosophy

> It is plausible *that what Wittgenstein has in mind is the sort of supposition that I noted in connection with Russell.*
> *What we have to acknowledge* is the primitiveness of the concept of a person. *What I mean by the concept of a person* is the concept of an entity. (**20**: 311)

> *That a retributivist theory, which is a particular application of a general principle, can account more satisfactorily for our notion of justice in punishment* is a positive reason in its support. (**47**: 66)

Abstract noun phrases—Political Science and Economics
Political Science

> *Expanded government aid* to insulate the dwellings of low-income persons might represent *a wise investment of some windfall tax proceeds,* as opposed to *a continuation of payments* that are simply intended to cover *rising household energy expenses.*
> (from *Report of the President's Commission for a National Agenda for the Eighties* [Washington, D.C.: U.S. Government Printing Office, 1980.])

> Montesquieu argued that citizens in classical republics had to be raised "like a single family"—with *a pervasive civic education in patriotism* reinforced by *frequent public rites and ceremonies, censorship of dissenting ideas, preservation of a single religion . . . , limits on divisive and privatizing economic pursuits,* and *strict restraints on the addition of aliens to the citizenry.* (**40**: 231)

Economics

> Concern has been voiced about *the desirability of advertising and product differentiation* in *monopolistically competitive and oligopolistic market structures.* (**33**: 665)

Writers use noun clauses and abstract noun phrases to pack information tightly together. Then they can put the closely packed information into other sentences as nominals (nouns). The fields of philosophy and political science are characterized by much discussion of ideas and theories. Discussion of theories and ideas involves the inclusion of enormous amounts of information. References to the relationships between and among various theories can be included if writers use carefully constructed combinations of noun clauses and abstract noun phrases. You have probably noticed that there are a lot of relative adjective clauses mixed in, too.

Gerunds—Business, the Physical and Biological sciences
Genetics

> Plasmids derived from *E. coli* cells play an important role in recombinant-DNA research, since they form one class of vectors, or carriers, into which segments of "foreign" DNA can be spliced prior to *their being reinserted* into an appropriate host to propagate, thereby *duplicating* not only their own native nucleotide sequence but also the foreign sequence. (**18**: 25)

Management

> Some responses to information overload may be adaptive tactics that can, at times, be functional. For example, *delaying the processing* of information until the amount is reduced can be effective. On the other hand, *withdrawing* from the task *of communicating* is usually dysfunctional. (**27**: 701)

Writers choose gerunds when no abstract noun phrases exist or to express movement and activity in some kind of process. Gerunds have stronger verbal force than noun clauses, infinitives, or abstract noun phrases. That means they put an emphasis on some kind of action.

The most common use of gerunds in academic writing is after a passive verb as the object of a preposition, especially "by." The meaning in these cases is adverbial. Such phrases express how something is done or occurs.

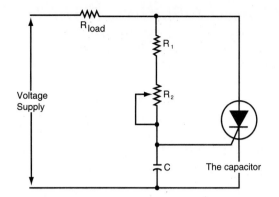

Figure 10-1 SCR gate control circuit. The capacitor provides a range of adjustment of the firing delay angle. (**37:** 204)

Infinitives—All types of academic prose
Electronics

> The reason for including R is *to limit* the large capacitive discharge current. . . . Resister R is of no use in actually suppressing the fast transients; its only purpose is *to limit* the discharge of capacitor C . . . a voltage proportional to motor shaft speed could be used as a feedback signal *to control* the firing delay angle. (**37:** 204)

Philosophy

> Ryle says *to speak* of the mind is really *to speak* of a set of dispositions possessed by intelligent beings.

Industrial Chemistry

> It is important *to realize* that it is not necessary *to know* the mechanism of a reaction in order *to develop* a chemical process.

Infinitives most commonly function as nouns in the complement position after the verb "be" and as subjects after certain predicate adjectives of judgment or opinion in a sentence beginning with "it."

As subjects, infinitive phrases are more formal than gerunds. The "it" construction is less formal. Experts believe that infinitives used as nouns represent an act or state as a whole, represent fairly strong verbal force, and express purpose. The main verbs in such sentences are usually in present or future tense.

Using Noun Clauses, Infinitives, Gerunds, and Abstract Noun Phrases in Writing

Writing Exercise 27: Read and React

Read the following selection, write a brief summary, and then write a critique of the ideas expressed in the article. You may agree or disagree with the author. Then review your summary to see if you used noun clauses, gerunds, infinitives, or abstract noun phrases. Here are some ways to begin your sentences.

The article states that   *What I want to know is*
It is a fact that   *The belief in UFOs is*
That UFOs exists is   *Believing in*
I (don't) believe that   *It is (im)possible to*

The abduction, interrogation, and examination of people

UFOS

One night in late November 1989, Maria says, she was asleep with her husband in their apartment on an upper story of a Manhattan building near the Brooklyn Bridge, when she awoke to find herself paralyzed, with three small gray figures in the room.

The beings caused her to float up off her bed and out the window, she says, into a beam of blue light, which drew her upward, as if on an invisible elevator, into a hovering UFO.

The story told by Maria is typical of those told by people who say they have remembered occasions—usually with the help of hypnosis—when they believe they were abducted by alien beings, subjected to medical examinations aboard an alien spaceship, interrogated, had tissue samples taken from them, and then were returned home.

Such tales were unheard of until recently. . . . Most people, and nearly all scientists, say such stories are so absurd as to not merit a response, let alone a serious investigation. A small but growing number of mental health professionals, however, is beginning to say the reports are widespread enough, and different enough from known psychological syndromes, to deserve serious analysis.

"These are valid experiences, and not some sort of mental aberration," says John Mack, a psychiatrist at Harvard University. "It's different from anything I could have imagined." "I could not put them in any kind of psychiatric category—except trauma," says Mack, who has practiced psychiatry for more than 30 years and was the founding director of the Cambridge Hospital psychiatry department. "But if it's trauma, then what is the source of the trauma?" asks Mack, after talking in detail about abduction experiences with 60 people.

Investigators make one key claim to bolster claims that UFO abductions are real, not just some kind of delusion. It is the startling similarity in the details of accounts given by people from all over the country who apparently never had contact with each other or any awareness of others' stories. More than a year after Maria had told Mack her story under hypnosis, he was independently contacted by two law-enforcement officers who had witnessed a UFO and saw a woman float out her window and into the craft, accompanied by three small beings. . . . Mack describes the men as being terrified and shaken.

(from David O. Chandler, "UFOs—Stories Gaining Serious Study," *The Des Moines Register,* July 27, 1992, pp. 1T–2T. Copyright © The Boston Globe. Reprinted with permission.)

Preparing for Standardized Tests

Practice Exercise 28

Choose the best answer to complete each of the sentences below.

1. Ecology is the study of _____ relate to one another and to their environment.
   a. how organisms
   b. what organisms
   c. where organisms
   d. organisms

2. Until the Middle Eastern oil crisis in 1973-74 and 1979, most people had never thought _____ out of resources.
   a. about that the world might run
   b. what the world would run
   c. how the world was
   d. that the world might run

3. Americans and Europeans seem _____ spectator sports with distinctly different characteristics.
   a. as if
   b. similar to
   c. like
   d. to value

4. It is argued that _____ bottled up inside individuals or societies, interpersonal conflict or war results.
   a. when too much aggressive tension is
   b. too much aggressive tension is
   c. how too much aggressive tension is
   d. too much aggressive tension is when

5. Sport reflects the amount of violence in a society and _____ .
   a. how is violence viewed
   b. how to view violence
   c. how violence is viewed
   d. what view of violence

6. _____ , Pascal published little but was in constant correspondence with many of the leading mathematicians of his day.
   a. A modest man
   b. It was important
   c. That he was a mathematician
   d. For to succeed

7. Sensory memory holds an exact copy of _____ .
   a. seeing or hearing that
   b. what seen or heard
   c. that is seen or heard
   d. what is seen or heard

8. Some theories of violent sports suggest _____ a form of social safety valve.
   a. what sports are served as
   b. that sport serves as
   c. what serves sports as
   d. that serving sports is

9. Jerome Cardan (1501–1576), _____ in genius and often devoid of princi-
    ple, was an Italian professor of mathematics and medicine with a most
    interesting and varied career.
    a. was rich   c. rich
    b. who rich   d. a rich

10. _____ the external demand for information is usually more difficult
    than other methods.
    a. Reduction   c. Reduce
    b. Reducing   d. To be reduced

11. It is probably no surprise _____ frequently cite communication
    breakdowns as one of their most important problems.
    a. to managers   c. that managers
    b. what managers   d. for what managers

12. It was the legislature _____ the cause of the Agricultural Extension
    Service.
    a. what furthered   c. furthered
    b. furthered what   d. that furthered

13. _____ the requirements of the Farm Aid Law was the objective of the
    county, state and federal governments.
    a. To meet   c. That the meeting
    b. A meeting   d. What meeting

14. Probability has been defined as the study of _____ in relation to all pos-
    sible alternatives.
    a. the frequency of appearance of a phenomenon
    b. a phenomenon in frequent appearance
    c. an appearing frequently phenomenon
    d. frequent phenomenon's appearances

15. Games of chance are probably as old as the human desire _____ some-
    thing for nothing.
    a. getting   c. to get
    b. for getting   d. for to get

Find and circle the letter of the *one* error in the following sentences. Then write the correct form above the error.

1. It is important to know the ramifications of <u>being</u> able to walk with

a

erect posture on two feet rather than <u>have</u> to use our hands to steady

b   c

<u>ourselves</u>.

d

2. Before 1945, it was believed <u>what</u> corn <u>developed</u> <u>from</u> wild grass in

a   b   c

either MesoAmerica, South America, <u>or</u> Southeast Asia.

d

3. The aim of a description of a foreign culture is <u>to make</u> it <u>clear</u> to the

a   b

reader just <u>that</u> it is like <u>to live</u> as an individual of the other culture lives.

c   d

4. <u>Being</u> assured of meeting <u>your</u> iron needs, it is best <u>to rely</u> on <u>foods</u>.

a   b   c   d

5. Not an industrialist <u>or</u> a manager <u>and</u> primarily a professor and scientist,

a   b

Babbage was a leading British <u>mathematician</u> who served as professor of

c

mathematics at Cambridge University <u>from</u> 1828 to 1839.

d

6. Statistics <u>has been</u> defined <u>as</u> the science and <u>art</u> of gathering,

a   b   c

analyzing, and <u>to make</u> inferences from data.

d

7. Rather than <u>stressing</u> competitive games among professional teams, the

a

<u>Swiss</u> place <u>relatively greater</u> stress on sharing their enjoyment of nature

b   c

and <u>maintain</u> good health.

d

8. The <u>United Nations</u> refusing <u>to consider</u> the conflict <u>in</u> Vietnam was a

          a   b   c

    problem for the members of the <u>security</u> council.

                                 d

9. The <u>general's</u> claiming <u>to have believed</u> that <u>his</u> superiors were aware of

         a   b   c

    his activities <u>were</u> false.

                d

10. One of <u>man's</u> discoveries was <u>what</u> fire could be used <u>to</u> frighten or <u>even</u>

         a   b   c   d

    kill large animals.

11. There are two main tasks involved <u>in</u> the <u>work</u> of the cultural

                                  a   b

    anthropologist, describing the cultures of <u>other</u> people and <u>to compare</u>

    them.

                                    c   d

12. The <u>environmental</u> factors <u>in</u> a region and the past history of a region

             a   b

    determine <u>that</u> <u>kinds</u> of organisms live there.

                c   d

13. Research shows <u>that</u> when parents tell a child to do one thing, <u>but</u>

                  a   b

    model a completely different response, children are <u>inclined</u> to imitate

                                               c

    what the parents do, and not <u>that</u> they say.

                            d

14. The value of <u>feedback</u> is one of the most <u>useful</u> lessons <u>to derive</u> from

                 a   b   c

    <u>psychological</u> studies of learning.

       d

15. Central America <u>made</u> it possible for organisms <u>moving</u> <u>between</u> <u>North</u>

                    a   b   c   d

    and South America.

16. The U.S. <u>Forest</u> Service has stopped <u>to control</u> fires in forests

               a   b

    containing species <u>for which</u> fire is a necessary event for the <u>sprouting</u> of

                         c   d

    seeds.

17. Legally, <u>slander</u> is the public <u>utter</u> of a statement that holds a person
              a   b

    <u>up for</u> contempt, <u>ridicule</u>, or hatred.
       c   d

18. What Mayo and his colleagues found, <u>based</u> partly on the earlier
                                 a

    <u>thinking</u> of Pareto, <u>were</u> to have a dramatic effect of management <u>thought</u>.
       b   c   d

19. The President urged that the Congressman <u>voted</u> <u>for</u> passage <u>of</u> the
                                      a   b   c

    <u>bill</u>.
      d

20. A recent study has revealed that <u>secondary</u> students in the United
                                         a

    States know very <u>little</u> geography. They will ask where <u>is</u> Russia located
                  b   c

    when <u>asked</u> to name the countries of Eastern Europe.
         d

Analysis Exercise 30: Building Templates for Noun Clauses, Gerunds, Infinitives, and Abstract Noun Phrases

Fill in the blanks with the names of structures you would expect to find (infinitives, gerunds, abstract noun phrases, or noun clauses). Some blanks may have more than one possibility.

Comparative Historical Methods

(1) _____ requires the study of events over time and the comparison of cases that differ in certain key respects but are similar in other important ways. For some problems this is possible only by (2) _____. In her study of revolutions, Theda Skocpol (1979) utilized (3) _____. This method is appropriate for (4) _____ explanations of large-scale historical phenomena of which only a few major cases exist. Skocpol's problem was (5) _____ and (6) _____ the causes of social revolutions. Her strategy was (7) _____ a few cases that shared certain basic features. (**35**: 45)

Modernization

Considerable research has been done to investigate (8) _____
_____ . Inkeles and Smith (1974) surveyed 6000 men from six
developing countries and found that some of them had
(9) _____ , characterized by a strong future orienta-
tion, confidence in the effectiveness of human action in the world, and
an openness to new ideas. Such"modern"attitudes were more likely
(10) _____ in educated men who had worked in a
factory-type (11) _____ than in farmers. (**35**: 521)

Dependency Theory

Dependency theory questions convergence theory's assumption (12)
_____ and will eventually reach the same "advanced"
stage as (13) _____ . Instead, dependency theory
suggests (14) _____ makes their prospects for
development quite different from those of (15) _____ .
(**35**: 523)

Exercise 31: Research Project—Noun Clauses, Gerunds, Infinitives and Abstract Noun Phrases

Use the journal article or textbook chapter from your major field that you have used for the previous research projects. Choose three or more paragraphs in different parts of the passage to see if the research done in the past is also true of writing in your field. Discuss your findings in class.

1. *Noun clauses*—Find the different types of noun clauses that are used in your article.
   a. Which are the most common?
   b. Where are they used? As subjects? objects? complements? appositives?

2. *Abstract Noun Phrases*—Find examples of abstract noun phrases. Are they common?

3. *Infinitive Phrases*—Find the infinitive phrases in your passage.
   a. Where are they used? As subjects? As subjects of sentences beginning with "it"? As objects? As complements? As adverbials? As appositives?
   b. Did you find any subjects of infinitives?

4. *Gerund phrases*—Find the gerund phrases in your passage.
   a. Where are they used? As subjects? As objects? As complements? As adverbials? As appositives?
   b. Did you find any subjects of gerunds?

5. Which forms are the most common: noun clauses, abstract noun phrases, infinitives, or gerunds? (count them)

REVIEW CHAPTER 1
PARTS OF SPEECH AND PHRASES

It is important for students of academic English to become familiar with commonly used grammatical terms and parts of speech as they are used to describe different elements in sentences and paragraphs. Review Chapter 1 begins with the most basic parts of speech and grammatical terms. We will review single words and phrases in Review Chapter 1 and then clauses and sentences in Review Chapter 2.

I. PARTS OF SPEECH

The English language is made up of thousands of words. Grammarians put these words into particular categories called "parts of speech."

Key Terms

PARTS OF SPEECH	EXAMPLE
Noun	*computer, love, Mrs. Johnson, apples*
Verb	*is, was, eat, believe, obtain*
Auxiliary verb	*is, was, have, has, had, have been*
Adjective	*beautiful, interesting, closed*
Adverb	*really, very, interestingly, fast*
Article	*a, an, the*
Preposition	*in, on, at, over, around, from, to*
Conjunction	*and, but, or, however, therefore, although*
Pronoun	*he, she, her, herself, their, one*
Interjection	*Help!*
Infinitive	*to be, to choose, to be chosen, to have been chosen*
Gerund	*choosing, running, swimming*
Participle	*choosing, chosen*
Verbal	an infinitive, participle, or gerund

Practice Exercise 1: Finding Parts of Speech in Context

This exercise will give you practice finding the parts of speech in context. Find the nouns, verbs, adjectives, adverbs, articles, pronouns, prepositions, and conjunctions, and mark them above the words in the paragraphs below.

> The computer has become a dominant force in society today. Business corporations, government agencies, and other organizations depend on the computer to process data and make information available for use in

decision-making. Computers are responsible, to a large extent, for our present standard of living. As the costs for computer equipment continue to decrease, computers will become an even more integral part of our daily lives. It is therefore essential that people gain a basic understanding of computers—their capabilities, limitations, and applications.

In this chapter, a basic description of the computer and its uses in data processing is given. The distinction between data and information is presented. A computerized example of payroll processing is used to demonstrate how computers can be programmed to provide meaningful information. Finally, some of the major advances and problems resulting from computers are presented as evidence of the growing impact computers have had on all parts of society. (31: 3)

Parts of speech do not act alone in sentences. As you have noticed, we almost never use words in isolation (except for interjections like *Help!*). As you worked with the exercise above, you probably were thinking about the groups of words surrounding the parts of speech that you were choosing. Many of the categories (parts of speech) are used together with other words in predictable ways to form parts of sentences.

Analysis Exercise 2: Identifying Parts of Sentences

Look at the groups of words below. Each column contains words or groups of words that can make up parts of sentences. Study the groups and think about how they are similar to or different from each other. Then answer the questions.

GROUP A	GROUP B	GROUP C	GROUP D
student	*in the morning*	*has been learned*	*a big problem*
run	*at the desk*	*is gone*	*my dear friend*
into	*in my opinion*	*will have*	*the interesting discussion*
a	*throughout the year*	*was stopped*	*an umbrella*
but	*near the highway*	*is being taught*	*some pretzels*
beautiful			
easily			

1. How does Group A differ from Group B, Group C, and Group D?
2. Groups B, C, and D have certain similarities. What are they?
3. Groups B, C, and D are also slightly different. In what ways are they different?
4. Write the names for each of the four groups.

Group A _____

Group B _____ _____

Group C _____ _____

Group D _____ _____

In general, groups of words with the characteristics of B, C, and D are known as _____s.

Now compare the facts you discovered with the following summary of the parts of speech.

Explanation—Parts of Speech

NOUNS

Nouns are words for the names of people, places, things, and ideas.

PEOPLE	PLACES	THINGS	IDEAS
woman	*Iowa*	*tractor*	*ability*
people	*the United States*	*library*	*intention*
Mary	*Latin America*	*speech*	*variation*
boy	*cities*	*cow*	*love*
students	*farm*	*title*	*information*

If they are countable nouns they have a singular or plural form.

one girl	*two girls*	*one ox*	*two oxen*
one student	*ten students*	*one goose*	*seven geese*
one variation	*three variations*	*one foot*	*six feet*

Some nouns are uncountable—they are always singular.

coffee, tea, information

Some nouns appear plural but are really singular; they are always the same.

The United States, news

DETERMINERS

Nouns are often used with determiners (also called articles, numbers, possessive adjectives, quantifiers).

a book	*five cows*	*some coffee*
the girl	*some farmers*	*several cities*
an army	*many people*	*my family*

ADJECTIVES

Nouns are also used with adjectives. Adjectives describe nouns.

a beautiful farm	*an interested student*
some hot, black coffee	*other beautiful places*
several tall, good-looking people	

Nouns sometimes have other nouns in front of them. These nouns act like adjectives and describe the main noun.

NOUN MODIFIERS	MAIN NOUN
a stone	*building*
ten John Deere	*tractors*

The combination of determiner, adjectives, noun modifiers, and main noun is called a **noun phrase.** In English sentences, the main noun is the last noun in a noun phrase. The main noun is the important noun in the phrase.

> *a gold metal table <u>lamp</u>.*
> *five small brown lamp <u>tables</u>*

PREPOSITIONS

Nouns can be followed by prepositional phrases that contain nouns or noun phrases. These are also part of the larger noun phrase.

> *a farm <u>in Iowa</u>*
> *three books <u>from the library</u>*
> *the talented student <u>in my class</u>*

Prepositions are words like:

in	*on*	*around*
by	*beside*	*near*
under	*from*	*at*

Prepositions are used with nouns. Combinations of prepositions, determiners, adjectives, and nouns are called **prepositional phrases**.

ADVERBS

Adjectives also have modifiers: adverbs. Adverbs modify the adjective in a noun phrase, not the noun.

> *a <u>very</u> large book*
> *an <u>extremely</u> heavy farm tractor*

The adverb in the phrases above describe "large" and "heavy," not "book" and "tractor."

Summary of Noun Phrases

determiner	adverb	adjective	noun modifier	main noun	prep. phrases
several	*really*	*large*	*John Deere*	*tractors*	*near the barn*

A noun phrase is made up of a main noun and its modifiers. Look at the underlined noun phrases. Notice how many adverb, adjective, and noun modifiers there are.

1. The existence of <u>seemingly contradictory approaches</u> is not unique to sociology.

2. The cause of republicanism provided a more obvious promise of <u>meaningful, morally worthwhile, and closely knit political communities in America.</u>

3. In the early years of the republic, most respectable American intellectuals endorsed the Enlightenment doctrines of human moral equality, expressed in <u>Princeton President Samuel S. Smith's essay</u>.

PRONOUNS

Pronouns are words that can take the place of nouns.

NOUNS

<u>Mary</u> is a <u>student</u>.
<u>John</u> gave <u>the book</u> to the <u>students</u>.

PRONOUNS

<u>She</u> is <u>one</u>.
<u>He</u> gave <u>it</u> to <u>them</u>.

Most of these pronouns can take the place of nouns in a sentence:

I, you, he, she, it, we, they   (subject forms)
me, you, him, her, it, us, them   (object forms)
(the) one, (the) ones
this, these, that, those
somebody, someone, everybody, everyone
anybody, anyone, anything, something
no one, nobody, nothing
another, other, others, (the)others
myself, yourself, himself, herself, itself, ourselves, themselves

VERBS

Verbs are generally action or state-of-being words.

Airplanes <u>fly</u>.
Farmers <u>enjoy</u> new tractors.
Few people <u>have</u> the ability to speak well.
The call number <u>indicates</u> the classification of the book.
The author <u>is</u> Delany.

Verbs have various tenses. Some verbs require a main verb and one or more auxiliary verbs.

	AUX VERB	MAIN VERB
The card	*will*	*tell you the location of the book.*
This chapter	*is not*	*intended to be a substitute.*
Libraries	*have always*	*been available to students.*
Students	*have often been*	*known to skip classes.*
Many people	*have*	*enjoyed playing basketball.*

Sometimes there are other verb forms after the main verb (see the second, fourth, and fifth examples above). What kinds of verblike words are these? There may also be adverbs like *not, always, usually,* and *often* between the first auxiliary verb and the main verb. A typical verb phrase:

(one or more auxiliaries)+ (adverbs)+ main verb+ infinitive or gerund

In an English sentence a verb must have a subject. The subject may be a noun, noun phrase, noun clause, pronoun, gerund, or infinitive. Sometimes the subject (you) is understood and not stated.

CONJUNCTIONS

Conjunctions are words that connect parts of sentences. **Coordinating conjunctions** connect single words, phrases, and clauses.

dogs and cats　　　　　　　*slowly but surely*
himself or herself　　　　　*up and down*
sink or swim　　　　　　　*down the street and to your left*
old but good　　　　　　　*a fancy house but no furniture*

Subordinating conjunctions connect different types of clauses.

I love you because you are you.
It is important that you arrive on time.
If I were you, I would study harder.
The assignment which he gave us was impossible to finish on time.
Whoever stole the computer will be caught.

II. PHRASES

A **phrase** is a group of words that are closely related.

Noun phrase:　　　　　　　*a big red tractor*
Prepositional phrase:　　　*in my class, on Monday*
Verb phrase:　　　　　　　*have been seen*

Some phrases can be combined (noun phrases and prepositional phrases) to make one big noun phrase.

the big red tractor behind the barn

Some phrases contain adverbs to modify the adjectives or verbs.

the very first step
have often been seen

Some prepositional phrases are used as adverbs to tell time or place.

on Monday, at school

In the sentence below, the noun phrases are underlined and the prepositional phrases are in parentheses. Notice how the prepositional phrases are used to modify the smaller noun phrases. Then the prepositional phrases themselves are part of the larger noun phrase. What part of speech is the word "little" in the example?

The definition (of manufacturing) (as the making) (of goods and articles) reveals little (about the complexity)(of the problem).

Analysis Exercise 3: Identifying Phrases

Study the following passages. Several phrases are underlined. Compare the phrases with the same number. What are they? How do they function in the sentences? Answer the questions after you have read the passage.

Cultural anthropology, as the term is commonly used today, generally refers to the study of existing peoples. Further, it is based upon a comparative approach, that is, its aim is

1

to understand and appreciate the diversity in human behavior,

1

and ultimately to develop a science of human behavior, through the comparison of different peoples throughout the world. In the United States we frequently make a distinction between two areas of cultural anthropology: ethnology and ethnography. Ethnology is the comparative study of culture and the investigation of theoretical problems

3   **1**

using information about different groups. . . . To avoid confusion we will

1

use the term cultural anthropology to cover both of these terms. There

3

are two main tasks involved in the work of the cultural anthropologist,

1   **1**

to describe the cultures of other peoples and to compare them. Such

2

description is not an easy task, since putting something from another

2   **4**

cultural context into the concepts and words available in the English

4   **1**

language is not always possible. The aim of the description is to make it

1   **1**

clear to the reader just what it is like to live as an individual of the other culture lives. Accurate descriptive work, cultural translation, is the essential basis for comparative studies, which after all are crucial

2

to understanding human behavior. (14: 16)

2

Figure 4 illustrates the labeling of the dissections of the pentagon and hexagon that are determined by the corresponding expressions of Fig-

3

ure 2. The converse procedure, involving the same initial labeling

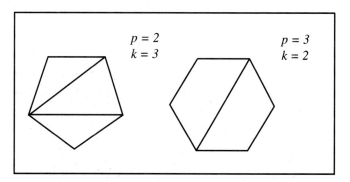

$$p = 2 \qquad\qquad p = 3$$
$$k = 3 \qquad\qquad k = 2$$

$$(s_1 ((s_2 \ s_3 \ ) \ s_4)) \quad (s_1 \ s_2 (s_3 \ s_4 \ s_5))$$

Figure 2. Left: An expression involving three applications of a binary operaton applied to 4 symbols and, at right,an expression involving two applications of a ternary operation applied to 5 symbols.

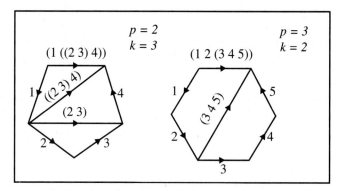

$$p = 2 \qquad\qquad p = 3$$
$$k = 3 \qquad\qquad k = 2$$

Figure 3. Left: A 5-gon subdivided into three 3-gons by two diagonals and, at right, a 6-gon subdivided into two 4-gons by one diagonal.

$$p = 2 \qquad\qquad p = 3$$
$$k = 3 \qquad\qquad k = 2$$

(1 ((2 3) 4))   (1 2 (3 4 5))

Figure 4. The dissected polygons of Figure 3, with diagonals and last side labeled. (All from Hilton and Pedersen, "Catalan Numbers," p. 65.)

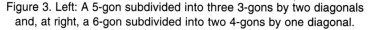

$$\overset{3}{\text{of the original sides}} \text{ of a dissected polygon, and } \overset{2}{\text{the successive}}$$

$$\overset{2}{\text{labeling of the diagonals}} \overset{3}{\text{introduced}}, \text{ leads to an expression that acts as label for the last (horizontal) side.}$$

(from Peter Hilton and Jean Pedersen, "Catalan Numbers; Their Generalization and Their Uses," *The Mathematical Intelligencer* 13, #2 [1991]: 66. Copyright © 1991 Springer-Verlag. Reprinted with permission.)

1. What do the phrases labeled "1" have in common? What are they called?
2. What do the phrases labeled "2" have in common? What are they called?
3. What do the phrases labeled "3" have in common? How are they different? What are they called?
4. What kind of phrase is number 4?

Compare your answers to the questions with the descriptions of the phrases that follow this exercise.

VERBALS

Participial, Adjective, and Appositive Phrases—Some nouns are preceded or followed by words ending with "-ing" or "-ed." These are called **participles**. Participles may function as part of the verb phrases or as adjectives and adverbs. Sometimes participles include other words as part of the phrase. In this case they are called **participial phrases**. Sometimes nouns are followed by adjectives or other nouns in a phrase. These are called **adjective phrases, noun phrase modifiers**, or **appositives**. Adjective phrases, appositives, and participial phrases describe the nouns they precede or follow.

Present participle:	*We have money <u>remaining</u> in the account.*
Past participle:	*American Indians had no <u>written</u> languages.*
	Books <u>written in the roman alphabet</u> were rare.
Adjective phrase:	*We have information <u>available for use</u>.*

Gerund Phrases—Gerunds are verblike words ending in "-ing" that function as nouns. They can do everything that nouns do. They act as subjects, objects, and complements in sentences. Sometimes gerunds have other words with them. These combinations of words are called **gerund phrases**.

Infinitive Phrases—Infinitives are verblike words preceded by the word *to*. Infinitives can have many functions. They can function as part of the verb phrase, as subjects, as objects, as complements, as adjectives, and as adverbs. Sometimes infinitives have other words with them. These combinations of words are called **infinitive phrases**.

Verbals—Participles, gerunds, and infinitives are sometimes called "verbals" because they are similar to verbs but function differently.

Practice Exercise 4: Finding Verbals

Find the participial phrases, gerund phrases, and infinitive phrases in the passage below.

> Language consists of spoken or written symbols combined into a system and governed by rules. It enables us to share with others our ideas, thoughts, experiences discoveries, fears, plans, and desires. Written language extends

our capacity to communicate through time and space. Language is the critical key to understanding any culture and any society. A person may be a superb athlete, mechanic, or cook, but teaching or talking about that skill requires language.

Language also provides clues to what a culture considers important. Farmers have many words to describe various types of soil, reflecting its importance to them. Our culture has numerous slang words for money (including "bread", "dough", "bucks" . . .) suggesting the importance of money in our culture. (**35**: 103)

CHART A-1 PARTS OF SPEECH

PART OF SPEECH	SINGLE WORDS	PHRASE	CLAUSE
NOUN / PRONOUN	book he, she, it	(ARTICLE)+(ADJECTIVE)+NOUN a red book my book	SUBORDINATOR + SUBJECT + VERB that you are studying what he said
VERB	go	AUX. + VERB + (INFINITIVE) will have gone to see	
ADJECTIVE	big, red	ADVERB + ADJECTIVE really big	SUBORDINATOR + (S) + V + COMPLEMENT/ OBJECT which John likes very much
ADVERB	slowly	INTENSIFIER + ADVERB very slowly	SUBORDINATOR + S + V + COMPLEMENT/ OBJECT although John is my friend
PREPOSITION	in, on, at	PREPOSITION + (ARTICLE) + NOUN in the morning	
ARTICLE	a, an, the		
CONJUNCTIONS COORDINATING SUBORDINATING	and, but, or although, when if, who, what, how, that		
GERUND	swimming	(SUBJECT) + (AUX) + GERUND Mary's studying His having been swimming	
PARTICIPLE	swimming delayed	PRESENT OR PAST PARTICIPLE having been swimming being delayed	
INFINITIVE	to see	(SUBJECT)+ INFINITIVE +OBJECT for her to see him for her to have seen him a letter for you to type	
ABSOLUTE		SUBJECT + PARTICIPIAL PHRASE the train being late "be" understood + phrase many of them only infants "with" +"be" understood + phrase with the police on all sides	
APPOSITIVE	NOUN / ADJECTIVE chairwoman	NOUN/ ADJECTIVE PHRASE a proud man	

Parts of Speech and Phrases   **343**

REVIEW CHAPTER 2
CLAUSES AND SENTENCES

I. CLAUSES

Analysis Exercise 1: Identifying Phrases and Clauses

Look at the groups of words below. Each group contains combinations of words that can make up parts of sentences. Study the groups and think about how they are similar to or different from each other. Then answer the questions.

GROUP A	GROUP B
has been	*after he finishes work*
in the morning	*when the professor arrived*
will go	*whom I met yesterday*
after work	*which is true*
the tall man	*that the government will endure*
an obvious answer	*whereas the legislature disagrees*
may be found	*although the summer is nearly here*
	because the exam was difficult

GROUP C
the ozone layer is disappearing
I exist
nobody is perfect
money talks
Russia has changed
Latin America was discovered first
the computer is part of the 20th century

1. How is Group A different from Group B and Group C?
2. How are Group B and Group C similar? What are they?
3. Groups B and C are also slightly different. In what ways are they different?
4. Can you think of a name for each of the three groups?

Explanation 1—Clauses

A **clause** is a group of words that are closely related, but a clause must have a subject and a verb. Clauses are *independent* or *dependent* (subordinate).

An **independent clause** can be a complete sentence or a part of a longer sentence.

subject	+	verb	(+ other words)
People		*talk.*	
The cards		*may be interfiled* in one or two sections.	
A card catalog		*is* an alphabetical listing of the books that a library owns.	

A **dependent** (subordinate) **clause** must be part of a longer sentence with an independent clause.

independent clause	subordinate clause
I know a man	who is a farmer.
John was a student	before he was a farmer.

A dependent (subordinate) clause contains a subject and a verb but it cannot stand alone as a sentence.

A subordinate clause begins with a word called a **subordinator** (subordinating conjunction).

before	*who*	*although*
after	*that*	*because*
which	*if*	*while*

Clauses contain phrases.

subordinator	noun phrase	verb phrase	noun phrase,
When	the students	have found	the necessary book,
pronoun	verb phrase	noun phrase	prepositional phrase
they	should consult	the librarian	at the desk.

Analysis Exercise 2: Identifying Independent and Dependent Clauses

In the paragraphs below, find and mark the independent and subordinate clauses.

[1] When C is large, the charge on the capacitator will be large for a given voltage across it. Since Q is measured in coulombs and V in volts, the unit of capacitance is coulombs per volt, which is called the farad(F). If one of the plates has an area A, and if the separation between the plates is d, it is possible to show that the capacitance of a parallel-plate capacitor is given by

$$C = \frac{E_o\, A}{d} \text{ parallel plates.}$$

(**2**: 427, 428)

[2] Strict vegetarians are most apt to be deficient in vitamin B_{12} because it is obtainable only from animal products, although they are likely to be well supplied with folic acid. As its name—related to foliage—implies, folic acid is found in vegetables and fruits. . . . The vegetarian's high intake of folic acid helps the red blood cells to develop to normal size and maturity, thus deceiving the physician who examines a blood sample for signs of abnormality. (**19**: 238)

Explanation 2—Formation of Subordinate Clauses

CHART A-2   HOW RELATIVE CLAUSES ARE FORMED

Sentences with "who" versus "whom"

Step 1.
Begin with two ideas.

Explanation
The two ideas must contain
the same noun or a synonym.

— same words or synonyms —

1. **The man** is over there.   2. Mary will marry **the man** (**him**).
1. **The man** is over there.   2. **He** will marry Mary.

Step 2.
Decide on the relative clause.

The most important idea or
the idea you want to
emphasize will be the main
clause.

main clause   relative clause
1. **The man** is over there.   2. Mary will marry **the man**.
1. **The man** is over there.   2. **He** will marry Mary.

Step 3.
Choose a subordinator to connect
the relative clause to the main clause.

If the noun or synonym in the
future relative clause is the
subject of the clause, choose
"who"; if it's the object, choose
"whom."

object
2. Mary will marry **the man**.
↓

subordinator
2. Mary will marry **whom**.

subject
2. **He** will marry Mary.
↓

2. **Who** will marry Mary.

Step 4.
Move the subordinator to the
front of the relative clause.

Notice that **who** doesn't
change position.

2. **whom** Mary will marry
2. **who** will marry Mary

Step 5.
Combine the two sentences.

Remember to put the relative clause as close as possible to the noun it describes.

(next to each other)

The man **whom** Mary will marry is over there.

main clause   relative clause   main clause ends
begins

(next to each other)

The man **who** will marry Mary is over there.

main clause   relative clause   main clause ends
begins

Sentences with "which" or "that" as Subjects or Objects

Step 1.
Begin with two ideas.

Explanation

same words or synonyms

1. **The office** is mine.   2. I showed you **the office**.
1. **The office** is mine.   2. **The office** is being painted.

Step 2.
Decide which idea will be the main clause and which will be the relative clause.

future main clause   future relative clause
1. **The office** is mine.   2. I showed you **the office**.
1. **The office** is mine.   2. **The office** is being painted.

Step 3.
Choose a subordinator to replace the noun or pronoun.

"That" is preferred in restrictive clauses. (no commas) "Which" must be used in non-restrictive clauses.

subordinator
2. I showed you **that** (or **which**)
2. **that** (or **which**) is being painted

Step 4.
Move the subordinator to the front of the relative clause.

       2. **that** I showed you
       2. **that** is being painted

Step 5.
Combine the two sentences. Put the relative clause after the noun it describes in the main clause.

(next to each other)

The office **that** I showed you is mine.

main clause relative clause main clause
begins   ends

(next to each other)

The office **that** is being painted is mine.

main clause relative clause main clause
begins   ends

Sentences with "which" or "whom" as Object of a Preposition

Step 1.
Begin with two ideas.

same words or synonyms

1. The latest *Newsweek* has arrived.   2. Her article was published **in** *Newsweek*.
1. **The editor** rewrote the article.   2. She relies **on the editor.**

Step 2.
Decide which sentence will be the relative clause.

    future main clause   future relative clause
1. The latest *Newsweek* has arrived.   2. Her article was published **in** *Newsweek*.
2. **The editor** rewrote the article.   2. She relies **on the editor**.

Step 3.
Choose a subordinator to replace the noun. Choose "which" for things, "whom" for people. (Notice the preposition remains)

                 preposition and
                 subordinator
        2. Her article was published **in which**
        2. She relies **on whom**

Step 4.

Move the subordinator and the preposition to the front of the relative clause.

> 2. **in which** her article was published
>
> 2. **on whom** she relies

Step 5.

Combine the two sentences. Put the relative clause after the noun it describes in the main clause.

(next to each other)

The latest *Newsweek*,   **in which** her article was published, has arrived.

The **editor**   **on whom** she relies   rewrote the article.

| main clause | relative clause | main clause ends |
| begins |

Informal: The latest *Newsweek*, **which** her article was published **in**, has arrived.
The editor **who**(**m**) she relies **on** rewrote the article.

Note: "Where" may be used in place of "in which." "That" may never be used when it is preceded by a preposition.
   The example sentences here show relative clauses following subjects of sentences. Relative clauses may follow any noun in a sentence.

CHART A-3   HOW NOUN CLAUSES ARE FORMED

Noun Clauses as Objects

Sentences with "that"

Step 1.	Explanation
Begin with two ideas.	The ideas are usually about thinking, believing, knowing, or understanding.

both are statements

I believe *something*.   You are a good student.

Step 2.

Choose the main clause and the noun clause.   The main clause is the one with verbs like "think" or "believe."

future main clause   object   future noun clause
I believe   *something*.   You are a good student.

Step 3.

Choose the subordinator.   "That" is the subordinator to combine statements.

Step 4.
Combine the two clauses with *that*.

The noun clause replaces the object in the main clause. "That" may be omitted.

main clause   noun clause
     subordinator
I believe (*that*) you are a good student.

Sentences with "whether" or "if"

Step 1.
Begin with two ideas.

Explanation
The ideas are usually about thinking, believing, knowing, or understanding.
One idea is a command, statement, or question with verbs like "tell" or "know"; the other idea is a "yes/no" question.

command, statement, question   "Yes/no" question

           object
Please tell me *something*.   Will we meet on Friday?
John knows *something*.   Does Mary like fish?
Would you tell me *something*? Did she lock the office?

Step 2.
Choose the main clause and the noun clause.

The main clause is the statement, command or question with verbs like "tell." The noun clause is the "yes/no" question.

future main clauses   future noun clauses
Please tell me *something*.   Will we meet on Friday?
Would you tell me *something*? Does Mary like fish?
John knows *something*.   Did she lock the office?

Step 3.
Choose a subordinator to combine the two ideas and add it to the beginning of the noun clause.

"Whether" or "if" are the subordinators for "yes/no" questions.

Step 4.
Change the word order of the future noun clause to statement word order.

subordinator statement word order
whether we will meet on Friday
whether Mary likes fish
if she locked the office

Step 5.
Combine the main clause and noun clause.

The noun clause replaces the object in the main clause.

main clause   noun clause
Please tell me *whether* we will meet on Friday.
John knows *whether* Mary likes fish.
Would you tell me *if* she locked the office?

There is no question mark at at the end unless the main clause is a question.

Sentences with "who," "whom," "which," "what," "when," "where," "how," and "why"

Step 1.
Begin with two ideas.

The ideas are usually about thinking, believing, knowing, or understanding.
One idea is a statement, command or question; one is "wh-" question.

command, statement, question

       object
Please tell me *something*.
I want to know *something*.
Can I ask you *something*?

Wh- question

What do you want to do?
Why did they fail the test?
Whom does Felix trust?

Step 2.
Choose the main clause.

The main clause is the statement, command, or question with verbs like "ask," and "tell." The noun clause will be formed from the "wh-" question. The "wh" word will be the subordinator.

future main clause

Please tell me something.
I want to know something.
Can I ask you something?

future noun clauses
subordinator
what do you want to do?
why did they fail the test?
whom does Felix trust?

Step 3.
Change the noun clause to statement word order.

Subordinator statement word order
what you want to do
why they failed the test
whom Felix trusts

Step 4.
Combine the main clause and the noun clause.

The noun clause replaces the object in the main clause.

main clause   noun clause
Please tell me what you want to do.
I want to know why they failed.

These two are statements.

Can I ask whom Felix trusts?

This has a question mark because the main clause is a question.

A Special Case: "who" and "what"

Case 1.
Combine two ideas.

future main clauses   future noun clauses
I want to know something.   Who is that man?
Please tell me something.   What is the big problem?

In the question "Who is that man?" "who" and the noun "man" mean the same person. Therefore, the question is put into *statement word order* when it is combined with the main clause.

                 statement word order
I want to know who that man is.

In the question "What is the big problem?," "What" and "big problem" mean the same thing. Therefore, the question is put into *statement word order* when it is combined with the main clause:

                 statement word order
Please tell me what the big problem is.

Case 2.
Combine two ideas.

future main clauses   future noun clauses
I want to know something.   Who is here?
Please tell me something.   What was said?
Should I explain something?   What is special about her?

In the question "Who is here?," "Who" and the adverb "here" do not have the same meaning. Therefore, the word order in the noun clause will not change.

            no change in word order
I want to know who is here.

no change in word order
I want to know what was said.

In the question "What was said?" "what" and the verb "was said" do not have the same meaning. Therefore, the word order in the noun clause will not change.

In the question "What is special about her?" "What" and the adjective "special" do not have the same meaning. Therefore, the word order in the noun clause will not change.

no change in word order
I want to know what is special about her.

Noun Clauses as Subjects

Sentences with "that"

Step 1.
Begin with two ideas.

The ideas express facts. The verbs are linking verbs like "be," "became," "seem," "remain," and "appear." The subject of one statement means the same as the other idea.

both are statements
same meaning

The world is round. *It* became scientifically accepted.

Step 2.
Choose the main clause and the noun clause.

The noun clause is the one that expresses a fact. It will replace the subject of the other clause.

future noun clause

The world is round.

future main clause
subject
It became scientifically accepted.

Step 3.
Combine the two clauses and add "that" to the beginning.

The noun clause replaces the subject in the main clause. "That" is the subordinator.

noun clause
subordinator   main clause
That the world is round became scientifically accepted.

Sentences with "what" and other "Wh-" words

Step 1.
Begin with two ideas.

Explanation
One idea is a "wh" question. The other is a fact. The verbs in the statement are linking verbs like "be," "became," "seem," "remain," and "appear." The subject of the statement means the same as the question.

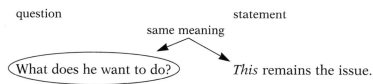

question   statement

same meaning

What does he want to do?   *This* remains the issue.

Step 2.
Choose the main clause and the noun clause.

The main clause is the statement. The noun clause is formed from the question. The "wh-" word will be the subordinator.

    future noun clause   future main clause
What does he want to do?   *This* remains the issue.

Step 3.
Change the word order of the future noun clause to statement word order.

    future noun clause
What he wants to do

Step 4.
Combine the two clauses.

The noun clause replaces the subject in the main clause.

noun clause   main clause
subordinator
What he wants to do remains the issue.

Sentences with "whether"

Step 1.
Begin with two ideas.

Explanation
One idea is a "yes/no" question; the other is a statement. The verbs in the statement are linking verbs like "be," "became," "seem," "remain," and "appear." The subject of the statement means the same as the question.

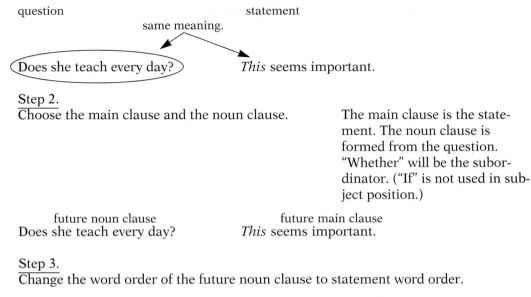

question   statement

same meaning.

Does she teach every day?   *This* seems important.

Step 2.
Choose the main clause and the noun clause.

> The main clause is the state-ment. The noun clause is formed from the question. "Whether" will be the subor-dinator. ("If" is not used in sub-ject position.)

future noun clause   future main clause
Does she teach every day?   *This* seems important.

Step 3.
Change the word order of the future noun clause to statement word order.

future noun clause
She teaches every day

Step 4.
Combine the two clauses.

> The noun clause replaces the subject in the main clause.

noun clause
subordinator   main clause
Whether she teaches every day seems important.

Note: It is also possible to combine two questions with a linking verb. Remember to change the question word order to statement word order in both questions.

noun clause   linking verb   noun clause
Who you are   is   what he wants to know.

II. SENTENCES

Analysis Exercise 3: Identifying Sentences

Look at the following groups of words and decide whether or not they are sentences. If they are sentences, write YES after them and then explain why. If they are not sen-tences, write NO after them and explain why.

1. The Genzyme Corporation, a fast-growing biotechnology company.

2. Regional economists are pointing to Genzyme's project.

3. If more local biotechnology companies stay here.

4. Henri Tremeer, head of Genzyme, at the company's proposed headquarters site in Boston.

5. Genzyme is

6. The accounting firm which does a yearly survey of biotechnology businesses.

7. When unemployment was 3 percent although there was attention to research.

8. Biotechnology will definitely play a role in the recovery.

9. By l995, when the plant operating, sales of the two drugs Genzyme plans to make there are expected to be above $200 million a year.

10. The most inviting—Rhode Island, North Carolina, and Puerto Rico—offered favorable tax rates and assurances of streamlined processes for obtaining permits.

Explanation 3—Types of Simple Sentences

English sentences are made up of phrases and clauses put together in a certain order.

A simple sentence = a subject + predicate.

The predicate includes the verb phrase and everything following it.

SUBJECT (NOUN PHRASE)	PREDICATE (VERB + REST OF SENTENCE)
The author	is Delany.
The call number	indicates the classification of the book.
Each card in the catalogue	carries some valuable information.
It	can help you find the book.
(You)	Look up the book in the catalogue.

TYPES OF SIMPLE SENTENCES

Type 1: subject + intransitive verb (+ adverbials of time, place, manner)

Money	talks.	
John	ran	into the house.
The librarian	worked	quickly.

Type 2: subject + linking verb + adjective or noun complement

Money	is	the root of all evil.
Jack	feels	sick.
The librarian	seems	worried.

Type 3: subject + transitive verb + direct object (+ adverbials of time, place, manner)

John	loves	Mary.	
The librarian	will find	the book	quickly.
I	always did	my homework	in the library.

Type 4: subject + transitive verb (+indirect object) + direct object

She will give *you the book.* OR She will give *the book to you.*

The librarian mailed the list of books for Mr. Johnson.

Type 5: subject + transitive verb + direct object   objective complement

The men	painted	the barn	red.
The people	elected	Bush	president.
The farmers	call	that building	a corn crib.

NOTE: Only certain verbs can be used in sentences of Type 5: *paint, color, call, name, elect,* and *choose* are a few of the most common.

Definitions of Sentence Parts and Terms

1. *Linking verb* (LV): a verb that connects subjects and complements in a sentence. Examples of linking verbs are *be, seem, appear,* and *become.*

2. *Transitive verb* (Vt): a verb that takes an object.

3. *Intransitive verb* (Vi): a verb that takes no object.

4. A *subjective complement* follows a linking verb. It is a noun in the predicate that means the same as the subject. An adjective in the predicate describes the subject.

5. *Objective complement*: a noun or adjective that describes the direct object; follows the object.

6. *Direct object*: receives the action of a transitive verb.

7. *Indirect object*: receives the benefit of the action to the direct object or receives the direct object itself; is usually a person.

Analysis Exercise 4: Finding Parts of Sentences and Identifying Types of Sentences

First find the subjects, verbs, objects, linking verbs, and subjective complements (predicate adjectives and predicate nouns) in the sentences below. Then examine each sentence and decide which type of simple sentence it is.

1. Computers can perform only three basic functions.

2. This chapter presents significant events leading to the development of the computer.

3. The King of England gave the backers of the Virginia Colony a charter granting them full power and authority to make laws.

4. Accounting machines could read data from punched cards, perform summary calculations such as addition and subtraction, rearrange data, and print results in a wide variety of formats.

5. Inventions and perfections of techniques and technologies brought entirely new processes to light.

6. Conflicts arise in societies.

7. We have been working to make the arts (and I include arts in the humanities) a required part of the Utah secondary school curriculum.

8. Statistical inference is an important aspect of scientific inference.

9. This marginal life is rich both in direct experience and in discussions of fundamentals.

III. COMBINING CLAUSES AND PHRASES INTO SENTENCES

All English sentences are made up of simple sentences (independent clauses) in combination with each other and/or in combination with subordinate clauses and phrases. Conjunctions join these phrases and clauses.

Explanation 4—Conjunctions

In Review Chapter 1 you identified some conjunctions. We have several kinds of conjunctions in English. Conjunctions fall into three groups.

1. **Correlative conjunctions:** Pairs of words like *either . . . or, neither . . . nor, both . . . and,* and *not only . . . but also* are used to connect words, phrases and sometimes clauses.

   He likes *neither* coffee *nor* tea.

2. **Coordinating conjunctions**—Words like *and, but, or, yet* may connect two or more nouns, noun phrases, verbs, verb phrases, adjectives, adjective phrases, adverbs, prepositional phrases, infinitives, and gerunds. Coordinating conjunctions like *and, but, or, yet* and conjunctive adverbs like *however* and *thus* may connect two independent clauses to form compound sentences. We will consider conjunctive adverbs to be the equivalent of coordinating conjunctions in this text.

   Managers try hard, *yet* they often fail.

   Communication is difficult; *nevertheless,* the manager tries.

3. **Subordinating conjunctions**: Words like *because, when, before, after, while, if, that, whether,* and *who* connect dependent (subordinate) clauses to independent clauses to form complex sentences.

> The manager must use simulations *even though* they seem unusual.

COMPOUND SENTENCES

Coordinating conjunctions and conjunctive adverbs connect simple sentences in order to form **compound sentences**.

Independent clause + *coordinate conjunction* + independent clause
S + V + (other words) + *coordinate conjunction* + S + V (+ other words).

> Most university libraries have adopted the Library of Congress system,
> (independent clause)

> but   local libraries   often use the Dewey Decimal system.
> (coordinating conjunction)   (independent clause)

> Encyclopedias   are   valuable sources of knowledge; however,
> (independent clause)   (conjunction)

> people   forget to use   them.
> (independent clause)

COMPLEX SENTENCES

Complex sentences are made up of at least one main independent clause and at least one dependent clause introduced by a subordinate conjunction. Dependent clauses fall into three basic groups:

1. Relative clauses

> The person *whom you should see i*s the Dean.
> The place *where they live* is nearby.

2. Noun clauses

> The President stated *that his adviser had resigned.*
> The police know *what they should do.*

3. Adverbial clauses

> *Before she left for the conference*, she confirmed her reservation.
> I would study *if I were you.*

COMPOUND–COMPLEX SENTENCES

Compound–complex sentences are made up of a combination of at least one compound sentence and at least one dependent clause.

> Sensory memory holds an exact copy of what is seen or heard, but it lasts for only one-half second or less.

1. How many dependent clauses are there in the example above?
2. How many independent clauses are there in the example above?
3. How many and what kinds of conjunctions do you see?

Practice Exercise 5: Identifying Types of Clauses and Conjunctions

Find the independent clauses, dependent clauses, and coordinating conjunctions in the sentences below. Do all of the conjunctions connect clauses? What structures do conjunctions connect? Identify the simple sentences, the compound sentences, the complex sentences and the compound–complex sentences.

[1]   Jefferson and Aaron Burr received equal numbers of electoral votes in the 1800 presidential contest, but Jefferson became president by a vote of the House of Representatives.

[2]   Short-term profit and productivity are the only things to consider. Long-term consequences are ignored, or it is assumed that technology can be developed to deal with them. Human desires are seen as the only important force in determining how the environment is shaped. Ponds may be drained for housing, rivers dammed, and highways carved into the sides of mountains. (**35**: 540)

[3]   Archaeology offers an opportunity to look into the distant past of the human species and try to reconstruct the picture. But it is like doing a jigsaw puzzle with most of the pieces missing, and without the picture of the finished puzzle on the box to work from. Archaeologists have a few things that fit together, they can guess about many others, but they really don't have enough to put it all together with complete confidence. (**14**: 11)

[4]   Most trees and shrubs lack fire-resisting specializations; however, some trees, such as sequoia and sugar pine, have evolved resistance to fire.

[5]   Cultural anthropology overlaps with every other social science in at least some areas of interest, yet it still retains its individuality.

[6]   Medieval philosophy was based on the belief that God had created and ordered the world for a certain purpose, and it took as its aim the explanation of that purpose.

Discussion: Problem 3 in Exercise 5 contains a sentence that begins with *But*. It doesn't fit readily into any of the simple sentence types, and it can't really be called a part of a compound sentence. One might classify the sentence as a simple sentence with a compound "flavor" because the conjunction *but* relates one simple sentence to another in the same way a compound sentence relates two independent clauses. In academic prose, the coordinating conjunctions and conjunctive adverbs are often used to start sentences and are *not* necessarily neatly placed between independent clauses and punctuated with semicolons and commas.

Practice Exercise 6: Finding Sentence Types

Find the simple, compound, and compound–complex sentences in the paragraphs below.

[1] In the unequal class structure that exists in capitalist societies, all the major social institutions, including the state, religion, and political economy, are characterized by what Marx called alienation. For him, alienation referred to the creation, by humans, of something that turns back upon people as an alien power. For example, people create religions but then let religion dictate what they should or should not do. People establish a state, but then the state's power may limit what people can do. They begin to use money to facilitate exchanges of goods and services, but money soon becomes an end rather than a means. In these and other ways, people become alienated from their own creations. (**35**: 15, 16)

[2] The Growth of Human Culture—Scavenging of some sort probably took place, putting early hominids in direct competition with other species. Plant food comes relatively easy in the forests where chimpanzees and gorillas live today, but it is, and was a constant problem on the savanna. Turning to meat, Australopithecus would have been compelled to beat off other scavengers, including jackals and hyenas as well as vultures, and presumably to carry hunks of meat into trees or rock shelters high on the sides of rocky slopes where it could eat in peace. It clearly had many reasons to fear lions and other large predators, but, if it was indeed a scavenger, it also benefited from their prowess. (**14**: 129)

IV. HOW PUNCTUATION AND PHRASE PATTERNS CAN HELP YOU CHOOSE ANSWERS IN MULTIPLE-CHOICE GRAMMAR TESTS LIKE THE TOEFL

English sentences are written in particular patterns. Some of the most difficult sentences contain several commas. The following patterns are likely to be found in the structure section of the TOEFL. Try it yourself on the "preparing for standardized tests" sections of this text.

PATTERN 1—COMMA IN THE MIDDLE OR NEAR THE END OF THE SENTENCE

A. _____ , _____ .
     main clause   phrase (prepositional,
                        participial, noun phrases)

B. _____ , _____ .
     main clause   coordinating + clause
                        conjunction
                        (*and, but, or*)

C. _____ , _____ .
     main clause   subordinating + clause
                       conjunction
                      (*whereas, while, which, who, where*)

D. _____ , _____ .
     main clause   subord. conjunction + phrase
                      (*while, when, if, thus, thereby*)

PATTERN 2—COMMA NEAR THE BEGINNING OR IN THE MIDDLE OF A SENTENCE

A. _____ , _____ .
  phrase (prepositional,   main clause
  participial, infinitive, noun)

B. _____ , _____ .
  subordinating conj. + clause   main clause
  (*although, even though, because,*
  since, when, while, whereas,
  before, after, once, as, if)

C. _____ , _____ .
  subordinating conj. + phrase   main clause
  (*although, when, while, if, once*)

PATTERN 3—TWO COMMAS IN THE MIDDLE OF A SENTENCE

A. _____ ,   _____ ,
  Beginning of main clause   subordinator + clause
            (*which, who, whom*)

_____ .
  main clause clause continued

B. _____ , _____ , _____ .
  Beginning of main   (subordinator + phrase   main clause continued
   clause   *although, if, when, while*)
          or
       (noun, prepositional, or
        participial phrase)

PATTERN 4—MORE THAN TWO COMMAS

A. _____ , _____ , _____ ,
   Beginning of   1st subordinate   2nd subordinate clause
   main clause   clause begins

_____ , _____ .
   1st subordinate clause   main clause continues.
   continues

B. Two or more commas may also indicate parallel structures.

PHRASE PATTERNS

The following phrase patterns are typical of English sentences, and so they are likely to be found in the error analysis portion of the TOEFL.

1. <u>Verb phrase patterns</u>
   A. adverb + verb or verb + adverb
      normally bloom   *react differently*

   B. aux. + adverb + main verb OR aux. + adverb + aux. + main verb
      is commonly   *known*   *has generally*   *been accepted*

2. <u>Noun phrase patterns</u>
   A. article/pronoun + adjective(s) + count noun

an	*important mining*	*state*
the	*public*	*health*
this	*difficult*	*language*
some	*happy*	*people*

   B. quantifier/ the/Ø + adjective + noncount noun/ abstract noun

a cup of	*hot*	*coffee*
the	*sour*	*milk*
	illegal	*money*
	disappointing	*love*

   C. article + adjective + noun modifier + noun

| *a* | *person's* | *body* | *size* |
| *the* | *beautiful* | *stone* | *wall* |

   D. article/ Ø + adverb + adjective + noun

| *a* | *comparatively* | *recent* | *development* |
| | *relatively* | *important* | *knowledge* |

3. <u>Prepositional phrase patterns</u>
   A. preposition + noun   prep. + article + noun
      in   *town*   *at*   *the*   *office*

   B. preposition + article + adverb + adjective + noun
      around   *a*   *relatively*   *difficult*   *subject*

C. subordinator + preposition + noun phrase

if	*in*	*a big hurry*
although	*near*	*death*
when	*at*	*work*
while	*in*	*the library*

4. <u>Participial phrase patterns</u>

A. verb + "ing" + noun phrase
   including   *most wood sculptures*

B. verb + "ing" + prepositional phrase(s)
   running   *down the stairs*

C. verb past
   participle + prepositional phrase(s)
   found   *in all parts of the world*
   used   *by art historians*

D. verb past
   participle + noun phrase + prepositional phrase
   inaugurated   *a second time*   *on March 4, 1901*
   having chosen   *the topics*   *for their essays*

E. subordinator + verb + "ing" + noun phrase + prep. phrase
   After   *winning*   *international renown as a pianist*
   While
   Thus
   Thereby

F. subordinator + verb past participle

if	*pushed*
when	*eaten*
once	*finished*
while	
when	
although	

Preparing for Standardized Tests

Practice Exercise 7: Parts of Speech and Parallelism

Choose the best answer to complete each sentence below.

1. As a plant matures, it provides not only for its own energy needs _____
   a. but also it provides food for the next generation.
   b. but also for food for the next generation.
   c. but also the next generation.
   d. but the next generation of food also.

2. Obesity is seen in more than 10 percent of school-age children in the United States, in about 15 percent of the people under the age of 30, and _____

   a. about 25 to 30 percent of the adults are too fat.
   b. in the adults, too.
   c. in 25 to 30 percent of the adults.
   d. adults, too.

3. Depending on their interests, psychologists may teach, _____ , administer psychological tests, or serve as consultants to business, industry, government, or the military.

   a. researching   c. research
   b. make research   d. do research

4. Humanists collect data and see evidence to support their ideas, but _____ to treat psychology as a science.

   a. the humanists tend to be less interested in attempts
   b. less interested in attempts
   c. not attempt
   d. are tending less interest in attempts

5. Horses, cattle, sheep, goats, rabbits, and cats were deliberately introduced to Australia; however, _____ .

   a. mice and rats introduced accidentally.
   b. rats were introduced accidentally like mice.
   c. the introduction of rats and mice was an accident.
   d. rats and mice were accidentally introduce.

6. The earthquake zone that includes Los Angeles is called the San Andreas fault, and _____ .

   a. including San Francisco devastated in 1906 by an earthquake and fire.
   b. it was responsible for the earthquake and fire that devastated San Francisco in 1906.
   c. in 1906 was devastating San Francisco with an earthquake and fire.
   d. because an earthquake and fire, San Francisco was devastated in 1906.

7. As more and more organisms live and die in a lake, _____ .

   a. there are more nutrients made available by microorganisms.
   b. microorganisms make more nutrients available.
   c. nutrients are made more available by microorganisms.
   d. more and more nutrients are made available by microorganisms.

8. Neither company organizations _____ is standardized.
   a. nor describing the organizational elements
   b. nor is the terminology used to describe organizational elements
   c. nor the terminology used to describe organizational elements
   d. nor to describe organizational elements.

9. Transactional analysis teaches people a theory of personality to use in be-coming more aware of themselves, their interactions with others, and _____.
   a. of how they live.   c. the life patterns they have.
   b. the way which they live.   d. the life patterns.

10. Monkeys are found in tropical rain forests in both _____.
   a. the New World and also the Old.
   b. the New and Old Worlds.
   c. the New World as well as the Old World.
   d. the New or Old Worlds.

11. Not only _____ but also the composition of the body fluids is vital to life.
   a. is the quantity   c. the quantity
   b. the quantity is   d. quantity

12. _____ of any kind have been domesticated in the last 2000 years, except tomatoes and coffee.
   a. No important new plants   c. Not newly important plants
   b. Neither important new plants   d. None important plants

13. The power of information is important, not only in revealing what the government is doing, but also _____.
   a. in determining what the government ought to do.
   b. to determine what the government should do.
   c. it is important to determine what the government ought to do.
   d. information should determine what the government ought to do.

14. Berne says that the personality has three basic parts or ego-states, known as the Parent, the Adult, and _____.
   a. the Childhood.   c. the Children.
   b. the Child.   d. the Childishness.

15. The persona is the "public self" presented to others when people adopt particular roles, or _____.
   a. when deeper feelings are shielded.
   b. when they shield their deeper feelings.
   c. when particular deep feelings shield people.
   d. when people are shielded by their deeper feelings.

16. No particular diet is magical, and no particular food must either be included _____.
   a. nor avoided. c. or avoided.
   b. not avoided. d. and avoided.

Practice Exercise 8

Find and circle the letter of the *one* error in the following sentences. Then write the correct form above the error.

1. <u>Persons</u> of the same sex, age, and <u>high</u> may differ in <u>weight</u> due to differing
      a   b   c
   <u>densities</u> of their bones and muscles.
      d

2. The Thirteenth Amendment (1865) <u>states</u> that <u>either</u> slavery nor
                        a   b
   <u>involuntary</u> servitude <u>shall</u> exist within the United States.
      c   d

3. A <u>plant</u> equipped with efficient machine tools and <u>serve</u> by the best
      a   b
   means of <u>material</u> movement and <u>assembly</u> can still lose money.
          c   d

4. Each gene is a <u>blueprint</u> that directs the <u>making</u> of the protein machinery
             a   b
   that <u>does</u> the cell's <u>works</u>.
      c   d

5. Americans are divided into <u>a</u> multitude of <u>ethnics</u>, religious, <u>regional</u>, and
                     a   b   c
   political <u>subgroups</u>.
      d

6. Jung <u>drew</u> <u>upon</u> art, religion, history, mythology, <u>alchemy</u>, literature, and
        a   b   c
   anthropology to build a rich and <u>complexity</u> theory of personality.
                        d

7. The cave <u>dweller</u> was <u>equipment</u> with a number of <u>drives</u> that helped
           a   b   c
   him <u>to</u> survive.
      d

8. Food <u>itself</u>—in the form of cattle, sacks of grain, and the <u>like</u>—used to be
   a b

   the <u>medium</u> of exchange because it was the important means of <u>survive</u>.
   c d

9. In <u>choosing</u> and developing processes, <u>their</u> impact on the environment
   a b

   (air and water pollution, <u>noise</u>, vibration, etc.) and on the safety and
   c

   <u>healthy</u> of operators and other people must be considered.
   d

10. Recent <u>work</u> by Wayne Hendrickson and his colleagues <u>at</u> Columbia
    a b

    University (New York, N.Y.) may go a <u>long</u> way to <u>elimination</u> this
    c d

    problem.

11. Gene transfer has <u>considerate</u> <u>potential</u> for the <u>genetic</u> improvement <u>of</u>
    a b c d

    farm animals.

12. In the <u>last</u> 50 years in the <u>industry</u> countries, <u>the</u> automobile has become
    a b c

    an extension of <u>the legs</u>.
    d

13. The U.S. Dietary Goals <u>recommendation</u> that the average person <u>consume</u>
    a b

    60 percent of his/her calories <u>as</u> carbohydrates and about 30 percent or
    c

    <u>less</u> as fat.
    d

14. Like the earlier plants, <u>flowering</u> plants captured the energy of the sun
    a

    and used <u>it</u> for their <u>own</u> needs such as the <u>grow</u> of stems and leaves.
    b c d

15. Scientists are making <u>innovation</u> use of the techniques of <u>mass</u>
    a b c

    <u>spectrometry</u>.
    d

16. Before an animal or plant is introduced <u>into</u> a new area, a very <u>big</u>
                                                     a   b

    deal should be <u>known</u> about the total ecology of the <u>situation</u>.
                            c   d

17. In the tropical rain forest <u>they</u> widespreading branches meet and their
                                       a

    dense foliage <u>forms</u> a <u>canopy</u>.
     a   b   d

18. The fear of new <u>foods</u> is so <u>strongly</u> that it seems to be <u>built into</u> our
               a   b   c   d
    genes.

19. The <u>relative</u> thin layer of water, <u>soil</u>, and air that <u>contains</u> the living
        a   b   c

    things <u>of</u> earth is called the biosphere.
          d

20. Of all the <u>great</u> variety of proteins in living organisms, the antibodies best
                a

    <u>demonstration</u> that the proteins are <u>specific</u> <u>for</u> one organism.
            b   c   d

21. The extinction of <u>various</u> large <u>land</u> mammals in different parts of the
                        a   b

    world coincided with the time <u>of entrance</u> of early people into their
                                      c

    biogeographic <u>regionals</u>.
                  d

22. <u>Early</u> in <u>its</u> evolution, the <u>species human</u> learned to <u>use</u> fire.
      a   b   c   d

23. <u>Throughout</u> the United States, all property owners <u>except</u> religious,
        a   b

    educational, fraternal, literary, <u>scientifics</u>, and similar <u>non-profit</u>
                                  c   d

    institutions must pay property taxes.

24. Vitamin C, <u>or</u> ascorbic acid, is <u>an</u> organic compound <u>with</u> a <u>certainly</u>
              a   b   c   d
    chemical structure.

25. People spend as many hours now as <u>formerly</u> performing the <u>work</u> <u>of</u>
    a   b c

    house and <u>children</u> care.
        d

26. Although there are some ocean <u>trenches</u> deeper <u>than</u> 9,000 meters
    a   b

    (29,800 feet), the average <u>deep</u> of the oceans is <u>about</u> 4000 meters (13,000
              c   d

    feet).

27. Bacterial and <u>mold</u> spores have been found <u>drifted</u> in <u>the</u> atmosphere at
         a   b c

    <u>great</u> heights.
     d

28. The <u>seasonal</u> accumulation of leaves and their <u>gradual</u> breakdown will
       a   b

    <u>eventual</u> lead to a <u>considerable</u> development of humus, teeming with all
      c   d

    sorts of life.

Analysis Exercise 9: Building Templates for Parts of Speech

Fill in the blanks in the sentences below with the parts of speech you would expect to find. Choose between determiner, noun, adjective, preposition, verb, adverb, conjunction, and pronoun.

Example: Marx **verb** that capitalism **verb** filled with **noun** which might prove to be its **noun** .

1. Herbert Spencer (1820–1903), an _____, contributed
   _____ _____ to _____ development
   _____ sociology.

2. He _____ that social _____ are subject to
   _____ law and hoped that the _____ study of
   _____ _____ world would _____ to improve
   _____ human condition.

3. Max Weber (1864–1920) _____ a German scholar _____
   interests ranged _____ religion, economics, cities,
   _____ music, among other _____.

4. Although its origins _____ European, _____ made big
   gains _____ _____ United States _____
   _____ _____ twentieth century.

5. The advantages of a _____ technology are obvious,
   _____ the problems that may arise are much more
   _____ to assess.

6. After _____ market is _____ , products are

   _____.

7. The positive terminal of the battery places a _____
   _____ on one _____ , _____ the negative terminal charges _____ other plate negatively.

8. In addition, if _____ plates are brought _____ together,
   the positive _____ will attract more negative charge
   _____ _____ battery to _____ negative plate.

9. The presidential primary campaign lasts officially _____ January
   _____ June of the election year, _____ the final
   _____ campaign heats up around Labor Day.

10. In Western Europe the age of exploration _____ discovery that
    followed the _____ of _____ Middle Ages saw an
    _____ interest in the _____ of peoples _____
    customs around the world.

APPENDIX 1—PREPOSITIONS
(and Other Words That Function as Prepositions)

Prepositions may express semantic ideas, such as time, and place meanings. **Prepositions may express structural or grammatical meanings. A preposition signals that a noun or a gerund will follow.**

> Preposition + Noun phrase = Prepositional phrase

The prepositional phrase may function as an adverb or an adjective.

I. SEMANTIC MEANINGS OF SOME PREPOSITIONS

TIME
A specific point in time: *on / at / in*

> Herbaceous plants bloom *in* the spring.

Extended period of time: *by / from - to* or *until / until/till / for / during, while /in, within / over / throughout*

> There is abundant evidence that *until* some 200 million years ago, all the continents formed one land mass.
>
> *Over* the past decade, bingo halls began popping up on reservations.
>
> Gradually, *throughout* millions of years, this land mass broke apart.

Sequence of time: *before /after /since /prior to /upon*

> *Prior* to Freud, most psychologists considered dreams to be meaningless.
>
> *Upon* analyzing his own dreams, Freud felt that many represented wish fulfillment.
>
> The number of technical publications has doubled about every twenty years *since* 1800.

Simultaneous time: *while / in / when*

> Compact units are the regions within the protein that have most effectively minimized hydrophobic surface area *while* maximizing internal atomic contacts.
> *In* designing experiments, it is frequently the case that we look ahead to the analysis of variance likely to result from data.

PLACE /AMOUNT
Position:

> the exact point: *in / inside* (in the pipe) */ on / at /* (*at* the bottom, *at* the proper level)

> The computer has become a dominant force *in* society today.

higher than a point: *over*
more than an amount: *above, over*

> Calvin Hall has collected and analyzed *over* 10,000 dreams.
>
> Only a small percent of the population scores *above* 140 on IQ tests.

lower than a point: *under / underneath /beneath / below*
close to (a) point(s): *near / next to / alongside / beside /between /opposite /*

adjacent to / in front/back of / within / against / among / before

His food and drink are placed *before* him in pottery vessels.

Communication must not only be seen as interaction *between* the sender and recipient of messages.

This was the only recorded example of multiple killings *among* primates in the wild.

Away from a point: *off*

The rocks ricocheted *off* the cliff.

Far away from a point: *beyond / out into*

It was *beyond* anything I even thought existed.

The atmosphere extends *out into* space.

DIRECTION

movement relative to a concrete or abstract point: *from-to, to-from / from-into / toward, towards / away from / in(to)-out of /up-down /around / through / past / by / as far as/ up to/ across/ along/ over*

Putting something *from* another cultural context *into* the concepts and words in the English language is not always possible.

The charge on the capacitor will be large for a given voltage *across* it.

The speed with which an impulse is transmitted *along* a nerve fiber is related to its size.

The 4700 system communicates *over* telephone lines.

CAUSE OR REASON: *as a result of / because of / due to / for / for lack of / for the sake of / for want of / in view of / on account of /owing to / thanks to / with*

The tribes also face stricter regulation, *thanks to* a crackdown by the National Indian Gaming Commission.

With the opening of Foxwoods, the $ 1 billion reservation gambling industry enters a new era of sophistication.

CONCESSION: *in spite of / despite / notwithstanding / regardless of /*

Despite the many gaps in our knowledge, there is a need to bring together the results of the various studies.

CONDITION: *in case of / in the event of*

PURPOSE: *for / for the purpose of / in order to*

When people are evaluating an idea *for* their own use, they consult with neighbors and friends.

TOGETHERNESS (OR LACK OF): *with, without / along with / together with*

Babbage developed a machine which could execute complex computations *without* human intervention.

Our language enables us to share *with* others our ideas, thoughts, experiences, and plans.

The existence of compact units follows from the observation of hierarchic architecture in proteins *together with* the close packed nature of the molecular interior.

ADDITION: *as well as*

COMPARISON /CONTRAST: *like / unlike / as*

The definition of manufacturing *as* the making of goods and articles reveals little about the complexity of the problem.

CONFLICT: *against / versus*

A single individual armed with a crude stone weapon stood little chance *against* an elephant or rhinoceros.

At the heart of the controversy was the issue of national government supremacy *versus* the rights of the separate states.

DEGREE: *according to / by*

The moveable pulley is drawn up by the cord causing the wiper to move up *by* the same amount.

People may be classified into categories *according to* the order in which they adopt new practices.

INSTRUMENT (HOW): *with / through*

It is gossip not ordinarily handled *through* normal channels.

MEANS: *by / with / through*

It's like doing a jigsaw puzzle *with* most of the pieces missing and without a picture.

Our language is a system governed *by* rules.

MANNER: *with / in*

The components interact *in* a dynamic manner.

They don't have enough information to put it all together *with* complete confidence.

ROLE (IN THE CAPACITY OF): *as*

Mass media have been relatively unimportant *as* information sources at the trial stage.

MATERIAL: *of / out of / from*

His razor is *of* steel.

He puts on his feet stiff coverings made *from* hide.

Masai tribesmen watched him spend half an hour making a chopper *out of* a handy rock.

SOURCE: *from*

Accounting machines could read data *from* punched cards.

SEPARATION: *from / with*

The task of control is to ensure that plans succeed by detecting deviations *from* plans.

ORIGIN /POSSESSION: *of / with, without (= have, don't have)*

Man's modern jet airplanes *with* their ever-increasing airspeeds and passenger capacities dangerously clog airlanes.

PARTS: *of*

Statistical inference is an important aspect *of* scientific inference.

APPOSITION: *of*

CHARACTERIZED BY SOME QUALITY: *of*

The ease with which an advantage *of* hybrid corn over open-pollinated varieties can be demonstrated no doubt has influenced its rapid acceptance.

EXCEPTION: *except (for) / but (for) / save (for) / apart from*

REFERENCE / CONCERNING: *with regard to / with respect to / with reference to / in regard to / in respect to / in reference to / about / as for / as to*

At this stage the individual knows little *about* the new idea beyond the fact that it exists.

There is a need for effective research to reduce the current uncertainty *as to* the risk of particular kinds of experiments.

REFERENCE TO AUTHORITY: *according to*

According to current thinking, *Australopithecus* adapted to life on the savanna.

EXAMPLE: *like / such as*

Some studies, *such as* that of hybrid corn in Iowa, indicate that salesmen are important in creating awareness of new ideas.

RELATIVE TO PERSON'S EXPERIENCE: *for / to*

For/to both Durkheim and Comte, writing about social change and social travel must have been like trying to convey the joys of world travel while desperately seasick.

II.   SOME STRUCTURAL/GRAMMATICAL MEANINGS OF PREPOSITIONS

Of

NOUN OR GERUND + OF + OBJECT OF NOUN OR GERUND

clarification of roles
discussions of fundamentals
exchanges of goods and services
the development of the computer
the labeling of the dissections
the making of goods
the processing of information

NOUN + OF + POSSESSIVE SUBJECT

a phenomenon of our time
every inch of the several hundred square miles
the top of the building
a form of organization
the definition of informal organization
the existence of norms
the importance of money
the science of human behavior
types of soil

III. SOME COMMON COMBINATIONS

TWO- AND THREE-WORD VERBS (* = may have an object before or after the preposition)

compensate for	*derive from**	*relate to**
act as	*escape from*	*rely on (upon)*
adapt to	*exist in*	*respond to*
approve of	*focus on**	*result in*
begin with	*give to**	*return to**
benefit from	*head for*	*serve as*
*bring about**	*hold in**	*succeed in*
*bring to**	*impose on /upon**	*talk about*
carry out	*increase in*	*use as**
code for	*lead to**	*vary with**
collide with	*listen to*	*wait for*
come upon	*occur to*	*wonder about*
communicate with	*operate on*	*work on*
comply with	*overload with*	*call attention to*
concentrate on	*participate in*	*do business with*
consist of	*pertain to*	*have respect for*
*contribute to**	*point out**	*pay attention to*
cope with	*react to*	*turn back upon*
deal with	*refer to*	
depend on		

ADJECTIVE OR PAST PARTICIPLE + PREPOSITION (*Be, become, seem, appear* and other linking verbs may precede the adjective.)

be accompanied by	*be classified into / as*	*be limited to*
be adapted to	*be composed of*	*be native to*
be affiliated with	*be concerned about*	*be referred to as*
be alienated from	*be dependent on*	*be regarded as*
be assigned to	*be derived from*	*be responsible for*
be attached to	*be elected to*	*be rich in*
be aware of	*be expected to*	*be rooted in*
be based on / upon	*be imposed on / upon*	*be used as*
be capable of	*be interested in*	*be wedded to*
be central to	*be involved in*	
be certain/uncertain about	*be knowledgable about*	
be characterized by	*be known as*	

NOUN + PREPOSITION

antagonism against	emphasis on / upon	part of
aspect of	evidence of	participation in
authority on	example of	place a value on
awareness of	existence of	preference for
basis for	explanation for	preoccupation with
cause for / of	flair for	problems of
certainty about	functions of	process of
cohesiveness of	improvement in	reason for
contributions to	increase in	resistance to
creation of	key to	search for
decrease in	lack of	show signs of
demand for	make provision for	skills in
description of	means of	symptoms of
diversity of / in	object of	uncertainty about
efficiency of	opposition to	views of

Prepositions Exercise

Use what you know about prepositions to fill in the blanks in the passage below with appropriate prepositions. When you are finished be prepared to explain why you chose the prepositions that you did.

[1]   *Anthropology*: Cultural anthropology, as the term is commonly used
        today, generally refers _____ the study _____ existing peoples. Further, it
        is based _____ a comparative approach, that is, its aim is to understand
        and appreciate the diversity _____ human behavior, and ultimately to
        develop a science _____ human behavior, _____ the comparison _____
        different peoples _____ the world. _____ the United States we fre-
        quently make a distinction _____ two areas _____ cultural anthropol-
        ogy: ethnology and ethnography. Ethnology is the comparative study
        _____ culture and the investigation _____ theoretical problems using
        information _____ different groups. . . . To avoid confusion we will use
        the term cultural anthropology to cover both _____ these terms. There
        are two main tasks involved _____ the work _____ the cultural anthropolo-
        gist, to describe the cultures _____ other peoples and to compare them.
        Such description is not an easy task, since putting something _____
        another cultural context _____ the concepts and words available _____
        the English language is not always possible. (14: 16)

[2]   *Light and Photosynthesis*

How a plant absorbs radiant energy _____ the sun and transforms it _____ sugars has been one ____ the most challenging problems _____ biology. It is also, of course, the key ____ life ____ this planet. _____ a very long time, this key was a mystery, and, even today, we don't have quite all the answers. But we know that ____ a complex series ____ reactions light energy is converted ____ chemical energy and stored _____ the chemical bonds ____ sugars. ____ this process oxygen is released.

It had long been assumed that the oxygen released ____ photosynthesis came _____ carbon dioxide. ____ the 1930s, C.B. van Niel, a graduate student ____ Stanford University, made the bold suggestion that the oxygen produced _____ photosynthesis was derived _____ water, not carbon dioxide. His reason was based _____ a study ____ the photosynthetic "sulfur bacteria." These unusual microbes thrive _____ sunlit stagnant pools ____ which hydrogen sulfide (H_2S) is produced ____ decay ____ organic matter. _____ most bacteria, they carry on photosynthesis. But instead ____ producing oxygen ____ a by-product, they release sulfur . . . Van Niel pointed _____ the parallel _____ this type of photosynthesis and that which occurs ____ algae and plants. He suggested that it was most logical to assume that one type _____ photosynthesis had evolved _____ the other and was therefore only a slightly different version _____ it. (**1**: 190)

[3]   Although business institutions ____ insurance, credit, and marketing were developed ___ the Middle Ages and although these and still others were well formed ____ the time ____ the industrial revolution ____ the nineteenth century, business was long regarded ____ a degrading occupation. Aristotle's characterization ____ buying and selling ____ "unnatural" moneymaking, Adam Smith's disparaging remarks concerning businessmen, and Napoleon's castigation ____ England ____ a "nation ____ shopkeepers" are evidences ____ this fact. Even _____ the past century, business was often regarded _____ the educated _____ a somewhat inglorious occupation. Indeed, one can say that only ____ the past half century has the businessman begun to hold a place ___ respect. (**27**: 30–31)

APPENDIX 2—ARTICLES

A/An

GENERAL USE: (Plural: *some*)
Meaning (with singular count nouns): "any," "one," or "each"

A table, derived from the National Income and Expenditures "Blue Book," is provided.

with noncount nouns: "a kind of," "the kind of," "some"

The guests were served *a* wine that no one recognized.

CLASSIFICATION: Used with singular count nouns that represent a class to emphasize one individual member of the class.

A heat pump can be used to heat *a* building.

A hypothesis is *a* tentative description or explanation.

IDENTIFICATION: Used for the first mention of a noun.

Faraday's law tells us that any change in the flux through *a* coil will induce *an* emf in the coil.

PRENOUN MODIFIERS:

1. after *so* or *too*: *so/too* + adjective + *a* + noun

   He had never seen *so* high *a* bridge over *so* narrow *a* river.

2. after *such* and *what*

   Wives retained an assured place in the long house where they were born, and the head woman in such *a* house was a person of power.

3. after *not*, *many*, *quite*, and *rather*

   There was not *a* taxicab in sight.

   August is quite *a* hot time of the year in Texas.

SPECIAL USES: *A/an* + noun quantifier + noun

A few students were late.
A little work remains to be done.

A/an + adjective or expression of percent + "majority" or "minority" + (*of* phrase)

He was elected by *a* 51 percent majority of the vote.
She won by *an* overwhelming majority.

TIME: Half *an* hour is a long time to spend on one problem.

We'll need *a* half hour to prepare for the class.

The

Definite "the" is specific, meaning "the only." "The" distinguishes known from unknown.

GENERAL USE: With count and noncount nouns to distinguish known objects / people/ ideas in a real situation.

> The Indian tribes of America were not uniformly warlike. *The* Siouan family was, especially *the* Dakotas, and so were *the* Nadene Apaches and *the* Aztec Tanoan Comanches.

CLASSIFICATION: With singular count nouns (often animals, humans, organs, and complicated mechanical or electronic machines) that represent a class to emphasize all of the class.

> Another useful organism in the fossil record is *the* ostracod, a very small crustacean.

IDENTIFICATION:

1. With familiar objects and people in the environment.

   > *The* Constitution is widely accepted today.

2. With things that are unique.

   > *The* solar system contains nine planets.

3. For subsequent mentions of a noun previously identified in the context.

   > Faraday's law tells us that any change in flux through *a* coil will induce an emf in *the* coil.

PRENOUN MODIFIERS: With nouns that are made specific in the following ways:

1. Restrictive adjectives preceding the noun.

   a. superlatives

   > The relations between employers and men form *the* most important part of the art of management.

   b. ordinal numbers

   > Innovators are *the* first to adopt new ideas.

   c. sequential chronological or spatial order words

   > The staff will be at a professional meeting the week of March 8th. *The* following week, they'll be on vacation.

   d. ranking adjectives

   > *The* primary responsibility rests in the manager charged with the performance of the particular plans involved.

POSTNOUN MODIFIERS: With nouns that are identified or made specific in the following ways:

1. Restrictive modifiers following the noun
   a. adjective clause

   Sediments were carried into *the* sea that lay in their midst by rivers and streams.

   b. participial phrase

   The articles found in *Psychology Today* are written for that sector of *the* public interested in psychological issues.

   c. prepositional phrase

   One might expect that political science would have been *the* father of a theory of management.

SPECIAL USES:

1. With adjectives used as nouns

   The Swiss place stress on sharing enjoyment of nature.
   The organisms seem *the* same.

2. With some indefinite pronouns

   One is an axon, *the* others dendrites.

3. With gerunds and abstract nouns + "of" phrases

   The law establishes *the* giving of instruction.

4. With expressions of quantity + *of* phrases

   The vast majority of neurons in the body are multipolar.

5. With special comparatives of proportion

   The bigger they are, *the* harder they fall.

TIME:

1. With seasons (*the* spring, *the* fall)
2. With many parts of the day (*the* morning, *the* afternoon)
3. With sequence of time (*the* past, *the* present, *the* future)
4. With historical periods (*the* 1990s, *the* nineteenth century)

PLACE:

1. *The* + noun + *of* phrase

   The universities of Florida and North Carolina participated in some of these experiments.

2. With some countries (*The* Sudan, *The* Netherlands)
3. With geographical or astronomical groups
    a. continents

    Following the discovery of *the* Americas, many agricultural crops were exchanged between the Eastern and Western hemispheres.
    b. mountain ranges (*the* Sangre de Cristo Mountains)
    c. groups of islands and archipelagos

    Malinowski was interned on a small group of islands, *the* Trobriands.
    d. astronomical groups (*the* stars, *the* planets)
4. Most bodies of water
    a   groups of lakes (*the* Great Lakes)
    b. rivers

    Nelson Mandela thought back on . . . the Tembu Krall by *the* Banshee River where he was born.
    c. oceans (*the* Pacific Ocean)
    d. seas (*the* Black Sea)
    e. canals (*the* Panama Canal)
    f. straits (*the* Straits of Magellan)
    g. gulfs (*the* Gulf of Mexico)
5. Types of land area and points of geography
    a. deserts (*the* Sahara)
    b. forests (*the* Black Forest)
    c. peninsulas (*the* Sinai Peninsula)
    d. points of the compass used as names of areas

    The Algonquins of *the* Old Northwest . . . became especially good marksmen.
    e. points on the globe (*the* eastern hemisphere, *the* Arctic, *the* equator)

OTHER PLACES:

1. some buildings (*the* World Trade Center, *the* Beverly Hills Hotel,
    the Library of Congress, *the* Peabody museum)
2. bridges (*the* Golden Gate Bridge)
3. tunnels (*the* Holland Tunnel)
4. towers (*the* Eiffel tower)

GOVERNMENT:

1. bills, laws, legislative acts

    The County Agricultural Extension Districts Law provided for a three person committee.
2. official titles

    The president urged his nominating committee to convene.

3. military groups (*the* army, *the* navy, *the* air force, *the* marine corps)
4. law enforcement groups (*the* police)
5. branches of government (*the* Senate, *the* House of Representatives)
6. names of political parties (*the* Democrats, *the* Republicans)
7. some wars (*The* Civil War, *The* Spanish-American War)

NO ARTICLE NEEDED

GENERAL USE:

1. With noncount concrete nouns in general statements

    Cereals are difficult to handle in tissue culture and to date *rice* is the only species reported in which regenerated plants have been obtained from protoplasts.

    Incomplete combustion may release combustible gases such as *carbon monoxide, hydrogen* and *methane.*

2. With noncount abstract nouns

    Your speech should not be based merely on *information* from encyclopedias.

CLASSIFICATION: With plural count nouns that represent a class

Cereals are difficult to handle in tissue culture . . .

POSTNOUN MODIFIERS: With a very general statement with a post modifier.

Denaturing is not necessary for *ethanol* produced on the farm.

TIME: With the names of most holidays (*Labor Day, Thanksgiving*)

PLACE:

1. With names of universities with no *of* phrase (*Florida State University*)
2. With single geographical or astronomical bodies
    a. continents (*South America*)
    b. most countries (*Taiwan, China, Korea, Japan*)
    c. single mountains (*Mount Fuji*)
    d. islands (*Block Island, Catalina Island*)
    e. lakes (*Lake Maracaibo*)
    f. names of bays (*Biscayne Bay*)
    g. names of planets (*Jupiter, Pluto, Neptune, Saturn, Earth*)
3. Types and points of geography: points of the compass used as adverbs meaning direction

    The pioneers traveled *west* in wagon trains.

OTHER PLACES:

1. cities (Washington, Paris, Bonn, Moscow)
2. states (New Mexico, Alaska)
3. some buildings (Carnegie Hall)
4. hotels and motels in which the word *hotel* or *motel* is first (Motel 6)
5. streets, avenues, and boulevards (Park Avenue, 42nd Street)
6. parks (Golden Gate Park, Central Park)
7. work, school, church, uptown, downtown
    While children go to *school*, adults go to *work*.

OTHER NONUSES:

1. most physical ailments (pneumonia, cancer)
2. names of magazines (*Newsweek, Time, National Geographic*)
3. most professional titles + personal names
    President Harry S. Truman once said, "The buck stops here."
4. plural numbers followed by "of " + plural noun
    Millions of dollars were spent last year.
    Thousands of people attended the concert.

Articles Exercise

The following exercises are from Business, American Government, and International Relations textbooks. Complete the exercises by filling in the blanks with *a*, *an*, *the*, or *Ø.* Be prepared to discuss why you made the choices that you did.

[1]   Information overload is _____ common phenomenon of our times; it is due, to _____ great extent, to technology. J.G. Miller reports that over 1,200,000 articles appear in _____ 60,000 books and _____ 100,000 reports every year. Moreover, _____ number of scientific and technical publications in _____ United States has doubled about every 20 years since _____ 1800. But _____ information overload can also be experienced within _____ enterprise, especially when _____ computer is used indiscriminately. When one of _____ authors of this text analyzed _____ control system, it was found that _____ controller was overloaded with information he neither used nor understood. Computer output sheets were piled up from _____ floor to _____ top of his desk _____ –output he never digested. _____ control system was designed

for maximum output rather than tailored to _____ specific needs of _____ user; _____ result was information overload. (**27**: 700)

[2] From 1960 through 1968, _____ Democrats, headed by Kennedy and Johnson, held national power. Republicans again came to power with _____ Nixon's victory in 1968 but lost prestige after _____ Watergate scandal forced his resignation on August 8, 1974. Although Republican Vice President Ford (_____ first person ever appointed to _____ vice presidency to become president) took over for _____ remainder of Nixon's second term, _____ Republicans were severely damaged by Nixon's resignation. For this and _____ other reasons, _____ Democrats were back in power in 1976. But Democratic President Jimmy Carter was unable to win reelection against Ronald Reagan in 1980. _____ Republicans also gained control of _____ Senate in 1980 and retained it in _____ elections of 1982 and 1984. In _____ next presidential election, Ronald Reagan became _____ oldest man to be elected to _____ presidency when he garnered _____ 59 percent majority of _____ popular vote . . . _____ Republicans lost two seats in _____ Senate and failed to gain enough seats in _____ House to ensure control. (**39**: 263)

[3] *Kinetic Energy* —If _____ object can do work, we say that _____ object possesses _____ energy. We define energy as follows:

Energy is _____ ability to do _____ work.

_____ object which is moving can do work. For example, _____ hammer does work on _____ nail as it drives _____ nail into _____ piece of _____ wood. Or _____ moving baseball does _____ work as it breaks _____ window. There are many other examples we could cite where _____ moving object does work as it slows down. As we shall see, this is _____ very important fact, and we shall make much use of it. Let us now examine how work and motion are related.

To begin our discussion, let us see how _____ object's motion depends on _____ unbalanced force which acts on it. Suppose _____ object of mass m is subjected to _____ constant resultant force F in the direction of _____ displacement s. During this displacement, _____ force does work given by

$$\text{Work} = Fs.$$

We wish now to relate this work to _____ change in motion of _____ object caused by _____ unbalanced force.

We know that _____ unbalanced force F is related to _____ acceleration of _____ object by $F = ma$. Therefore, _____ above equation for work becomes

$$\text{Work} = mas.$$

Suppose _____ object had _____ original velocity v_0 and _____ final velocity v_f after _____ work was done. Then, since

$$v_f^2 - v_0^2 + 2as,$$

we can substitute $\frac{1}{2}(v_f^2 - v_0^2)$ for as in _____ work equation to obtain

$$\text{Work} = \frac{1}{2}\,mv_f^2 - \frac{1}{2}\,mv_0^2.$$

This is _____ very important relation. Let us summarize our result: _____ work done by _____ resultant force on _____ object leads to _____ change in motion of _____ object. (**2**: 94-95)

[4] Most often imperialism has been rationalized as bringing civilization to _____ uncivilized. Even _____ ancient Greek city-states established colonies in _____ Italy and _____ Sicily, in _____ Aegean Islands, or on parts of _____ Asia Minor, primarily to accommodate their surplus populations. _____ period of _____ imperial age however reached its heights with _____ movement of _____ Western European states— primarily _____ Portugal, _____ Spain, _____ France, _____ England, _____ Netherlands, _____ Belgium, and _____ Germany — into _____ Americas, _____ Africa and _____ Asia. Various rationales, from spreading _____ God's work to _____ concept of _____ white man's burden, were used as justifications for what was essentially greed behavior to get _____ resources and lands of _____ other peoples. (**12**: 113)

[5] _____ transmission electron microscope (TEM) uses _____ beam of electrons rather than light rays and focuses _____ beam by using electromagnets instead of glass lenses. _____ resolving and magnifying power of _____ TEM is as much as 400 times that of _____ light microscope.

[6] _____ lipids are used for energy storage in both _____ animals and _____ plants. _____ fats are defined as _____ lipids that are generally solid at _____ room temperature and are produced by _____ animals; _____ lard and _____ butter are examples. _____ oils such as _____ corn oil and _____ olive oil, are produced by _____ plants and are generally liquid at _____ room temperature. (**1**: 109, 78)

APPENDIX 3—VERBS THAT TAKE INFINITIVES AND/OR GERUNDS

Verb + Infinitive

Consumers often *want to know* what kind of bread is the most nutritious.

afford	endeavor	need	swear
agree	expect	offer	tend
appear	fail	plan	threaten
arrange	get	prepare	used
ask	guarantee	pretend	volunteer
aspire	happen	promise	wait
beg	help	refuse	want
care	hesitate	request	wish
claim	hope	resort	work
consent	intend	seek	would hate
decide	learn	seem	would like
demand	manage	struggle	would love
desire	mean		

Verb + Object + Infinitive

The relative effects *will have a chance to manifest* themselves.

We *chose design to describe* the plan.

adopt	direct	lead	request
advise	drive	like	require
allow	elect	love	reserve
appoint	employ	meant	select
ask	enable	name	send
assign	encourage	need	teach
authorize	engage	notify	telephone
beg	expect	oblige	tell
call	forbid	order	tempt
cause	force	pay	train
challenge	get	permit	trust
choose	have	persuade	urge
command	help	pick	use
conduct	hire	prefer	want
contract	inspire	prepare	warn
convince	instruct	push	wire
dare	intend	raise	would hate
depend on	invite	rely on	would like
design	involve	remind	write
desire			

Verbs + Gerunds

The law *establishes the giving* of instruction and practical demonstrations.

admit	discuss	miss	report
advise	dislike	picture	resent
anticipate	enjoy	postpone	resist
appreciate	escape	practice	resume
avoid	establish	protest	risk
can't help	finish	quit	save
complete	imagine	recall	stop
confess	include	recommend	suggest
consider	involve	regret	tolerate
debate	mention	relate	understand
delay	mind	remember	welcome
deny			

(subject of gerund)
Verb + Possessive Noun or Pronoun + Gerund

An example *is the body's handling* of alcohol.

admit	enjoy	miss	remember
applaud	forget	picture	report
appreciate	depend on	prefer	resent
approve	hate	protest	risk
be	imagine	recall	save
concede	like	recommend	salute
deny	mention	regret	welcome
disapprove	mind		

Common Verbs + Infinitive or Gerund

Critics of modern management *prefer to refer / referring* to the ideal group operation as a team effort.

attempt	forget	like	remember
begin	go	neglect	start
bother	hate	prefer	stop
choose	intend (rare	try	
continue	with gerunds)	regret	
deserve			

Some Adjectives + Infinitives

It is *presumptuous to present* this result as evidence.
It may be *difficult to design* an "ideal" experiment.

able	eager	motivated	smart
afraid	easy	necessary	sorry
amazed	expected	nice	stupid
anxious	foolish	pleased	strange
apt	fortunate	possible	stunned
ashamed	free	predicted	supposed
astonished	fun	prepared	sure
bound	glad	presumptuous	surprised
careful	good	proud	terrible
certain	happy	qualified	unable
content	hard	quick	upset
delighted	hesitant	ready	welcome
depressing	important	relieved	willing
determined	inclined	reluctant	wise
difficult	kind	sad	wonderful
disappointed	likely	shocked	wrong
disturbed	lucky	slow	

REFERENCES

1. Barrett, James M., Peter Abramhoff, and A. Krishna Kumaran. *Biology*. Englewood Cliffs, N.J.: Prentice-Hall, 1986. Reprinted by permission of Prentice-Hall, Inc.

2. Bueche, F. *Principles of Physics*, 4th ed. New York: McGraw-Hill, 1982. Reprinted by permission of McGraw-Hill, Inc.

3. "Cables and Allied Products." *Electrical Communication* 61, #3 (1987): 359–365.

4. Carlson, John. "Scientists hunt for clues to massive apes' demise." *The Des Moines* (Iowa) *Register*, December 3, 1988, pp. 1B–4B. Copyright ©1988 The Des Moines Register and Tribune Company. Reprinted with permission.

5. Clausen, Chris A. III, and Guy Mattson. *Principles of Industrial Chemistry*. New York: John Wiley & Sons, 1978.

6. Cochrane, Williard W. "The Impact of Different Forms of Foreign Assistance on Agricultural Development." *World Food Conference Proceedings*. Ames: Iowa State University Press, 1977. Pp. 183–193.

7. Coon, Dennis. *Introduction to Psychology: Exploration and Application*. St. Paul, Minn.: West Publishing Company, 1980. Reprinted with permission.

8. Ember, Carol R., and Melvin Ember. *Anthropology*, 5th ed. Englewood Cliffs, N.J.: Prentice-Hall, 1988. Reprinted by permission of Prentice-Hall, Inc.

9. Erlich, Paul, Richard W. Holm, and Irene L. Brown. *Biology and Society*. New York: McGraw-Hill, 1976. Reprinted by permission of McGraw-Hill, Inc.

10. Russell, John F.A. "Essential Ingredients of an Effective Extension Service and Some Issues Arising from World Bank Experience in Sub-Saharan Africa." Paper presented at Zimbabwe's Annual Project Review Conference, Iowa State Extension Service, May 1985.

11. Fetrow, Jacquelyn S., Michael Zehfus, and George D. Rose. "Protein Folding: New Twists." *Biotechnology* 6 (February 8, 1988): 167–170. Reprinted by permission of Bio/Technology Nature Publishing Company.

12. Findlay, David J., and Thomas Hovet, Jr. *7304: International Relations on the Planet Earth*. New York: HarperCollins, 1975. Reprinted with the permission of HarperCollins Publishers.

13. Folks, Leroy. *Ideas of Statistics*. Copyright ©(1984: John Wiley). Reprinted by permission of John Wiley & Sons, Inc.

14. Friedl, John, and John E. Pfeiffer. *Anthropology: The Study of People*. New York: HarperCollins, 1977. Reprinted with the permission of the authors.

15. Fritz, Sandy. "Who Was the Iceman?" *Popular Science* (February 1993): 46–88. Copyright © Sandy Fritz. Reprinted with permission of the author.

16. Gilles, Anthony E. *The Evolution of Philosophy: An Overview of Western Thought as It Relates to Judeo-Christian Thought*. Staten Island, N.Y.: Alba House, 1987. Reprinted with permission.

17. Goodman, Jeffrey. *American Genesis*. New York: Summit Books, 1981. Copyright ©1981 by Jeffrey Goodman. Reprinted with permission.

18. Grobstein, Clifford. "The Recombinant-DNA Debate." *Scientific American* (July 1977): 24–31. Copyright ©1977 by Scientific American, Inc. All rights reserved. Reprinted with permission.

19. Hamilton, Eva May, and Eleanor Whitney. *Nutrition: Concepts and Controversies*. St. Paul, Minn.: West Publishing Company, 1979. Reprinted with permission.

20. Hamlyn, D.W. *A History of Western Philosophy*. Hammondsworth, Middlesex, England: Viking, 1987.

21. Hoskins, H. Preston, J.V. LaCroix, and Karl Mayer, eds. *Canine Medicine*, 2nd ed., rev. Goleta, Calif.: American Veterinary Publications, 1959. Reprinted with permission of American Veterinary Publications.

22. "How Farm People Accept New Ideas." Special Report 15, North Central Regional Publication No. 1. Ames: Iowa State University Cooperative Extension Service, 1981.

23. Husted, Stewart W., Dale Varble, and James R. Lowry. *Principles of Modern Marketing*. Boston, Mass.: Allyn and Bacon, 1989.

24. Josephy, Alvin M., Jr. *Indian Heritage of America*. New York: Alfred A. Knopf, 1968. Copyright ©1968 by Alvin M. Josephy, Jr. Reprinted by permission of the author.

25. Kenney, Martin. "Is Biotechnology a Blessing for the Less Developed Nations?" *Monthly Review—An Independent Socialist Magazine* 34, #11 (April 1983): 10–17.

26. Kish, Leslie. "Some Statistical Problems in Research Design." *American Sociological Review* 24, #3 (1959): 328–338. Reprinted with permission.

27. Koontz, Harold, Cyril O'Donnell, and Heinz Weihrich. *Management*, 7th ed. New York: McGraw-Hill, 1980. Reprinted by permission of McGraw-Hill, Inc.

28. Lightner, James E. "A Brief Look at the History of Probability and Statistics." *The Mathematics Teacher* 84, #8 (November 1991): 623–635. Reprinted with permission.

29. Linton, Ralph. *The Study of Man*. Englewood Cliffs, N.J.: Prentice Hall, 1936, © renewed 1964. Reprinted by permission of Prentice-Hall, Inc.

30. Maloney, Timothy J. *Industrial Solid State Electronics: Devices and Systems*, 2nd ed. Englewood Cliffs, N.J.: Prentice-Hall, 1986. Reprinted by permission of Prentice-Hall, Inc.

31. Mandell, Steven L. *Computers and Data Processing: Concepts and Applications*. St. Paul, Minn.: West Publishing Company, 1979. Reprinted with permission.

32. Mark, Kathleen. "Ancient Ocean Rocks—High in the Sangre De Cristo Mountains." *Sea Frontiers* (January/February 1988): 22–29. Reprinted with permission.

33. Miller, Roger L. *Economics Today*. New York: HarperCollins, 1991. Copyright ©1991 by Harper & Row Publishers, Inc. Reprinted with the permission of HarperCollins Publishers.

34. Oxendine, Joseph B. *American Indian Sports Heritage*. Champaign, Ill.: Human Kinetics Books (a Division of Human Kinetics Publishers), 1988. Copyright ©1988 by Joseph B. Oxendine. Reprinted by permission.

35. Persell, Caroline Hodges. *Understanding Society: An Introduction to Sociology*. New York: HarperCollins, 1984. Copyright ©1987 by Harper & Row Publishers, Inc. Reprinted with the permission of HarperCollins Publishers.

36. Pfeiffer, John E. *The Emergence of Man*, 3rd ed. New York: HarperCollins, 1978. Reprinted by permission of HarperCollins Publishers, Inc.

37. Schey, John A. *Introduction to Manufacturing Processes*, 2nd ed. New York: McGraw-Hill, 1987. Reprinted by permission of McGraw-Hill, Inc.

38. Schmidt, Steffen W. "Clientelism and Agricultural Modernization: Some Observations on Technology, Equity and Decision-Making." *Third World Review* 4, #2 (Fall 1978): 64–78. Reprinted with permission of the author.

39. Schmidt, Steffen W., Mack C. Shelley, and Barbara A. Bardes. *American Government and Politics Today*, 3rd ed. St. Paul, Minn.: West Publishing Company, 1989. Reprinted with permission.

40. Smith, Rogers M. "The 'American Creed' and American Identity: The Limits of Liberal Citizenship in the United States." *Western Political Quarterly* 41 #2 (June 1988): 225–249.

41. Smith, Ronald C., and Cameron K. Andres. *Principles and Practices of Heavy Construction*, 3rd ed. Englewood Cliffs, N.J.: Prentice Hall, 1986. Reprinted by permission of Prentice-Hall, Inc.

42. Stout, B.A. *Energy Use and Management in Agriculture*. Belmont, Calif.: Breton, 1984.

43. Thompson, Dick, and Sharon Thompson. "Regenerative Agriculture—Thompson's On-Farm Research." *Thompson on Farm Research Summary*. Boone, Iowa, 1986.

44. Tulchin, Joseph S., ed. *Latin America in the Year 2000*. Reading, Mass.: Addison-Wesley, 1975.

45. Wilde, Daniel U. *An Introduction to Computing: Problem-Solving, Algorithms, and Data Structures*. Englewood Cliffs, N.J.: Prentice-Hall, l973. Reprinted by permission of Prentice-Hall, Inc.

46. Wilson, William B. "The Deeper Necessity—Folklore and the Humanities." *Journal of American Folklore* 101, #400, 156–167.

47. Wolff, Robert Paul. *Introductory Philosophy*. Englewood Cliffs, N.J.: Prentice-Hall, l979.

48. Yarbrough, Paul, and Gerald E. Klonglan. "Adoption and Diffusion of Innovations: Basic Concepts." *Community Dental Health: Organizing for Action*, ed. John L. Tait and John E. Goodrich. Sociology Report No. 113. Ames: Iowa State University Department of Sociology and Anthropology, 1974.

INDEX

NOTE: Page numbers in *italics* denote charts, figures, and tables.